The Best American History Essays 2007

The Best American History Essays 2007

Edited by
Jacqueline Jones
for the
Organization of American Historians

THE BEST AMERICAN HISTORY ESSAYS 2007
© Organization of American Historians, 2007.

First published in 2007 by
PALGRAVE MACMILLAN™
175 Fifth Avenue, New York, N.Y. 10010 and
Houndmills, Basingstoke, Hampshire, England RG21 6XS
Companies and representatives throughout the world.

PALGRAVE MACMILLAN is the global academic imprint of the Palgrave Macmillan division of St. Martin's Press, LLC and of Palgrave Macmillan Ltd. Macmillan® is a registered trademark in the United States, United Kingdom and other countries. Palgrave is a registered trademark in the European Union and other countries.

ISBN-13: 978–1–4039–7659–8 (hardcover)
ISBN-10: 1–4039–7659–7 (hardcover)
ISBN-13: 978–1–4039–7660–4 (paperback)
ISBN-10: 1–4039–7660–0 (paperback)

Library of Congress Cataloging-in-Publication Data

The best American history essays 2007 / edited by Jacqueline Jones for the Organization of American Historians.
    p. cm.
Includes bibliographical references and index.
ISBN 1–4039–7659–7 (alk. paper)—ISBN 1–4039–7660–0 (alk. paper)
    1. United States—History. 2. American essays. 3. United States—Historiography. I. Jones, Jacqueline, 1948– II. Organization of American Historians.

E178.6.B53 2007
973—dc22   2006050719

A catalogue record for this book is available from the British Library.

Design by Newgen Imaging Systems (P) Ltd., Chennai, India.

First edition: April 2007

10 9 8 7 6 5 4 3 2 1

Printed in the United States of America.

Contents

List of Illustrations

Acknowledgments

The 2007 edition of the *Best American History Essays* was prepared by its editor, Jacqueline Jones, and the hardworking individuals who comprised the editorial board: Anthony J. Badger, John M. Belohlavek, Ellen Carol DuBois, Eric Foner, Sharon Harley, M. Ruth Kelly, John Saillant, and Elliott West. We would like to thank them for their efforts in selecting the ten articles from the hundreds of journals and magazines they scoured looking for the best American history published between the summers of 2005 and 2006. In addition, we want to acknowledge and thank those involved in producing the inaugural edition of the *Best American History Essays* in 2006. Under the careful editorship of Joyce Appleby, University of California, Los Angeles professor emerita, and past president of the Organization of American Historians (OAH), the following American historians invested their time and energy to assemble the 2006 volume: Anthony J. Badger, John Belohlavek, Flannery Burke, David Goldfield, M. Ruth Kelly, Jill Lepore, John Saillant, George Sanchez, and Gordon Wood.

We would also like to thank the following staff at the Organization of American Historians executive office, whose hard work behind the scenes helped bring these editions to print: Kevin Byrne, Amanda Dollar, Keith Eberly, Susan Ferentinos, Terry Govan, Jason Groth, Kara Hamm, Phillip Guerty, Matthew Laird, Susanna Robbins, Amy Stark, and Annette Windhorn. We must also thank OAH Publications Director Michael Regoli and former OAH Deputy Director John Dichtl.

Finally, we want to thank Brendan O'Malley who first brought the idea of a *Best American History Essays* volume to OAH more than three years ago. We also appreciate the efforts of our colleagues at Palgrave Macmillan, especially editor Alessandra Bastagli, Erin Ivy, and Emily Leithauser, who made these volumes possible.

—*Lee W. Formwalt*
Executive Director, Organization of American Historians

Introduction

Jacqueline Jones

For avid readers of history, the historical essay offers all the pleasures of a book, compressed; here, in just thirty pages or so, are the elements that make historical scholarship such a compelling literary genre—a good story, well told and thoroughly researched, a narrative that illuminates the past and, in some cases, inspires fresh ways of looking at the present. Indeed, a case can be made that the history essay compares to a book the same way a short story compares to a novel: The shorter work provides the gratification and intellectual stimulation of the longer one, but the story moves more briskly, and the reader is rewarded more quickly.

And so it is lamentable that most history readers never encounter the very best essays, many of which are published and widely scattered in more than three hundred journals devoted to historical scholarship. The vast majority of these journals are highly specialized and readily available only to members of professional historical organizations and to scholars and students with access to extensive libraries. The purpose of this volume is to gather between two covers ten essays that represent the best in current scholarship, and to bring to a wider audience outstanding works in American history that would otherwise reach only a small audience.

These essays were chosen by a hardworking committee of eight people, all members of the Organization of American Historians, the largest professional organization of historians of the United States. The committee's task was to survey an impressive variety and number of scholarly journals and general interest magazines, and to choose from them a handful of essays notable for their overall excellence and for their accessibility to a wider audience. Committee members included Anthony J. Badger, John M. Belohlavek, Ellen Carol DuBois, Eric Foner, Sharon Harley, M. Ruth Kelly, John Saillant, and Elliott West. The group followed a grueling schedule that spanned five months and culminated in mid-May, when most members faced a crushing end-of-year workload. In the spring of 2006, that workload included not only the usual tasks of grading papers and preparing for commencement exercises, but also the challenge of voting for ten essays out of a shortlist of thirty-seven nominees. Essays on the shortlist appeared in thirty-one different (for the most part highly specialized) publications, including, among others, *Montana: The Magazine of Western History, Sport History Review, Columbia Journal of Law, Journal of Urban History, New Political Science, Teachers College Record*, and *Journal of Military History*.

Taken together, these ten essays are a testament to the richness and vitality of current scholarship in the field of American history. In theme and time period, they range widely over the vast landscape of the American past, in all its fascinating detail and diversity—from the late eighteenth-century borderlands inhabited by Indians, French, and Spanish to contentious debates over slavery in the Baptist churches of early nineteenth-century Kentucky; to Civil War battlefields with their bloody harvests of corpses; to twentieth-century Midwestern airports evolving from parklands to noisy centers of commercial transportation; and recent debates over any number of historical events and developments, including the Lewis and Clark expedition of 1804–1806 and the civil rights movement of the mid-twentieth century. Of course American history encompasses far more than whatever transpired on American soil; several essays suggest the necessity of transcending national borders—to examine debates over Chinese immigrant workers, or the housekeeping skills of wives of Foreign Service diplomats—if we are to gain an appreciation of American history that is broadly defined. The historians represented in this collection have employed a number of different research methodologies and have examined an array of historical sources, including, to name but a few, legal and literary texts, courtroom testimony, sermons and minutes of church meetings, federal and local government records, Congressional testimony, city recreation commission reports, letters, diaries, oral history testimony, travelers' accounts, newspapers, advertisements, records of commercial transactions, census data, and political speeches. The footnotes of these works tell a story in themselves, and suggest historians' new and creative ways of recapturing the country's past.

Published in nine different journals, these essays also illustrate the excellence of specialized publications. Fittingly, the *Journal of American History*, which publishes in all fields, is represented by two articles in this collection. The other journals include *American Quarterly, Journal of the Early Republic, American Literary History, Southern California Quarterly, Technology and Culture, Southern Cultures, Journal of Southern History*, and *Journal of Women's History*. Most of these journals find their way into the hands only of the dues-paying members of the professional organizations that publish them—for example, the Organization of American Historians (*Journal of American History*), the Southern Historical Association (*Journal of Southern History*), and the American Studies Association (*American Quarterly*). However, like many other articles published in these journals, the ten included here deserve a wide and appreciative readership.

Certainly the art of the historical essay has received far less attention than the art of the short story. The relatively short length of the essay belies the amount of time necessary to perfect it. In many cases, article-length manuscripts undergo a lengthy process of revision and resubmission to a particular journal, or even, in some instances, to several different journals, before they are accepted for publication. Editors send manuscripts to as many as seven different readers, who in some instances offer wildly contradictory reports to the author. Overall favorable reviews are no guarantee that a manuscript will be accepted; instead, such reviews often contain multiple suggestions for revisions and additional research, prompting intensive rewriting. The whole unwieldy process can consume many months, or even a number of years, from initial submission to final publication. In several essays, either in the first note or in prefatory material to the notes, the author acknowledges the comments and suggestions offered by an array of friends, colleagues, students, conference participants, and anonymous journal readers. Like a book, the history essay, then, is often the product of a grueling regimen and of a broader collective effort than the lone author's name might imply.

These essays explore a variety of topics that range widely over time and space, with some narrowing in on a case study and others taking a more capacious view of the past. At the same time the essays illustrate a number of interlocking themes and overlapping research methodologies revealing of the state of historical scholarship in the early twenty-first century. Several introduce us to relatively new fields, such as the history of the environment and the "new" foreign relations history. Taken individually and as a group, the essays also reveal the creative strategies of historians who are bringing women into stories about the past. A number focus on the problem of slavery and other tangible forms of racial ideologies that transcend a black-white binary. The authors represented here also explore the politics of remembering—how we as a nation memorialize the past and construct stories to illuminate it. Several consider the ways that different groups of Americans have constructed, acknowledged, and honored the notion and the reality of citizenship. Additionally, the essays offer pointed critiques of bland textbook renderings of the past, and of national mythologies that are marketed by enterprising merchandisers and entertainment companies. Readers will find these essays stimulating and provocative, and in some cases disturbing. In other words, these works will evoke a range of emotional and intellectual responses in ways that good literature always does.

In order to provide a more accurate view of the past, recent historians have broadened traditional subfields of history, and opened up new areas of inquiry. For example, scholars working in the traditional field of American diplomatic history tended to focus on international conflicts and high-level negotiations; these writers looked to the decisions made by presidents, prime ministers, and generals to explore America's place in the world. In contrast, scholars working in the field of the "new" foreign relations history look beyond the roles of heads of state and military officials in crafting foreign policy. These historians take a broader perspective that takes into account international labor relations, changing ideas of race and other notions of social difference, and the effects of domestic political and social developments on the relations between the United States and other countries. For example, in his essay, "Outlawing 'Coolies': Race, Nation, and Empire in the Age of Emancipation," Moon-Ho Jung explores the mid-nineteenth-century debate over the importation of Chinese workers called "coolies," a largely derogatory term connoting unfree, or enslaved, slave labor.[1] Jung explores a question that increasingly preoccupied landowners all over the world: How best to deploy large labor forces in the sugar, cotton, and rice fields in response to an expanding global market for staple crops? Jung views the United States as part of a larger system of transnational labor migrations in the nineteenth century, and relates this debate to the controversy over slavery in antebellum America, where abolitionists and their adversaries were contemplating a nation—and a world—purged of unfree labor. Thus he shows that the concern over importing large numbers of Chinese workers was not just an American story, but one linked to the wider imperial policies of European powers shaping the Caribbean and Asia throughout this period. In the United States, some slave owners and employers saw these workers as a transitional work-force bridging the institution of slavery and free labor, and hence a group to be welcomed, or feared, depending on one's perspective. Jung reminds us of the spectrum of labor systems that have shaped American history—not just slavery and free labor at either extreme, but also indentured servitude and apprenticeship in between.

Writing about a completely different topic, Molly M. Wood nonetheless joins with Jung in challenging the traditional view of American foreign relations as a domain inhabited only by powerful men crafting diplomacy in the suites of palaces and the offices of the U.S. State Department. In "Diplomatic Wives: The Politics of Domesticity and the 'Social Game' in the U.S. Foreign Service, 1905–1941," she suggests that the U.S. households established abroad carried great symbolic and practical significance within the realm of diplomatic overtures and negotiations.[2] The Foreign Service diplomatic corps consisted of husbands and wives who forged partnerships to conduct diplomacy outside formal meetings—at parties and receptions and around the dinner table. Within these informal venues, women as wives and mothers served as highly visible ambassadors of American prosperity as well as agents of formal diplomatic initiatives. Wood also explores the ways that wives' interaction with native-born servants revealed the American women's own class and cultural assumptions. And she discusses the hierarchy of age and status among the wives themselves, a hierarchy that encouraged older women to serve as mentors to their young counterparts, instructing them in their daunting responsibilities. At a time when relations with other countries were assuming an ever more critical role in U.S. politics and society, the politics of domesticity was a game, its rules being shaped by highly stylized forms of etiquette that women as well as men were able to—and forced to—master. The women who hoped to "win" this game had to be well trained and well informed; the stakes were high: advancing their husbands' careers as well as promoting the stipulated foreign policy interests of the United States.

If the new foreign relations history reveals fresh ways of looking at the past, so too does the history of the environment, an emerging field that stresses the social meanings and functions of the natural and built environment. Writing about the complex interplay between technology and the environment, Janet R. Daly Bednarek explores the evolution of the modern airport in her essay "The Flying Machine in the Garden: Parks and Airports, 1918–1938."[3] For the most part, the earliest airports had functions quite different from those of today. At the dawn of air travel, many people saw airports as parkland, as places of recreation. Indeed, cities often paired various forms of leisure—from swimming to horseshoes—with expansive pieces of real estate that also included landing strips. During these early years, people flocked to airports not to travel to distant places, but to relax with their families, enjoy a picnic lunch, and watch the planes. Air races and daredevil stunts and celebrity appearances and other forms of mass entertainment were all part of the function of the early airport. Only later in the century did city parks and recreation departments cede their airports to private companies that specialized in the transportation of people, mail, and goods.

Like many good stories, this one is evocative: while reading it I began to think back to the 1950s and the Sunday afternoons I spent with my parents and two brothers at the New Castle County airport, a small regional airport in northern Delaware. During World War II, my father, a licensed pilot and technical sergeant, had served as Central Fire Control ("top gun") on a B-29 "Superfortress" bomber. Stationed in the South Pacific on the island of Saipan, he and his crewmates flew thirty missions, most of them over Japanese cities during the last nine months of the war. But a decade later, on any particular Sunday afternoon, he could be found piling his wife and daughter and two sons into the family's red Ford station wagon and driving twenty minutes or so to the airport. There we would enjoy dinner together and watch the planes land and take off. For my father, the airport had now become a site not of danger, but of postwar domesticity, a place of leisure and family togetherness. Contemplating the nature and function of today's airport, more resembling an armed camp than a green space oasis, it is difficult to imagine fighting one's way through security barriers and police checks for the sole purpose of sharing a family meal, let alone finding a place to spread out the picnic blanket. Bednarek's work introduces us to a new dimension of the not-so-distant past, when flying machines and natural landscapes complemented and did not war against each other.

Bednarek makes her case about the evolving functions of airports by examining the cities of Wichita, Omaha, and Minneapolis. Her work reminds us that case studies can help to reveal not just the particulars of American history, but broader themes as well. Monica Najar's essay, " 'Meddling with Emancipation': Baptists, Authority, and the Rift over Slavery in the Upper South," focuses on debates over slavery in Kentucky Baptist churches around 1800.[4] By taking a relatively narrow view, she is able to provide local texture to this widening crisis in American political life. At the national level, politicians crafted tortuous compromises between the free North and the slaveholding South, compromises that were reworked and renewed through the 1850s. But at the local level, smaller bodies—in this case church congregations—erupted into open conflict over the issue of slavery, as the question of human bondage spilled out of the realm of religion and into the realm of economy and society. In the young state of Kentucky, homesteaders faced the arduous tasks of chopping down trees, clearing the land, and planting and harvesting crops. Because these tasks often outstripped the energies of any one family, and because slavery was such a widely accepted system of labor exploitation, many white Kentuckians embraced the institution unequivocally.

However, Baptists faced a particular set of dilemmas: First, their faith, and in many cases church membership rolls, presumed an equality among congregants, rich and poor, male and female, black and white, slave and free. Second, Baptist doctrine established church authority over their members' social relations; but when certain ministers and congregants began to speak out against human bondage, they provoked bitter controversy within and among individual Baptist churches. By examining church minutes and other records, Najar is able to reconstruct the conflict that tore congregations apart and ultimately led Baptists in general to cede authority over the master-slave relation to civil institutions such as state legislatures and courts. In contrast to broader studies of slavery, Najar's essay shows the nuances of localized debates within a literature that often casts the controversy in broader, North-South terms.

In addition to Najar, several other authors take up the question of slavery and its legacy as the great moral burden of a nation conceived in liberty and freedom. Kentucky Baptists engaged in a bitter debate over the seeming contradiction between their own high-minded egalitarianism on one hand and the grim realities of homesteading on the other. More generally, this disjuncture—between professed ideals of the nation's founders and the brutal reality of chattel slavery—is a topic of enduring and widespread concern among historians. In her essay titled, "Revisiting Nashoba: Slavery, Utopia, and Frances Wright in America," Gail Bederman focuses on a British reformer and author determined to set in motion single-handedly a great abolitionist project within the antebellum United States.[5] Frances Wright viewed the United States as the most enlightened republic in the world, and believed that bondage was but an aberration, a blot on the country's character that, with some effort and determination, could be lifted from the fabric of the young nation. Wright founded an experimental community she called Neshoba, where, presumably, collective labor would enable a small number of slaves to work hard and earn enough money to free themselves. Yet Wright was a victim of her own ignorance and naiveté, according to Bederman. The reformer underestimated southern planters' dependence on enslaved labor. Wright also failed to live up to her own egalitarian principles, treating the enslaved residents of Nashoba as inferior beings who must be shipped out of the country, to Haiti or Liberia, if and when they earned their freedom.

Like Moon-Ho Jung and his work on Chinese "coolies," Juliana Barr shows that the issue of slavery in general and unfree labor more particularly is not one that we can confine within black-white dichotomies. Barr, in her essay "From Captives to Slaves: Commodifying Indian Women in the Borderlands," calls our attention to a diversity of slave systems within territory that would eventually become part of the United States.[6] She suggests that a relatively narrow view of slavery, one that focuses only on people of African descent performing forced labor, ignores significant departures from that particular form of bondage—specifically, the systems that developed in areas of the Lower Mississippi Valley and the Southwest occupied by Indians, French, and Spanish in the late eighteenth century. Barr focuses on the plight of Indian women and children captives, and contributes to our understanding of the multiple ways groups in addition to people of African descent were enslaved, and the various meanings attached to these forms of slavery. In this borderlands area, French traders treated Indian women captives as pawns in negotiations, sources of prestige, currency of exchange, a means of bonding between men of different cultural groups, and potential sexual partners and wives in an area where women of French descent were in short supply. While the French willingly enslaved Indian women, they refrained from holding their coreligionists, the Spanish, in bondage. For their part, Spanish colonial officials incorporated into their military strategies the use of Indian women and children as captives of war and as political hostages in a contested land marked by sporadic warfare and persistent violence. Barr shows the multiple uses of enslaved persons—not just as sources of exploitable labor, but as human pawns useful to powerful men of all kinds.

Barr forces us to rethink the problem of racial ideologies—those ever-changing notions of difference based on "racial" categories. Similarly, Michelle Brattain's work stresses the fluidity of those notions, and more particularly, the near impossibility of defining "racial" identities with any precision, whether in the workplace or in a court of law. In "Miscegenation and Competing Definitions of Race in Twentieth Century Louisiana," she examines the efforts by Louisiana lawmakers, judges, and employers to enforce a black-white definition of race.[7] Meanwhile, Louisiana (like all other states) was populated by residents whose skin color and background defied such easy categorization. Examining the testimony of witnesses in antimiscegenation cases, Brattain finds ordinary individuals wrestling with state-imposed racial definitions that remained at odds with their own relationships revolving around kin, friends, neighbors, coworkers, and sexual partners. In Louisiana and no doubt all over the United States, people defied the imperatives of a rigid "racial" segregation, identifying themselves and other people along various lines of heritage, culture, and (for people with a light skin color), individual choice. Indeed, Brattain suggests that people constructed their own identities on the basis of whom they lived with and established relationships with, and not on the basis of state-sanctioned forms of "racial" difference.

Several authors introduce their essays by noting they hope to get beyond glib textbook generalizations about the American past. For example, Gale Bederman begins her subject, revisiting Nashoba, with the observation that many textbook authors describe that community as a beacon of harmony, a successful example of interracial living in the wilderness of American proslavery sentiment. In this view, Frances Wright was a visionary who challenged prevailing ideas about the proper role of women and black men. On the contrary, Bederman, asserts, Wright had no intention of treating blacks as equals, and she failed miserably at running a collective enterprise.

Stephen Aron revisits a famous episode in his essay, "The Afterlives of Lewis and Clark."[8] The two explorers have received a great deal of attention recently—not just from textbook authors, but also from museum curators and merchandisers of everything from dolls to cookbooks and playing cards. Aron points out that in the last few years the expedition has often been rendered in broad strokes for the general public as a milestone in multicultural goodwill. In this view, William Clark and Meriwether Lewis established friendly relations with the Indians they encountered, and integrated an Indian, Sacagawea, and a black slave, York, as full and equal members into their Corps of Discovery. Aron disputes this view by looking into the posttrek careers of both Lewis and Clark, when Lewis served as the governor of the new, expansive Louisiana Territory, and Clark went on to become a brigadier general of the Louisiana territorial militia and superintendent of Indian affairs. In contrast to their two-and-a-half years exploring the Northwest, when they remained sensitive to the delicate intricacies of cultural negotiation and commercial exchange with Indians, later in their careers both men found themselves under pressure to preside over the dispossession of vast numbers of natives. Although President Thomas Jefferson had commissioned the Corps to find a water route to the Pacific, one that would facilitate trade, subsequent policies of the federal government aimed to remove Indians from their land, or otherwise deprive them of the full and unfettered use of it.

Aron challenges what he calls the "feel-good myth of the Lewis and Clark epic," and provides an account of York's life after the trek. Citing recently discovered correspondence, Aron shows that, contrary to the myth, Clark refused to grant York his freedom as a reward for his vital role in the journey, and instead kept the black man in bondage, forcing him to continue living apart from his wife. As York grew increasingly resentful, Clark grew increasingly abusive, beating him and threatening to sell him to another owner as punishment. Rather than foreshadowing a nation of great tolerance and freedom, the posttrek history of Lewis and Clark reveals much about the hardening of prejudice toward Indians and blacks in the early nineteenth century, according to Aron. This more accurate version of events calls into question the historical basis of recent energetic efforts to market a happy ending to the Lewis and Clark story.

Aron's work reminds us of the significance of memory and memorials—how and why we reconstruct the past, and the meanings we today attach to past events. In her essay, " 'The Dread Void of Uncertainty': Naming the Dead in the American Civil War," Drew Gilpin Faust examines the problem of remembering and honoring the dead who have fallen in war.[9] In her essay she illuminates larger questions of citizenship arising from the sacrifices of American soldiers and their families, northern and southern, in the Civil War. Faust notes the unprecedented scale of the slaughter—the fact that more than 600,000 soldiers lost their lives in the conflict, more than all the American war fatalities from the Revolution to the present combined. This vast carnage, together with emerging ideas of federal responsibility, prompted Confederate and U.S. officials alike to develop more systematic procedures for identifying the dead, recording their names and the circumstances of their death, and notifying their families. Before and during much of the Civil War, these grim tasks were considered to come under the purview of individual military officers and the comrades of the deceased, who, on an ad hoc basis and in their own good time, were informally responsible for contacting the dead man's kin. Yet the huge numbers of Civil War fatalities, and the fact that in some cases human remains were literally obliterated by lethal forms of modern warfare, meant that officials would find the traditional methods of identification and notification unequal to the task at hand.

By the end of the war, and with the prodding of energetic and determined reformers such as Clara Barton, the United States had established formal procedures for accounting for the battlefield fallen. In the process, Faust argues, Americans began to recognize that the nation was a collection of affective relationships organized around households and kin networks. By demonstrating patience and by sacrificing their loved ones to a patriotic cause, the living too deserved honor and respect from a grateful nation. Thus the state recognized the rights of mothers and wives to know how and why a son or brother had died, and where he was buried. This process was integral to emerging definitions of citizenship and government accountability.

Faust recognizes that the narrative of individual deaths—who died, where, and under what conditions—carried great significance. It was a narrative that the parents, wives, and children of fallen soldiers needed to know, had a right to know. Jacquelyn Dowd Hall also focuses on the power of stories about the past to inform us about ourselves and about the broader contours of American history. Hall's essay, which was also her OAH presidential address in 2004, is titled "The Long Civil Rights Movement and the Political Uses of the Past." She begins with the premise that embedded within stories, including works of history, lurk potentially dangerous and divisive truths.[10] Today, Americans often look not to professional historians but to "public story tellers"—political pundits, museum curators, film directors, and corporate executives—for an understanding of who we are as a nation, and of ways change can or cannot be effected. It is within this context that Hall describes what she calls the "dominant narrative" of the American civil rights movement enshrined in textbooks and in current public discussions of the successes and failures of modern American politics.

This "dominant narrative," Hall suggests, focuses on Martin Luther King, Jr., and the activism of other southern black leaders, and begins with the *Brown v. Board* Supreme Court decision of 1954 and ends with the Civil Rights acts of 1964 and 1965. Hall suggests that recently, conservative politicians and ideologues have reinforced this narrative in order to argue that the civil rights project was a narrow and contained effort led by a few high-minded men. These conservatives regard the movement as a relatively limited project that culminated in the passage of federal legislation in the mid-1960s. The result of this legislation was a newly "color-blind" society where discussions of racial ideologies and their legacies had no place. Such "color blindness," Hall charges, provides a license for indifference toward not only the ongoing struggles of people of color, but also indifference or contempt toward a longer and deeper campaign that encapsulated the rights of workers and women as well.

Hall begins her counternarrative in the early twentieth century with the great migration of black people out of the South, continues the story through the 1930s with the surge in federal power, and ends it in the 1980s, with the Reagan devolution of federal power to the states. In the process, Hall reconfigures the history of the civil rights movement, and encourages us to consider the way the histories of unions, women's rights organizations, and civil rights advocacy groups were entwined. This perspective, she suggests, allows for little of the complacency characteristic of the purveyors of the "dominant narrative" of civil rights history. In describing the "long civil rights movement," she sees not triumph and closure, but an unfinished project on behalf of the struggles of blacks, workers, and people of color.

In conclusion, the ten essays in this volume are notable for the way that their interlocking stories provide us with new ways of looking at the past. Several authors aim to overturn conventional views about the black-white binary, suggesting that discourses about and practices related to notions of racial and cultural hierarchy are broader and deeper than a single-minded focus on African American history might suggest. It is also worth noting here that most historians integrate into their analysis issues of gender as a matter of fact—a matter of historical fact—in order to provide a more accurate view of the country's past. Portrayed here are not only women as wives and mothers, but women as reformers, workers, and as agents of change on the national and the international scene. Even women's tasks that might have once been viewed as purely domestic—keeping house and raising children—can, within contexts as divergent as eighteenth-century borderlands and twentieth-century Foreign Service households, assume tremendous political and even international significance. And finally, the historians represented here understand keenly the power of stories to shape not only national identity and our vision of the past, but also, at least in some cases, our priorities for the future. Together these essays reveal the power of history as a source of enlightenment, entertainment, and enduring fascination for readers everywhere.

Notes

Jacqueline Jones is Harry S. Truman Professor of American History at Brandeis University. A MacArthur Foundation Fellow (1999–2004), Jones is the author of several books on labor, the Civil War, and the American South, including *Saving Savannah: Civil Wars in the Georgia Lowcountry, 1854–1872* (forthcoming), *Creek Walking: Growing Up in Delaware in the 1950s* (2001), *American Work: Four Centuries of Black and White Labor* (1998), *The Dispossessed: America's Underclasses from the Civil War to the Present* (1992), and *Labor of Love, Labor of Sorrow: Black Women, Work, and the Family from Slavery to the Present* (1985).

1. *American Quarterly* 57 (September 2005): 677–701.
2. *Journal of Women's History* 17 (Summer 2005).
3. *Technology and Culture* 46 (April 2005): 350–73.
4. *Journal of the Early Republic* (Summer 2005): 157–86.
5. *American Literary History* (Fall 2005): 438–59.
6. *Journal of American History* (June 2005): 19–46.
7. *Journal of Southern History* (August 2005): 621–58.
8. *Southern California Quarterly* (Spring 2005): 27–46.
9. *Southern Cultures* (Summer 2005): 7–32.
10. *Journal of American History* (March 2005): 1233–63.

Chapter 1

From Captives to Slaves: Commodifying Indian Women in the Borderlands

Juliana Barr

From *The Journal of American History*

On July 21, 1774, fray Miguel Santa María y Silva, the leading Franciscan missionary stationed in the mission district of Los Adaes on the border between Texas and Louisiana, reported to the Spanish viceroy in Mexico City on his trip through that region as part of a delegation seeking renewed peace with powerful Wichita and Caddo nations. In 1769, in the aftermath of the Seven Years' War, Spain had officially established administrative control of the former French province of Louisiana, and the mission to reconfirm Wichita and Caddo alliances sought to represent the new unity of Spaniards and Frenchmen in Louisiana and Texas. Many, however, could not put aside past rivalries so easily, and Santa María y Silva was no exception. Rather than detail this first peace council sought by the Spanish government with leading Indian nations, the Franciscan spent page after page lamenting an "infamous traffic of the flesh" he had witnessed being carried on by Frenchmen living in and among Caddoan Indian villages along the Red River. To discredit Frenchmen, Santa María y Silva could have deplored the skyrocketing numbers of enslaved Africans and African Americans in Louisiana by the 1770s. Or, given the hostile relations between the Spanish government and many independent and powerful Indian nations in the lower Plains, the missionary could have bemoaned the fate of Spanish women and children from New Mexico who had been taken captive by Indians armed with guns obtained from French traders. Yet, strikingly, the traffic in humans on which Santa María y Silva chose to focus was one in Indian women and their children, captured by Indian warriors in the Southern Plains and Texas and traded east as slaves to French buyers in Louisiana— women thus consigned to "perdition" by "such cruel captivity," grieved Santa María y Silva.[1]

Given the growing proliferation of studies of Indian slavery, notably the works of James F. Brooks and Alan Gallay, the Franciscan's lament seems not at all surprising.[2] Increasing attention to the enslavement of Indians has pushed United States historians beyond identifications of North American slavery as primarily an African American experience and of North American captivity as primarily a white experience. As Brooks's study of New Mexico demonstrates, scholars are beginning to focus attention also on women as the victims of that slave trade. Their scholarship is deepening understandings of the roles of Indian women in their peoples' interactions with Europeans. Women often stood in unique positions to learn languages, to act as translators and emissaries in cross-cultural communications, and to create ties between cultures.[3] Though scholars have recognized that the conflicting European and native systems of power in which native women operated constrained the women's opportunities, an emphasis on women's agency has obscured the more coercive traffics in women that were equally central to Indian-European relations. In seeking to redeem the humanity of such women and to recognize their important roles in trade and diplomacy, scholars have often equated agency with choice, independent will, or resistance and de-emphasized the powerlessness, objectification, and suffering that defined the lives of many. Perhaps the best-known example of this trend in American history and popular culture is Sacagawea, whose capture at the hands of raiding Hidatsas turned into enslavement when she was purchased by the French Canadian trader Toussaint Charbonneau—bondage that continued through her time with the Lewis and Clark expedition. The violence and coercion that reduced her to the status of a slave among Euro-Americans has been lost, as popular preference casts her as Charbonneau's "wife" and a celebrated mediator of Indian-European diplomacy.[4]

The scholarly focus on mediation and accommodation as women's characteristic activity in Indian-European relations often leads us to overlook the importance of women in political economies of war and imperial rivalry. Multiple coercive traffics in women became essential to European-Indian interaction long before Sacagawea fell into the hands of her captors. Recognition of the diversity of trafficking not only enriches our understanding of the gender dynamics of European-Indian diplomacy and conflict, but also enables us to move beyond the homogeneous conception of slavery suggested by using only African American enslavement, specifically, racial chattel slavery (defined here as a form of property and system of compulsory labor entailing permanent and hereditary status) to explore bondage and unfreedom in America. In fact, the very heterogeneity of Indian bondage suggests comparisons with the range of slave practices in Africa, Asia, the Mediterranean, and other parts of the world where at different times and places, persons—primarily women—were held and used as not only economic, but also as social and political capital. These are comparisons that resonate with growing scholarly discussions of slavery in a global perspective.[5]

The confluence of Spanish, French, and Indian peoples in the areas later known as Comanchería, Apachería, Spanish Texas, and French Louisiana (figure 1.1) makes them an ideal venue for exploring the forms that traffic in women might take and the kinds of currency that women might represent to Indian and European men who exchanged them. Distinct systems of captivity, bondage, and enslavement developed in a matrix of expanding Indian territories, French mercantilism, and Spanish defensive needs during the eighteenth century. At the end of the seventeenth century, steadily increasing numbers of Spaniards coming north from Mexico and Frenchmen coming south from Illinois and Canada began to invade the region and establish neighboring, competing provinces. At the same time, the territories of bands of Apaches and later Comanches and Wichitas were shifting to include increasingly large areas of present-day north and north-central Texas. As those groups converged in the eighteenth century, European and Indian men—as captors, brokers, and buyers—used captured and enslaved women to craft relationships of trade and reciprocity with one another. A key difference between such exchanges and those involving inter-marriage was that the women whom men captured and enslaved were

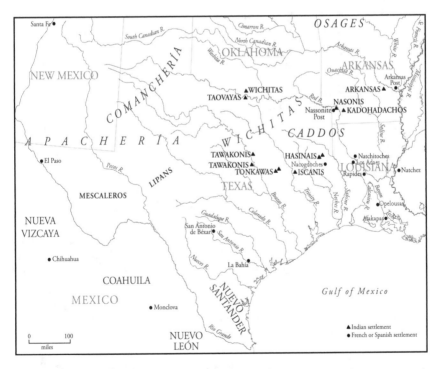

Figure 1.1 Major Indian, Spanish, and French settlements in Spanish Texas, French Louisiana, Apachería, Comanchería, and the territories of Caddo and Wichita peoples in the mid-eighteenth century.

Source: Organization of American Historians.

strangers or enemies to their kinship systems. When Indian bands brokered marital unions in the service of diplomacy, a woman's own family or band leaders usually negotiated on her behalf, as in the fur trade of Canada, the Great Lakes region, and the American Southeast. In contrast to such women, who may have expanded their existing social and economic authority through intermarriage, enslaved Indian women in Texas and Louisiana remained outside the kin relations of the households that made them objects of exchange.[6] If efforts to cement diplomatic and economic ties did not succeed—as often happened between Indians and Spaniards—military and state officials made punitive war, seeking out captives and hostages in retribution for failed negotiations. Thus hostility as much as accommodation was the context for the traffic in women. The political and commercial aspects of the exchanges also set them apart from most Indian practices of captivity and from European systems of enslavement: Indians did not take the women to avenge or replace the dead, as they took most captives; nor did Europeans intend to use them as a servile labor force, as they used most slaves. Instead, the exchanges interwove the categories of captivity and slavery and thereby transformed Indian women into valuable commodities of cross-cultural war, diplomacy, and power.

Writing in 1774, Santa María y Silva demonstrated a certain disingenuousness in focusing only on Frenchmen, since Spaniards had been reducing select Indians from the region to bondage for much of the eighteenth century. But that misdirection highlights the way the trade in Indian women may explicate geopolitical relations among European and native powers in colonial America. In his attempts to accent Spanish-French differences, the Franciscan downplayed the contentious relations between Spaniards and neighboring Indians that had made the diplomatic mission to the Wichita and Caddo bands a necessity in the first place. In such a world, Indian women in the hands of enemy Indian men became key objects of captive raiding and hostage exchange as the women's Indian captors sought economic and diplomatic gain with both native and European allies. In the hands of Spanish and French buyers and enslavers, women faced fates from sexual servitude, to consignment to labor camps, to use as political capital in attempts to win or impose alliances or to signal the failure of those efforts. The multiplicity of experiences reflected not only differences of culture or race, but also different understandings of how to govern, how to express power, and how to seek and build political relationships with other men and the nations they represented, whether native or European. This, then, is the story I would like to explore: the ways Spanish, French, and Indian men sought to forge or coerce bonds of obligation through a trade in female pawns. The diverse conditions to which such women were reduced reveal new ways of understanding bondage and unfreedom.

Our story begins with French-Indian captive trade across the Plains and along the Texas-Louisiana border. Initial European observations at the end of the seventeenth century suggest that natives in the Southern Plains and the Red River valley did not maintain captives as a source of labor. Instead,

Indian peoples took a few captives in warfare only for ritualized ceremonies of revenge or, less often, for adoption. Men rarely allowed themselves to be captured, preferring death on the battlefield; those captured most often were destined for torture, which furnished the opportunity for the honorable warrior's death denied them in battle (the honor acquired by enduring pain). In contrast, captors deemed women and children easier to incorporate into their communities, though adoption was not always their fate either. An early French observer, Henri Joutel, a survivor of René-Robert Cavelier, sieur de La Salle's ill-fated expedition of 1684–1687, recorded that during his visit to Hasinai Caddos in 1687, warriors returned from a battle with scalps and two captives for victory celebrations. Of the two captives, both women, one was turned over to Caddo women to be tortured and killed, the other was scalped but not killed, given a bullet and powder, and sent back to her people as a warning. Outside the realm of war, exchanges of women and children more often took a peaceful form, particularly in the service of diplomatic alliance. Intermarriage often united bands in political and economic relationships, such as the Hasinai, Natchitoches, and Kadohadacho confederacies created by the alliance of various Caddo bands by the end of the seventeenth century. Children might also be exchanged among Wichita and Caddoan bands and adopted into their communities as signs of alliance and insurance of peace.[7]

Three years after Joutel's encounters with Caddos, Henri de Tonti and several other Frenchmen arrived in Caddo lands in search of survivors of La Salle's expedition, and Kadohadacho warriors tried to persuade the Frenchmen to accompany them into war against Spaniards to the southwest of their lands. As enticement, the warriors promised the Frenchmen any money found, but "as for themselves," Tonti recorded, "they only wished to take the women and children as slaves." The Frenchmen declined, trying to make clear that the decision derived from a reluctance to take Christian captives, since the women and children targeted were in Spanish settlements. The Caddo men, however, could not be blamed for presuming French interest in slaves, since the Frenchmen showed no reluctance to trade in enslaved or captive *Indians*. In fact, Tonti had brought with him two Kadohadacho women whom he had purchased from Arkansas Indians at his Illinois trading post on the Mississippi River. The Frenchman hoped that returning the women to their people would put him in the Caddos' good graces—and he was right; it did. It may also have helped establish an image of Frenchmen as purveyors of Indian slaves in the minds of Caddoan peoples.[8]

After the French province of Louisiana was established in 1699, French officials, following these earlier promising contacts, decided to orient their trade interests to the west and north. In 1706, the Spanish expedition leader Juan de Ulibarri reported to New Mexican officials that Wichitas in the Southern Plains had begun to sell captive Apache women and children to the French (whom the Wichitas then identified as the "Spanish in the east"). Attempts to find routes to New Mexico put the French in contact with

Indian bands whose reactions to the French newcomers further signaled their spreading reputation as slave raiders. In 1719, for instance, when the French trader Claude-Charles Dutisné first approached a northern Wichita village in the Plains, warriors twice raised a war club over his head as he struggled to convince them that he had not come to enslave them. A warning from neighboring Osages regarding French intentions, he soon learned, had preceded his arrival.[9]

Dutisné's protestations to the contrary notwithstanding, the French presence quickly introduced a commercial element into native captive taking in the Southern Plains and Red River valley in the early eighteenth century. The same year he faced death on the Northern Plains, Dutisné also recorded that a Mento (Wichita) chief had visited him at a new French post along the Red River to sell Indian slaves (most likely Plains Apaches). Another French trader, Jean Baptiste La Harpe, reported a mix of old and new ways of treating captives in Wichita villages he had visited. At a Tawakoni (Wichita) village on the South Canadian River, a Wichita chief gave La Harpe an eight-year-old Apache boy in an exchange of ceremonial gifts and speeches. In the same breath, the chief added that had La Harpe arrived a month earlier, he could have given (or sold) him seventeen more Apaches, but, alas, they had been killed in a public festival.[10]

Frenchmen next attempted to open trade with Apaches, the very people who were losing relatives to French enslavement. In 1724, Etienne de Bourgmont sent a twenty-two-year-old woman and a teenage boy of sixteen whom he had purchased from Kansas Indians back to their village among Plains Apaches. Three months later, he traveled there and tried to build on this gesture in seeking trade relations with Apache leaders. Standing in the midst of trade goods he had carefully laid out for display—rifles, sabers, pickaxes, gunpowder, bullets, red cloth, blue cloth, mirrors, knives, shirts, scissors, combs, gunflints, vermilion, awls, needles, kettles, bells, beads, brass wire, and rings—Bourgmont both symbolically and rhetorically made the case that the Apaches would derive advantage from trade with Frenchmen. Apache leaders, though, saw quite a different gain to be had and quickly grabbed the opportunity. "We will go to visit the French, and we will bring horses to trade with them," an Apache chief first informed Bourgmont. The next day, as negotiations continued, he neatly and publicly committed the French to supplying much more than the goods so carefully advertised by Bourgmont. Standing before more than two hundred warriors and an equal number of women and children who served as audience to the ceremonial meetings, the Apache leader announced: "You see here the Frenchman whom the Great Spirit has sent to our village to make peace with us. . . . Henceforth we shall be able to hunt in peace. . . . They will return to us our women and children whom they have taken from us and who are slaves in their country in exchange for horses that we will give them. The great French chief has promised this to us." But both men's machinations would be in vain.[11]

Despite Bourgmont's peaceful intentions and the Apache chief's persuasive rhetoric, French posts in western Louisiana had already become, and would remain throughout the eighteenth century, nuclei of a slave trade in Apache captives brought by Caddos, Wichitas, and later Comanches. Having identified the numerous and prosperous Caddoan peoples along the Red River as crucial targets for efforts to establish profitable trade alliances, Frenchmen had established a military post near a village of Natchitoches Indians in 1716, naming it Fort St. Jean Baptiste aux Natchitoches. They built a subsidiary trading post further upriver among Nasonis, another Caddo band, in 1719 (followed later by posts along the Red River at Rapides, Avoyelles, Ouachita, Opelousas, and Atakapas). A 1720 report of the French government addressing the commercial potential of the Natchitoches post and its hinterlands asserted that the most profitable trade with Indians there was in slaves, horses, deerskins, and bison hides. In 1726, Sieur Jean-Baptiste Le Moyne de Bienville reiterated that, although few Frenchmen had yet pursued it, "trade would be very good" with Wichita bands, and he implicitly connected the value of that trade to Wichitas' prowess as a "truly warlike" people who successfully took many captives from Apaches. Once Caddo, Wichita, and Comanche warriors had ascertained their own families' safety from French enslavement, they willingly obliged French desires by trading to them the enemy women and children they had captured in war.[12]

The Indian peoples with whom Frenchmen sought trade enjoyed powerful positions in the region, and almost all of them used the European presence to maintain and even strengthen those positions. Caddo, Wichita, and Comanche willingness to trade war captives to Frenchmen in exchange for European material goods indicates that the three groups—displaying a range of socioeconomic systems—did not secure captives with the intention of keeping them in their own communities for labor or other purposes. Caddoan peoples maintained three affiliated confederacies, spread thickly over hundreds of square miles in present-day Louisiana, Texas, Arkansas, and Oklahoma. The multiple communities in those confederacies rested economically on steadily intensifying agricultural production and a far-reaching commercial exchange system, involving trade in hides, salt, turquoise, copper, marine shells, bows, and pottery with New Mexico, the Gulf Coast, and the Great Lakes.[13] By the end of the seventeenth century, Wichita-speaking peoples had moved into the lower Southern Plains to establish fifteen to twenty consolidated, often palisaded villages scattered across the northern regions of present-day Texas, most in fertile lands along rivers where they could successfully farm without jeopardizing their defensive capabilities. The trade connections Wichitas then developed over the first half of the eighteenth century with Frenchmen and Caddos to the east and newly allied Comanches to the west secured a steady supply of guns and horses as well as critical alliances needed to defend their populous and productive communities against Osage and Apache raids.[14] Like Wichitas, Comanches had moved onto the Southern Plains by the early eighteenth century, operating as independent, bison-hunting groups loosely tied to one another in defensive and economic alliances.[15] By mid-century Comanche, Wichita, and Caddo bands had formed mutually beneficial trade relationships that brought European material goods, Plains hides, and Spanish horses together for exchange. All three also shared common enemies—multiple bands of Apaches living in mobile encampments across central Texas and western New Mexico—and all three took increasing numbers of Apache captives for trade in Louisiana.

The economic visions of Frenchmen in Louisiana dovetailed with those of native groups, as the French extended their involvement in the native trade networks that crisscrossed the Southern Plains and lower Mississippi Valley. Though plantation agriculture increasingly garnered the attention of Frenchmen in south and central Louisiana, the Indian hide trade remained an important component of the province's economy to the end of the eighteenth century. Thus, a satellite system of trading posts gradually began to line the western and northern reaches of the French province with a mandate to establish and maintain the economic and diplomatic relations that underwrote that trade. The Frenchmen of the outlying posts did not have the numbers or force to subjugate Indians or dispossess them of their lands, nor did they wish to. Rather, they sought to establish profitable exchange, and as a result, they entered into egalitarian relations with dominant Caddo, Wichita, and, by extension, Comanche peoples. Frenchmen offered European trade goods that the Spaniards in Texas would not, thus stealing a march on their rivals to the west. French demographic and settlement patterns further contributed to their success as traders. In the Louisiana hinterlands, French social and familial intermixing with Indians was widespread, as the French built their trading and military posts in or near native villages and consequently joined with Indians not only for trade, but also for subsistence, family building, and daily life. Community ties, in turn, brought Frenchmen into the heart of Indian political economies and offered foundations for long-lasting alliances.[16]

As such ties developed, bands of Caddos, Wichitas, and Comanches found female Indian captives to be as valuable as hides and horses in French markets in Natchitoches and other western Louisiana posts. In exchange, French trade offered native groups guns and ammunition essential not only for hunting, but also for defense in the context of increasing competition and militarization among the region's native peoples. To its Indian participants, the developing slave trade represented two sides of native conventions of reciprocity.[17] Caddos, Comanches, and Wichitas obtained their trade goods from a range of sources: the hides from hunting, the horses from raids on Spanish settlements in Texas, and the captives from warfare with native enemies (primarily Apaches). One aspect of native conventions dictated that the three groups took captives only from those they designated enemies or "strangers" to systems of kinship and political alliance—thus they took captives only in the context of war. On the flip side, once captive women became desirable commodities in Louisiana, they also served as tools Comanche, Wichita, and Caddo men could use to build trade relations with Frenchmen. In the eighteenth century, therefore, the French markets gave new value to an old by-product of warfare.

The trade in women following their capture resulted in more than individual benefit or profit, however. Like diplomatic exchanges, the Indian slave trade brought together men of French and Indian nations in an exchange that served both utilitarian and prestige purposes. Reciprocal relations both required and created kinship affiliation. Participation in exchanges made groups less likely to engage in confrontation and violence and brought them into metaphorical, if not real, relations of kinship. Caddo, Comanche, and Wichita men cast trade alliances in terms of fictive kinship categories of "brotherhood" and male sodalities. The women who were the objects of the exchange did not create or constitute the tie of personal or economic obligation. The exchange process itself created relationships, binding men to each other in the act of giving and receiving. Practices of intermarriage, adoption, and symbolic kinship relations among different Indian peoples and among Europeans and Indians meant that "kinship" expanded to include relations beyond those of only familial (biological) descent. Economic ties could not be separated from political ones, and trading partners were also military and political allies. Quite simply, one did not fight with brothers, just as one did not trade with enemies. Conversely, the predominance of "Canneci" (Apache) women in the enslaved Indian population in Louisiana became so pronounced by mid-century that the governor of Louisiana, Louis Billouart de Kerlérec, identified it as the primary hindrance to any hope of adding Apache nations to the list of Louisiana's native trade allies. Since successful trade with some groups made trade with others impossible, the slave trade put its own limits on French commercial expansion.[18]

Though the relations formed by the trade were between men, the female sex of the majority of enslaved Indians determined the supply, the demand, and thus the very existence of the trade network. Women were what Frenchmen wanted, and women were what Indian warriors had for exchange. Caddo, Comanche, and Wichita men traded only captive Indian women and children to Frenchmen (captive men were tortured and killed). In turn, the French market for female captives was not merely a response to the availability of such commodities in native societies, but also represented the needs of soldiers and traders in such French frontier settlements as Natchitoches. Unlike settlers in the British colonies and New France (Canada), those in French Louisiana made little systematic attempt to exploit enslaved Indians as a labor force. Louisiana colonists did hold as slaves some Indians whom French forces had defeated in wars—notably the Chitimachas in the 1710s and the Natchez in the 1730s—but such enslavement was an isolated practice belonging to the early period of French invasion and colonization. As early as 1706, French officials in Louisiana began lobbying their imperial superiors for permission to trade those Indian slaves for enslaved African Americans from the West Indies. A 1726

Louisiana census listed enslaved Africans as outnumbering enslaved Indians, 1,385 to 159, and the difference continued to expand due to an ever-increasing African population, especially in the 1780s when the Spanish government's renewal and legalization of the African slave trade led to a "re-Africanization" of Louisiana. Yet despite the growth in the enslaved African population, the number of enslaved Indians held steady, indicating that the size of the two populations bore little relation to one another.[19] More specifically, even as the importation of African American slave laborers replaced Indian slaves and the importation of French women made Indian concubinage and intermarriage unnecessary in regions of Louisiana with a larger European population, enslaved Indian women remained fixtures of Indian trade and French family life in outpost settlements in the west. The minimal use of Indian slaves in the establishment of French plantation agriculture and the French preference for enslaved African Americans as a servile labor force indicated that the continuing *Indian* slave trade held importance primarily for male domestic demands in the hinterlands of French settlement.

French settlers and traders by and large came from Canada rather than France and brought with them a social and cultural heritage of intimate association with Indian peoples. Intimate unions with women of allied nations and later with female slaves acquired for sexual exploitation were thus not new to the Frenchmen who emigrated to Louisiana. Because single male traders and agents, who often lived among their native trading partners, originally predominated in the French occupation of Louisiana, Frenchmen needed to intermarry if they were to have wives and families. Abbé Guillaume-Thomas-François de Raynal, writing in the 1770s and looking back over the century, argued that the French had brought to Louisiana "the custom of living with the savages, which they had adopted in Canada" and which often involved marrying Indian women with the "happiest results." "There was never observed the least coolness in the friendship between these two so diverse nations whom matrimony had united," Raynal continued, because "they have lived in this intercourse and reciprocity of mutual good-will, which made up for the vicissitudes of events brought by the passage of time."[20]

In this spirit, Frenchmen at posts such as Fort St. Jean Baptiste aux Natchitoches formed marital unions with their Caddo trading partners and sexual unions with the captive Apache women who were the objects of French-Caddo trade. Sexual and marital relations solidified French relationships with Caddoan peoples as demonstrable acts of permanence and commitment. The slave trade played a crucial role in supplementing the female population at Natchitoches throughout the eighteenth century. French colonial officials linked the Indian slave trade directly with a "licentious" mode of living that they considered a challenge to the colonization and development of Louisiana. The French missionary François le Maire bemoaned the trade in "savage female slaves" who, though reputedly bought to perform domestic services, in actuality became concubines. Such practice "had become established usage among the French at all levels, from governor Lépinay to a company officer, and from one of Crozat's [trade] agents to a private soldier," according to the historian Marcel Giraud. Sexual relations between Frenchmen and enslaved native women further merged commercial and marriage practices. The traffic in women via the slave trade, like French-Caddo intermarriage, developed out of the French-Indian trade and settlement nexus and strengthened the ties of interdependency. The consequent sexual relationships, whether licit or illicit, became widespread and significant enough to inspire heated complaints from French imperial and ecclesiastical officials that degeneracy marked social and familial relations in Louisiana. They helped fuel escalating demands for greater immigration of Frenchwomen as the eighteenth century progressed and led to official surveillance of interracial cohabitation and sexual intercourse. Despite such concerns at the imperial and provincial levels of church and state, however, the number of Apache women among enslaved populations and in Louisiana households steadily increased as trade networks in hides, horses, and captives grew between the French and Caddos and, through Caddos, extended to Wichitas and Comanches.[21]

On the other side of the Texas-Louisiana border, Indian enslavement exerted quite a different influence on the early invasion and settlement of the Spanish province of Texas. The advance of the Spanish frontier northward over the sixteenth and seventeenth centuries into the regions claimed as the provinces of Nueva Vizcaya, Coahuila, and Nuevo León (south of what became the province of Texas) had brought with it the spread of European diseases and the intrusion of slave-raiding expeditions seeking forced labor for Spanish mines and ranches—inexorable forces that preceded much of the colonization of those regions. Epidemics that began in the 1550s had, by the 1700s, scythed 90 percent of the native population of those northern regions of Mexico. Under law, moreover, the Crown might assign to Spaniards the labor and tribute of a specific Indian community in an arrangement termed an *encomienda*. Consequent Spanish demands for labor on farms and ranches and in mines brought their own brand of annihilation. By 1600, trafficking in enslaved Indians had become an established way of life in Nuevo León. Once the Spaniards there had killed off all the nearby Indian peoples by congregating them in crowded, unsanitary work camps where disease or overwork devastated their numbers, they extended the relentless reach of their slave raids ever northward. A 1672 royal cedula reiterated the royal prohibitions against the enslavement of Indians—first expressed in the New Laws in 1542 and reconfirmed in the 1680 Recompilation of the Laws of the Indies—and required their Christian conversion instead. But the Spaniards in the region merely renamed their *encomiendas*, calling them *congregaciones* (Indian communities nominally congregated for acculturation and religious instruction) and continued their raids into the mid-eighteenth century in search of Indian bodies for labor, not souls for salvation.[22]

Just as Indian groups had done when they encountered the early French traders on the Plains, Indians in Texas quickly learned what would be of value to the Spaniards whose expeditions had targeted the region even before permanent Spanish settlement was attempted in the 1690s. For some time rumors and evidence had been reaching them that the Europeans from Mexico and New Mexico were both buyers and actual enslavers of Indians. Jumanos, who lived in present-day southwest Texas and acted as middlemen in trade networks linking Caddo groups along the Red River to peoples in New Mexico and Coahuila, spread news of Spanish slaving practices. Not surprisingly, when Spaniards first made contact with Caddo peoples along the Texas-Louisiana border in the 1690s, their reputation as slavers had apparently preceded them. When Franciscan missionaries asked that a Hasinai Caddo chief allow his brother, nephew, and two other relatives to return with the Spaniards to Mexico to receive gifts to bring back to the chief, the leader feared for their return. He gave permission only after admonishing fray Damián Mazanet: "Do not permit anyone to demand service from these men who you take with you, nor to make them work."[23]

Others sought their own advantage in Spanish labor systems and thereby pulled native peoples from the Southern Plains into an increasingly commercialized exchange system to the west in New Mexico. Many eastern Apache groups, who had been victims of Spanish slave raiding in New Mexico, began to bring their own captives to New Mexican markets. As early as the 1650s, the Franciscan missionary Alonso de Posada reported that in addition to hides and chamois skins, some Apaches now sought "to sell for horses some Indian men and women, girls and boys" taken from Wichita bands from the lands of Francisco Vásquez de Coronado's fabled Quivira (the Southern Plains). Such Wichita women and children became members of a population of detribalized and enslaved Indians known as *genízaros* that grew to be a significant element in the New Mexico settlements. *Genízaros* aided the expansion and defense of New Mexico's borders as members of slave militias and frontier communities.[24]

To the east, as Spaniards sought a toehold in Texas in the 1710s, they focused on building a cordon of mission-presidio complexes as bulwark to protect the silver mines of New Spain's northern provinces against French aggressors. Having failed to establish settlements among Caddos in the 1690s, Spaniards focused instead on south-central Texas. There remnants of innumerable Indian bands from south of the Rio Grande had gathered after fleeing north to escape the reach of both Spanish slave raiding and European diseases. In south-central Texas they clustered together with kin and allies and, in the eighteenth century, sought a new form of alliance with Spaniards through joint settlement in newly established presidio-mission complexes at San Antonio de Béxar and La Bahía. Throughout the eighteenth century, however, the Spanish government faced serious problems attracting settlers, soldiers, and native converts to populate colonial centers so far north. The Spanish population of the Texas province at its height in 1790 was only 3,169. Spanish colonial development also remained rigidly hemmed in by far more populous and powerful Indian nations—both indigenous to the region (such as Caddos) and newly arrived (such as Lipan Apaches and later Comanches and Wichitas). Spaniards thus found that even in the limited areas claimed by Spanish settlement, their imperial policies regarding Indians involved, not imposing rule on others, but defending themselves against superior native rivals. The resulting weakness of New Spain's position in the region made it crucial for provincial authorities to secure peace and alliances with the independent and dominant native peoples who surrounded them. Yet their efforts would be fraught with difficulty. The Crown's prohibition against trade with *indios barbáros* (independent Indian peoples) shackled local Spaniards' ability to make diplomatic overtures like those of the French, while the horse herds of mission, civilian, and presidial settlements attracted native raiders against whom Spanish forces could offer little defense. Over the eighteenth century, then, Spaniards struggled to maintain their small foothold in the area against vying Apache, Caddo, Comanche, and Wichita powers.[25]

Of the four native powers, Lipan Apaches were the first to challenge the Spanish presence in Texas; as a result Spanish-Indian relations there took a different path than did the relations enjoyed by the French to the east, and the path led to a different form of bondage—one defined by punitive war. Though now less well-known than their western relatives, Lipan Apaches represented a widespread and formidable power throughout the eighteenth century. Eastern Apaches living in what is now Texas had gained an early advantage among Indians there with horses acquired in the seventeenth century through trading and raiding in New Mexico. By the 1740s, "Lipan" had become the designation used by Spaniards to refer to the easternmost Plains Apache groups. Their economy centered on hunting and raiding for bison and horses, which did not allow permanent settlement, though they did practice semicultivation. Social units farmed and hunted in rancherías (a Spanish term for Indian encampments) that might cluster together for defense and ceremonial ritual. Usually numbering around four hundred people, such units aggregated ten to thirty extended families related by blood or marriage that periodically joined together for horse raids, bison hunts, and coordinated military action. No central leadership existed, and group leaders made decisions in consultation with extended family headmen, but unity of language, dress, and customs maintained collective identity and internal peace. An estimated twelve groups of Lipan Apaches, each incorporating several rancherías, lived in central Texas and used horses to expand their range and control over bison territories and to secure their individual rancherías from attack during the agricultural cycles that alternated with bison hunting over the year. As horses rose in importance, so too did the raiding that maintained their herds and sustained their economy.[26]

Apache economies came under attack in the early eighteenth century, however, as Comanches and Wichitas migrated south to challenge Apache bands for the rich bison territories of northern and north-central Texas.

Hostilities that pitted Apaches against Comanches and Wichitas as well as the Spaniards quickly erupted, and the treble embattlement gradually weakened Apaches' defenses, making them increasingly vulnerable to all three opponents. Apache women and children thus became the focus not only of raids by Comanche and Wichita warriors seeking captives for French markets in Louisiana, but also of Spanish military campaigns seeking prisoners whom the Spaniards could use to coerce or punish their Apache foes. Throughout the 1720s, 1730s, and 1740s, Lipan Apaches mounted raids on the horse herds of San Antonio de Béxar missions, civilian ranches, and presidio to sustain a supply of horses crucial to the mobility and defense of their family bands amid mounting conflicts. In turn, Spanish fear and frustration escalated when presidial forces proved unable to stop the warriors' attacks and led to desperate bids by the Spaniards to stem the raids. Spanish officials, making war to achieve peace, ordered Apache women and children to be taken captive to force diplomacy, arguing that the best way to manipulate native groups was through their captive kinsmen or, more accurately, kinswomen. Sometimes the Spaniards went so far as to single out as political hostages the wives, daughters, sisters, and mothers of leading chiefs and warriors.[27]

Spanish captive policy devastated many Lipan Apache bands by preying on their women and children (figure 1.2). Indian captive taking involved small numbers of individuals; Spaniards introduced captive taking on a scale unimaginable to most Indian nations. To use captives for political coercion may have seemed a logical tactic to Spanish officials, who could refer to long traditions of prisoner and hostage exchange in European warfare. Yet, when Spanish forces attacked Apache rancherías, took captives, and then tried to force peace with the bands they had attacked, they sought to forge alliance through an act of hostility. Moreover, even by Spanish terms of hostage exchange, their captive policy was fundamentally unequal because it never represented an exchange of Indian women for Spanish women. Unlike the Comanche warriors in New Mexico who took Spanish women and children as well as horses as the booty of their raids, Apache men in Texas focused their raiding on horse herds.[28]

Not surprisingly, Spanish actions brought only more hostilities with Apaches. For the Apache women and children held prisoner in San Antonio de Béxar, the situation worsened. As captivities lengthened from months into years, officials distributed the Apache women and children as "servants" among soldiers and civilians in Texas and other provinces to the south. Spaniards, who had for long found ways around the crown's legal prohibitions against the enslavement of Indians, now rationalized their decision to keep such women and children in bondage by claiming the necessities of defense. By sleight of interpretation, they deemed the only *cautivos* in New Spain's northern provinces to be Spaniards captured by Indians— Apache women and children captured by Spanish forces were *prisioneros* (prisoners of war). Critics, however, clearly saw that officials and civilians alike sought profit rather than peace through such enslavement. Fray Benito

Figure 1.2 Lipan Apache Indians North of the Rio Grande, ca. 1834–1836. Watercolor by Lino Sánchez y Tapia after the original sketch by José Maria Sánchez y Tapia. Lipan Apaches were the main victims of both punitive Spanish policies and the ready market for enslaved Indians in French Louisiana.

Source: Gilcrease Museum, Tulsa, Oklahoma.

Fernández de Santa Ana, for instance, argued in 1740 that raids against Apache rancherías only increased Apache hatred; it was "ridiculous" that soldiers and citizens pledged to serve the king instead sought their own gain through the "capture of horses, hides, and Indian men and women to serve them." He concluded that with such vile intentions, their actions would result in an equally vile outcome.[29]

Some of the Apache women distributed by Spanish authorities may have remained as slaves in Spanish communities and households, but unlike Indian women in French trading posts, they were not often involved in intimate unions with their captors. Although, like the French in Louisiana, Spaniards needed to increase their settler population, there is no indication that they intermarried with either the native peoples they sought as allies or the native captives whom they manipulated in the service of peace. Intermarriage with Indians was not uncommon in Spanish America, but by the eighteenth century it was no longer used as a means of diplomacy and alliance with *independent* Indian nations. Rather, Spanish-Indian sexual relations and intermarriage took place only within Spanish society, involving

Indian individuals who had been incorporated into that society as subjects of the Spanish church and state. Some of the enslaved Apache women may have become the consorts of Spaniards or of mission Indians in the lower ranks of Spanish communities. Yet in contrast to the large *genízaro* population that grew steadily in New Mexico, the women and children held in bondage in Texas were few, and as warfare with Apache peoples increased across the northern provinces over the eighteenth century, they were likely to be deported to Mexico City and later the Caribbean.[30]

The experiences of Apache family bands targeted by Spanish military policy are illustrated most poignantly by the story of one headed by the chief Cabellos Colorados. In 1737, accompanied by eight men and eight women, he approached San Antonio, seeking trade with Spanish residents there. The equal number of men and women in the party suggested their peaceful intent. Yet to find Apaches close to town just when Spanish forces were looking for someone to nab for past horse raids and when Spanish officials were seeking to reestablish the effectiveness of their arms in the eyes of a desperate citizenry and doubting viceregal authorities was too providential an opportunity to pass up. When twenty-eight armed soldiers rode out, Cabellos Colorados and his men were clearly not expecting a fight and did not put up a defense; they were therefore quickly surrounded and captured. In further indication that the Spaniards had no evidence to prove the group were raiders, they insisted on hearings to gather such evidence—something they had never felt necessary before.[31]

In June 1738, Prudencio de Orobio y Bazterra, the governor of Texas, thus proceeded to gather testimony on the "infidelity" of Apaches in violating a 1733 peace treaty that did not exist, and Cabellos Colorados and his people were the designated subjects of the frame-up. The "evidence" against them amounted to assertions based only on coincidence, rumor, and prejudice. First, the Spaniards saw it as suspicious that, of the known Apache rancherías, that of Cabellos Colorados and his people was the closest to San Antonio. Second, soldiers testified that no "assaults" had taken place since their capture, so the raiders must be the ones in jail. Third, the presidial commander José de Urrutia identified Cabellos Colorados as a man of standing and reputation among Apaches—so much so that Urrutia claimed it was rumored that the leader had bragged to the *capitáne grande* of the Apache nation (a position that did not exist) that he would raid all the presidial horse herds of San Antonio, Coahuila, San Juan Bautista, and Sacramento (quite a task for one man), then slaughter all the inhabitants (a war tactic that did not exist among Apaches). Clearly, Cabellos Colorados was a powerful man whose downfall might powerfully enhance the reputation of the Spaniard who brought him down.[32]

In the meantime, Cabellos Colorados tried to negotiate with his captors, relying on female hostages as mediators by requesting that the Spaniards allow one of the women to return to his ranchería to get horses with which to buy their freedom. Between the December capture and the June hearings, Apache women traveled back and forth between Apache and Spanish settlements, trying to exchange horses for the captives, but an attack on their ranchería by Caddos who killed twelve men, captured two boys, and stole all their horses severely limited their ability to produce enough horses to appease Spanish officials. Instead, the women brought bison meat for their captive kinsmen and bison hides as goodwill gifts for Spanish officials. In August, an elderly man accompanied the women and brought news that, though they could not supply any horses, he had visited all the Apache bands and asked them to stop all raids, and he now offered this peace agreement to the officials in exchange for the captives. The governor refused. The elderly man then tried to exchange a horse and a mule for his elderly wife, who was among the captives. The governor refused again.[33]

No peace offering could offset the desire of the Spaniards to punish someone for the deeds of Apache raiders who had made a mockery of their presidial forces in the preceding years. Ultimately, Orobio consigned Cabellos Colorados and his entire family to exile and enslavement. In his order of February 16, 1739, the governor refused to spare the women or even an infant girl, declaring that "the thirteen Indian men and women prisoners in the said presidio, [shall be taken] tied to each other, from juris-diction to jurisdiction, to the prison of the capital in Mexico City, and that the two-year-old daughter of chief Cabellos Colorados, María Guadalupe, shall be treated in the same manner." The *collera* of Apache prisoners—seven men, six women, and one child—left on February 18 escorted by a mixed guard of soldiers and civilians.[34]

They traveled for 102 days on foot—the men shackled each night in leg irons, stocks, manacles, or ropes—before reaching Mexico City in late May where they were incarcerated in the viceregal prison, Real Carcel de la Corte (the Acordada). Two of the fourteen died en route to Mexico City, and less than six months later, seven more succumbed in the disease-ridden prison or in workhouses. Whether any of the other five survived is unknown; the last records indicate that prison officials sent two men to a hospital while consigning two women, although very ill, to servitude in private homes of prominent Spaniards. The last of the five, little María Guadalupe, was separated from her mother (one of the two sent into servitude), and later efforts to return her to her mother failed when the appointed guardian absconded with the wife of Cabellos Colorados. They would not be the last Apaches to suffer such a horror-filled fate.[35]

Having proclaimed defensive needs as their *carte blanche* for wartime enslavements, militia groups made up of soldiers and civilians devastated Apache family bands, causing repeated loss of kinswomen and children, and nearly brought on their own destruction at the hands of infuriated Apache leaders and warriors until a peace treaty in 1749 ended hostilities for twenty years. During those twenty years, Apache leaders would strive without success to regain family members lost in the 1730s and 1740s. By the 1760s, intensifying Comanche and Wichita pressures on both Apaches and Spaniards brought their brief experiment with peace to an end. By then,

Spanish officials had decided to ditch Apaches as allies, preferring their more powerful Comanche and Wichita enemies.[36]

It is at this point, in the late 1760s, that our two stories (and the two slave networks) come together. French trade relations with powerful Caddo, Wichita, and Comanche bands—relations underwritten by the traffic in women—had been all too clear to watchful Spanish eyes since the beginning of the century. For as long as French traders had been operating in the region, Spanish missionaries and military officials in Texas had been trying to effect alliances of their own in the hope of offsetting the influence of their French rivals. Throughout the first half of the century, however, such efforts had met with abject failure even as the Spaniards watched Indian-French ties steadily strengthen.[37] Reports filtered in from all across the Plains and New Mexico detailing how Frenchmen had expanded their native alliances and their slave trade.[38] Imperial Spanish officials feared that growing trade relations signaled military alliance and the potential for a united French-Indian attack on Spanish territories. Such laments remained focal points of Spanish rhetoric as they watched first Caddos, then Comanches and Wichitas, build economic ties to the French colony. The ever-increasing military power of Comanche and Wichita nations soon became far more daunting than that of the French, however. The armaments acquired through French trade had equipped Comanche and Wichita bands better for the raids that from the 1740s on plundered Spanish horse herds in civil and mission settlements in both Texas and New Mexico. By 1758, officials in Mexico City even feared Comanche *invasion* of the Spanish provinces south of the Rio Grande.[39]

Yet without the finances to offer competitive trade of their own or the military power to stop French-Indian alliances by force, the Spaniards in Texas found they could do little to offset French advantage. It was not until the 1760s that the cession of Louisiana from French to Spanish rule following the Seven Years' War opened up new possibilities for Spanish officials. Spanish law officially prohibited the enslavement and sale of Indians, and Alejandro O'Reilly, then serving as governor of Louisiana, extended that prohibition to the province with the formal assumption of Spanish power in 1769. Spanish officials saw an opportunity to cut off the trade that put guns into the hands of native groups deemed "hostile" to the Spanish government. Local imperatives ensured the enforcement of the ban in the Red River valley along the Texas-Louisiana border, particularly among Wichitas and Comanches. Spanish officials finally had the means to sever the commercial ties that had allied native bands in Texas and the Southern Plains with Frenchmen. Thus in response to O'Reilly's edict, officials in Natchitoches forbade the trade in horses, mules, and slaves from those Indian nations, and they recalled from their subposts or homes among "hostile" Indians all licensed traders, hunters, and illicit "vagabonds"— many of whom the Natchitoches commander Athanase de Mézières described in 1770 as men "who pass their scandalous lives in public concubinage with the captive Indian women whom for this purpose they purchase among the heathen, loaning those of whom they tire to others of less power, that they may labor in their service, giving them no other wage than the promise of quieting their lascivious passion."[40]

Once at Natchitoches, the traders and hunters had to answer questions about their native trade relationships and to register their Indian slaves. In fear of losing their slaves, some Frenchmen sought to secure the women by whatever means possible. Though government officials recognized provisional ownership pending a royal decision on the status of enslaved Indians in the province, some men clearly chose not to let their fate rest on the vagaries of a royal decree. Many married their slaves or promised freedom if the women swore to remain with them as servants or consorts. Intimate relations thereby became a means of prolonging women's servitude. François Morvant, for instance, in 1770 declared his ownership of a twenty-five-year-old Apache woman named Marie Anne as well as their son, age twelve. Sometime thereafter, however, her status was transformed, as she was enumerated as Morvant's wife, "Ana Maria, of Apache nationality," in later Spanish censuses for the nearby settlement of Nacogdoches, Texas. Tellingly, though their relationship had existed for at least thirteen years, it was not until Morvant faced losing ownership of her that he married Marie Anne. By 1805 they had three more sons, a daughter, and one grandson living with them. Similarly, in 1774 Jacque Ridde freed an eighteen-year-old Apache girl, Angélique, whose ownership he claimed, but only after she pledged to remain in his service, and Pierre Raimond married Françoise, another Apache woman, following her manumission.[41]

Governing officials in Spain never ruled on the status of Indian slaves, and the extension of Spanish law into Louisiana freed no enslaved Indians except for a very few whose owners voluntarily manumitted them in the aftermath of O'Reilly's edict in 1769 or in 1787 when the ordinance was republished in response to a legal case involving runaway Indian slaves in St. Louis. The existence of a law tells us very little about whether the law was enforced or obeyed—and the reiteration of legal prohibitions suggests a lack of compliance. Between 1790 and 1794, a handful of slaves also sued successfully for manumission in Spanish courts on the grounds of Indian identity (their own or that of their mothers), but all those cases were heard in New Orleans, and such legal opportunities did not exist for enslaved Indian women or their children in outpost settlements far from urban centers, such as Natchitoches. In the wake of the slave uprising in Saint Domingue in 1791, such opportunities quickly disappeared for all, as Spanish officials decided that any challenges to the slave system were dangerous.[42]

Meanwhile, reports from Natchitoches indicate that despite the new trade prohibitions on the books, the slave traffic along the Texas-Louisiana border kept up a steady, if illicit, flow of women from west to east on the ground. As late as the 1780s, peltries (primarily deerskins) still made up a significant portion of Louisiana's exports, indicating the continued importance of Indian trade and the extensive network of trading posts that supported

European-Indian exchange. Marriage and baptism records in Natchitoches were testament to the continued role of enslaved Apache women as consorts, wives, and mothers through the end of the eighteenth century. Maria Modesta, the "natural" daughter of Marie Magdalena, an Apache slave of Jean Louis le Court, grew up to marry Jean Laurent Bodin and have a son, while Therese Lecompte, the natural daughter of an enslaved Apache woman also named Therese, married Louis Metoyer, a free man of color. Another Apache woman named Marie Rosalie married Louis Guillori, an Opelousa Indian. The unions of the two Louises indicate that French traders were not the only men in the market for Indian wives. Unlike the black population in urban New Orleans, the black residents of Natchitoches, both slave and free, were predominantly male, leaving them with fewer potential consorts among enslaved or free women—a demographic factor that may have encouraged their intermarriage with Indian women. Official censuses only hinted at the numbers, and sacramental records—listing almost two hundred enslaved Indian women and children in the Natchitoches area over the century—also offer only a partial accounting. Nevertheless, by 1803 almost one-quarter of the native-born European population in northwest Louisiana counted Indian slaves in their ancestry, and 60 percent of that number claimed descent directly from an enslaved Indian parent or grandparent.[43]

In 1806, an Anglo-American report discussing the still-prevalent Apache women who had been "brought to Natchitoches, and sold amongst the French inhabitants, at forty or fifty dollars a head," concluded that the women had become "servants in good families, and taught spinning, sewing, &c. as well as managing household affairs, married natives of the country [Frenchmen and *métis*], and became respectable, well behaved women; and have now, grown up, decent families of children, have a language peculiar to themselves, and are understood by signs by all others."[44] Most enslaved women, however, appear in records only as the subjects of baptism at the behest of their French owners or as mothers of natural children whose fathers usually, but not always, went unnamed in sacramental registers. Thus the lives of most enslaved Indian women rested on the whims of their owners, and a woman might find her world turned suddenly upside down if she were used to pay medical bills, exchanged for horses, seized for debt, or enumerated in a will.[45] The experiences of these women began in war, when they were torn from their communities by brutal force, and culminated in their sale into sexual and labor relations defined by coercion.

It was in response to such stories that fray Santa María y Silva had issued his denunciation of French traders after the Indian slave trade into Louisiana had become illicit in the 1770s. Yet, even Santa María y Silva, if pressed, would have needed to acknowledge that as Spanish officials in Texas sought to stem the eastward flow of captive Indian women into Louisiana, they created in its stead a more deadly southward flow of hostages into Mexican prisons and labor camps.[46] Though French traders associated with the Natchitoches and Arkansas posts remained active covertly and British traders soon began pushing into the region, Comanche and Wichita economies were hindered. The need to diversify their trade contacts more and more turned Indian eyes to the Spaniards in Texas. Though Comanches and Wichitas continued their raids on Spanish settlements in Texas to maintain their horse supply, the challenge of picking up the slack in arms and material goods formerly provided by Louisiana markets remained. To solve this problem, they found new ways to benefit from an exchange of women, selling war captives to the Spaniards for horses and goods that Spanish officials preferred to term "ransom" and "redemption" payments. The new diplomatic traffic would put even more Apache women and children into Spanish bondage. Yet, it took years before economic exchange completely replaced battlefield violence among Spaniards, Wichitas, and Comanches.

During the transitional period of alternating war and diplomacy, Comanche and Wichita men at first took advantage of Spanish diplomatic needs to pursue personal rather than commercial ends. The tales of two Indian couples, one Wichita and one Comanche, illustrate the twists and turns that newly emerging captive exchanges might take in Spanish-Indian relations. Both stories unfolded over the spring and summer of 1772. That spring word reached a principal chief of a Taovaya (Wichita) band that his wife—who had been taken from him by Apache raiders—had been sold by her captors to a Spaniard in Coahuila. As the chief was soon to travel to San Antonio de Béxar as part of a diplomatic party sent to ratify the first treaty between Wichitas and the Spanish government, he recognized that Spanish officials' desperation for peace could be the means of saving his wife in circumstances where he himself could not. As soon as the chief reached San Antonio that summer, he explained his plight to the Spanish governor, Juan María de Ripperdá. "She is so much esteemed by him," Ripperdá reported to the viceroy, "that he assures me that she is the only one he has ever had, or wishes to have until he dies, and, as she leaves him two little orphans, he begs for her as zealously as he considers her delivery [return] difficult."[47]

The governor quickly grasped that the fate of the captive woman would determine the fate of the newly completed peace treaty and promised the Taovaya chief he would use the "strongest means" to secure her. If he failed to grant the chief's request for help, Ripperdá warned the viceroy, "all that we have attained and which is of so much importance, would be lost." Thus it was with exultation that Ripperdá wrote to the viceroy a month later, assuring his superior that, in answer to his urgent requests, the governor of Coahuila had found and returned the chief's wife. Indeed, Ripperdá had orchestrated her delivery to his own home in San Antonio where she was to be turned over to her husband (surely to convince the Taovaya chief that it was the Texas official to whom he was beholden for his wife's return). Optimistically, the governor reiterated "that she may be the key that shall open the way to our treaties." In March 1773, Ripperdá finally concluded his private captive exchange, writing to the viceroy that the happy husband and a delegation of Taovayas were in Ripperdá's home and the Taovaya couple had been reunited.[48]

The governor might well choose to dwell on that auspicious moment, because his negotiation of a similar situation with Comanches had taken a far rockier, less promising path. In fact, Ripperdá very nearly bungled the whole thing. The second story began in February 1772 when a detachment from the Béxar presidio returned to the town of San Antonio with an unexpected prize—not Apache but Comanche captives—three women and one girl. Ripperdá already had three other Comanche women, captured months before, who had been held so long in one of the San Antonio missions that all three had been baptized and two married off to mission neophytes. Because of their baptisms, those three could not be returned to live among their people in what Spaniards considered apostasy, but the four new captives provided the governor an opening for diplomatic overtures to Comanche leaders. Since the Spanish government had recently completed new peace agreements with bands of Taovayas and Caddos, he hoped he might likewise attract (or coerce) Comanches to the negotiating table for the first time. Ripperdá therefore sent two of the women back to their village under military escort, carrying goodwill gifts to present to their chief, Evea, while he kept the other woman and little girl as hostages to draw the chief to San Antonio.[49]

A month later, Evea sent a response to San Antonio in the form of emissaries led by a woman carrying a cross and a white flag. The woman at the head of the party was one of the female captives freed by Ripperdá and was also the mother of the little girl still held hostage. Others in the party included the hostage girl's father, the husband of the other hostage woman held by the governor, and the brother of two of the three Comanche women held in the missions. The governor's gambit had not drawn out the chief, but he certainly had attracted a diverse group seeking to recover lost family members. Initially, meetings went well as the Comanche visitors reunited with Ripperdá's two hostages and exchanged diplomatic courtesies with the governor. As they departed, however, they sought retribution for their troubles by taking four hundred horses from the Béxar presidial herd. They also tried to liberate the three other Comanche women held in the mission, but Spanish soldiers thwarted that rescue operation. In despair at her failed escape, one of the women from the mission tried to kill herself upon recapture by the Spaniards. Unfortunately for the Comanche party, they too failed in their getaway. A group of Apache warriors attacked the party as it fled the region, killed seven men, captured half the horses and four of the women, and promptly turned them over to the Spaniards. Ripperdá, angered at what he labeled the Comanches' "treachery" for using women to feign peace, consigned all the women to different forms of bondage in Coahuila. The three missionized Comanche women were destined for Coahuila missions, accompanied by their neophyte husbands, while the others went to labor camps.[50]

Comanche leaders, however, did not give up, and in the summer of 1772, they traveled to San Antonio (this time in the company of Wichita allies) to retrieve the women now even farther from their reach, in Coahuila.

Human

Chief Evea himself joined the conference. Following ceremonies reaffirming peace agreements with Wichita bands, Ripperdá attempted to shame the Comanche men by displaying the "false" white flag of truce carried earlier by the Comanche woman. Though he claimed to the viceroy to have sent the Comanches away empty-handed, the men he confronted—including the husband of one captive woman—ultimately had the advantage; the governor could not risk offending representatives of such a powerful Indian nation. Tellingly, in the same letter in which he bragged of cowing Evea with the false flag, Ripperdá reported that he had advised the governor of Coahuila to ensure that the Comanche woman was not baptized, so that she could be returned to her husband. Records fail to tell whether she was. If she was redeemed, it did not buy the Spaniards peace for long, since hostilities continued unchecked until 1785 when the two peoples signed their first peace treaty. The position of power enjoyed by Comanches and Wichitas stood in stark contrast to that of Apaches, as the Comanche and Wichita women who fell prey to Spanish bondage were few and Comanche and Wichita men more easily regained those who did.[51]

Spanish officials increasingly chose to negotiate truce and alliance with Comanche and Wichita warriors by ransoming from them any enemy captives they took in war. In the process, the Spaniards also attained for themselves, by commercial rather than violent means, captive Indian women to use in diplomatic relations with the women's families and peoples. Most commonly, they purchased Apache captives from Comanche and Wichita men. Native captive raiding may have risen in response to Spanish attempts to broker deals with family members of the victims. Fray Juan Domingo Arricivita asserted that while Apaches might take captives in war to sell to other nations, they equally took them "to exchange them for some of their relatives who have been made prisoners."[52] Spanish diplomatic traffic in women was not limited to transactions with Comanches and Wichitas. For instance, when eighty Apache warriors led by seven chiefs captured a woman, one girl, and two boys in a revenge raid on a Tonkawa ranchería in 1779, Texas governor Domingo Cabello offered eight horses for the captives. He claimed to want the children because they "could become Christians by virtue of their youth," but his desire for the woman was purely political, since she could be restored to the Tonkawa band as "proof of friendship." Interestingly, the Apache men refused to give him any of the captives, not because eight horses was an unfair price, but because they saw little political gain to be had from the Spanish governor at that time. Further proof of the Apache men's careful assessment of where their interests lay came when chief El Joyoso chose instead to give one of the children, a ten-year-old Mayeye girl, to his "good friend Don Luis Menchaca," a Spanish merchant in San Antonio who had long traded with Apache peoples and shown them good faith (sometimes against the wishes of the provincial government).[53]

Caddos and Wichitas also found remuneration by ransoming Spanish women whom they had acquired from Comanches who had captured them in New Mexico. The payment received by Taovayas (Wichitas) from the trader José Guillermo Esperanza for a New Mexican woman, Ana María Baca, and her six-year-old son spoke to the possible profits. For Ana María Baca, Taovayas received "three muskets, three netted cloths, two blankets, four axes, three hoes, two *castetes* with pipe, one pound of vermilion, two pounds of beads, ten knives, twenty-five gunflints, eight steels for striking flints, six ramrods, six awls, four fathoms of wool sash, and three hundred bullets with necessary powder." For Baca's son, Esperanza gave Taovayas "one otter hide, one hundred bullets with necessary powder, one ax, three *castetes* with pipe, one and one-half quarter pounds of vermilion, one net-ted cloth, one blanket, and one musket." Notably, in this exchange Taovayas were not the only ones who planned to profit from Ana María Baca's captivity. The Nacogdoches lieutenant Christóbel Hilario de Córdoba, to whom Esperanza had related his purchase, reported with out-rage that Esperanza went on to say that he planned to take the woman and sell her in Natchitoches "where there could not but be plenty of Frenchmen to purchase her and bother her, as is their custom, since she still is attractive." Córdoba forestalled the woman's sale into concubinage by taking her and her son into protective custody. Córdoba's intervention (which Spanish officials vehemently supported) made clear how aberrant it was that Ana María Baca's Spanish identity had not excluded her from the category of women whom Esperanza felt he might acceptably sell into the sex trade.[54]

Although Spanish officials spent much time bemoaning the loss of Spanish women to Indian captivity, the charge remained rhetorical in eighteenth-century Texas. Spanish captives were few in number, and the new Spanish-Indian traffic in "redeemed" captives remained primarily one of Indian women. The rhetoric about Spanish female captives in Indian hands was meant to appeal to government superiors in Mexico and thereby to gain more military men and supplies with which to defend the province against indomitable Comanche and Wichita forces, but that tactic often failed. In response to complaints from the commandant of the Interior Provinces that Texas officials had failed to contribute to the alms that Spanish law demanded all settlements in the provinces collect for the ransoming of Christian captives held by Indians, Cabello explained that no captives from Texas had been taken and thus little local imperative to give to such a fund existed in Texas.[55] In Texas, then, fictitious Spanish women were objects of persuasion and real Indian women were the objects of exchange—whether in French trade markets or in Spanish diplomatic negotiations.

The gradual stabilization of relations among Spaniards, Comanches, and Wichitas in the waning years of the century meant only ill for Apaches, as the maintenance of the three groups' peace agreements often involved the enslavement of Apaches still deemed enemies by them all. Whether captured by Spanish presidial forces or ransomed to them by Comanche or Wichita warriors in diplomatic exchange, Apache women and children continued to fall victim to punitive Spanish policies that sent younger children to missions for conversion and all others to labor camps or prisons in Mexico City and, beginning in the 1780s, in the Caribbean. Many died in transit to Mexico. Most never saw their homes again. Despite the impossibility of return, back home their husbands and fathers received promises of the women's return if they agreed to treaty negotiations. Thus when, in one instance, Apache men arrived at a meeting site and did not find their wives among the women brought for exchange, officials responded by offering them their pick of other women captured elsewhere. For those Spanish officers, Apache women had become so commodified that they were interchangeable. Spanish records rarely detail the suffering of women themselves, but a handful of incidents give mute testimony to it, and none more powerfully than the stories of women who tried to take their own lives rather than remain captive. The Comanche woman who tried to kill herself upon recapture after she escaped from the San Antonio mission in 1772 was not alone in preferring death to enslavement. Jean Louis Berlandier recorded that another Comanche woman captured early in the nineteenth century "asked for a knife to remove a thorn she said was hurting her foot, but when they gave it to her she plunged it into her heart." The fate of these captive and enslaved Indian women signified irremediable moments of Spanish-Indian interchange in eighteenth-century Texas. Theirs is the story that remains to be written.[56]

Beyond telling of warfare and its spoils, the stories of enslaved Apache women and children document the ways European and Indian men used them as social and political capital in efforts to coerce and accommodate one another. Looking at how bands and empires or traders and diplomats transformed women into currency allows one to see multiple sources and forms of bondage: from pre-Columbian indigenous warfare that created captivity as an alternative to battlefield deaths, to captive raiding and commercial trade that created human commodities, to hostage taking and deportation that created prison labor. Pressed into service, women became objects for sex, familial reproduction, and reciprocal trade relations; gifts that made peaceful coexistence possible for their captors; or victims who paid the price for their captors' hostility. This diversity of slaveries unfolded from the confrontations and collusions of European and native political systems that structured economic behavior, battlefield enmity, and diplomatic maneuvering. Putting standardized categories of slavery and unfreedom to the test in complicated borderlands where two imperial powers sought to negotiate multiple configurations of Indian social and political organization show how wanting those categories can be. Slavery in North America has been cast as a monolithic, chattel-oriented system of coerced labor, thus making it a distinctive and anomalous model when compared with forms of bondage instituted in other times and places. Meanwhile the forms of captivity and exchanges of women involved in European-Indian relations in the Americas have fallen into categories often perceived to be more benign. If bondage could prove such an infinitely variable institution in just one region of colonial North America, imagine what we may find as we piece together experiences across the entire continent. Explicating such diversity will bring American practices of slavery into better global perspective and more fruitful comparison with colonial geopolitics and cultural geographies around the world.

Notes

Juliana Barr is an assistant professor at the University of Florida. She wishes to thank Sean P. Adams, Jeanne Boydston, James F. Brooks, Indrani Chatterjee, Laura F. Edwards, Alan Gallay, Ramón A. Gutiérrez, Nancy A. Hewitt, Joseph C. Miller, Jennifer M. Spear, David J. Weber, the participants in the 2002 Avignon Conference on Forced Labour and Slavery, and the anonymous readers for the *Journal of American History* for their valuable comments on earlier drafts of the essay.
Readers may contact Barr at jbarr@history.ufl.edu.

1. Fray Miguel Santa María y Silva to Viceroy Antonio Bucareli y Ursúa, July 21, 1774, in *Athanase de Mézières and the Louisiana-Texas Frontier, 1768–1780,* trans. and ed. Herbert Eugene Bolton, 2 vols. (Cleveland, OH, 1914), 2: 74–75.

2. James F. Brooks, *Captives and Cousins: Slavery, Kinship, and Community in the Southwest Borderlands* (Chapel Hill, NC, 2002); Alan Gallay, *The Indian Slave Trade: The Rise of the English Empire in the American South, 1670–1717* (New Haven, CT, 2002); Russell M. Magnaghi, *Indian Slavery, Labor, Evangelization, and Captivity in the Americas: An Annotated Bibliography* (Lanham, MD, 1998). Recent conference programs of historical organizations (notably the Omohundro Institute of Early American History and Culture) indicate that numerous studies, particularly dissertations, of Indian slavery across colonial North America are in the works. For a recently completed example, see Brett H. Rushforth, "Savage Bonds: Indian Slavery and Alliance in New France" (PhD diss., University of California, Davis, 2003).

3. Susan Sleeper-Smith, *Indian Women and French Men: Rethinking Cultural Encounter in the Western Great Lakes* (Amherst, MA, 2001); Jennifer S. H. Brown, *Strangers in Blood: Fur Trade Company Families in Indian Country* (Vancouver, 1980); Jacqueline Peterson, "The People In Between: Indian-White Marriage and the Genesis of a Métis Society and Culture in the Great Lakes Region, 1680–1830" (PhD diss., University of Illinois, Chicago, 1981); Sylvia Van Kirk, *Many Tender Ties: Women in Fur Trade Society, 1670–1870* (Norman, OK, 1980); Nancy Shoemaker, ed., *Negotiators of Change: Historical Perspectives on Native American Women* (New York, 1995); Tanis C. Thorne, *The Many Hands of My Relations: French and Indians on the Lower Missouri* (Columbia, 1996); Greg O'Brien, *Choctaws in a Revolutionary Age, 1750–1830* (Lincoln, NE, 2002); Theda Perdue, *Cherokee Women: Gender and Culture Change, 1700–1835* (Lincoln, NE, 1998).

4. On historians' definitions and uses of agency, particularly in relationship to slavery, see Walter Johnson, "On Agency," *Journal of Social History* 37 (Fall 2003): 113–24. On the limits of agency for women caught in the exchanges of men, see Brooks, *Captives and Cousins;* and Albert L. Hurtado, *Intimate Frontiers: Sex, Gender, and Culture in Old California* (Albuquerque, NM, 1999). On Sacagawea's experience with the Lewis and Clark expedition as well as her escape from slavery and her life afterward—lost to history by past tendencies to cast her as a tragic heroine who died young—see Thomas P. Slaughter, *Exploring Lewis and Clark: Reflections on Men and Wilderness* (New York, 2003), 86–113. On the mythologizing of Sacagawea, see Donna Barbie, "Sacajawea: The Making of a Myth," in *Sifters: Native American Women's Lives,* ed. Theda Perdue (New York, 2001), 60–76.

5. Igor Kopytoff, "Slavery," *Annual Review of Anthropology* 11 (1982): 207–30; Joseph C. Miller, "The Problem of Slavery as History," inaugural lecture of the David Brion Davis Lecture Series at the Gilder-Lehrman Center, Yale University, February 7, 2005 (in Joseph C. Miller's possession); James L. Watson, "Slavery as an Institution: Open and Closed Systems," in *Asian and African Systems of Slavery*, ed. James L. Watson (Oxford, 1980), 1–15. Historical and anthropological discussion of African slavery is threaded throughout the text and notes of Brooks, *Captives and Cousins*. The annual Avignon Conference on Forced Labour and Slavery brings together scholars whose research ranges over times from antiquity to the recent past and over places across the globe to discuss systems of slavery in comparative perspective.

6. Discussing Claude Levi-Strauss's theory of marriage as a form of gift exchange, Gayle Rubin explained, "If it is women who are being transacted, then it is the men who give and take them who are linked, the woman being a conduit of a relationship rather than a partner to it." See Gayle Rubin, "The Traffic in Women: Notes on the 'Political Economy' of Sex," in *Toward an Anthropology of Women*, ed. Rayna R. Reiter (New York, 1975), 174. Jane Fishburne Collier, *Marriage and Inequality in Classless Societies* (Stanford, CA, 1988).

7. William C. Foster, ed., and Johanna S. Warren, trans., *The La Salle Expedition to Texas: The Journal of Henri Joutel, 1684–1687* (Austin, TX, 1998), 227–29; Fray Francisco Casañas de Jesús María to the Viceroy of Mexico, August 15, 1691, in "Descriptions of the Tejas or Asinai Indians, 1691–1722," trans. Mattie Austin Hatcher, *Southwestern Historical Quarterly* 30 (January 1927): 217; Ralph A. Smith, trans. and ed., "Account of the Journey of Bénard de la Harpe: Discovery Made by Him of Several Nations Situated in the West," ibid. 62 (July 1958): 75–86; *Southwestern Historical Quarterly* (October 1958): 246–59; ibid. (January 1959): 371–85; ibid. (April 1959): 525–41; David La Vere, *The Caddo Chiefdoms: Caddo Economics and Politics, 700–1835* (Lincoln, 1998), 1–14, 33–35; Timothy K. Perttula, *"The Caddo Nation": Archaeological and Ethnohistoric Perspectives* (Austin, TX, 1992), 85, 217–20; Karl Schmitt and Iva Osanai Schmitt, *Wichita Kinship: Past and Present* (Norman, n.d.), 23; Gordon M. Sayre, *Les Sauvages Américains: Representations of Native Americans in French and English Colonial Literature* (Chapel Hill, NC, 1997), 14, 266.

8. Henri de Tonti, "Memoir Sent in 1693, on the Discovery of the Mississippi and the Neighboring Nations by M. D. La Salle, from the year 1678 to the Time of his Death, and by the Sieur de Tonty to the year 1691," in *The Journeys of Rene Robert Cavelier, Sieur de la Salle*, ed. Isaac Joslin Cox, 2 vols. (New York, 1973), 1: 41–44, 46, esp. 42.

9. Juan de Ulibarri, "The Diary of Juan de Ulibarri to El Cuartelejo, 1706," in *After Coronado: Spanish Exploration Northeast of New Mexico, 1696–1727*, trans. Alfred Barnaby Thomas (Norman, OK, 1935), 59–77; Charles Wilson Hackett, trans., *Pichardo's Treatise on the Limits of Louisiana and Texas*, 4 vols. (Austin, 1931), 2:179–87; Mildred Mott Wedel, *The Wichita Indians, 1541–1750: Ethnohistorical Essays* (Lincoln, NE, 1988), 101; Kate L. Gregg, "The Missouri Reader: Explorers in the Valley, Part II," *Missouri Historical Review* 39 (July 1945): 511.

10. Gregg, "Missouri Reader," 512; Smith, trans. and ed., "Account of the Journey of Bénard de la Harpe," 529; Wedel, "Claude-Charles Dutisné," 102, 106.

11. Etienne de Bourgmont identified the Indians as "Padoucas"—a French ethnonym that some scholars have asserted referred to Comanches. But Thomas W. Kavanagh and other Plains historians have convincingly argued that until 1750 it described Apaches. Frank Norall, trans., "Journal of the Voyage of Monsieur de Bourgmont, Knight of the Military Order of Saint Louis, Commandant of the Missouri River [which is] above That of the Arkansas, and of the Missouri [Country], to the

Padoucas," in *Bourgmont, Explorer of the Missouri, 1698–1725*, by Frank Norall (Lincoln, NE, 1988), 125–61, esp. 152 and 154–55; Henri Folmer, "De Bourgmont's Expedition to the Padoucas in 1724, the First French Approach to Colorado," *Colorado Magazine* 14 (July 1937): 124–27; Henri Folmer, "Etienne Véniard de Bourgmont in the Missouri Country," *Missouri Historical Review* 36 (April 1942): 279–98; Thomas W. Kavanagh, *The Comanches: A History, 1706–1875* (Lincoln, NE, 1996), 65–66.

12. Pierre François Xavier de Charlevoix, *History and General Description of New France*, trans. John Gilmary Shea, 6 vols.(New York, 1872), 6: 32–38; Daniel H. Usner Jr., *Indians, Settlers, and Slaves in a Frontier Exchange Economy: The Lower Mississippi Valley before 1783* (Chapel Hill, NC, 1992); archival material from Correspondence Générale, French Dominion, Mississippi Provincial Archives, vols. 9, 3, cited in Almon Wheeler Lauber, *Indian Slavery in Colonial Times within the Present Limits of the United States* (New York, 1913), 75; Sieur Jean-Baptiste Le Moyne de Bienville, "Memoir on Louisiana, the Indians and the Commerce that Can Be Carried on with Them" (1726), in *Mississippi Provincial Archives, French Dominion, vol. III: 1704–1743*, ed. Dunbar Rowland and A. G. Sanders (Jackson, 1932), 532; Russell Magnaghi, "Changing Material Culture and the Hasinai of East Texas," *Southern Studies* 20 (Winter 1981); W. W. Newcomb and W. T. Field, "An Ethnohistoric Investigation of the Wichita Indians in the Southern Plains," in *Wichita Indian Archaeology and Ethnology: A Pilot Study*, ed. Robert E. Bell, Edward B. Jelks, and W. W. Newcomb (New York, 1974).

13. Twenty-member bands of these confederacies and at least three other independent Caddo bands clustered in fertile valleys along the Angelina, Neches, Sabine, and Red rivers. Town centers, surrounded by temple mounds built by the Caddoans' ancestors, still served as the residence of paramount chiefs and the locus for public gatherings and ceremony. People in the ranked, matrilineal societies, with well-developed political and ceremonial governing structures, lived in kin-based hamlets located near the agricultural fields radiating out from the town centers. La Vere, *Caddo Chiefdoms;* Perttula, *"Caddo Nation."*

14. Agriculture played a central role in Wichitas' socioeconomics and tied them to their grass-lodge villages much of the year, but they spent the fall and winter in mobile camps while men hunted deer and bison. Their extensive crop cultivation and centralized role in French-Indian market exchange created subsistence and economic practices more sedentary than those of their Comanche neighbors. Wichita bands active in Texas included Tawakonis, Taovayas, Iscanis, Wacos, and Wichitas proper. Early French identification of Wichitas as "Panis Piques" or "Pani-piquets" in reference to their tattoos and linguistic similarities to Pawnees later confused distinctions between Wichitas and Pawnees (known simply as "Panis"). Pawnees, unlike Wichitas, constituted a significant number of the Plains Indians sold north into slavery in New France. W. W. Newcomb Jr., *The People Called Wichita* (Phoenix, AZ, 1976); Elizabeth A. H. John, "A Wichita Migration Tale," *American Indian Quarterly* 7 (Fall 1983): 57–63; Susan C. Vehik, "Wichita Culture History," *Plains Anthropologist* 37 (November 1992): 311–32; F. Todd Smith, *The Wichita Indians: Traders of Texas and the Southern Plains, 1540–1845* (College Station, TX, 2000).

15. Comanches were a branch of northern Shoshones of the Great Basin region whose acquisition of horses had led to their rapid evolution into a mounted, mobile, military power. During the seventeenth century, Comanches had moved into the plains of eastern Colorado and western Kansas and then turned south, pulled by abundant bison herds, Spanish horses ready for the taking, and French trade goods ready for the bartering. Identified as eastern-dwelling bands of Kotsotekas and western-dwelling bands of Jupes and Yamparicas, Comanches operated as independent, kin-based

hunting and gathering groups rather than as united confederacies such as those of
Caddo bands of east Texas and Wichita bands of northern Texas. Thomas W.
Kavanagh, *Comanche Political History: An Ethnohistorical Perspective, 1706–1875*
(Lincoln, NE, 1996); Morris Foster, *Being Comanche: A Social History of an
American Indian Community* (Tucson, 1991); Gerald Betty, *Comanche Society:
Before the Reservation* (College Station, 2002); D. B. Shimkin, "Shoshone-
Comanche Origins and Migrations," in *Proceedings of the Sixth Pacific Science
Congress of the Pacific Science Association* (Berkeley, CA, 1940), 17–25.

16. Usner, *Indians, Settlers, and Slaves in a Frontier Exchange Economy*, 116–22, 244–75;
Joseph Zitomersky, "The Form and Function of French-Native American Relations in
Early Eighteenth-Century French Colonial Louisiana," in *Proceedings of the Fifteenth
Meeting of the French Colonial Historical Society, Martinique and Guadeloupe, May
1989*, ed. Patricia Galloway and Philip P. Boucher (New York, 1992).

17. Clarence H. Webb and Hiram F. Gregory, *The Caddo Indians of Louisiana* (1978;
Baton Rouge, LA, 1986); Hiram Ford Gregory, "Eighteenth Century Caddoan
Archaeology: A Study in Models and Interpretation" (PhD diss., Southern Methodist
University, 1973); Dayna Bowker Lee, "Indian Slavery in Lower Louisiana during
the Colonial Period, 1699–1803" (MA thesis, Northwestern State University of
Louisiana, 1989). On reciprocity and political economies, see Patricia C. Albers,
"Symbiosis, Merger, and War: Contrasting Forms of Intertribal Relationship among
Historic Plains Indians," in *The Political Economy of North American Indians*,
ed. John Moore (Lincoln, NE, 1993), 94–132; Marcel Mauss, *The Gift: The Form
and Reason for Exchange in Archaic Societies*, trans. W. D. Halls (1924; New York,
1954); Marshall Sahlins, *Stone Age Economics* (Chicago, 1972); and Claude Lévi-
Strauss, *The Elementary Structures of Kinship*, trans. James Harle Bell and John
Richard von Sturmer, ed. Rodney Needham (1949; Boston, MA, 1969). La Vere,
Caddo Chiefdoms; Daniel A. Hickerson, "Trade, Mediation, and Political Status in
the Hasinai Confederacy," *Research in Economic Anthropology* 17 (1996): 149–68.

18. Brooks, *Captives and Cousins*, 177–97; Louis Billouart de Kerlérec, "Projet de paix
et d'alliance avec les Cannecis et les avantages qui en peuvent résulter, envoyé par
Kerlérec, gouverneur de la province de la Louisianne, en 1753," in "Un Mémoire
Politique du XVIII Siécle Relatif au Texas" (An Eighteenth-Century Political Memoir
Relating to Texas), by M. Le Baron Marc de Villiers du Terrage, *Journal de la Société
des Américanistes de Paris* 3 (1906): 67–76.

19. J. Leitch Wright, *The Only Land They Knew: The Tragic Story of the American
Indian in the Old South* (New York, 1981); Marcel Trudel, *L'esclavage au Canada
Français: Histoire et conditions de l'esclavage* (Slavery in French Canada: History
and Conditions of Slavery) (Quebec, 1960); Brett Rushforth, " 'A Little Flesh We
Offer You': The Origins of Indian Slavery in New France," *William and Mary
Quarterly* 60 (October 2003): 777–808; Daniel H. Usner Jr., "From African
Captivity to American Slavery: The Introduction of Black Laborers to Colonial
Louisiana," *Louisiana History* 20 (Winter 1979): 25–48; James T. McGowan,
"Planters without Slaves: Origins of a New World Labor System," *Southern
Studies* 16 (Spring 1977): 5–26; Gwendolyn Midlo Hall, *Africans in Colonial
Louisiana: The Development of Afro-Creole Culture in the Eighteenth Century*
(Baton Rouge, LA, 1992); Kimberly S. Hanger, *Bounded Lives, Bounded Places: Free
Black Society in Colonial New Orleans, 1769–1803* (Durham, NC, 1997); Gilbert
C. Din, *Spaniards, Planters, and Slaves: The Spanish Regulation of Slavery in
Louisiana, 1763–1803* (College Station, TX, 1999), 3–17.

20. Sleeper-Smith, *Indian Women and French Men;* Brown, *Strangers in Blood;* Peterson,
"People In Between"; Van Kirk, *Many Tender Ties;* Jennifer M. Spear, " 'They Need
Wives': Métissage and the Regulation of Sexuality in French Louisiana,

1699–1730," in *Sex, Love, Race: Crossing Boundaries in North American History*, ed. Martha Hodes (New York, 1999). For the statement of abbé Raynal, see Hackett, trans., *Pichardo's Treatise on the Limits of Louisiana and Texas*, 1: 258.

21. Marcel Giraud, *A History of French Louisiana, vol. II: Years of Transition, 1715–1717*, trans. Brian Pearce (Baton Rouge, LA, 1993), 129; Jennifer M. Spear, "Colonial Intimacies: Legislating Sex in French Louisiana," *William and Mary Quarterly* 60 (January 2003): 75–98; Carl A. Brasseaux, "The Moral Climate of French Colonial Louisiana, 1699–1763," *Louisiana History* 27 (Winter 1986); Carl A. Brasseaux, "The Administration of Slave Regulations in French Louisiana, 1724–1766," ibid., 21 (Spring 1980); *Charles Edward O'Neill, Church and State in French Colonial Louisiana: Policy and Politics to 1732* (New Haven, 1966); Mathé Allain, "Manon Lescaut et Ses Consoeurs: Women in the Early French Period, 1700–1731," in *Proceedings of the Fifth Meeting of the French Colonial Historical Society*, ed. James J. Cooke (Lanham, MD, 1980); Elizabeth Shown Mills, *Natchitoches, 1729–1803: Abstracts of the Catholic Church Registers of the French and Spanish Post of St. Jean Baptiste des Natchitoches in Louisiana* (New Orleans, LA, 1977); Bolton, trans. and ed., *Athanase de Mézières and the Louisiana-Texas Frontier*, 1: 48, 64, 90, 91, 162, 168, 2: 76; Lee, "Indian Slavery," 87, 92.

22. Peter Gerhard, *The North Frontier of New Spain* (Princeton, 1982), 328, 344–48; Daniel T. Reff, *Disease, Depopulation, and Cultural Change in Northwestern New Spain, 1518–1764* (Salt Lake City, UT, 1991); José Cuello, "The Persistence of Indian Slavery and Encomienda in the Northeast of Colonial Mexico, 1577–1723," *Journal of Social History* 21 (Summer 1988): 683–700; Susan M. Deeds, "Rural Work in Nueva Vizcaya: Forms of Labor Coercion on the Periphery," *Hispanic American Historical Review* 69 (August 1989): 425–49; Peter Bakewell, *Silver Mining and Society in Colonial Mexico: Zacatecas, 1546–1700* (Cambridge, UK, 1971); Vito Alessio Robles, *Coahuila y Texas en la época colonial* (Coahuila and Texas in the Colonial Period) (Mexico City, 1978); Silvio Zavala, *Los Esclavos Indios en Nueva España* (Indian Slaves in New Spain) (Mexico City, 1967), 179–349.

23. Brooks, *Captives and Cousins;* L. R. Bailey, *The Indian Slave Trade in the Southwest* (Los Angeles, 1966); Nancy Parrott Hickerson, *The Jumanos: Hunters and Traders of the South Plains* (Austin, TX, 1994), 32–33, 48, 80, 103–4, 113–14; Fray Damián Mazanet to Don Carlos de Sigüenza, 1690, in *Spanish Exploration in the Southwest, 1542–1706*, ed. Herbert Eugene Bolton (New York, 1916), 282.

24. Alfred Barnaby Thomas, trans., *Alonso de Posada Report, 1686: A Description of the Area of the Present Southern United States in the Late Seventeenth Century* (Pensacola, FL, 1982), 36–37; Brooks, *Captives and Cousins*, 121–42.

25. Thomas R. Hester, "Texas and Northeastern Mexico: An Overview," in *Columbian Consequences, vol. 1: Archaeological and Historical Perspectives on the Spanish Borderlands West*, ed. David Hurst Thomas (Washington, DC, 1989), 191–211; *The Indians of Southern Texas and Northeastern Mexico: Selected Writings of Thomas Nolan Campbell* (Austin, TX, 1988); Donald Chipman, *Spanish Texas, 1519–1821* (Austin, TX, 1992), 182–83, 205–7, 249–50.

26. Morris Edward Opler, "The Kinship Systems of the Southern Athabaskan-Speaking Tribes," *American Anthropologist* 38 (October 1936): 620–33; Morris E. Opler, "Lipan Apache," in *Handbook of North American Indians*, ed. William C. Sturtevant, vol. 13; *Plains*, ed. Raymond J. DeMallie (Washington, DC, 2001), part 2, 941–52; Thomas F. Schilz, *Lipan Apaches in Texas* (El Paso, 1987); Dolores A. Gunnerson, *The Jicarilla Appaches: A Study in Survival* (DeKalb, 1974); Gary Clayton Anderson, *The Indian Southwest, 1580–1830: Ethnogenesis and Reinvention* (Norman, OK, 1999), 105–44; José Cortés, *Views from the Apache*

Frontier: Report on the Northern Provinces of New Spain, ed. Elizabeth A. H. John, trans. John Wheat (Norman, OK, 1989).

27. William Edward Dunn, "Apache Relations in Texas, 1718–1750," *Quarterly of the Texas State Historical Association* 14 (January 1911): 198–274.

28. James William Brodman, *Ransoming Captives in Crusader Spain: The Order of Merced on the Christian-Islamic Frontier* (Philadelphia, PA, 1986); Jarbel Rodriguez, "Financing a Captive's Ransom in Late *Medieval Aragon,*" *Medieval Encounters: Jewish, Christian, and Muslim Culture in Confluence and Dialogue* 9 (April 2003): 164–81; Brooks, *Captives and Cousins*; Dunn, "Apache Relations in Texas"; Juliana Barr, " 'Traces of Christians': A Spectrum of Indian Bondage in Spanish Texas," in *Indian Slavery in Colonial America*, ed. Alan Gallay (Lincoln, NE, forthcoming).

29. Ana María Alonso, *Thread of Blood: Colonialism, Revolution, and Gender on Mexico's Northern Frontier* (Tucson, AZ, 1995), 37; Fray Benito Fernández de Santa Ana to Fray Guardian Pedro del Barco, February 20, 1740, in *The San José Papers: The Primary Sources for the History of Mission San José y San Miguel de Aguayo from Its Founding in 1720 to the Present, part I: 1719–1791*, trans. Benedict Leutenegger, ed. Marion A. Habig (San Antonio, TX, 1978), 64; Proceedings concerning the Infidelity of the Apaches, June 28, 1738, Béxar Archives (Center for American History, University of Texas, Austin); Fray Benito Fernández de Santa Ana to Viceroy Archbishop Juan Antonio de Vizarron, June 30, 1737, in *Letters and Memorials of the Father Presidente Fray Benito Fernández de Santa Ana, 1736–1754: Documents on the Missions of Texas from the Archives of the College of Querétaro*, ed. Benedict Leutenegger (San Antonio, TX, 1981), 26–27.

30. Brooks, *Captives and Cousins*, 121–42; Gilberto M. Hinojosa and Anne A. Fox, "Indians and Their Culture in San Fernando de Béxar," in *Tejano Origins in Eighteenth-Century San Antonio*, ed. Gerald E. Poyo and Gilberto M. Hinojosa (Austin, 1991), 109–10; Jesús F. de la Teja, *San Antonio de Béxar: A Community on New Spain's Northern Frontier* (Albuquerque, NM, 1995), 122–23.

31. Don Prudencio de Orobio y Bazterra, Order for Investigation and Questionnaire, June 25, 1738, Proceedings concerning the Infidelity of the Apaches; Testimony of lieutenant Mateo Pérez, chief constable Vicente Alvarez Travieso, captain José de Urrutia, alférez Juan Galván, and corporal Juan Cortina, June 26–28, 1738, ibid.; Dunn, "Apache Relations in Texas," 244–45.

32. Testimony of Mateo Perez, Vicente Alvarez Travieso, and José de Urrutia, Proceedings concerning the Infidelity of the Apaches; Dunn, "Apache Relations in Texas," 245–47.

33. Statement of Don Prudencio de Orobio y Bazterra, August 18, 1738, Proceedings concerning the Infidelity of the Apaches; Dunn, "Apache Relations in Texas," 245–46.

34. Order of Governor Don Prudencio de Orobio y Bazterra, February 16, 1739, Proceedings concerning the Infidelity of the Apaches; Benito de Fernández de Santa Ana to Viceroy Archbishop Juan Antonio de Vizarron, November 24, 1739, in *Letters and Memorials of the Father Presidente Fray Benito de Fernández de Santa Ana*, ed. Leutenegger, 32.

35. Max L. Moorhead, "Spanish Deportation of Hostile Apaches: The Policy and the Practice," *Arizona and the West* 17 (Autumn 1975): 210–11, 215, 217.

36. Dunn, "Apache Relations in Texas," 248–62; Elizabeth A. H. John, *Storms Brewed in Other Men's Worlds: The Confrontations of Indians, Spanish, and French in the Southwest, 1540–1795* (College Station, TX, 1975), 273–303, 336–405.

37. Casañas de Jesús María to the Viceroy of Mexico, August 15, 1691, in "Descriptions of the Tejas or Asinai Indians, 1691–1722," trans. Hatcher, 208; Juan Bautista

Chapa, *Texas and Northeastern Mexico, 1630–1690,* ed. William C. Foster, trans. Ned F. Brierley (Austin, TX, 1997); Fray Francisco Hidalgo to the Viceroy, November 4, 1716, in "Descriptions of the Tejas or Asinai Indians, 1691–1722," trans. Mattie Austin Hatcher, *Southwestern Historical Quarterly* 31 (July 1927): 60; Fray Isidro de Espinosa, "Ramón's Expedition: Espinosa's Diary of 1716," trans. Gabriel Tous, *Preliminary Studies of the Texas Catholic Historical Society* 1 (April 1930): 4–24; Don Domingo Ramón, "Captain Don Domingo Ramón's Diary of his Expedition into Texas in 1716," trans. Paul J. Foik, ibid., 2 (April 1933): 3–23; Fray Francisco Céliz, *Diary of the Alarcón Expedition into Texas, 1718–1719,* trans. Fritz Hoffmann (Los Angeles, CA, 1935), 83.

38. Don Antonio Valverde y Cosio, governor of New Mexico, to Marquis de Valero, November 3, 1719, in *Pichardo's Treatise on the Limits of Louisiana and Texas,* trans. Hackett, 1:193, 206; Testimonies of Luis Febre, Pedro Satren and Joseph Miguel Riballo before Governor Tomás Vélez Cachupín, April 13, 1749, and March 5, 1750, ibid., 3: 299–320; testimony of Felipe de Sandoval, March 1, 1750, ibid., 320–24; Statement of Antonio Treviño to Governor Angel Martos y Navarrete, July 13, 1765, Béxar Archives.

39. Pedro de Rivera, "Diary and Itinerary of What Was Seen and Examined During the General Inspection of Presidios in the Interior Provinces of New Spain," in *Imaginary Kingdom: Texas as Seen by the Rivera and Rubí Military Expeditions, 1727 and 1767,* ed. Jack Jackson (Austin, TX, 1995), 35; Marqués de Rubí, "Dictamen of April 10, 1768," trans. Ned F. Brierley, ibid., 182–83; Paul D. Nathan, trans., Lesley Byrd Simpson, ed., *The San Sabá Papers: A Documentary Account of the Founding and Destruction of San Sabá Mission* (San Francisco, CA, 1959), 71, 107–15, 136, 145.

40. Alexandro O'Reilly, Proclamation, December 7, 1769, in *Spain in the Mississippi Valley, 1765–1794,* ed. Lawrence Kinnaird (Washington, DC, 1949), 2: 126–27; Alejandro O'Reilly to Athanase de Mézières, January 23, 1770, in *Athanase de Mézières and the Louisiana-Texas Frontier,* ed. and trans. Bolton, 1: 135–36, 152; de Mézières to Governor of Louisiana Luis Unzaga y Amezaga, May 20, 1770, ibid., 166–68, esp. 166.

41. On the actions of François Morvant, Jacque Ridde, and Pierre Raimond in 1770, see Lee, "Indian Slavery," 83–85; and Mills, *Natchitoches, 1729–1803,* entries 1016, 1101, 1619, 1953, 2297, 2901. For the first and last appearances of the Morvant family in the town censuses, see Censuses of Nuestra Señora del Pilar de Nacogdoches for 1784 and 1805, Béxar Archives.

42. Stephen Webre, "The Problem of Indian Slavery in Spanish Louisiana," *Louisiana History* 25 (Spring 1984): 117–35; Hans W. Baade, "The Law of Slavery in Spanish Louisiana, 1769–1803," in *Louisiana's Legal Heritage,* ed. Edward F. Haas (Pensacola, FL, 1983), 43–86; Winston de Ville, ed., *Natchitoches Documents, 1732–1785: A Calendar of Civil Records from Fort St. Jean Baptiste in the French and Spanish Province of Louisiana* (Ville Platte, LA, 1994), 10, 17, 35.

43. Present-day Ebarb in Sabine Parish in northwestern Louisiana is populated by descendants of enslaved Lipan Apaches, indigenous Caddos, and immigrant Choctaws, and Louisiana officially recognizes the Choctaw-Apache People of Ebarb among the state's American Indian groups. See *Official Home Page of the Choctaw-Apache Tribe of Louisiana* at http://cate.50megs.com/index.htm (accessed March 24, 2005). N. M. Miller Surrey, *The Commerce of Louisiana during the French Régime, 1699–1763* (New York, 1916), 226–49; Usner, *Indians, Settlers, and Slaves in a Frontier Exchange Economy,* 116–22, 244–75. On Maria Modesta, see Mills, *Natchitoches, 1729–1803,* entries 2391, 2876, 2973. On Therese, see ibid., entries 2392, 2447, 2992, 3448. On Marie Rosalie, see ibid., entries 2354, 2425, 2524,

2863, 3013, 3394. See also Elizabeth Shown Mills, *Natchitoches, 1800–1826: Translated Abstracts of Register Number Five of the Catholic Church Parish of St. François des Natchitoches in Louisiana* (New Orleans, LA, 1980), entry 43 for Marie Modesta; and Elizabeth Shown Mills, *Natchitoches Colonials: Censuses, Military Rolls, and Tax Lists, 1722–1803* (Chicago, 1981). Gary B. Mills, *The Forgotten People: Cane River's Creoles of Color* (Baton Rouge, LA, 1977), 50–51, 83–88; H. Sophie Burton, "Free People of Color in Spanish Colonial Natchitoches: Manumission and Dependency on the Louisiana-Texas Frontier, 1766–1803," *Louisiana History* 45 (Spring 2004): 180; Charles R. Maduell, *The Census Tables for the French Colony of Louisiana from 1699–1732* (Baltimore, MD, 1972); Elizabeth Shown Mills, "Social and Family Patterns on the Colonial Louisiana Frontier," *Sociological Spectrum* 2 (July–December, 1982): 238.

44. John Sibley, "Historical Sketches of the several Indian tribes in Louisiana, south of the Arkansas river, and between the Mississippi and river Grande" 1806, in *American State Papers*, vol. 1 (Washington, DC, 1832), 721–31, esp. 723; Pueblo de Nuestra Señora del Pilar de Nacogdoches: List of Families in the Said Pueblo Taken by Captain and ommandant, Don José Joaquín Ugarte," January 1, 1804, Béxar Archives; "Report of the Missions Occupied by the Priest of the College of Our Lady of Guadalupe de Zacatecas in Said Province [Texas], Their Progress to the End of 1804 . . . ," December 31, 1804, ibid.; "Pueblo of Nuestra Señora del Pilar de Nacogdoches: Census of the families who live in the aforesaid pueblo, compiled by Commandant José Joaquín Ugarte," January 1, 1805, ibid.; José María Guadiana, "Jurisdiction of the Pueblo de Nuestra Señora del Pilar de Nacogdoches: Houses located on the eastern side of the Sabinas River," November 1805, ibid.; Sebastian Rodriguez, "Pueblo de Nuestra Señora de Pilar of Nacogdoches: Census of the families living in said town and its jurisdiction," January 1, 1806, ibid.; "Report on the Barbarous Indians of the Province of Texas, Dec. 27, 1819," in "Texas in 1820," trans. Mattie Austin Hatcher, *Southwestern Historical Quarterly* 23 (July 1919): 47–53.

45. A few men did register their paternity of children at baptism. See, for example, the children of Pierre Sebastian Prudhomme and Naillois, "an Indian woman," and Jean Baptiste Samuel and Jeanne, "a woman of the Canneci (Apache) nation," in Mills, *Natchitoches, 1729–1803*, entries 2245, 3444, 3049. For uses of women as objects of exchange, see Lee, "Indian Slavery."

46. Moorhead, "Spanish Deportation of Hostile Apaches"; Christon I. Archer, "The Deportation of Barbarian Indians from the Internal Provinces of New Spain, 1789–1810," *Americas* 29 (January 1973): 376–85.

47. Barón de Ripperdá to Bucareli y Ursúa, July 5, 1772, in *Athanase de Mézières and the Louisiana-Texas Frontier*, trans. and ed. Bolton, I, 322.

48. Ripperdá to Bucareli y Ursúa, March 30, 1773, Béxar Archives; Ripperdá to Bucareli y Ursúa, July 5, August 2, 1772, in *Athanase de Mézières and the Louisiana-Texas Frontier*, trans. and ed. Bolton, I, 322, 335; Ripperdá to governor of Louisiana Unzaga y Amezaga, September 8, 1772, ibid., 348.

49. Bucareli y Ursúa to Ripperdá, March 24, April 28, 1772, Béxar Archives; Ripperdá to Unzaga y Amezaga, May 26, 1772, in *Athanase de Mézières and the Louisiana-Texas Frontier*, trans. and ed. Bolton, I, 273.

50. Bucareli y Ursúa to Ripperdá, June 16, 1772, Béxar Archives; Ripperdá to Unzaga y Amezaga, May 26, 1772, in *Athanase de Mézières and the Louisiana-Texas Frontier*, trans. and ed. Bolton, I, 274.

51. Ripperdá to Bucareli y Ursúa, July 5, 1772, in *Athanase de Mézières and the Louisiana-Texas Frontier*, trans. and ed. Bolton, I, 321–22.

52. Fray Juan Domingo Arricivita, *Apostolic Chronicle of Juan Domingo Arricivita: The Franciscan Mission Frontier in the Eighteenth Century in Arizona, Texas, and*

the Californias, trans. George P. Hammond and Agapito Rey, 2 vols. (Berkeley, CA, 1996), 2: 25.

53. Though long identified as indigenous to Texas, Tonkawas, like Comanches and Wichitas, appear to have been Plains peoples who migrated south into present-day Texas in the late seventeenth century. Living up to their name "Tonkawa" (a Wichita [Waco] name meaning "they all stay together"), they had joined with other cultural and linguistic groups for defense by the late eighteenth century. Tonkawas and their new allies lived in nonsedentary hunting and gathering communities that were organized into matrilineal clans, with many clans representing once-autonomous groups of Mayeye, Yojuane, Ervipiame, Sana, and Tonkawa proper. Domingo Cabello to commandant general of the Interior Provinces, Teodoro de Croix, March 18, 1779, Béxar Archives; William W. Newcomb Jr. and Thomas N. Campbell, "Tonkawa," in *Handbook of North American Indians*, 12, ed. DeMallie, part 2, 953–64.

54. Christóbel Hilario de Córdoba, Interim Lieutenant at Nacogdoches, Report, Aug. 26, 1786, Béxar Archives. For Spanish captives in Indian hands on other Spanish frontiers, see Brooks, *Captives and Cousins*, 179–93; and Susan Migden Socolow, "Spanish Captives in Indian Societies: Cultural Contact along the Argentine Frontier, 1600–1835," *Hispanic American Historical Review* 72 (February 1992): 73–99.

55. Cabello to commandant general Felipe de Neve, August 3, 1784, Béxar Archives.

56. Archer, "Deportation of Barbarian Indians from the Internal Provinces of New Spain"; Al B. Nelson, "Juan de Ugalde and Picax-Ande Ins-Tinsle, 1787–1788," *Southwestern Historical Quarterly* 43 (April 1940): 450; Jean Louis Berlandier, *The Indians of Texas in 1830*, ed. John C. Ewers, trans. Patricia Reading Leclercq (Washington, 1969), 41.

Chapter 2

"Meddling with Emancipation": Baptists, Authority, and the Rift over Slavery in the Upper South

Monica Najar

From *The Journal of the Early Republic*

In 1808, a crisis occurred in the Mount Tabor Baptist Church of Kentucky. In the ten years since its 1798 constitution, the members had communed closely, addressing each other as brother and sister, ritually washing each other's feet in keeping with early Christian practice, watching over each other's conduct, remonstrating one another when necessary, and celebrating the Eucharist. Their fellowship was shattered in April 1808 when John Murphy, clerk of the church, rose from his seat and "declared nonfellowship with the church on account of slavery." Following Murphy's lead, Elijah Davidson then rose and withdrew from the church because it tolerated slaveholding among its members. In the following five months, two men and four women left the church for the same reasons.[1] Far from a singular event, this rupture was repeated in churches across the state and was the culmination to a decades-long debate within Baptist churches in the Upper South over the issue of slaveholding. Before the crisis was settled, Baptists would be forced to rethink their doctrines, worldview, and relationship to the new republic.

As Baptists began to evangelize the Upper South, they addressed the complicated issue of slaves and slavery. Slaves were part of the early audiences for Baptist itinerants in the 1760s and 1770s, and, after the War for Independence, slaves began to join churches in increasing numbers. This phenomenon forced Baptists into the quagmire of slavery as they constructed a coherent theology and a network of churches in a revolutionary age. The churches they built were biracial with white and black members. White and black evangelicals together faced the contradictions between their theology that emphasized the equality of souls, and the institution of

slavery that reified inequality. Churches became the arenas in which southerners debated what slavery meant in an evangelical society and what
religion meant in a slave society.[2]

The ongoing efforts of Baptists to claim an expansive authority for their
churches and to draw a divide between their members and "the world"
created a variety of thorny issues for them, ranging from the most intimate
(such as sexual conduct and marriage) to the decidedly public (such as business practices and political behavior). But it was their debates about slavery
that soon constituted the most serious crisis in early evangelical churches.
As with all other issues facing their members, Baptist churches claimed an
oversight of the relationships and behavior of masters, mistresses, and
slaves—a claim that allowed churches to intrude on the authority of white
male householders and to serve as the final arbiters of treatment of slaves.
Some Baptist ministers even attempted to inscribe the theology of the equality of all souls into church policy, issuing declarations against slaveholding
and creating emancipation plans. These efforts, met by hostility, rapidly created dissension within and among church congregations, so much so that in
the 1790s, many Baptists began to distance themselves from antislavery
statements to quell developing conflicts. Consequently, antislavery seemed
to disappear in the region. But, in fact, antislavery Baptists, or as they were
known, "emancipation" or "emancipating" Baptists, far from going quietly,
became more radical. Most vocal partisans migrated to Kentucky, making it
a battleground between those for and against slaveholding that would result
in a clash that would divide brethren and rupture churches.

The debate over the morality of slaveholding, then, was not so much a
political compromise as a hard-fought battle that divided churches, pitted
old friends against one another, and ultimately marginalized the antislavery
position both geographically and politically. Slavery was consequently redefined as a political issue outside the province of churches. While Baptists
continued to insist on their broad authority over their members, a claim that
included master-slave relations, they ceded the issue of the morality of
slavery to the civil state when it proved too divisive.

In their efforts to define their authority, Baptists self-consciously drew
upon the parallel process underway in the nascent governmental bodies.
In the early republic, the nature, structures, and powers of both state and
local governments were in flux, and individuals and groups sought to
define the boundaries and authority of government, a dynamic that has
been recently explicated in the burgeoning and innovative literature on
the emerging state and its political culture. This process, significantly,
ought not to be understood as wholly governmental or even wholly
secular. There was an analogous process underway in a number of
denominations, as sectarian groups sought to determine the appropriate
boundaries of the religious realm and, hence, the civil realm. Here, too,
these institutions sought to define and expand their authority, sometimes
by limiting the authority of the state over their members and at other
times seeking to create new arenas of power. In the Upper South, these

efforts encouraged the broad redefinition of the sacred and secular realms, as well as the reestablishment of the "proper" relationship between religion and society. "Sacred" and "secular" are social constructs that change and assume meaning in historical contexts. As R. Lawrence Moore points out, " 'secular' as a category for understanding historical experience depends for its meaning on the existence of something called 'religion,' and vice versa." As one changes, so does its binary opposite.[3] A significant intersection of the different, and often competing, efforts to determine authority in the new republic was slavery, as both church and state had legitimate claim to this issue.

For the evangelical Baptists of the Upper South, defining their relationship to the state and the civil realm was an imperative struggle, dictated by God, to protect the converted from the corrupting influences of worldly society and to build godly communities on earth. Baptists insisted that God retained sole authority over ministers and religious worship, and that to allow civil government any degree of power in the matter compromised God's supremacy; God, and God alone, could rule their consciences, and human law held no relevance. In that spirit of fervent defiance, Virginia Baptists not only resisted colonial restrictions on their practices, they also embarked, as early as the 1760s, on what was eventually a successful political campaign to limit state authority over religious beliefs and practices. By the 1780s, they were quite self-conscious about defining their authority against the power of government. Thus, as Americans debated not simply how the state was defined, but who was defining it, Baptists intended to be a coherent voice among the clamor seeking to shape civil bodies. Moreover, they wanted to use state power—and the very concept of the state—to resolve their own dilemma about the relationship between race and evangelical fellowship.[4]

At the heart of this issue are the significance of evangelicals' opposition to slavery and their subsequent rejection of that stance. Many works in the last twenty years have identified this compromise of early principles as a key component of their subsequent success at gaining southern white converts. Both the Baptists and the Methodists took a similar trajectory. In the early decades of their southern proselytizing (1770s and 1780s for Baptists and 1780s and 1790s for the Methodists), both sects issued statements against slavery, and in some cases, investigated ways to limit or eliminate it. Around the turn of the nineteenth century, each came to reject public declarations or actions against slavery by its churches or ministers, and by the antebellum era, both had come full circle, participating in public, explicit support for slavery. For the Methodists, this transformation has been well documented, since the hierarchical structure of the church allowed for consistent, if changing, policies.[5] Due to the congregational structure of Baptist churches, which gave each individual church the authority to determine its own policies, this process has proven more difficult to trace. Yet studying the anatomy of the Baptists' struggle with antislavery has much to teach us about the tenacity of antislavery evangelicals as well as the evangelicals' efforts, both conscious and unwitting, to define a division between religious authority and civil authority in the new republic.

In the late eighteenth and early nineteenth century, Baptists' efforts to reach consensus on the morality of slaveholding threatened to divide the young denomination permanently. Baptist theology itself forced congregants and churches to face the question directly. In particular, the Baptist belief in the equality of souls conflicted with the social practices of their communities, churches, and, for slave owners, their homes. Baptists commonly cited New Testament doctrines to articulate a vision of believers that valued a relative egalitarianism over "earthly" divisions of gender, race, and status. Baptists insisted that their mission was to strive for a pure covenanted community that rooted out all sin. Other churches (such as the Presbyterian Church and the Anglican-Episcopal Church) did not expect human society to approach the perfection of the heavenly realm. Evangelical Baptists, however, could not accept such distinctions, and they sought to create a godly haven in an imperfect world. This required church congregations to confront the presence of slavery in their midst. How to reconcile their theology with the reality of slaves and slave owners in their churches became the subject of frequent and often intense debate. In the 1780s and 1790s, that debate was only beginning, and no clear consensus had yet emerged.

In the years immediately following the War for Independence, some Baptists in Virginia and its Kentucky territory came to believe that the doctrine of the equality of all souls before God necessitated the abolition of slavery. In the 1780s and 1790s, a number of Baptist churches and associations (regional bodies designed to guide otherwise autonomous churches) made a brief and wavering commitment to antislavery. A wavering commitment is, of course, a contradiction in terms, but contradiction perhaps best captures white Baptists' struggles with slavery. One of the earliest debates came in 1785 (a year after the Methodists issued and quickly repealed a bold antislavery policy) when the Baptist General Committee of Virginia took up the issue of slavery. Formed in 1782, this committee of ministers was organized to apply pressure to the state government to disestablish the Anglican-Episcopal Church and eliminate its traditional privileges. It was explicitly and exclusively intended to be the "political mouth . . . to the State Legislature" on church-state relations. Despite its narrow charge, the General Committee repeatedly issued declarations against slavery to be circulated among its member churches. The 1785 meeting, when the committee first took up the question of slavery, resulted in a statement that avowed "hereditary slavery to be contrary to the word of God." Whereas the Methodist Conference more definitively laid out its position rejecting slaveholding and formulated plans for ministers as well as the laity to emancipate their slaves, the Baptist position was more moderate. In defining slavery in opposition to God's word, it implied that holding slaves could be, and even ought to be, defined in the churches as an excommunicable offense, but it left any such conclusions unstated.[6]

In 1790, the General Committee took a more forceful stand when the attendees again considered the "equity, of Hereditary Slavery." The committee had difficulty formulating a statement so it deferred to the leadership and words of minister John Leland. Leland submitted a resolution that the General Committee then issued in its minutes:

> Resolved, That slavery, is a violent deprivation of the rights of nature, and inconsistent with a republican government; and therefore recommend it to our Brethren to make use of every legal measure, to extirpate the horrid evil from the land, and pray Almighty God, that our Honourable Legislature may have it in their power, to proclaim the general Jubilee, consistent with the principles of good policy.

With this statement, the General Committee broadened the position from which it attacked slavery; having already found slavery at odds with the word of God, it also declared slavery contrary to republicanism and natural rights. Indeed, it was this latter, more secular assault that dominated this second statement against slavery. And it boldly encouraged Baptists to take legal steps to eliminate slavery, though it again avoided drawing the logical conclusion that slaveholding must therefore be a sinful act that required church intervention. Significantly, because Baptists valued consensus, it is likely that most, if not all, of the forty-two ministers and church representatives in attendance would have had to agree to this declaration before it could be passed. The General Committee's minutes were published for wide circulation among the represented churches as well as other associations in Virginia, North Carolina, and Kentucky.[7]

As this document circulated, the decentralized structure of Baptist institutions ensured that these antislavery resolutions would be the subject of great debate and likely strong opposition. Each church was an independent body that could make its own rules and policies. While this congregational structure protected the autonomy of each covenanted community, in practice, Baptists valued consensus and continuity, which promised the converted relative harmony and gave them confidence in the godliness and purity of their practices. To ensure this stability, Baptists relied on specific structures and practices to maintain continuity across time and across churches. In particular, regional associations played an important role here as they guided churches on thorny issues. Associations consisted of church representatives that met annually or semiannually to discuss theology, practices, and discipline and then circulated published minutes of their debates and decisions to their churches and other regional associations. Church representatives thus had a chance to consider and debate a host of questions on which they could bring their collective judgment to bear and distribute their conclusions to member churches and to other associations that might be faced with the same problem. While information on a variety of issues such as heresy, price setting, Freemasonry, and consanguineous marriage commonly circulated, none of these provoked the backlash of antislavery resolutions.

In 1790, when the General Committee circulated its strong statement against slavery, the clamor from some quarters was so loud and immediate that the following year the committee had to reconsider its statement as well as the one of 1785. Indeed, some church representatives were so disturbed by the resolution of the previous year that they requested that the association entertain the question of whether it had deviated from its original design. Seeking greater agreement among Virginia Baptists, the General Committee agreed that the antislavery policy should be "again referred to the district association, and from thence to their respective churches for their consideration, desiring them to take the matter into consideration, and shew [sic] their opinion on this subject to the general committee." By returning the issue of slavery to local associations and their member churches, the representatives hoped to signal the General Committee's respect for the appropriate lines of communication (from independent churches to representative bodies) and for the authority of the churches. Finally, since the committee's consideration of the morality of slavery appeared to have inadvertently raised the specter of oppression from a centralized body, the representatives took pains to assure their member churches that they did not consider themselves a supervisory committee and that their sole goal was to promote the political liberty of the sect.[8]

By returning the question of the morality of slavery to the churches and regional associations, the General Committee hoped to see a consensus emerge. Divisions, however, emerged instead. The Strawberry Baptist Association agreed to advise the General Committee "not to Interfere" in slavery. The Roanoke Association was quite troubled by this issue, explaining that their members wished to be governed by the "spirit of humanity," and yet they were "not unanamously [sic] clear in [their] minds whether the God of nature ever intended, that one Part of the human species should be held in an abject state of slavery to another part of the same species." Nonetheless, the association did not believe that the General Committee should meddle in slavery, citing concerns about how slaves would support themselves as well as about the general complexity of the issues. The Ketocton Association was apparently unconvinced by the General Committee's nod to congregational autonomy and went so far as to suggest that the General Committee was "dangerous to the liberties of the Churches." It was two years before the General Committee came to any type of agreement. When it did, it not only radically departed from its own position of just a few years earlier, it also signaled a major transformation in Baptists' understanding of religious and civil authority. In 1793, the committee again debated hereditary slavery and voted "by a majority (after considering it a while) that the subject be dismissed from this committee, as believing it *belongs to the legislative body*." This was a remarkable rejection of contemporary Baptist theology and practice. Baptists intended to build a distinct society within society, a community that would maintain broad authority over their congregants' lives to ensure the righteousness of each individual and the purity of the church. Having established a religious movement founded on the claim that virtually every issue relating to their members concerned the church, some Baptist leaders were now willing to sacrifice a major issue to the civil state, defining it as outside of the province of the churches and more properly the concern of the government.[9]

While the General Committee backed away, other Baptists continued to press the issue. John Leland was clearly not persuaded by the opponents to an antislavery position, and he worked to galvanize southern Baptists. In the same year that he wrote the General Committee's statement, he published his own essay in which he decried the evils of slavery and the slave trade, which he denounced as "the horrid work of bartering spirituous liquor for human souls." Leland objected to the legal structures of slavery that eliminated a slave's ability to testify in court against a white person, leaving the slave no legal redress if abused; he also complained of federal law which, under the Constitution, decreed slaves were "possessed of three-fifths of a man, and two-fifths of a brute." Using a language that presaged rhetoric by antebellum abolitionists, Leland warned that "the whole scene of slavery is pregnant with enormous evils. On the master's side, pride, haughtiness, domination, cruelty, deceit and indolence; and on the side of the slave, ignorance, servility, fraud, perfidy and despair." Shortly after the publication of this essay, Leland moved with his family to New England, and a leading voice for antislavery in the region was lost.[10]

Other Baptist ministers and unordained leaders shared Leland's antislavery beliefs and attempted to unite brethren in the region against slavery, working against the emerging coalition of evangelicals that wished to define slavery as a civil issue. As representatives of their churches to regional associations, church leaders worked together to issue statements against slavery on behalf of their churches. In 1796, the Portsmouth Baptist Association, representing some twenty-two churches, complained of the "*Covetousness* [that] leads Christians, with the people of this country in general, to hold and retain, in *abject slavery* a set of our poor fellow creatures *contrary to the laws of God and nature*." Churches and associations also tried to initiate debate and so posed "queries" for congregations and associations. In 1796, the Kehukee Association, which represented churches from North Carolina and Virginia, debated the question, "*Whether Negro Slavery Be Lawful in the Sight of God or not.*" Happy Creek Church of Virginia wanted its regional association to take up the issue of slavery as well, asking "Can the present practice of holding Negroes in slavery be supported by scripture and the true principles of a republican government?" But it was disappointed when the association "refused to take it up, considering it as an improper subject of investigation in a Baptist Association, whose only business is to give advice to the Churches respecting religious matters, and considering the subject of this query to be the business of government, and a proper subject of Legislation."[11]

For many Baptist activists, antislavery agitation was one radical effort among many to limit the authority of slave owners and to reshape the institution of slavery. In the early 1790s, as the General Committee was backing away from its public opposition, minister David Barrow worked to ameliorate slavery, seizing and creating opportunities to highlight slavery's injustices to his brethren. When the Virginia Portsmouth Association was asked to consider whether an unnamed male slave could remarry after his wife was forcibly removed to a great distance, the representatives debated it for so long that it was referred to the following yearly meeting. Here too, they engaged in an extensive debate before the question was withdrawn for unnamed reasons. Barrow was one of a three-member committee that was authorized to construct a substitute question. Barrow and his fellow committee members submitted: "What ought Churches to do with Members in their Communion, who shall either directly, or indirectly separate married Slaves, who are come together according to their custom as Man and Wife?" From judging the appropriate behavior of one particular slave, Barrow and his committee asked a far broader question about the behavior of slave owners, a question with the potential to limit owners' ability to sell, lend, or will their slaves.[12]

While ministers' names were most frequently identified with antislavery, the laity played a crucial role in driving the issue of slavery to the center of debate within congregational life. In late eighteenth- and early nineteenth-century churches, laypeople not only had the right, but also the responsibility to secure the "purity" of the covenanted community and therefore could, and did, raise questions for debate, propose new rules, and instigate disciplinary proceedings. Antislavery Baptists took advantage of this opportunity to agitate on the immorality of slavery. Just before a major conflict over slavery erupted in his church, Brother Palmer charged Brother and Sister Stephens of mistreating their slave, Nancy, an act that required a church inquiry into their home. After the couple was acquitted of that charge, Palmer brought similar charges against them four months later. Similarly, Brother Samuel Richardson asked his congregation to debate whether slavery could be justified by scripture or consistent with republican government. Women were often restricted from raising formal queries, but they too became important actors in the local dramas. Antislavery women often outnumbered antislavery men, creating a sizeable enough faction to disrupt the working of churches. In South Fork Church, when the antislavery faction declared themselves, they included six men (including the minister) and ten women. By exiting their church en masse, these individuals were able to hinder the remaining body's ability to function. The actions of the laity belie the idea that antislavery was promoted primarily by the ministry who were alienated from the mainstream views of their congregants, an argument that has encouraged scholars to conclude that evangelical antislavery never ran deep and quickly dried up from a lack of support. To be sure, ministers who used their positions and pulpits to attack slavery became more notorious in their communities, but laymen and laywomen acted as well to force congregations to debate slavery and to shelter those ministers who took public stands against slaveholding.[13]

In the 1780s and 1790s, some antislavery Baptists wanted to move beyond general statements of opposition and sought to promote bolder action among their brethren, though they still worked within the confines of consensus building. Pushed by the antislavery agitation by Happy Creek and Back-Lick churches, the Ketocton Association in Virginia circulated a plan for gradual emancipation. The Dover Association also believed that with member churches it should create a plan to emancipate their slaves gradually and asked people to aid abolition efforts. Moved by revolutionary spirit and egalitarian theology, some individual Baptists, such as ministers George Smith, Hampton Pangburn, and David Barrow, as well as a number of laypeople including the very wealthy planter Robert Carter, manumitted their slaves. It is impossible to know how many individuals manumitted slaves under the influence of Baptists' arguments, but it is clear that even ardent antislavery Baptists did not seek to demand bold collective action before 1800. They did not, for instance, attempt to make slaveholding an excommunicable offense, and emancipation plans were circulated, not mandated. Some sects in the region offered models for stronger action. In the 1760s and 1770s, the Quakers, who in the early eighteenth century had reluctantly tolerated slaveholding among their brethren, took aggressive steps to eliminate it, agreeing to expel Friends who refused to manumit their slaves. The Methodists, too, briefly attempted to purge slaveholding among their ministers and members. In 1784, the Methodist Annual Conference decreed that ministers could not participate in the slave trade and must free their slaves where it was legal to do so. Emboldened church leaders agreed a few months later that members must emancipate their slaves, though local Methodists reacted with such immediate hostility that these new policies were suspended within a few months of their introduction. Such an effort on the part of Baptists might have been easier to attempt (and sustain) because of the congregational structure that empowered individual churches to pass their own rules. Ironically, it may have been the Baptist ethic of consensus building—to compensate for the lack of institutional structures creating unity—that limited rather than expanded possible strategies.[14]

Beginning in the 1790s, this debate shifted geographically and rhetorically to new territory. Many devoted antislavery Baptists—both ministers and laypeople—moved west, including many of the leaders of the antislavery contingent, and "western parts," or what would become Kentucky, quickly became the battleground between Baptist pro- and antislavery factions in the Upper South. The West seemed to offer more opportunity for those that Ronald Hoffman has called "the disaffected." Just as political dissenters, tax revolters, and land squatters had sought refuge in the western fringes of white settlement in the late eighteenth century, so did antislavery Baptists seek a greater chance to create their vision of a godly society. The West was an exciting prospect for many evangelicals. It offered them the opportunity to shape community at its broadest level. To be sure, Baptists were strong believers in the separation of political and church authority and did not envision a western theocracy or even an evangelical version of a church establishment. Nonetheless, the promise of the West lay in the possibility of creating pure covenanted communities in a region unfettered by a church establishment or a society that was hostile to evangelicals. It promised not just the financial and personal opportunities that drew so many migrants westward, but also a spiritual hope to have church and faith precede, and ultimately guide, state and society. It seemed to be a wilderness free of such abhorred social conventions as dancing schools, theatres, gaming, and, for antislavery Baptists most significantly, slavery. David Barrow saw Kentucky as idyllic farmland with rich soil, fatted calves, and hardworking settlers in a land "entirely exempt from the horride [sic] course of negro slavery." For men such as Barrow, antislavery ideals joined with financial incentives to influence their decision to migrate. Kentucky farmland, Barrow explained in his departure letter, would allow him to do justice to his ministry and support his family without having to turn to the unsavory practices of speculation or slaveholding. With high expectations of a better life in a better land, antislavery Baptists, such as Barrow, William Hickman, and Carter Tarrant, moved their families and made their homes in Kentucky. This migration, though, spatially marginalized the debate over slavery to this frontier region: after 1800, debate virtually ceased in Virginia, North Carolina, and Tennessee churches and district associations.[15]

The consolidation of the emancipating Baptists, however, did not lead to an easier path because there they met with an increasingly intransigent antiemancipation faction that was determined to eliminate evangelical debate about slavery. The West, of course, also beckoned those who saw slavery as a significant and desirable tool for financial success. In the 1780s and 1790s, Virginians journeyed over the Cumberland Gap in pursuit of many kinds of opportunity; cheap land, a growing economy, and an underdeveloped legal system all made Kentucky a playground for those hoping to make their fortunes. Some of these migrants, Baptists and non-Baptists alike, saw slave owning as the foundation of their economic strategy. After all, the rich farmland in the region did not come without risks. Although there were few permanent settlements of Native Americans in the Kentucky region in the late eighteenth century, a number of Indian nations still claimed the land as hunting grounds. As the number of white migrants increased, so did the conflicts between the Indians and white settlers, which quickly became fierce struggles over control of the land. And since white "ownership" of the land often meant no more than occupying and improving it, the traumas of the wars threw the American land tenure process into chaos. Settlers' rude dwellings and young crops were abandoned and destroyed, perhaps to be reclaimed by former occupants, or new ones, but often with different boundaries and only until the next violent conflict, failed crop, or migratory urge. As successive occupants improved and therefore claimed the land, they set the stage for decades of conflicts over competing rights of "legitimate" ownership. Within this turmoil, slaves served as a valuable asset in quickly clearing land and planting and harvesting crops. That was certainly Jacob Creath's expectation when he moved to

Kentucky in 1803. Like Barrow, he was a minister struggling to support his family, but, unlike Barrow, Creath hoped Kentucky would allow him to compete effectively as a small slave owner. And there were many who shared his expectations: as early as 1792, there were already over 11,600 slaves in Kentucky. By 1800, that number more than tripled to nearly 36,000.[16] Kentucky then combined antislavery sentiment born of evangelical and revolutionary optimism, hopes of greater fortune, and the absence of strong civil authority, all in a region fiercely claimed by competing groups. This combination proved explosive in both the civil and religious arenas.

In the civil arena, Kentucky was home to intense debates over emancipation in the 1790s, particularly during the two campaigns preceding its two constitutions (1792 and 1799). In both campaigns, slavery proved the most divisive issue and one that incorporated other large questions of political representation, economic development, tax structures, population growth, class structure, and, at its broadest level, the future of Kentucky society. If the stakes were high, the possibilities were many, particularly before the ratification of the first constitution. Emancipationists had settled in considerable numbers, feeling that western territories were a good place to work for emancipation because of the relatively weak slave structure. Slavery proponents, on the other hand, saw the constitution as the key opportunity to determine the value of their property (slaves and land) and their place in the developing local economy. While these groups did not neatly align with religious affiliation, the evangelical churches, as Joan Wells Coward argues, provided the core of antislavery activism during the debates of 1791 and 1792. Seven ministers, all opposed to slavery, were elected to serve at the convention. The Elkhorn Baptist Association even attempted to influence the delegates and drafted a memorial address to the convention on the topics of slavery and religious liberty. But these efforts by evangelicals failed dramatically. Evangelicals failed to weaken or eliminate slaveholding, and proslavery leaders were able to pass constitutional protection of slave property.[17]

While the passage of the proslavery article was a substantial blow to the antislavery movement, emancipation again emerged as a legitimate political agenda during debates in the late 1790s about whether Kentucky should create a new state constitution. A provision of the 1792 constitution provided for such a prospect, and antislavery activists were one voice among many that sought a constitutional convention. However, even in the few years between the 1792 constitution and the 1798 campaign, antislavery opportunities had declined in Kentucky. With Ohio lands opening up after the Battle of Fallen Timbers, some devout emancipators migrated westward, while the constitutional protection of slavery had made Kentucky a more appealing place for slaveholders. Indeed antislavery was such a controversial stance during these debates that some supporters of a constitutional convention downplayed the possibility of any reconsideration of slavery and even accused their political opponents of raising the issue to discredit a new convention. Nevertheless, emancipation was a political issue in this process, and again, evangelicals, notably Presbyterian minister David Rice among them, were a leading voice. In this case, the antislavery activists won the battle but lost the war. They succeeded in calling for a constitutional convention, but their opponents waged a determined and ultimately successful effort to control the convention. The election of delegates proved a fierce contest that pitted Governor James Garrard, a Baptist preacher opposed to slavery, and his supporters against some of the most prominent Kentucky politicians, including George Nicholas and John Breckinridge. It exposed regional fault lines as Lexington emerged as largely antislavery while the Bluegrass region was solidly proslavery, and it engulfed national debates over the Alien and Sedition Acts when antislavery activists attempted to tap into opposition to those despised acts. Profound divisions emerged in the counties of Montgomery, Logan, and Mason. But ultimately the majority of voters was unwilling to reconsider the issue of slavery and elected proslavery representatives who ensured that the 1799 constitution kept the controversial guarantee of slave property.[18]

Even as opportunities were being closed off in the political arena, conflicts over slavery erupted again in the religious realm. Frustrated that other members of their sect were dragging their feet, some antislavery Baptist ministers and churches began to abandon the moderate consensus model, preaching outright emancipation and refusing to remain in churches and associations with slaveholders or those who tolerated slaveholding. Rollings Fork Church of Kentucky transitioned from agitation to separatism in just seven years. In 1789, the church asked its association to consider whether it was "lawful in the sight of God for a member of Christ's Church to keep his fellow creature in perpetual slavery?" Since the church had only been admitted to the association the previous year, the other representatives may have considered the controversial question unnecessarily aggressive; in any case, the other attendees were in no mood to debate such a topic and so, while conceding the matter was critical, they ruled it was improper for them to consider it. By 1796, the Rollings Fork congregation was frustrated enough by the association's refusal to take a stand on the topic to withdraw altogether from the association. The solidly antislavery church at Mill Creek took similar action in 1794, withdrawing from its association when it refused to consider a query about slavery.[19]

After the turn of the century, an increasing number of emancipating Baptists proclaimed in word and deed that quiet coexistence with slavery was itself a sin and that they would no longer live with that transgression. Insisting they wanted to worship in churches that wholly reflected their doctrine and that were untainted by antiemancipation beliefs, they began to create new churches specifically organized around antislavery principles. Minister Carter Tarrant, a vocal proponent of emancipation, joined John Sutton in forming the New Hope Church specifically for antislavery Baptists. Antislavery members of the Church at Clover Bottom sought such an opportunity and asked the other members to dismiss them so they could join a church that supported emancipation. In what was an even more shocking move to their fellow brethren, by 1804, ministers such as David Barrow and Carter Tarrant began to use their pulpits to preach emancipation as a moral necessity. While these early sermons did not survive, complaints about them suggest that their position was adamant, blunt, and, perhaps worst of all, spoken to audiences that were increasingly biracial. As Ellen Eslinger demonstrates, while relatively few African Americans joined Kentucky churches before 1800 (considerably fewer than had joined Virginia churches), slaves increasingly sought membership during the revivals that began in 1800. Whether influenced by the growing number of slaves in their churches or disappointment that Kentucky was looking increasingly like the slaveholding Virginia that they had left behind, these emancipators adopted a new stand that more aggressively and publicly challenged their Baptist brethren.[20]

This newly radicalized antislavery faction quickly clashed with equally intransigent antiemancipation Baptists. In this new conflict that spread through much of Kentucky, neither side sought unanimity or consensus; each sought to identify godliness with their own position and sin with the other. Antiemancipation Baptists rejected out of hand the idea that slaveholding was a sin that required church discipline; in this, they repeated arguments from the earliest debates over a Baptist position on slavery. But they went even further. They now sought to make an *antislavery stance* an actionable offense that required church discipline. As these individuals sought to reframe the debate about emancipation and evangelicalism, they aimed at the most prominent of the antislavery Baptists: the ministers. In 1805, David Barrow found himself at the center of a controversy that would divide associations and churches and would force longtime colleagues to turn against him and one other. Barrow was not new to the debate and had in fact been a voice against slavery for some decades. He freed his own slaves in the 1780s and publicly spoke against slavery in several venues, including in a published letter announcing his departure to Kentucky. His public antislavery beliefs appeared to be no barrier to active leadership in either Virginia (where he remained until the late 1790s) or in Kentucky. Upon his arrival in Montgomery County, Kentucky, he became pastor to three churches and was frequently called to leadership in the regional associations where he served on committees, as association moderator, and as the voice of the association in sermons and circular letters.[21]

By 1805, however, Barrow's decades-long attack on slaveholding and slaveholders had become a thorn in his ministerial brethrens' side. At the subsequent two meetings of the North District Association, representatives from another association came and charged Barrow with "Meddling with emancipation" and "preaching the doctrine of emancipation, to the hurt and injury of the feelings of the brotherhood." These charges were unprecedented, and the unusual method of bringing charges to an association (which had no authority to discipline individual Baptists) rather than Barrow's church suggests his accusers' belief that they would have a more sympathetic audience in this body as well as their determination to see action taken. The strategy proved effective: the North District Association agreed to consider the charges and rebuked emancipationists in its annual "Circular Letter" to the churches. The association warned the brethren against people who professed godliness and yet were "so far deluded, that their printing, preaching, and private conversation, go to encourage disobedience in servants, and a revolution in our Civil Government." In 1806, it required Barrow to be "tried" before a committee of five ministers. Rather than exhibit remorse and repentance, Barrow spoke, as the meeting minutes report, "in justification of his conduct on that subject, and brother Barrow manifest[ed] no disposition to alter his mode of preaching, as to the aforesaid doctrine." The representatives then took the extraordinary step of expelling him from his seat in the association.[22]

The drama of Barrow's trial and expulsion sent shockwaves through the regions' churches and associations. A prominent and celebrated leader, Barrow was among the first generation of southern Baptist converts, and he was baptized just before joining the ministry. He was a veteran of the Revolutionary War, but, to this cohort of southern Baptists, he was a hero because of his engagement in another kind of battle. He was a survivor of the religious persecution in the 1760s and 1770s, having been nearly drowned by some men during a preaching appointment. Stories of these early persecutions signified to Baptists their status as a chosen people, repeating the experiences of the first Christians, and consequently the stories were told, retold, collected, and published. No doubt the badge of having suffered for the cause of Christ followed Barrow into his pastorates at various Virginia and Kentucky churches and contributed to his frequent calls to leadership, but it did not insulate him from attack once the conflict heated up. As news of Barrow's trial and expulsion spread throughout the region, Baptists lined up to take sides in this increasingly polarized debate, and the next thirty-six months witnessed a bitter and rancorous dispute. The North District Association did not stop at expelling Barrow; it also sent a committee to his church to instigate discipline there. Proslavery Baptists took heart from this ruling and acted against emancipationists in their midst. Churches dismissed their antislavery ministers and revoked their right to preach. Emancipationists left churches to set up new ones. Proslavery majorities excommunicated proemancipation minorities. Ministers on both sides denounced congregants and colleagues. Hostage to these two adamant positions, many churches in Kentucky broke apart. Minister John Sutton left his church, Clear Creek, to join an antislavery church; the following month Clear Creek expelled him for that action, as well as for speaking contemptuously of other ministers. South Fork Baptist Church's minister declared himself an "amanspater," and within six months the church had become divided and the emancipationists left the congregation. Similar conflicts divided such churches as Lick Creek, Bracken, Clear Creek, Hillsborough, and Clover Bottom, and this controversy extended across the Kentucky counties of Woodford, Bracken, Washington, Clarke, Shelby, Fleming, Montgomery, Barren, Jefferson, Hardin, and Warren, among others.[23]

Forks of Elkhorn Church provides a window into the demise of these church communities. Formed in 1788, Forks of Elkhorn was, like most southern churches, biracial and even included some slaves who were owned by the governor. The church had faced normal theological, procedural, and disciplinary issues: in the years preceding the conflict over slavery, the church considered such matters as the proper time for the Lord's Supper, its present method of receiving new members, the Son of God's equality with the Father, and the discipline of members for such offenses as lying, drinking to excess, gambling, adultery, fighting, fraud, spousal abuse, and disobedience to a master. Like other churches in the region, Forks of Elkhorn also was swept into the divisive debate about slavery and emancipation. Their minister, William Hickman, was one of the early opponents of slavery. It is likely that some white members of the church were equally uncomfortable with slavery, or, at the very least, with how their white brethren treated their slaves, as evidenced by Brother Palmer's accusations against Brother and Sister Stephens for mistreating their slave.[24]

Forks of Elkhorn Church became polarized over this issue between 1806 and 1807 when the majority began to reject the antislavery minority led by the popular minister, William Hickman. In May 1806, the church asked whether "Baptist Preachers are authorized from the word of God to Preach Emancipation" and soon agreed with the recent ruling of the Elkhorn Association that ministers should not meddle in this "political Subject." The church again confronted Hickman when he allowed excommunicated abolitionist minister Carter Tarrant to preach at his home. By September of the next year, tension had built in the church, and it reached a climax when Hickman went on the offensive, informing "the Church that he was distressed on account of the practice of Slavery as being tolerated by the members of the Baptist Society, therefore declared himself no more in Union with us, or the Elkhorn Association." The church responded to his withdrawal by excluding him. Other members who agreed with Hickman also formally withdrew or simply stopped attending the church. Brother Sisk took the opportunity to withdraw from the church at the same meeting and was likewise excluded. Lewis Palmer was called to task for absenting himself. In response he charged the church with "acting tyrannically in expelling her former Pastor," an accusation that got him excommunicated. While other members who stopped attending church meetings chose not to give a reason, one woman's declaration rocked the church, not simply for her words but also for who and what she was. Winney was a slave (owned by a Baptist woman) who had converted to Christianity and had been admitted to the church. Her conversion and faith, she explained, convinced her that no true Christian would own slaves, and she said as much, condemning slavery as well as slaveholders. Winney avowed that she had "once thought it her duty to serve her Master & Mistress but since the lord had converted her, she had never believed that any Christian kept Negroes or Slaves." Furthermore, she contended that there were "thousands of white people Wallowing in Hell for their treatment to Negroes[,] and she did not care if there was as many more." (Ironically, it was likely the church's horror at her words that inspired the church clerk to record Winney's declarations in greater detail than white emancipationists' statements.) In linking her religious conversion directly to her defiant stand against slavery and slaveholders, Winney embodied what many southerners feared most about evangelicalism. Doctrines such as the equality of all souls together with practices that downplayed social distinctions seemingly threatened to disrupt the slave system, a charge that many evangelicals had worked hard to counter. The Forks of Elkhorn Church made it clear that Winney's statements were unacceptable by expelling her from the church one month after she leveled the accusations.[25]

The polarization of Baptists on the question of slavery was soon felt on an institutional level as a vocal coterie of emancipationist Baptists in Kentucky agreed to unite in their own association. In 1807, David Barrow joined other antislavery Baptists in creating the "Baptized Licking-Locust Association, Friends of Humanity." In their first meeting, they welcomed representatives from nine small churches and most of the prominent Baptist abolitionists in the region. The representatives indicted slave owning in general and Christian slave ownership in particular. They rejected the stance of other Baptists, explaining, "We are now distinguished from our former brethren, by reason of our professed abhorrence to unmerited, hereditary, perpetual, absolute unconditional Slavery." Seeking to highlight the discordance of Christianity and slaveholding, they marveled that "(strange as it may appear in other nations and to future generations,) there are professors of christianity in Kentucky, who plead for [slavery] as an institution of the God of mercy; and it is truly disgusting to see what pains they take to drag the holy scriptures of truth, into the service of this heaven daring iniquity." Slave apologists, they continued, use such erroneous Scriptural justifications for slavery as the curse of Noah, or Philemon's servant, Onesimus. In rejecting these justifications, the emancipators challenged an increasingly common Baptist practice which was to "exchange the word slave for servant," a rhetorical turn, they argued, that obscured the reality of the system and allowed appeals to biblical discussions of the duties of servants. They criticized those ministers who remained silent on the issue of slavery as well as laypeople who were opposed to slavery but remained in fellowship with slaveholders. And they publicly denounced their former brethren by naming the associations who countenanced this obscenity. They identified the Bracken, Elkhorn, and North District associations as having issued "cruel censures against the Friends of Humanity [.] Blinded by covetousness and intoxication with the cup of Babylon, they call evil good and good evil." With these ringing denouncements of their former brethren, the Licking-Locust Baptists signaled that there was no room for negotiation or compromise in this showdown between good and evil.[26]

For these emancipation Baptists, the evils of slavery required that they combine their political and religious identities. Rejecting the antiemancipationists' bifurcation of religious and civil responsibilities, they embraced a dual identity as citizens and as Christians, insisting that each required them to take an active position to end slavery. "As a political evil," they declared, "every enlightened wise citizen abhors it; but as it is a sin against God, every citizen is in duty bound to testify against it." They scorned those who tried to defer this issue to the civil state, "as if the church was beholden to the world for assistance in matters of religion, and had no king nor constitution of her own, and as if the laws of Kentucky constrained men to commit wickedness in the land, a stigma on our constitution." Carter Tarrant also embraced his civil identity when in his own speeches and writing about slavery he insisted that it was his constitutional right as a "free citizen" to speak on this topic. His views, he argued, were entirely in keeping with both the Constitution and the Bible. And, with mock concern that his opponents appeared unacquainted with the Constitution, he repeated a few passages he found relevant; in addition, calling upon a series of civil "proof texts" to stand alongside his biblical ones, he quoted liberally from Thomas Jefferson's *Notes on the State of Virginia* and one of Jefferson's speeches on the close of the international slave trade to demonstrate the justice of his cause. In his appeal to "republican principles," he reminded his listeners that the Revolution and the Bill of Rights demanded liberty as a birthright: "Your late gallant struggles with British fury, adamantly declare that you mean to maintain those rights sacred and inviolate . . . but oh! how horridly have we abused this liberty." African Americans, he argued, had "never forfeited their natural right to liberty, and that an attempt to take it from them is a violation of nature, reason, philosophy and the word of God." Seamlessly combining religious and political language that authorized his brethren's antislavery actions, Tarrant declared simply, "We are republicans and will hear who we please, even the Pharisees." These references did not necessarily display a sophisticated engagement with contemporary political theory, but they were a consistent component of emancipating Baptists' speeches and writings, and they allowed these individuals to mark themselves as true republicans, as well as true Christians.[27]

Both sides of this sectarian debate, then, self-consciously appealed to the state in their arguments. Emancipationists saw their cause as one with that of republican government. "Republican principles" mirrored Christian principles; the Bill of Rights and the Constitution reiterated the message of the Bible. These twin authorities presented a unified message in regards to slavery that made easy the path to good principles and to right action. For the antiemancipationists, the state served a very different role, one that established a distinct authority for human behavior. For these Baptists, the boundary between church and state became of supreme importance because it allowed them to mark slavery as a "political" and "legislative" matter and, therefore, not their concern. Drawing upon a well-established rhetoric that divided the godly from the worldly, these Baptists used the boundary between God and Mammon to delineate the limits of their authority, and, in the process, they saved themselves and their sect the difficulty of reconciling egalitarian theology with the profound inequities of slaveholding. They drew upon this rhetoric, but they could not incorporate it wholly. Originally, this initial effort to delineate the "religious" from the "secular" arose from the desire to protect the spiritual realm from being corrupted by secular authorities and led Baptists to be strong proponents of the disestablishment of the Anglican-Episcopal Church at the same time that churches took on many civil responsibilities and demanded an expansive authority over their congregants. But the antiemancipationists argued that unity among the churches required them to relinquish this authority to the secular powers that they usually mistrusted. For them, slavery was a "legislative concern" outside of the province of the church, a designation unshaken by churches' regular involvement in business disputes, price setting, and politics. It was this compromise that won out in the debate over slavery. Even the Elkhorn Association, which had publicly opposed slavery in 1791 to the Kentucky Constitutional Convention, joined its sister associations in designating slavery a political issue in 1805.[28]

As this settlement emerged as the dominant Baptist practice, Baptists healed the rifts in their churches and associations quite rapidly with the aid of significant shifts in their population. The Kentucky emancipationists lost a number of their most prominent leaders, losses that, given their small numbers and the hostility of some of the population, must have been profoundly felt. A number of these individuals died during these years. They had been part of the cohort of early Baptists converted in the 1770s and 1780s as young adults, and by 1810, many of them were in their sixties and seventies. David Barrow, for instance, died in 1819 at the age of sixty-six. Likewise, seventy-three-year-old George Smith died in 1820; his younger brother George Stokes Smith died in 1810, and fifty-one-year-old Carter Tarrant died in 1816. Some of the younger generation gave up on Kentucky altogether, often moving to Ohio and Illinois, including Joshua Carman (who had founded an early emancipation church), Donald Holmes, and Thomas Whitman. There was enough migration out of Kentucky that another Friends of Humanity Association was established in Illinois in 1822, explicitly following the model established by the Kentucky society.[29]

Many of the remaining emancipationists finally accepted the now established definition of slavery as a "civil" matter and returned to their churches. A significant step toward this reconciliation occurred in March of 1808 with Carter Tarrant's published announcement in the *Kentucky Gazette* that there would be an attempt to form a secular abolition society in which "No religious acknowledgement" was necessary. Later that year the Kentucky Abolition Society was founded. After that year, participation in the Friends of Humanity declined precipitously, so much so that a prominent Baptist historian who had traveled through the region to research his 1813 history believed they had dissolved. Friends of Humanity finally disbanded in 1820, just months after the death of David Barrow. The decline of this association provided an incentive for emancipationists to return to their old churches; these churches were also eager to heal the rifts, and they not only accepted the former members but quickly restored them to their former positions. Elijah Davidson, who had declared "nonfellowship" with his church in 1808, returned two years later; just two months after his read-mission, he was appointed treasurer of the church, and in 1812, the church elected him as a deacon. In the following years, other emancipating members drifted back. In February 1814, a former preacher in the church, John Murphy, returned with his wife Rachel; two months later, the church restored his license to preach. Other churches also experienced these years as period of reconciliation, including South Fork, Forks of Elkhorn, and Bracken. Indeed, even the abolitionist slave Winney had her membership restored in 1812.[30]

The brokered compromise with slavery after 1810 meant Baptists no longer would debate the morality of the institution of slavery; instead churches that were so inclined would consider only specific cases to amelio-rate some aspects of slavery. Individual incidents involving slaves, masters, and mistresses would continue to be adjudicated in churches, and these matters would be accepted, investigated, and determined entirely on the local level without implying or leading to broader reevaluations of the institution itself. The deliberations of the Concord Association in 1812 reveal the contours of this settlement. In a circular letter distributed to member churches and other associations, the association gave advice on good "family discipline," first evaluating husbands', wives', and children's duties, before turning reluctantly to "servants." The association explained that "on this subject we dwell with unpleasant sensations," and they avoided any use of the terms "slaves," "slavery," or even designations of race, such as "blacks" or "Negroes." But, even at this date, the representatives did acknowledge slavery to be "an evil [as] all agree, but how to Remedy it none can devise." Rather than take up that issue, the association settled for instructing masters to use moderation in exercising authority over their slaves and to be just in what they distributed to their slaves. White members who failed to exercise moderation, separated married slaves, or denied their slaves basic needs faced the possibility that they could be called before their churches to answer for their conduct. But no longer would Kentucky churches and asso-ciations debate the larger issues of slavery and slaveholding. Now, following the practices common to other southern states, they would, at best, seek to ameliorate some aspects of slavery for individual black members.[31]

In the late eighteenth century, Baptist churches had claim a broad juris-diction over all aspects of their member's lives. Baptists believed they answered a divine calling to build covenanted churches of the faithful, and they asserted godly authority wherever they could. They demanded the right to judge each others' business practices, land disputes, parental deci-sions, leisure activities, and marital relations. In this context, it was natural that churches would insist on their right to monitor master-slave relations and to debate the morality of slaveholding. But efforts to resolve the con-tradictions between the belief in the equality of all souls and the presence of slaves and slaveholders in their churches threatened to tear the denomination apart. To stem the developing crisis, Baptists redefined slavery to be a civil rather than a moral and religious issue. This solution meant that individual cases involving specific slaves and masters would remain within the purview of the local church, but that Baptists would relinquish any authority over the question of slavery as an institution. For the first time, they defined an issue as being outside the province of the churches and exclusively the concern of the civil government. Thus, the "separation of church and state"—often understood as a legal delineation enacted in Virginia and Kentucky during the revolutionary era—was not a straightforward process, nor was it strictly legal. It was, instead, the political and legal face of a broader reconceptualization of secular and sectarian bodies in the postrevolutionary era. In other words, as debates over slavery reveal, it was a reconstruction of civil and religious authority. At the same time that civil authorities embraced a new relationship between religion and government, church members too sought to define the appropriate boundaries between the religious and civil realms in the early republic, a shift that required they welcome the presence and authority of the state over a matter that had been a church matter and that they reshape their understanding of their religious authority.

Notes

Monica Najar is an associate professor in the Department of History at Lehigh University and a recent fellow at the Center for the Study of Religion at Princeton University. She wishes to thank all those who read and commented on drafts of this article, including Jeanne Boydston, Charles Cohen, Bethel Saler, Sarah Fatherly, Elizabeth Dolan, John Lauritz Larson, Ellen Baker, and the *JER* anonymous readers.

1. *Mount Tabor Church Minutes, Barren County, Kentucky, vol. 1, November 5, 1798 through December 1829*, presented by Sandra K. Gorin (Glasgow, KY, 1994), Third Sat. in April, 1808, Third Sat. in July 1808, and Third Sat. in September, 1808, 33–34.

2. Itinerant preachers deliberately sought out and included slaves in their meetings. As early as the 1780s, some churches were evenly divided between black and white members. By 1790, most Baptist churches in the region were biracial congregations, and African Americans made up nearly one-third of all Virginia Baptists (30.35 percent). Robert G. Gardner, *Baptists of Early America: A Statistical History, 1639–1790* (Atlanta, GA, 1983). Because membership was not a right that could be secured through simple attendance, parental membership, or an owner's membership, these numbers represent conscious choices by slaves.

   The broader relationship between slavery and evangelicalism is crucial to understanding the values of the evangelical sects and their position within southern society before the Civil War. For important voices in the debate, see Sylvia Frey, *Water From the Rock: Black Resistance in a Revolutionary Age* (Princeton, 1991); Christine Heyrman, *Southern Cross: The Beginnings of the Bible Belt* (New York, 1997); Rhys Isaac, *The Transformation of Virginia, 1740–1790* (1982; repr., Chapel Hill, NC,1999); Donald G. Mathews, *Religion in the Old South* (Chicago, 1977); and Randolph Scully, " 'Somewhat Liberated': Baptist Discourses of Race and Slavery in Nat Turner's Virginia, 1770–1840," *Explorations in Early American Culture 5* (2001): 328–71.

3. R. Lawrence Moore, *Selling God: American Religion in the Marketplace of Culture* (New York, 1994), 7–8. Baptists division of the world into secular and sacred realms would seem to have much in common with the public and private spheres, posited in Jürgen Habermas, *The Structural Transformation of the Public Sphere: An Inquiry into a Category of Bourgeois Society*, trans. Thomas Burger in association with Frederick Lawrence (Cambridge, MA, 1989). Baptists did often use the words "public" and "private" to encapsulate the outside society (public) from church matters (private). But they did not understand, nor do I mean to invoke, a division between a civic society of politics, opinions, and discourse and a private world of family and economy. Instead, their division between the godly and the secular centered on members and nonmembers, not on specific issues or locations of discourse. For recent literature on state formation, see Saul Cornell, *The Other Founders: Anti-Federalism and the Dissenting Tradition in America, 1788–1828* (Chapel Hill, NC, 1999); David Waldstreicher, *In the Midst of Perpetual Fetes: The Making of American Nationalism, 1776–1820* (Chapel Hill, NC, 1997); Joanne B. Freeman, *Affairs of Honor: National Politics in the New Republic* (New Haven, CT, 2001); John Lauritz Larson, *Internal Improvement: National Public Works and the Promise of Popular Government in the Early United States* (Chapel Hill, NC, 2001); Richard R. John, *Spreading the News: The American Postal System from Franklin to Morse* (1995; repr., Cambridge, MA, 1998); and Simon P. Newman, *Parades and Politics of the Street: Festive Culture in the Early Republic* (Philadelphia, PA, 1997).
4. On Virginia Baptists involvement in debates over church and state, see Thomas E. Buckley, *Church and State in Revolutionary Virginia, 1776–1787* (Charlottesville, VA, 1977), and Rhys Isaac, " 'The Rage of Malice of the Old Serpent Devil': The Dissenters and the Making and Remaking of the Virginia Statute for Religious Freedom," in *The Virginia Statute for Religious Freedom: Its Evolution and Consequences in American History*, ed. Merrill D. Peterson and Robert C. Vaughan (Cambridge, MA, 1988): 139–70.
5. James Essig, *The Bonds of Wickedness: American Evangelicals Against Slavery, 1770–1808* (Philadelphia, PA, 1982) provides the most comprehensive study of this topic. Essig finds a vital movement during the revolutionary era that combined evangelical theology with a strain of republican ideology. Heyrman, however, argues that evangelicals willingly sacrificed antislavery in order to secure greater respectability within southern society, see *Southern Cross*, particularly 24, 92–93, 138, and 155. See also Jewel Spangler, "Salvation was Not Liberty: Baptists and Slavery in Revolutionary Virginia," *American Baptist Quarterly* 13 (1994): 221–23. For Methodists and slavery, see Cynthia Lynn Lyerly, *Methodism and the Southern Mind, 1770–1810* (New York, 1998); Donald G. Mathews, *Slavery and Methodism: A Chapter in American Morality, 1780–1845* (Princeton, NJ, 1965); and John H. Wigger, *Taking Heaven by Storm: Methodism and the Rise of Popular Christianity in America* (New York, 1998).
6. Minutes of the Baptist General Committee, May 1791, 8, 5 (Virginia Baptist Historical Society, University of Richmond, Richmond, VA; hereafter VBHS).
7. Ibid., May 1790, 6–7.
8. Ibid., May 1791, 5, 4, 8.
9. Records of the Strawberry Baptist Association (October 1787 to May 1822), May 1792 (Archives, Library of Virginia, Richmond, VA; hereafter LVA); Roanoke District Baptist Association Minute Book (1789–1821), June 1790, LVA; Ketocton Baptist Association Minutes, 1792, VBHS; (italics mine), *Minutes of the Baptist General Committee, Holden at Muddy-Creek Meeting-House: Powhatan County, Virginia. May,1793* (Richmond, VA, 1793), 4, VBHS.

10. John Leland, "The Virginia Chronicle" in *The Writings of the Late Elder John Leland Including Some Events in his Life Written by Himself*, ed. L. F. Greene (New York, 1845), 95, 96, 96–97.

11. Minutes of the Virginia Portsmouth Baptist Association, 1796, 5, VBHS; *Minutes of the Kehukee Baptist Association, Holden at Parker's Meeting-House, on Meherrin, Hertford County, North-Carolina, September, 1796* (Halifax, 1796), 4; *Minutes of the Ketocton Baptist Association Held at Thumb Run, Fauquier County, Virginia, August 1796* (Dumfries, 1796), 4.

12. Minutes of the Virginia Portsmouth Baptist Association, May 17[9]3, 4, VBHS; ibid., May 1792, 2. Barrow may have engaged in some devious actions here to give his substitute query a public forum. The minutes from 1794 meeting indicate that the representatives agreed that Barrow's substitute question was to be "expunged" from the official records. However, Barrow, who was assigned to prepare the minutes, neglected to remove his question. Minutes of the Virginia Portsmouth Baptist Association, May 1794, 5, VBHS.

13. Forks of Elkhorn Baptist Church Minutes, Kentucky, 1788–1831, January 1806, April 1806 (Southern Baptist Theological Seminary, Louisville, KY; hereafter SBTS); "Minutes of the Proceeding of the Church at Waterlick (in Shenandoah County) Consolidated on the Fifteenth of Apr. AD. 1787," August 13, 1796, VBHS; South Fork Baptist Church Minutes, December 19, 1807, July, the third Sat., 1808, SBTS. There were, of course, limits on laypeople's rights of participation that were only extended in their fullest sense to white men. White women and African Americans experienced various restrictions, yet could utilize "backdoor" opportunities to raise a variety of issues. It was quite easy to instigate a disciplinary investigation, for instance, which often led to full church debate.

14. When the majority of the churches sent word to the association that they rejected the plan, it agreed to drop it. Minutes of the Ketocton Baptist Association, August 1798, 3–4 (Virginia Historical Society, Richmond; hereafter VHS); *Baptist Dover Association held at Bestland Meeting-House, Essex County, Virginia, October 14th, 1797*, 4, VBHS; Carter Tarrant, *A History of the Baptised Ministers and Churches in Kentucky, &c. Friends to Humanity* (Frankfort, KY, 1808), 15, 18, 47 (Rare Book Room, Library of Congress, Washington, DC). Robert Carter was heavily influenced by Baptist antislavery beliefs as well as economic and political arguments when he decided to gradually manumit his 422 slaves; he eventually left the Baptist faith and became a Swedenborgian. Robert Baylor Semple, *History of the Baptists in Virginia*, revised and extended by G. W. Beale, with Introduction by Joe M. King (1810 [1894]; repr., Lafayette, TN, 1976), 178. Jean Soderlund, *Quakers and Slavery: A Divided Spirit* (Princeton, NJ, 1985); Hiram H. Hilty, *Toward Freedom For All: North Carolina Quakers and Slavery* (Richmond, IN, 1984), 13–43; Mathews, *Slavery and Methodism*, 3–26.

15. Ronald Hoffman, "The 'Disaffected' in the Revolutionary South" in *The American Revolution: Explorations in the History of American Radicalism*, ed. Alfred F. Young (Dekalb, IL, 1976). "Diary of David Barrow of His Travel Thru Kentucky in 1795" 5 (typescript at North Carolina Baptist Historical Society, Wake Forest University, Winston-Salem, NC); Carlos R. Allen, Jr., ed., "David Barrow's Circular Letter of 1798" *William and Mary Quarterly* 3rd ser., 20 (July 1963): 445.

16. Semple, *History of the Baptists in Virginia*, 182–83; Frank M. Masters, *A History of Baptists in Kentucky* (Louisville, KY, 1953), 178; Joan Wells Coward, *Kentucky in the New Republic: The Process of Constitution Making* (Lexington, KY, 1979), Table 1, 37; Table 6, 63.

17. Six of the sixteen antislavery votes came from the ministers, the seventh minister, David Rice, having resigned before the vote. Five of the remaining ten votes came

from active laymen in Baptist and Presbyterian churches. Coward, *Kentucky in the New Republic*, 38, 36–38, 45; Lowell H. Harrison, *Kentucky's Road to Statehood* (Lexington, KY, 1992), 103–11; "Minutes of the Elkhorn Baptist Association, Kentucky, 1785–1805" in William Warren Sweet, ed., *Religion on the American Frontier: A Collection of Source Material, 1783–1830*, 4 vols. (New York, 1931), 1: 444. The following meeting was attended by many prominent emancipationists, including George Stokes Smith, William Hickman, and James Garrad, but the fifteen new representatives enabled enough of a shift that this meeting voted to "disapprove" of the memorial. "Elkhorn Minutes" in Sweet, ed., *Religion on the American Frontier*, 1: 447.

18. Coward, *Kentucky in the New Republic*, 107–09.
19. J. H. Spencer, *A History of Kentucky Baptists From 1769 to 1885*, 2 vols. (Cincinnati, OH, 1885), 2: 47; 2: 47–49, 1: 184.
20. Ibid., 1: 189; *Minutes of the Elkhorn Association of Baptists, Begun and held agreeable to appointment, at David's Fork Meeting-House, State of Kentucky, the 2d Saturday in August, 1807*, 2 (Special Collections, Margaret I. King Library, University of Kentucky, Lexington); *Minutes of the North District Association of Baptists; Held . . . the first Saturday in October, in the year of our Lord one thousand eight hundred and six*, 3 (Special Collections, Margaret I. King Library, University of Kentucky, Lexington); Ellen Eslinger, "The Beginnings of Afro-American Christianity Among Kentucky Baptists" in *The Buzzel about Kentuck: Settling the Promised Land*, ed. Craig Thompson Friend (Lexington, KY, 1999), 203–6.
21. Allen, ed., "David Barrow's Circular Letter," 445, 450. See Baptist General Committee, May 1790, 6; Portsmouth Baptist Association, May 17[9]3, 4; Portsmouth Baptist Association, May 1794.
22. *Minutes of the North District Association of Baptists . . . October 1805*, 2, SBTS; *North District Association*, October 1806, 3; *North District Association*, October 1805, 5; *North District Association*, October 1806, 3.
23. South Fork Baptist Church Minutes, December 19, 1807, July, the third Sat., 1808, SBTS; Tarrant, *A History*, 7. For more on Barrow, see Essig, *The Bonds of Wickedness*, 74–78.
24. Forks of Elkhorn Church Minutes, January 1806, April 1806.
25. Ibid., May 1806; "Elkhorn Minutes" in Sweet, ed., *Religion on the American Frontier*, 1: 508; Forks of Elkhorn Church Minutes, September 1807, August 1808, January 1807, June 1806, December 1806, February 1807. For other members expelled for nonattendance for unnamed reasons, see ibid., July 1807; October 1807, May 1808, June 1808, and July 1808.
26. "Minutes of the Baptized Licking-Locust Association, Friends of Humanity" in Sweet, ed., *Religion on the American Frontier*, 1: 566–67, 567, 567–68, 568, 569.
27. Ibid., 1: 566–67, 568. Carter Tarrant, *The Substance of a Discourse Delivered in the Town of Versailles, Woodford County, State of Kentucky, April 20, 1806* (Lexington, KY, 1806), 4–7, 32, 9; Tarrant, *A History*, 1, 42. See also Essig, *The Bonds of Wickedness*, chap 4.
28. "Elkhorn Minutes" in Sweet, ed., *Religion on the American Frontier*, 1: 508. For more on the construction of sacred and secular authority among the Baptists, see Monica Najar, "Evangelizing the South: Gender, Race, and Politics in the Early Evangelical South, 1765–1815" (PhD diss., University of Wisconsin, Madison, 2000).
29. Spencer, *A History of Kentucky Baptists*, 1: 192–97; 1: 191–92; 2: 21–23; 1: 189–90; 1: 163; 1: 190; 1: 250; Sweet, ed., *Religion on the American Frontier*, 1: 570–72.
30. March 15, 1808, *Kentucky Gazette and General Advertiser*, Lexington, KY (Kentucky Historical Society, Frankfort, KY); David Benedict, *A General History of the Baptist Denomination in America and Other Parts of the World*, 2 vols.

(Boston, MA, 1813), 2: 248; *Mount Tabor Church Minutes*, third Sat. in August 1810; third Sat. in October 1810; third Sat. in August 1812; third Sat. in February 1814 and third Sat. in April 1814. See also third Sat. in April 1813 and third Sat. in April 1814. South Fork Baptist Church lost five men and ten women over slavehold-ing; by 1812, four of the women and three of the men had returned, with the men quickly returning to their positions of authority. South Fork Baptist Church, third Sat. in July 1808, fourth Sat. in December 1811, fourth Sat. in February 1812, fourth Sat. in March 1812, fourth Saturday in April 1812; fourth Sat. in July 1812; Spencer, ed., *A History of Kentucky Baptists*, 1: 264; Forks of Elkhorn Church Minutes, September 1807, November 1809, August 1812.

31. "Minutes of the Concord Baptist Association Held at Hopewell Meetinghouse Sumner County West Tennessee Sept. 26, 27 & 28th, 1812," 12 (Southern Baptist Historical Library and Archives, Nashville, TN). See also Minutes, Tennessee Baptist Association, 1802–1932, October 1808, October 1810 (Southern Baptist Historical Library and Archives, Nashville, TN); Forks of Elkhorn Church Minutes, January 1806, April 1806, and May 1806. For the continuation of this pattern through the antebellum period, see Gregory A. Wills, *Democratic Religion: Freedom, Authority, and Church Discipline in the Baptist South, 1785–1900* (New York, 1997), chap 3.

Chapter 3

The Afterlives of Lewis and Clark

Stephen Aron

From *Southern California Quarterly*

This essay maps the fall and rise of Lewis and Clark by exploring what happened to the explorers following the return of the Corps of Discovery to St. Louis in September 1806. Charting the personal descent of Meriwether Lewis and the political undoing of William Clark, the article ties the sad fate of the cocaptains to the far sadder fate of race relations on the American frontier. Turning, then, from the lives of Lewis and Clark after the expedition to their afterlives, it tracks how, in the years since the deaths of Lewis and Clark, Americans have forgotten and now remember them, how the cocaptains have been joined by Sacagawea and York in the American imagination, and what this resurrection tells us about them—and us.

As historical celebrities go, Meriwether Lewis and William Clark are as hot as they come right now. Fifteen years ago, Lewis and Clark placed seventh in a survey of the collective memory of Americans about pre–Civil War historical figures. If that survey were taken again today, the duo would surely rank even higher. In recent years, *Time* magazine featured Lewis and Clark on its cover, and they have been the subject of the biggest of big screen treatments in an IMAX film. In the fall of 2003, the Autry National Center staged scenes from "Lewis and Clark: The Musical," which, if all goes according to plan, will premiere on Broadway in the not-too-distant future. There, it may compete with "Lewis and Clark: The Opera," a production of the St. Louis Opera Company. St. Louis is also the site at which the Official National Bicentennial Exhibition opened to overflowing crowds in the winter of 2004. What is surprising, given the public's fascination with all things Lewis and Clark, is that no major motion picture is under development. Thus, it appears that movie fans will still have only "The Far Horizon," starring Fred McMurray as Meriwether Lewis, Charlton Heston as William

Clark, and that famous American Indian actress Donna Reed as Sacagawea.[1]

If movie makers have missed their opportunity, merchandisers have not. Consumers have an astonishing array of Lewis and Clark commodities from which to choose. T-shirts abound, including my favorite, which carries the slogan "Lewis and Clark: The original guys that didn't need directions." At the gift shop for the Autry National Center's Museum of the American West, several shelves of wares tempt customers, who can select among Lewis and Clark coins, "authentic" foods from the journey, Corps of Discovery playing cards, Trail West jigsaw puzzles, action figures, and Sacagawea dolls. Most of all, there are books, probing the Lewis and Clark expedition from seemingly every conceivable angle and for all ages. There are, for example, a number of new Lewis and Clark cookbooks—presumably essential for those who purchase Lewis and Clark foods. For wilderness enthusiasts eager to follow in the Corps of Discovery's footsteps, there are a variety of guide books. Recently published biographies of Lewis and Clark, of the other men in the Corps, and of Sacagawea spill off the shelves. Lest animal lovers feel left out, Lewis's dog, Seaman, has been the subject of several tomes (figure 3.1). And all of this merchandise and all of these publications have appeared before the actual bicentennial of the exploration commences! Two hundred years after Thomas Jefferson instructed Meriwether Lewis and William Clark to go forth "for the purposes of commerce," it seems that they have fulfilled their mission.[2]

That aura of commercial success has not always enveloped Lewis and Clark. True, the Corps of Discovery received a hero's welcome when it arrived back in St. Louis in 1806. Residents ran to the shoreline to cheer the members of the expedition, then sang songs in their honor and feted them in their homes. The high note continued for several months. Through the fall of 1806 and winter of 1807, newspapers across the country celebrated the journey's completion. President Thomas Jefferson, who had authorized the expedition and provided the explorers with their instructions, exulted that "never did a similar event excite more joy through the United States" than did the homecoming of Lewis and Clark. Soon after their return to St. Louis, Jefferson appointed Lewis governor of the Louisiana Territory. A week later, William Clark got his reward, accepting an appointment as brigadier general of the territorial militia and its superintendent of Indian affairs. For the thirty-two-year-old Lewis and the thirty-six-year-old Clark, these were heady days, with the rest and seemingly best of their lives ahead of them. But happily ever after is not how their postexpedition careers played out. For Lewis, the aftermath of the expedition turned quickly to personal and political despair, culminating in his premature death in 1809. For Clark, the fall was not nearly so calamitous, but in the last thirty years of his life, he suffered a crushing political defeat, provoked the poisoning of his relationship with his slave and fellow explorer York, and participated in a transformation of American-Indian relations that in many ways undid the promise of the Lewis and Clark expedition. So undone were

Figure 3.1 Epitomizing the new "feel good" version of the Lewis and Clark saga, this toy features Lewis's dog Seaman at the bow of a canoe with Clark, Sacagawea, York, and Lewis.

Source: Stephen Aron.

these promises that the Lewis and Clark expedition faded into relative obscurity in the years after Clark's death. Only in the last few years of the twentieth century were Lewis and Clark resurrected and placed at the center of a new, "feel good" frontier history.[3]

* * *

Contrary to their current acclaimed status, the glow about Lewis and Clark subsided shortly after their journey's end. In part, the problem was that the mission did not fulfill Jefferson's instructions, or at least what the Corps discovered did not meet Jefferson's hopes. First and foremost, Thomas Jefferson had directed the explorers to find "the most direct and practicable water communication across the continent, for the purposes of commerce." Although Lewis and Clark thought they had done this, their tortuous route up the Missouri and over the Bitterroot Mountains to the Columbia was not the Northwest Passage of Jefferson's dreams, nor was their trail a viable highway for large volume trade or human transportation. In fact, what

Lewis and Clark found out about the North American West blasted Jefferson's Enlightenment expectations about continental geography. Instead of a symmetrical design, in which West mimicked East, Lewis and Clark learned that the Missouri did not mirror the Ohio and that the Rockies were far more difficult to cross than the Appalachians. In the wake of Lewis and Clark's expedition, the illusion of the Rockies as a single ridge, which typified wishful imaginations about North American geography, disappeared from maps of North America. But what good was this negative knowledge, especially as the bills for the exploration came due? The ultimate cost of Lewis and Clark's journey has been estimated at $40,000. That exceeded the initial appropriation of $2,500 by 3,000 percent, and it gave Jefferson's political opponents grounds on which to attack the expedition and the expenditure as wasteful and worthless.[4]

More immediate were the local political problems that burdened Lewis and Clark. Governing the vast Louisiana Territory was, as Lewis soon learned, a tougher task than commanding the Corps of Discovery. In both endeavors, Lewis had to lead a diverse assortment of people. But as governor, his authority was more contested, and the often conflicting interests of the territory's colonists—who were divided between long-settled French-speaking farmers, creole fur traders based primarily in St. Louis, and more recent waves of American emigrants—made governing a trial. Adding to Lewis's difficulties was the very limited budget that the federal government granted him, and the constant demands that his superiors made for still greater economy.[5]

For Lewis and also for Clark, the most pressing problems were traceable to the management of Indian affairs. Here, in contrast with their lack of experience in the general administration of territorial governance, Lewis and Clark seemed exceptionally well prepared. During their expedition, the captains had largely fulfilled Jefferson's dictum that in their "intercourse with the natives," they should "treat them in the most friendly and conciliatory manner which their own conduct will permit." Although much has been made of the education that Lewis received before the expedition from his mentor and from the nation's leading scientists and scholars, the mission's diplomatic successes owed less to information gleaned in Jefferson's library or in Philadelphia salons than to lessons from French traders in St. Louis and *métis* members of the corps. From these sources, Lewis and Clark learned the importance of respecting the rules and rituals of Indian diplomacy and exchange. Consequently, Lewis and Clark brought a supply of peace medals to bestow upon native leaders and, in St. Louis, they bought additional commodities to give as presents. The encounters they had during the twenty-nine-month excursion reinforced these precepts and protocols. As Clark discerned, "it requires time and a little smoking with the Indians, if you wish to have peace with them" and [he might have added] if you wish to conduct trade with them.[6] That Lewis and Clark had mostly peaceful encounters with Indians traced as well to relations fashioned outside formal councils, to the more *intimate* diplomatic intercourse that occurred between the men in the Corps of Discovery and diverse Indian women. To be sure, the men who participated in this intercourse did not often think themselves diplomats. Nor did Lewis (who likely abstained) or Clark (who was rumored to have fathered a child by a Nez Percé woman) appreciate the diplomatic character of sexual contacts between their men and Indian women. Raised to believe that all Indian women were "squaw drudges," the captains viewed sexual advances by Indian women as solicitations from "lechous" and "lude" prostitutes. What Lewis and Clark could not grasp was the status that Indian women held in many native societies as principal agriculturalists or the powers they acquired through sexual contact with outsiders. In part, the gains were material; as sexual partners, Indian women secured favorable access for themselves and their kin to trade goods. Equally important were the spiritual powers transmitted through copulation and, in turn, transmittable to Indian partners.[7]

For reasons, then, that Lewis and Clark did not themselves fully understand, as the Corps of Discovery made its way across the continent, the American emissaries managed to stay on the good side of most of the Indians through whose countries they traveled. As Meriwether Lewis wrote near the end of the two-and-a half-year odyssey, "so long have our men been accustomed to a friendly intercourse with the natives, that we find it difficult to impress on their minds the necessity of always being on guard with rispect [sic] to them." Therein lay the promise of the Lewis and Clark expedition that American expansion might be accomplished through friendly intercourse with the natives.[8]

For the most part, amicable relations between Native Americans and Europeans had also prevailed in and around St. Louis, especially so long as fur trading interests were in control of that town and its commercial hinterlands. Thus, during the 1790s, even the emigration of various eastern Indian groups, principally Shawnees and Delawares, and the first wave of American colonists from the Ohio Valley, the most famous of whom was Daniel Boone, did not disturb the peace. To the contrary, although these same Indians and Americans had turned the Ohio Valley into a dark and bloody ground, the former enemies coexisted quite harmoniously while establishing new settlements along the middle Mississippi and lower Missouri rivers. Indeed, in their joint pioneering into what was still Spanish territory, both Indians and Americans had developed novel arrangements, blending material cultures, subsistence systems, and common landscapes, and joining together to hunt, race horses, gamble, drink, and dance. As among the French colonists in the region, marital unions sometimes facilitated this easy familiarity and peopled a still-melting pot with mixed-ancestry children.[9]

But the transfer of Louisiana to the United States and the continuing influx of American settlers compounded the challenges for territorial officials. Initially, Thomas Jefferson had contemplated transferring populations to separate Indians and whites. Under this scheme, French and American colonists living on the western side of the Mississippi would exchange their lands for holdings in the Ohio Valley, while eastern Indians would relocate to the Missouri River Valley. This plan, however, met resistance from all parties, and Jefferson had neither the money nor the manpower to enforce the transfer of peoples and the restriction of movement. "Nothing but a cordon of troops will restrain our people from going over the [Mississippi] River and settling themselves down upon the western bank" was the judgment of Massachusetts Senator Rufus King. Bowing to political reality, Jefferson retreated from his plan, and Americans continued to move across the Mississippi in an unregulated fashion, squatting on whatever lands they deemed vacant.[10]

To stem encroachments onto their lands, the Osages, long the most powerful nation in the lower Missouri Valley, struck out against trespassers. By 1808, depredations attributed to the Osages led Governor Lewis to declare the nation beyond the protection of the United States and to recall traders from among them. Following Jefferson's views, Lewis believed "the policy of withholding merchandise" superior to "the chastisement of the sword." Deprived of trade goods, the Osages would, in Lewis's view, soon seek peace and the resumption of the trade on which they had grown dependent. In this case, he was proven right when several Osage leaders signaled their desire to negotiate. Accordingly, William Clark headed up the Missouri again, this time to construct a fort in the heart of Osage country and to broker a treaty with Osage headmen. The resulting compact saw the Osages cede much of their claims to all but the western parts of Missouri and Arkansas. Trade resumed, and peace, if not good feelings, was restored, at least for the moment. Privately, William Clark expressed concerns about his part in this transfer of land from the Osages to the United States. It was, he later acknowledged, "the hardest treaty" that he ever made. Indeed, he confided that if he were "damned hereafter, it would be for making" the 1808 treaty with the Osages.[11]

Clearing Osage claims opened land not only for white American pioneers but also for those whom Lewis described as "intimately friendly Indians." These were the Shawnees and Delawares of the lower Missouri valley, whose relations with American neighbors in the Louisiana Territory had been startlingly convivial. As Clark recorded, the Shawnees and Delawares were "peaceable and well disposed" peoples who had been "of great service to our frontier settlements." But the continuing influx of newcomers from Kentucky and Tennessee placed more and more squatters on Shawnee and Delaware lands and built pressure for their dispossession. One solution, favored by both Lewis and Clark, was to convince the Shawnees and Delawares to sell these lands in exchange for those made available by the recent Osage cession.[12]

At this point, though both Lewis and Clark encouraged the Shawnees and Delawares to leave their lands, they refused to force them out. When Shawnees and Delawares balked at trading current tracts for lands given up by the Osages, Governor Lewis courageously rebuffed demands from white pioneers that he unilaterally compel the Indians to move. Quite the opposite, Lewis responded to protests from Shawnee and Delaware villagers by issuing a proclamation in April 1809. In this manifesto, he ordered the white intruders off Indian lands, lest "the peace and tranquility so happily subsisting between the United States and those tribes be wantonly interrupted."[13]

Lewis's edict contained more bark than bite (figure 3.2). Just as Jefferson could not keep Americans from crossing the Mississippi, so Lewis could not prevent their trespasses on Shawnee and Delaware claims. Ineffectual though it was, Lewis's stand further alienated him from a citizenry already angry about the failings of his administration. Indeed, during the last

Figure 3.2 Portrait of Meriwether Lewis by Charles Willson Peale, from life, 1807.

Source: Independence National Historical Park.

months of his life, Lewis became an increasingly unpopular figure in the territory. Embarking in September 1809 on what was to be his final trip east, Lewis had, according to the Secretary of the Territory, "fallen from the Public esteem & almost into the public contempt."[14]

On September 4, 1809, just short of three years since his triumphant return with the Corps of Discovery, Meriwether Lewis set off from St. Louis. No cheering, singing crowds sent him on his way, and he never reached his destination. On October 10, 1809, Lewis met his end in central Tennessee. For nearly two centuries, the mysterious circumstances surrounding Lewis's death have stirred some controversy. Was he murdered? Possibly, but far more likely, the gunshots that killed Lewis were fired by his own hand. Earlier in this his final journey, he had been drinking heavily, and he may have attempted to commit suicide. Tellingly, when his closest friends heard about Lewis's demise, they accepted that he had taken his own life. "I fear this report has too much truth" was William Clark's initial reaction to a report that his despondent comrade had killed himself.[15]

*   *   *

Lewis's probable suicide cost the Shawnees and Delawares a valuable ally; the outbreak of the War of 1812 made their hold on lands in the territory even more fragile(figure 3.3). Ironically, this weakening occurred despite the continuing loyalty of these Shawnees and Delawares to the United States. During the war, Shawnees in the Missouri Valley resisted efforts by their tribal brother Tecumseh to join in a pan-Indian, anti-American crusade. Nonetheless, the raids of other Indians against American settlements along the lower Missouri led to calls for indiscriminate vengeance. All too typical was the sentiment of a St. Louis resident who recommended "slaying every Indian from here to the Rocky Mountains."[16]

Against this tide stood William Clark, who in 1813 added the office of territorial governor to his duties as the superintendent of Indian affairs. To be sure, in protecting the Shawnees and Delawares, Clark was partially motivated by expediency. Facing a difficult military situation, he recognized that the "Missouri Tribes must either be engaged for us; or they will be opposed to us without doubt." And yet, Clark did not forget the services of allied Indians. After the war, Governor Clark issued a proclamation that echoed Lewis's earlier one. The intrusion of white persons on Indian lands "in violation of laws and disregard of the executive authority of the territory . . . can no longer be permitted." The government, Clark declared in 1815, must run off white squatters. In other words, while his constituents cried for punishment against all Indians, Clark tried to protect at least some of them. Needless to say, that was not a recipe for popularity for Clark, who, especially in the postwar period, found himself caught between the increasingly irreconcilable demands of settlers, Indians, and the federal government.[17]

Figure 3.3   Portrait of William Clark by Charles Willson Peale, from life, 1807–1808.
Source: Independence National Historical Park.

After the war, a flood of new settlers moved to the lower Missouri Valley in search of farmland. In these years, farmers decisively supplanted fur traders as the dominant group in what had become the Territory of Missouri. Where fur traders depended on the goodwill and labor of Indian hunters and trappers, farmers demanded only land from Indians. As the population of Missouri skyrocketed in the years after 1815, it also graduated to higher stages of territorial government, which meant more local control. And here, demography and democracy doomed the Indians of Missouri, as well as those public officials who were seen as sympathetic to them. "Clark is too good to the Indians," summarized one of the growing number of his critics. Already in 1816, a prominent Missourian estimated that "nine-tenths" of the territory's citizens no longer wanted Clark as governor. That year, the territorial Assembly, which, unlike the governorship, was popularly elected, undermined Clark's proclamation. The Assembly petitioned the United States Congress to guarantee the improvements made by white squatters and remove Shawnee and Delaware claimants to unoccupied lands to the west.[18]

For Clark, the cheers that had greeted him upon his return to St. Louis in 1806 had long since dissipated. When, on the eve of statehood, the governorship of Missouri became an elective office, Clark stood for office, expecting that his heroic accomplishments and his long public service would guarantee him election. Political opponents, however, stepped up their charges against Clark's too friendly intercourse with Indians. Adversaries spread rumors that Clark had fathered a child by an Indian woman. On election day in August 1820, Clark was swamped, losing by a better than two-to-one margin.[19]

Clark's electoral downfall did not end his government service. He soon won reappointment as Superintendent of Indian Affairs, overseeing relations with tribes across the Upper Mississippi and Missouri valleys. True to the convictions that had contributed to his electoral defeat, Clark remained a foe of squatters who illegally occupied Indian lands. In the spring of 1824, in response to continuing incursions, he determined that whites "settled on lands designed for the Delawares and Shawnees will be required to remove." Those words sounded very much like the proclamation he had issued in 1815, suggesting that Clark's views had not changed.[20]

Or had they? Barely eighteen months after his latest defense of Shawnee claims, Clark affixed his signature to a treaty by which those same Shawnees relinquished their lands near Cape Girardeau. In exchange for giving up their Spanish grant, the Shawnees received $14,000 and a tract near the junction of the Kansas and Missouri Rivers, just beyond the western border of the state of Missouri. And this pact was no aberration. If the 1808 treaty with the Osages was the "hardest" one he made, compelling land concessions from Indians became much easier for Clark, especially during the 1820s and 1830s. In all, he signed thirty-seven treaties with Indians, far more than any other agent. With those secured by his direct subordinates included in the total, Clark had a hand in more than 20 percent of all of the ratified treaties between the United States and Indian nations. Taken together, Clark's treaties dispossessed tens of thousands of Indians from hundreds of thousands of acres, and, as Superintendent of Indian Affairs, he oversaw a policy of forced removals that amounted to state-sponsored "ethnic cleansing." Certainly, Clark's conduct seemed very distant from the "friendly intercourse" that had characterized relations between Indians and the Corps of Discovery.[21]

In part, changing times explained Clark's changing views. Accepting the inevitability of Indian removal, he reasoned that since "the Government will sooner or later have to do this . . . the sooner it was done the better." Delay would only increase "the difficulties of purchasing" Indian lands and deepen the dissatisfactions among those forced to abandon their improvements. The challenge facing Clark during the 1820s was to make removal as orderly as possible. Accordingly, in June 1829, Clark once more decried "the encroachment of the whites" onto "that part of Shawnee lands yet remaining on White River." By this time, however, Clark's "regret" was not the trespassings themselves. What upset Clark was that the incursions interfered with the efficient execution of "the removal of those Indians," which "would most probably have been effected in the course of the next year."[22]

Before damning Clark for betraying the promise of the Lewis and Clark expedition or for bowing to political realities, his actions and his ideas should be put in context. That Clark concluded so many pacts attested to the trust that so many Indians retained in him. In an era in which his compatriots called for "slaying every Indian from here to the Rocky Mountains," Clark remained committed to protecting the welfare of Native Americans. If Clark used military force—or the threat of military force—to discipline Indian groups deemed hostile to the United States, he insisted that peaceable peoples be treated humanely. "In my present situation of Superintendent of Indian Affairs," wrote Clark to Jefferson in 1825, "it would afford me pleasure to be enabled to meliorate the condition of those unfortunate people placed under my charge, knowing as I do their [w]retchedness and their rapid decline."[23]

Clark justified removal as the most compassionate policy left to him and for Indians. In the mid-1820s, he explained that the changing circumstances of Indians now necessitated their departure "from within the limits of the States." With the Indians' power "broken, their warlike spirit subdued, and themselves sunk into objects of pity and commiseration . . . justice and humanity require us to cherish and befriend them." That entailed transplanting them to a country "where they could rest in peace," by which he did not mean, as some other Americans wished, they would go to die. Rather, Clark held on to the belief that, given time and proper instruction, Indians might yet be fully incorporated into the American republic. These hopes were a rhetorical commonplace among Jacksonian champions of removal. The difference was that Clark genuinely believed that if Indians were "kept close to [agricultural] work and dissuaded from hunting as much as possible," they could become like white Americans. To that end, Clark understood that removal imposed an obligation on the government of the United States "to teach them to live in houses, to raise grain and stock, to plant orchards, to set up landmarks, to divide their possessions, to establish laws for their government, [and] to get the rudiments of common learning, such as reading, writing, and ciphering." Assimilating Indians also required that the government shield them from pernicious influences.[24]

Among the influences from which Clark wished to isolate Indians were unregulated and unscrupulous traders. At one point, he proposed that a thirty-year transition period be established in which the Indians would be completely sequestered from all traders. Instead, all intercourse would continue to be conducted through government-run factories, which would insure that Indians were not ripped off by price-gouging merchants. After Congress closed government-operated posts in the early 1820s, Clark advocated strict regulation of traders to prevent their taking advantage of Indians.[25]

These ideas about commerce were increasingly anachronistic, as was Clark's position on the assimilability of Indians. No doubt, his views made him unelectable and cost him considerable popularity. Yet, when Clark died in 1838, the glories of his life were ardently recalled. Hundreds of mourners gathered at the home of his son Meriwether Lewis Clark. Thousands poured onto the streets of St. Louis for the funeral procession. "The name of GOVERNOR CLARK must ever occupy a prominent place on the pages of the history of this country," a Missouri newspaper eulogized.[26]

*   *   *

The names of both Clark and Lewis, however, became ever less prominent on the pages of nineteenth-century histories. By the mid- and late 1800s, school primers devoted little space to the Corps of Discovery. Other explorers enjoyed far more renown. The rediscovery of Lewis and Clark happened primarily not in the first century after their expedition, but over the last one hundred years. The centennial of the expedition in the early twentieth century brought major expositions in St. Louis and Portland that saluted the Lewis and Clark expedition and tied its success to the story of American progress. In these centennial celebrations, Sacagawea and York gained a new prominence. She especially was featured in plays, books, magazine articles, and statues.[27]

During the run-up to the expedition's bicentennial, the cult of Lewis and Clark grew larger, and the spotlight on Sacagawea grew brighter. Yet for all the attention that has been focused on her, much about her biography remains uncertain. Where she was born and what she looked like still summon no definitive answers. Her name, too, is the source of continuing debate. In the expedition's journals, she is mentioned more than one hundred times, but only eleven times is she named—ten times by some spelling of Sacagawea and once by Clark as "Janey." Today, various pronunciations of Sacagawea compete, with different ways of saying her name connoting different meanings and different stories about her life before encountering Lewis and Clark. Uncertainties about her name and her biography get even more tangled when considering what happened to Sacagawea after she parted ways with Lewis and Clark. According to written records, including Clark's, which historians have generally accepted, Sacagawea died of a "putrid fever" in 1812. But native oral traditions, which historians have now come to see as equally plausible, tell of an eventful and extended life. In these stories, Sacagawea took on the name Porivo and did not meet her end until 1884.[28]

Although the riddles of her life, particularly of her life after the expedition, will likely never be resolved, the search for Sacagawea continues to occupy researchers and inspire new publications. Indeed, in recent versions of the Lewis and Clark myth, Sacagawea has become almost as prominent as the cocaptains of the expedition, and, in her afterlife, she has emerged as the most famous of American Indians. Until the last few years, when I asked students to name the Indians whose names come first to mind, their answers were Geronimo, Sitting Bull, and Crazy Horse. These were warriors, whose reputation rested on having catalyzed militant resistance to American expansion. Now almost always, students cite Pocahontas (they did grow up watching the Disney movie) or Sacagawea.

What should we make of the shift in gender and in the reconfiguration of intercultural relations that my students' choices suggest? In Disney's Pocahontas and in the Sacagawea of our new dollar coin, we undoubtedly locate a softer past. We reveal a preference for an alternative frontier process in which Indian-American relations were defined not by destructive conquest, but by a kinder, gentler history of peaceful accommodations and mutual acculturations.

The same wishes explain why York has moved from the edges to the center of the myth of Lewis and Clark. As with Sacagawea, the journals of the Corps provide numerous references to York, but they give him no voice of his own. That, however, has not stopped interpreters from seeking York and speaking for him. In the new, "feel good" version of the Lewis and Clark story, attention focuses on the moment when the Corps, having reached the Pacific Ocean, had to decide on which bank of the Columbia River to situate their winter camp. In a seeming departure from military hierarchy, Lewis and Clark opted to leave the matter to a ballot of the entire Corps. That York was given a vote has been depicted as a reflection of the cocaptains' liberalism, suggestive of an equality that York supposedly enjoyed during the expedition. No wonder the creators of "Lewis and Clark: The Musical," seeking a happy ending for their production, made this moment the final scene.

In fact, such an interpretation drastically overstretches the evidence of York's treatment on the journey and stands in sharp contrast with his postexpedition fate. As with Sacagawea, what happened to York after the exploration remains in some dispute. Very questionable is a newly published article that dates York's death to 1879. More plausible, though impossible to verify, was the story told by fur trader Zenas Leonard, who claimed to have met a black man in 1832 living among Crow Indians in what is today northern Wyoming. According to Leonard, the man introduced himself as York.[29]

What is no longer in dispute is York's continuing slavery after the Corps of Discovery returned to St. Louis. To later interviewers, Clark intimated that he had emancipated York upon the completion of the journey, a story that makes a fitting conclusion to the "feel good" story and seems true to the supposedly egalitarian spirit of the West Coast vote. Yet newly discovered—and now published—letters from William Clark to his brother Jonathan contradict this uplifting ending. From these letters, we learn that Clark rejected York's plea for freedom on the basis of his participation in the expedition. Instead, Clark decided that his slave's "services" had not "been so great." Rather than emancipation, Clark required that York stay in St. Louis. Thus separated from his wife in Louisville, York, in Clark's words, turned "insolent and sulky." Repeatedly, Clark complained about York's attitude. On more than one occasion, he gave his slave a "trouncing." Clark also worried that York was planning to run away. Should York have tried or should he have continued "to refuse to" perform "his duty as a Slave," Clark would have him "[s]old, or hired out to Some Severe master until he thinks better of Such Conduct."[30]

York escaped being sold down river. Some time after the War of 1812, he gained his freedom and returned to Kentucky. From there however, the trail of York gets much harder to follow. But what we know of York's life after the journey deprives us of the good feelings that have surrounded the expedition and its aftermath. Still, it is easy to see why we are so attached to versions of the Lewis and Clark expedition in which York enjoys equality and Sacagawea mediates peace between Indians and Americans. In York's elevation from slave to Corps member, we escape the brutality of bondage and enter what appears to be a far more humane interracial landscape. Likewise, we are captivated by stories of the captive Indian woman Sacagawea because, through her, we glimpse a past about which we can be truly proud. In that sense, the feel-good myth of the Lewis and Clark epic tells us less about who we were or who we are than it does about whom we would like to be.

Maybe, though, we should be satisfied with who they were. Yes, this review of the postexpedition careers of Meriwether Lewis and William Clark shows that the cocaptains shared the racial attitudes of their time. But it also highlights the uncommon principles that the expedition's principals demonstrated as government officials. Their defense of Indian rights was not all we might have wanted, but it did injure both Lewis and Clark politically. Surely, we can appreciate how in sacrificing popularity they manifested a "courage undaunted" that matched their accomplishments as explorers.

Notes

Stephen Aron, professor of history at the University of California, Los Angeles, and executive director of the Institute for the Study of the American West at the Autry National Center, is a specialist in frontier and western American history. He is author of *How the West Was Lost: The Transformation of Kentucky from Daniel Boone to Henry Clay* (1996) and *American Confluence: The Missouri Frontier from Borderland to Border State* (2005), and coauthor of *Worlds Together, Worlds Apart: A History of the Modern World from the Mongol Empire to the Present* (2002).

1. For survey, see Jay H. Buckley, "William Clark: Superintendent of Indian Affairs at St. Louis, 1813–1838" (PhD Dissertation, University of Nebraska, 2001), 1; *Time*, July 8, 2002. Carolyn Gilman, *Lewis and Clark: Across the Divide* (Washington, DC: Smithsonian Books, 2003), is a superb catalogue for the Bicentennial Exhibition.

2. The book whose sales best attest to the public's fascination with the expedition is Stephen Ambrose, *Undaunted Courage: Meriwether Lewis, Thomas Jefferson, and the Opening of the American West* (New York: Simon and Schuster, 1996). I have reviewed a number of the more recent books in "Rediscovering Lewis and Clark," *Convergence* 1 (Summer 2004): 12–15.

3. Jefferson quoted in Betty Houchin Winfield, "Public Perception of the Expedition," in Alan Taylor, ed., *Lewis and Clark: Journey to Another America* (St. Louis: Missouri Historical Society Press, 2003), 187. A report on the reception given to Lewis and Clark on their return to St. Louis appeared in the Frankfort, Kentucky, newspaper, *The Western World* on October 11, 1806, and is reprinted in James P. Ronda, ed., *Voyages of Discovery: Essays on the Lewis and Clark Expedition* (Helena, MT: Montana Historical Society Press, 1998), 203–05.

4. Thomas Jefferson to Meriwether Lewis, June 20, 1803, in Gunther Barth, ed., *The Lewis and Clark Expedition: Selections from the Journals Arranged by Topic* (Boston, MA: Bedford, 1998), quotation on 18; Anthony F. C. Wallace, *Jefferson and the Indians: The Tragic Fate of the First Americans* (Cambridge, MA: Belknap Press, 1999), 266; James P. Ronda, *Finding the West: Explorations with Lewis and Clark* (Albuquerque, NM: University of New Mexico Press, 2001), 12; Donald Jackson, *Thomas Jefferson and the Stony Mountains: Exploring the West from Monticello* (Urbana, IL: University of Illinois Press, 1981).

5. I discuss the political situation that Lewis confronted in the Louisiana Territory in detail in Stephen Aron, *American Confluence: The Missouri Frontier from Borderland to Border State* (Bloomington, IN: Indiana University Press, 2005), chapter 4.

6. Thomas Jefferson to Meriwether Lewis, June 20, 1803, in Barth, ed., *The Lewis and Clark Expedition*, quotation on 20; Clark quoted in Buckley, "William Clark," 113. On the education of Lewis and Clark and their reeducation from St. Louis merchants, see James Ronda, *Lewis and Clark among the Indians* (Lincoln, NE: University of Nebraska Press, 1984), 1–16; John Logan Allen, "Imagining the West: The View from Monticello," in James P. Ronda, ed., *Thomas Jefferson and the Changing West* (Albuquerque, NM and St. Louis, MO: University of New Mexico Press and Missouri Historical Society Press, 1997), 3–23; William E. Foley, "The Lewis and Clark Expedition's Silent Partners: The Chouteau Brothers of St. Louis," *Missouri Historical Review* 77 (January 1983): 131–146; William E. Foley and C. David Rice, *The First Choteaus: River Barons of Early St. Louis* (Urbana, IL: University of Illinois Press, 1983), 89–96.

7. Carolyn Gilman, "A World of Women," *Gateway Heritage*, 24 (Fall 2003–Winter 2004), quotation on 46; Ronda, *Lewis and Clark among the Indians*, 36–37, 62–64, 106–07, 208–10, 232–33. For a Nez Perce version of the Lewis and Clark expedition, including details about William Clark's reputed offspring, see "William Clark's Nez Perce Son: A Tsoopnitpeloo Legend As Told by Otis Halfmoon of the Nez Perce Tribe," Discovering Lewis and Clark: A Legacy Website, http://www.lewis-clark.org/index.htm (accessed November 14, 2006).

8. Meriwether Lewis, February 20, 1806, in Gary E. Moulton, ed., *The Journals of the Lewis and Clark Expedition*, 13 vols. (Lincoln, NE: University of Nebraska Press, 1983–2001), quotation on 6: 331.

9. For the furthering of this process of cultural borrowings between Indians and Anglo-Americans in the Ohio Valley, see Stephen Aron, "Pigs and Hunters: 'Rights in the Woods' on the Trans-Appalachian Frontier," in Andrew R. L. Cayton and Fredrika J. Teute, eds., *Contact Points: American Frontiers from the Mohawk Valley to the Mississippi 1750–1830* (Chapel Hill, NC: University of North Carolina Press, 1998), 175–204; Stephen Aron, *How the West Was Lost: The Transformation of Kentucky from Daniel Boone to Henry Clay* (Baltimore,

MD: Johns Hopkins University Press, 1996), 1–57, 102–23. And for the fruition of these developments in the lower Missouri Valley, see John Mack Faragher, "'More Motley Than Mackinaw': From Ethnic Mixing to Ethnic Cleansing on the Frontier of the Lower Missouri, 1783–1833," in Cayton and Teute, eds., *Contact Points*, 304–26.

10. Rufus King to Christopher Gore, September 6, 1803, in Charles R. King, ed., *The Life and Correspondence of Rufus King*, 6 vols. (New York: G. P. Putnam's Sons, 1897), quotation on 4:303; William E. Foley, "James A. Wilkinson: Territorial Governor," *Bulletin of the Missouri Historical Society* 25 (October 1968): 14–15; Bernard Sheehan, *Seeds of Extinction: Jeffersonian Philanthropy and the American Indian* (Chapel Hill, NC: University of North Carolina Press, 1973), 245–50.

11. Meriwether Lewis to Thomas Jefferson, December 15, 1808, McCarter & English Indian Claim Cases, Mudd Library, Princeton University, Box 18, Folder 4, Exhibit 144 (quotation); Clark quoted in J. Frederick Fausz, "Becoming 'a Nation of Quakers': The Removal of the Osage Indians from Missouri," *Gateway Heritage* 21 (Summer 2000): 37; William Clark to the Secretary of War, September 23, 1808, in Clarence E. Carter, ed., *The Territorial Papers of the United States: Volume 14: The Territory of Louisiana-Missouri, 1803–1806* (Washington, DC: United States Government Printing Office, 1948), 224; Jerome O. Steffen, *William Clark: Jeffersonian Man on The Frontier* (Norman: University of Oklahoma Press, 1977), 64–65. The full text of the 1808 treaty is in Kate L. Gregg, ed., *Westward with Dragoons: The Journal of William Clark on His Expedition to Establish Fort Osage, August 25 to September 22, 1808* (Fulton, MO: Ovid Bell Press, 1937), 64–68.

12. Lewis quoted in Lynn Morrow, "Trader William Gilliss and Delaware Migration in Southern Missouri," *Missouri Historical Review* 75 (January 1981): 151; William Clark to James Madison, April 10, 1811, in Carter, ed., *The Territorial Papers of the United States: Volume 14*, quotation on 445.

13. Proclamation by Governor Lewis, April 6, 1809, in Carter, ed., *The Territorial Papers of the United States: Volume 14*, quotation on 261.

14. Frederick Bates to Richard Bates, July 14, 1809, in Thomas Maitland Marshall, ed., *The Life and Papers of Frederick Bates*, 2 vols. (St. Louis, MO: Missouri Historical Society, 1926), quotation on 2: 68.

15. William Clark to Jonathan Clark, October 28, 1809, in James J. Holmberg, ed., *Dear Brother: Letters of William Clark to Jonathan Clark* (New Haven, CT: Yale University Press, 2002), quotation on 216; Gary E. Moulton, "Meriwether Lewis," in Christensen, et al., eds., *Dictionary of Missouri Biography* (Columbia, MO: University of Missouri Press, 1999), 486; Paul Aron, *Unsolved Mysteries of American History* (New York: J. Wiley, 1997), 79–84; Kathryn Moore, "The Lost Years of Meriwether Lewis," *Journal of the West* 42 (Summer 2003): 62–65. Although suicide is currently the dominant view of Lewis's death, see J. Frederick Fausz and Michael A. Gavin, "The Death of Meriwether Lewis: An Unsolved Mystery," *Gateway Heritage* 24 (Fall 2003–Winter 2004): 66–79, for an interrogation of the evidence that suggests the case should not yet be considered closed.

16. Christian Wilt to Joseph Hertzog, August 6, 1814, Christian Wilt, Letterbook, War of 1812 Papers, Missouri Historical Society, St. Louis (quotation).

17. William Clark to the Secretary of War, August 20, 1814, in Carter, ed., *The Territorial Papers of the United States: Volume 14*, quotation on 786; Governor William Clark, A Proclamation, December 4, 1815, in Clarence E. Carter, ed., *The Territorial Papers of the United States: Volume 15: The Territory of Louisiana-Missouri, 1815–1821* (Washington, DC: United States Government Printing Office, 1951), quotation on 192.

18. Buckley, "William Clark," quotation on 143; John G. Heath to Frederick Bates, January 14, 1816, in Marshall, ed., *The Life and Papers of Frederic Bates*, quotation on 2: 297; Resolutions of the Territorial Assembly, January 22, 1816: To the Honorable the Senate and House of Representatives of the United States of America in Congress, in Carter, ed., *The Territorial Papers of the United States: Volume 15, 106–107*; Resolutions of the Territorial Assembly Referred, January 24, 1817: Resolutions Concerning the Indian Title in the Counties of St. Genevieve and Cape Gerardeau, in ibid., 235.

19. William E. Foley, "After the Applause: William Clark's Failed 1820 Gubernatorial Campaign," *Gateway Heritage* 24 (Fall 2003–Winter 2004): 104–11; Jerome O. Steffen, "William Clark: A New Perspective of Missouri Territorial Politics, 1813–1820," *Missouri Historical Review* 47 (January 1973): 171–97.

20. William Clark to J. C. Calhoun, April 29, 1824, U.S. Superintendency of Indian Affairs, St. Louis, Records, Kansas State Historical Society, Topeka (quotation).

21. Fausz, "Becoming 'a Nation of Quakers,' " 38; Walter A. Schroeder, *Opening the Ozarks: A Historical Geography of Missouri's Ste. Genevieve District, 1760–1830* (Columbia: University of Missouri Press, 2002), 194, 381–82; Buckley, "William Clark," 114; John L. Loos, "William Clark: Indian Agent," *Kansas Quarterly* 3 (Fall 1971): 33–37. For the argument that removal amounted to state-sponsored ethnic cleansing, see Faragher, " 'More Motley Than Mackinaw,' " 304–26.

22. William Clark (St. Louis) to the Secretary of War, December 8, 1823, McCarter & English Indian Claim Cases, Box 18, Folder 2, Exhibit 91 (quotation); William Clark to Secretary of War, June 1, 1829, ibid., Box 24, Folder 2, Exhibit 205 (quotation).

23. Clark quoted in Jerome O. Steffen, *William Clark: Jeffersonian Man on the Frontier* (Norman: University of Oklahoma Press, 1977), 150.

24. William Clark to Secretary of War, March 1, 1826, in Walter Lowrie and Walter Franklin, eds., *American State Papers, Class 11, Indian Affairs*, 2 vols. (Washington, DC: Gales and Seaton, 1834), quotations on 2: 653; John Dougherty to William Clark, September 10, 1828, in John A. Dougherty, Letterbook, 1826–1829, Western Historical Manuscripts Collection, State Historical Society of Missouri, Columbia, C2292, Letter 65 (quotation).

25. Landon Y. Jones, Jr., *William Clark and the Shaping of the American West* (New York: Hill and Wang, 2004), 296–334.

26. Buckley, "William Clark," quotation on 268.

27. On the waning and waxing of popular interest in Lewis and Clark, see Winfield, "Public Perception of the Expedition," 178–99; John Spencer, " 'We are not dealing entirely with the past': Americans Remember Lewis & Clark," in Kris Fresonke and Mark Spence, eds., *Lewis and Clark: Legacies, Memories, and New Perspectives* (Berkeley, CA: University of California Press, 2004), 159–83.

28. Virginia Scharff, *Twenty Thousand Roads: Women, Movement, and the West* (Berkeley, CA: University of California Press, 2003), 11–33; Thomas P. Slaughter, *Exploring Lewis and Clark: Reflections on Men and Wilderness* (New York: Knopf, 2003), 86–113; Laura McCall, "Sacagawea: A Historical Enigma," in Kriste Lindenmeyer, ed., *Ordinary Women, Extraordinary Liues: Women in American History* (Wilmington, DE: SR Books, 2000), 39–54; Angela Cavender Wilson, "A New Encounter: The Native Oral Tradition of Lewis and Clark," in Taylor, ed., *Lewis and Clark*, 196–97, 208–10.

29. Robert B. Betts, In *Search of York: The Slave Who Went to the Pacific with Lewis and Clark* (Boulder, CO: University Press of Colorado, 2000, rev. ed.), 135–43; Slaughter, *Exploring Lewis and Clark*, 114–33; Winfield, "Public Perception of the Expedition," 194–95.

30. William Clark to Jonathan Clark, May 28, 1809, in Holmberg, ed., *Dear Brother*, quotations on 201; William Clark to Jonathan Clark, December 10, 1808, in ibid., quotation on 184; William Clark to Jonathan Clark, November 9, 1808, in ibid., quotations on 160; James J. Holmberg, " 'A Notion about Freedom': The Relationship of William Clark and York," *Gateway Heritage* 24 (Fall 2003–Winter 2004): 80–87.

Chapter 4

Revisiting Nashoba: Slavery, Utopia, and Frances Wright in America, 1818–1826

Gail Bederman

From *American Literary History*

In 1825, Frances Wright, British author and protégée of the aging Marquis de Lafayette, proposed an antislavery experiment that became known as Nashoba. Although Nashoba soon failed, it has made its way into the broad narrative of U.S. history (and many U.S. history textbooks) as an inspiring interracial utopia—a noble, if transient, step on the road to abolitionism and racial equality. As one recent textbook puts it, "Influenced by Robert Owen and New Harmony, Frances Wright established an interracial utopian community, Nashoba, near Memphis, Tennessee" (Clark et al. 459). Another characterizes Nashoba as "a bold plan to set up a utopian community of whites and freed slaves who would live together in full equality" (Henretta et al. 336).[1]

Although this optimistic description fits nicely into textbook depictions of U.S. history moving inevitably toward ever-increasing freedom, it bears little relationship to Nashoba's actual character, nor to Wright's true aims in establishing her "utopia." Wright's original goal was never to form an interracial community. Rather, she hoped to perfect American liberty by ridding the United States of both slavery and former slaves, through a complex financial scheme that would support universal colonization. An English radical, Wright chafed at the British political repression of the 1810s and viewed the United States, in contradistinction, as a utopia of liberty; she planned Nashoba accordingly. She wanted to get rid of the U.S.'s slaves, so the world's only true bastion of liberty could flourish.

The history of Nashoba is thus a complex story of political misrecognition. Naively idealizing America as a bastion of late eighteenth-century republican principles, Wright misrecognized the United States as the perfect republic—the opposite of 1810s British political corruption. Following this logic, she misrecognized slavery as a vestigial remnant of British colonial tyranny rather than an intrinsic part of U.S. political culture. In turn, subsequent U.S. historians and history textbooks—with little understanding of the transatlantic complexity of Wright's racial and civic identifications—have misrecognized "Nashoba" as an early example of the type of interracial community we would wish to see (but almost never do) in the United States' distant past. In reality, Nashoba was never an "interracial community." Wright's relationship with her slaves was no different from that of any other benevolent slave mistress, and her slaves bore the brunt of her visionary schemes. In founding Nashoba, Wright was motivated not by interracial sympathy, but by a profound political, racial, and civic identification with the patriots of 1776, especially republican slaveholders such as Thomas Jefferson and James Madison. Nashoba's inevitable failure was caused by this ironic misrecognition.

Late Enlightenment Middle-Class British Radicalism and Wright's Youth

In 1825, when Wright began to plan Nashoba, her political philosophy was radical in Britain but absolutely mainstream in the United States. In Britain, her politics fit into the current known today as philosophic radicalism, a type of middle-class radicalism espoused by thinkers such as Jeremy Bentham, William Godwin, Joseph Priestley, and Mary Wollstonecraft. In Britain, philosophic radicalism had been firmly suppressed since the outbreak of war with revolutionary France in 1793. Yet in the United States, Wright's early political enthusiasms were quite ordinary—even old-fashioned—and echoed Revolutionary era republicanism.[2]

Wright was drawn to republican ideals partly in reaction to the Tory relatives who raised her. Born in 1795 to a Scottish merchant with radical sympathies, Wright was orphaned at the age of two and raised by her mother's Tory father and sister, whom she grew to detest. Growing up during the Napoleonic wars when political radicalism of all sorts was associated with the French enemy—hearing, no doubt, political aspersions cast on her dead, liberty-loving father—the young girl intuitively identified with the radicalism of the 1790s (figure 4.1).[3]

Then, around 1812, Wright discovered America—or more accurately, she read Carlo Botta's epic history of the birth of North American liberty, *History of the War of Independence of the United States of America* (1809), which had just been translated from Italian into French. Written to reaffirm erstwhile Girondists' faith in republicanism after the excesses of the French Revolution, Botta's stirring history seemed to her like a dream come true: "From that moment," Wright wrote years later "[I] awoke, as it were, to a new existence. . . . There existed a country consecrated to freedom, and in which man might awake to the full knowledge and extent of his power"

Figure 4.1   Frances Wright.
Source: Library of Congress, Prints and Photographs Division, Washington DC.

(D'Arusmont 11). Having satisfied herself that the United States of America really existed despite the fact that none of her grandfather's friends ever spoke of it, Wright quietly vowed to visit it.[4] Because she and her sister had inherited small fortunes from their uncle, an officer with the East India Company, she would have extraordinary opportunities to pursue her utopian vision of distant American liberty (Morris 7).

Although Wright had been relatively well educated at her grandfather's house, her paternal relations finished her education in Enlightenment principles and opposition politics. As soon as she was eighteen, she fled from her maternal relations and, with her devoted sister Camilla in tow, joined the household of her uncle James Mylne, who held the chair of moral philosophy at Glasgow University. Although Wright herself always depicted her radical politics as entirely self-generated, she was certainly deeply influenced by the "aspiring women and Scottish Whigs" of the Mylne family and its network of friends and relations (Rendall). In Wright's own telling, however, she spent her three years in Glasgow deepening her knowledge of the United States. Her uncle helped Wright gain access to the university library, where she spent the next three winters poring over "all that had yet appeared in print respecting the American colonies" (D'Arusmont 13).[5] During these months, Wright also imbibed an anachronistic, 1790s version of Anglo-American republicanism from a woman she soon began to call "Mother," Robina Craig Millar. In 1795, Millar, related by marriage to Wright's uncle Mylne, had settled in Philadelphia as part of the great emigration of radicals who, like Joseph Priestley, fled to the United States to escape anti-Jacobin repression. Millar and her husband had been part of Benjamin Rush's Pennsylvania circle of British expatriates, until John Millar's unexpected death eighteen months later had forced Robina to return to Scotland, where she continued to see herself as a patriot and to correspond with Rush until he died in 1813.[6]

Millar's Revolutionary-era republicanism reinforced the idealistic literary depictions of the United States that Wright devoured in the Glasgow University Library. Together, they confirmed Wright's belief that the United States was a progressive republican utopia. At the same time, they left her singularly unprepared to understand the less egalitarian aspects of nineteenth-century U.S. society. Steeped in late-Enlightenment radicalism, including a belief that talented women should ignore their sex and take up important work, Wright reached the age of twenty-three imbued with ideas that were radical in Britain but absolutely mainstream in the United States.

"A country where the dreams of sages, smiled at as utopian, seem distinctly realized": *Views of Society and Manners in America* (1821)

In 1818, Wright announced to her startled friends and relations that she and Camilla were about to embark on a trip to America. Her uncle Mylne tried to convince his nieces that a grand tour of Italy and Greece would be more suitable. His arguments fell on deaf ears. Wright, objecting that her heart would break to see the Italians—the heirs of Roman republicanism—under the Austrian yoke, asked rhetorically whether "a young country inhabited by freemen, was not more worthy to attract curiosity than countries in ruin, inhabited by slaves?" (D'Arusmont 14).[7] She seems to have been relatively unconcerned that her beloved America, too, was "inhabited by slaves."

The United States did not disappoint its young enthusiast. From the moment she first glimpsed the New York coastline, Wright contrasted American liberty and prosperity to British despotism and inequality. She described this sight to Millar in her first letter, "Here was seen no great proprietor, his mighty domains stretching in silent and solitary grandeur for uninterrupted miles, but thousands of little villas or thriving farms, bespeaking the residence of the easy citizen or tiller of the soil" (Wright, *Views* 8–9). Wright spent most of the next twenty-one months in the United States, which seemed to her a veritable utopia of democracy.[8]

Wright postponed entering slave territory until a month before her departure, when she finally visited Washington, DC. Slavery's reality was more shocking than she had expected. As she wrote in her final letter, "The sight of slavery is revolting everywhere, but to inhale the impure breath of its pestilence in the free winds of America is odious beyond all that the imagination can conceive" (Wright, *Views* 167). Slavery, encountered late and incompletely on her travels, marred America's near-perfection.[9]

Wright returned to England ambitious to advance the linked causes of America and liberty and ready to step upon the public stage. British radicalism had slowly begun to revive after the close of the Napoleonic wars, and Wright was eager to help it along. Encouraged by her relations, she decided to revise and publish her letters home to counter Tory travel literature about American social and political backwardness. In six months, *Views of Society and Manners in America* (1821) was ready for publication.[10]

Views of Society depicts the United States of America as a republican utopia: "It is singular to look round upon a country where the dreams of sages, smiled at as utopian, seem distinctly realized, a people voluntarily submitting to laws of their own imposing . . . respecting the voice of a government which their breath created and which their breath could in a moment destroy" (Wright, *Views* 188). Political liberty had allowed Americans, masters of their own political fate, to banish poverty, misery, and ignorance.

All Britain's problems had been solved in America. Every dwelling in New York City was comfortable. There were no dark alleys, "no hovels, in whose ruined garrets or dank and gloomy cellars crowd the wretched victims of vice and disease" (Wright, *Views* 13). In America "there seem to be neither poor nor uneducated" (16). Women could leave their shopping on the pavement and return later, for nobody would steal anything (17). Love of liberty had even led to the proscription of all corporal punishment: "in the schools, in the prisons, on shipboard, in the army—everywhere, in short, where authority is exercised it must be exercised without appeal to the argument of a blow" (217). Most strikingly utopian was Wright's assertion that universal manhood suffrage had transformed American men into liberal philosophers. Americans were "well-informed and liberal philosophers, who can give you, in half an hour, more solid instruction and enlightened views than you could receive from the first *corps littéraire* or *diplomatique* of Europe by listening to them for a whole evening" (65). Democratic participation combined with universal education had made American citizens into embodiments of enlightenment (98–99).[11]

Wright contrasted the fruits of American liberty with British want and corruption. English farmers suffered from high tithes and taxes, official corruption, and "anxious fears" about their children's futures. In contrast, American farmers enjoyed "plenty at the board, good horses in the stable, an open door, a friendly welcome, light spirits and easy toil—such is what you find with the American farmer. In England . . . ." Wright finished by quoting a poem about the fall of Rome, adding darkly that she hoped that Britain still retained enough vigor to "work her own regeneration" (Wright, *Views* 98–99).

Britain had caused the one odious imperfection in America's utopia— slavery, "the blot which defaces a portion of the Union" (Wright, *Views* 41). Yet like an inkblot on an immaculate linen cloth, slavery had been imposed from outside upon America's otherwise perfect liberty. British colonialism had saddled the United States with slavery. Perhaps Wright learned this argument from Millar, for it was as old as the nation itself. In an early draft of the Declaration of Independence, Jefferson had listed the institution of slavery as one item on a long list of intolerable royal offences, although slaveholding interests made him strike the phrase. Now Wright updated this old argument by insisting that, since 1776, U.S. legislators had invariably tried to get rid of slavery, first by abolishing the slave trade under the Constitution and later by gradually abolishing slavery in the Northern states (37–39). Wright even managed to explain the five new slave states admitted to the union since 1776 as residual effects of French and British colonial slavery (202–05).

Race prejudice, too, was a British import, Wright insisted. Perhaps she spoke from experience: her description of a European's disgusted reaction to a group of free blacks in Philadelphia suggests her own visceral racism and, perhaps, her shame at that response:

> When [a European] sees a crowd of black faces assembled at the corner of a street, or descries the sable cheeks and clumsy features of a negro girl under a pink silk bonnet, the sight offends him from its ugliness, and an immediate distaste at the country, defaced by a mixture of so novel and unseemly a population, takes possession of his mind. (Wright, *Views* 41)

Wright insisted however, that Americans, unlike Europeans, felt sorry for free Negroes and treated them with gentleness and benevolence (41).

Although Wright condemned racial prejudice, she did not believe that recently freed "Negroes" or their immediate descendants were capable of being good republican citizens—an opinion she would retain when she planned Nashoba. Generations of enforced slavery, she explained, had rendered American Negroes inferior to whites in both character and appearance. Despite a few laudable exceptions in New England, most of America's freed Negroes remained morally lax, lazy, frivolous, and unable to plan for the future (Wright, *Views* 41–44). Slavery's abjection had raised a "barrier between the American and the negro, similar to that which separates the higher from the poorer and less polished classes of society in Europe. The black and the white man are a distinct race, and the distinction is, as yet, no less marked in the internal than the external man" (43). Perhaps generations of benevolent education could uplift the Negroes of the United States. Perhaps not. She could not predict, although she hoped the experiment would be tried (43, 44, 267–70).

These ambiguous views on race and slavery, basically unchanged, would underlie Wright's own antislavery experiment five years later. She believed that American Negroes as a class, like ignorant European peasants, were intrinsically inferior to America's white "citizen philosophers." Yet, as with European peasants, their inferiority—however difficult to stamp out—stemmed not from intrinsic racial character but from the lasting degradation caused by slavery. She admired Haiti, particularly its educated mulatto leadership, who, generations away from slavery, had achieved great things. For example, three years later she admiringly described the Haitian emissary Jonathas Granville. Granville, she explained, like many educated Haitians, had served in Europe in the French army and possessed all the attributes of an enlightened European himself: He "has the air & manners, information & conversation of a polite European—his color very dark mulatto features good & countenance pleasing" (Wright to Julia Garnett, November 12, 1824, quoted in Payne-Gaposchkin 230). She particularly admired Granville's modest demeanor in the United States and his patience with ignorant whites, who, unaware of his education, background, and character, treated him disrespectfully. In short, although Wright had little faith in the capacity of people who had lived as slaves themselves, she never believed that racial character was immutable—that is, for future generations untainted by slavery.[12]

Race plays a relatively small role in *Views of Society and Manners in America*, but one that would set the stage for Wright's abolitionist experiment at Nashoba. The book's final paragraph reconciles the incongruity of a slaveholding republic rhetorically, linking the republican past with the utopian future—the heroic revolution of 1776 with the ultimate abolition of slavery. Wright wrote that she had seen in America "so bright a dawning of national glory, so fair a promise of a brilliant meridian day" that she regarded with "regret, impatience and anxiety . . . every stain that rests upon [America's] morals" (Wright, *Views* 270). Slavery stained America's past and present—but must it stain her future? Americans single-handedly bore the "awful responsibility" of safeguarding "the liberties of mankind" and "the honor of freedom" (270):

> [T]he agents of tyranny are active in one hemisphere; may the children of liberty be equally active in the other hemisphere! May they return with fresh ardor to the glorious work which they formerly encountered with so much success—in one word, may they realize the conviction lately expressed to me by their venerable President that "the day is not very far distant when a slave will not be found in America!" (270)

Little did she imagine when she concluded her book that within five years, she herself would undertake precisely that task.

Published in Britain in May 1821, Wright's ostensibly apolitical travelogue launched her political career. Tories were outraged at her utopian portrait of the United States. The *London Literary Gazette* called *Views* "a tissue of impertinence, injustice, and falsehood" (quoted in Morris 47). The *Quarterly Review*—nasty, but not inaccurate—called it "a most ridiculous and extravagant panegyric" (quoted in Morris 47).

Yet British readers who longed for a rebirth of radical principles delighted in Wright's portrait of American liberty. Charles Maclaran, Whig editor of *The Scotsman*, rejoiced to discover in Wright's pages "what I wished to be true, yet was afraid to rely on, so amply confirmed by the result of your experience and observation" (quoted in Perkins and Wolfson 58). Jeremy Bentham, probably delighted with Wright's assertion that universal manhood suffrage had made Americans into citizen-philosophers, immediately invited her to visit, and soon became one of her mentors. In at least one letter to Bentham, Wright—underlining for emphasis—refers to the United States as "*our Utopia*" (Wright to Bentham, September 12–15, 1821, quoted in Conway 10:392).

Preserving the American Utopia by Abolishing Slavery: Planning Nashoba as Model Farm, February–December 1825

The story of Nashoba begins in late 1824, when the Wright sisters returned to the United States. Frances had spent the previous three years enmeshed in radical French politics as the self-styled "adopted daughter" of the Marquis de Lafayette, hero of the American Revolution, who admired her book and who materially reinforced her identification with the generation of 1776.[13] Yet as Celia Morris has shown, soon after Frances arrived in New York with Camilla on September 11, 1824, ready to accompany Lafayette on his triumphal farewell U.S. tour, she realized that she could no longer serve as Lafayette's assistant—she would need to find a different avenue for her political energies (Morris 79–83).

As Lafayette toured during the winter of 1824–1825, Wright began to ponder how to rid America of its one great flaw—slavery. On this trip, unlike their first, the Wright sisters spent most of their time in the South, where Frances had the opportunity to observe slavery in detail. The experience both sickened and obsessed her. A month after her arrival, she was traumatized by the sight of a boatload of manacled slaves, destined for the Southern slave markets. She frequently repeated the story in her letters: "My heart is sick. . . . I have seen [my fellow creatures] manacled when sold on board a vessel bound for New Orleans. . . . I cannot write on this subject and yet it preys so continually on my mind that I find it difficult to write on any other" (Wright to Garnett, October 30, 1824, quoted in Payne-Gaposchkin 228).[14]

In 1825, slavery was not yet a white woman's issue in the United States. A number of women had been active in the successful British campaign against the slave trade between 1808 and 1815, and by 1826, British women would begin to form the ladies' antislavery societies that would have so much impact on abolitionism in Britain and, after 1830, the United States. Yet there is no evidence that Wright knew or cared about any of these British female forerunners. She eschewed typical feminine antislavery tactics. She conducted no petition drives, spent no time fundraising for other activists, and wrote no antislavery literature.[15] Moreover, unlike most other female abolitionists, Wright scorned religion as irrational and unnatural. Her antislavery motivations were secular and pragmatic. America could not achieve its true republican greatness—could not be the perfect utopia of liberty depicted in *Views of Society*—while slaves resided within her borders.

In short, Wright's strategies made her a most atypical female antislavery activist. Independently wealthy, and used to acting as Lafayette's assistant in France, she tried to manipulate the levers of power by lobbying powerful male politicians to support her project, as she had previously done in Europe on Lafayette's behalf and in his name. She spent the winter of 1824–1825 in Washington, DC, hobnobbing with congressmen and taking every opportunity to study slavery's laws, observe its practice, and discuss it with the wealthy planters who, she believed, best understood it. Particularly influential was a week she spent with Lafayette at Monticello, where she discussed slavery with Jefferson, whose support of state-sponsored colonization she admired (Wright to Garnett, November 12, 1824, quoted in Payne-Gaposchkin 229–30).[16] Still assuming, as she had in her book, that Americans sincerely wanted to rid their country of slavery but lacked the means to do so, she took upon herself the task of developing and implementing an effective plan of abolition.

By summer 1825, Wright had developed her plan, which was based on, first, the principles of cooperative labor used by George Rapp's religious community in Indiana and, second, her profound misunderstanding of planters' complaints about slavery. Wright had gleaned both while traveling through the United States. To gather more information on slavery, Wright took Camilla on a two-month spring tour through the interior and down the Mississippi to New Orleans, where they planned to meet Lafayette. On the way, they spent several days with James and Dolley Madison at their plantation—Wright enjoyed spending time with powerful U.S. politicians—then traveled inland to southern Indiana, where they stopped to visit Harmonie, the large, prosperous religious community led by German pietist Rapp. Harmonie's comfort and prosperity, which the Rappites themselves ascribed to their unique way of organizing work, contrasted so markedly with the surrounding countryside that no doubt seemed possible—cooperative labor's productivity was as superior to that of individual labor as the productivity of ordinary free labor was to slave labor. A seed was planted: might "united labor," as practiced by the Rappites, contribute to slavery's abolition?[17] By the time Wright reached New Orleans, she had begun to imagine a large model farm, organized on the Rappite system, on which slaves could earn the price of their purchase through their labor. She began to drop hints to Louisiana slaveholders about her emancipation plan.[18]

Wright profoundly misunderstood New Orleans's slaveholders' responses to her hints about the dangers of slavery and the desirability of abolition. Yet her confusion is understandable, if unfortunate. Southerners were still panicked about Denmark Vesey's alleged rebellion three years earlier. Still terrified of being murdered in their beds by mutinous slaves, they were only too happy to agree that slavery was a frightening and dangerous institution, albeit one they were stuck with. Moreover, given the date, it is unlikely that any educated slaveholder gave Wright any reasoned defense of slavery. In 1825, arguments that slavery was "a positive good" had not yet made their way into general circulation. Hearing slaveholders speak passionately about slavery's dangers rather than its benefits, Wright seems to have taken literally planters' hyperbolic protestations that they wished slavery would disappear.[19] Understandably misreading slave owners' ubiquitous complaints as a widespread appetite for abolition, Wright convinced herself that Southerners longed desperately for a plan to abolish slavery before race war broke out and their slave property became worthless.[20]

Wright returned from New Orleans confident that the most influential Southerners would support abolition, if it could be accomplished safely and with no financial loss. By June 8, she had finished her plan and received Lafayette's blessing.[21] By the end of July, she had printed up copies of her prospectus and, with Lafayette's help, was soliciting subscriptions and support from leading U.S. politicians for this project, which eventually became Nashoba.

Although Nashoba, as Wright originally planned it, was grandiose in scope, it was not itself a utopia. Rather, Nashoba was a scheme to abolish all U.S. slavery in order to save Wright's true utopia, the United States. Wright explained her scheme in her prospectus, entitled "A Plan—for the gradual abolition of slavery in the United States, without danger or loss to the citizens of the south." Slavery, she began, presented self-evident dangers to the U.S.'s future—disunion, bloodshed, "servile wars of extermination" (Wright, "Plan" 58).[22]

Yet two conditions must be met in any practical emancipation scheme. First, planters must be convinced that emancipation would not cause them any pecuniary sacrifice. Second, all emancipated slaves must be settled outside the borders of the United States. The latter was not an unusual demand: in the 1820s, colonization remained the main focus of most white abolitionists, and although Wright privately ridiculed Americans' color prejudice as irrational, she was perfectly happy to humor it to abolish slavery and perfect American liberty. Satisfying these conditions, Wright believed, would gain planters' support and assuage their terror of race war (Wright to Garnett, June 8, 1825, quoted in Payne-Gaposchkin 240–41). Above all, Wright promised that if put into practice, her plan would abolish slavery and remove all former slaves from the United States in about eighty-five years ("Plan" 58–59).

To demonstrate the feasibility of her scheme, Wright proposed to open a pilot project—a large model farm populated by at least one hundred slaves who would work the fields according to George Rapp's superproductive "united labor" system. Within five years, Wright calculated, the average slave working under this system would produce enough to cover the entire costs of the enterprise. The efficiencies of united labor would allow him to produce enough to pay his owner a fair price for his purchase, to cover the project's overhead, and to transport him and his family, with all necessary farming implements, to a foreign colony such as Liberia or Haiti. In addition, this superproductive labor system would allow each slave to earn enough to pay for the purchase of an additional slave to replace him (Wright, "Plan" 58).

In other words, Wright's plan was a pyramid scheme that depended upon highly inflated expectations of "united labor." Under this plan, each slave would raise the money to purchase himself and another, and so double the number of slaves in the emancipation pipeline every five years. As the great productivity of this united labor rendered traditional slave labor unprofitable, others would open similar Rappite farms. Unable to sell their produce as cheaply as that produced by free or united slave labor, slaveholders would eagerly send their slaves to these farms to recoup their investment before the bottom fell out of slavery. Gradually, as hundreds of thousands of slaves were resettled abroad, not only slavery but also the former slaves themselves would disappear from the United States, leaving it a land of perfect liberty ("Plan" 58).

Wright's scheme would thus reimburse the slaveholder, educate the slave for freedom, open the South for free white labor, and banish both Negroes and slavery from America forever. Wright even included a table demonstrating how long it would take to "redeem the whole slave population of the United States" beginning with 100 slaves (eighty-five years), or with 800 slaves (sixty years) ("Plan" 59). She included, in addition, a detailed budget estimating how much it would cost to open, equip, populate, and run such an establishment for the first year: $42,168 ("Plan" 59).

In short, when Wright planned Nashoba, she had no intention of establishing a community of any sort, utopian or otherwise. Nashoba would be successful only if its residents *departed* from the premises as expeditiously as possible. The whole purpose of her plan was to facilitate slaves' permanent removal from both Nashoba and the United States, while safeguarding slave owners' pecuniary interests (Wright, "Plan" 58–59).[23] In this original Plan, Nashoba was simply a means to perfect Wright's true utopia—the United States, which she still saw as the antithesis of British corruption.

Wright had every faith that her plan would succeed because she believed that white politicians such as Jefferson, Henry Clay, and Madison would support it. Together, she and Lafayette tried to put her plan into effect using traditional male political methods—that is, by working his network of influential and powerful friends. By the end of August, Lafayette had asked four past or future Presidents—Jefferson, Madison, James Monroe, Andrew Jackson—as well as Chief Justice John Marshall to support Wright's plan.[24]

Wright herself, who had learned political organizing from Lafayette, likewise contacted prominent U.S. politicians, sending her prospectus and requesting advice, sponsorship, and financial contributions.[25] Wright's surviving letter to Clay, for example, politely requests his advice and sponsorship while assuring him of the great support her plan had already received from "many distinguished citizens in the South and North" (Wright to Clay, July 28, 1825, in Hopkins 557).

Now, for the first time, Wright's American utopia began to disappoint. By December, no one had offered to finance her plan except Lafayette, whose proffered $8,000 she lovingly refused.[26] Throughout these months, Wright seems to have misinterpreted good wishes and vague promises as serious support. Used to acting as a sort of honorary man when aiding Lafayette, she did not understand how differently men responded when she attempted to achieve her own political aims.[27]

Madison's response, however, ought to have given Wright pause, for the experienced planter wrote forthrightly that her plan was financially unworkable. He rightly predicted that Wright would be hard pressed merely to produce a surplus over what was necessary to keep her farm afloat, let alone repay the purchase price of her slaves. He doubted "that there is such an advantage of united over individual labor as is taken for granted" in her plan (Madison 497). Madison surely feared but did not say that Wright, who knew nothing about farming, would be lucky to avoid bankruptcy, let alone make staggering profits from an untried system of labor. He urged her to commence her project "on a scale smaller than that assumed in the prospectus" (498).

Lacking any investors, Wright adopted this advice perforce. Nashoba began on a much smaller scale than she had envisioned. Wright used her own money to purchase about 1,240 acres of unimproved "second rate" land in western Tennessee. Significantly, she located the land with the aid of Jackson—the only instance in which Lafayette's political network came through for her (Morris 109). Here, the colonialist nature of Wright's project becomes most visible. The land she purchased from the United States' most famous Indian fighter had belonged to Chickasaw Indians until 1818, when Jackson himself maneuvered Congress into giving him the ability to force the Indians to cede it. There is no evidence Wright herself thought much about its previous owners, however.[28] Purchasing recently confiscated Native American land with profits her uncle had amassed in British India, Wright prepared to put her abolitionist plan into effect.

Bitterest of all, without donations of money and slaves, Wright could not afford the hundred slaves needed to reap the financial rewards of "united labor." Instead, Wright purchased eight people of her own with whom to begin her "experiment": Willis, Jacob, Grandison, Redick, Henry, Nelly, Peggy, and Kitty. Still hoping that early success would convince planters to send dozens of slaves later, she named her new farm, "Nashoba."[29]

Wright's Plan Fails; Nashoba Becomes a Non-Interracial, Utopian Community of Free White Trustees, December 1826

Only seven months after Nashoba's official opening, it had become clear that Wright's highly publicized experiment in abolishing slavery through "united labor" had failed utterly. The necessary funding to make the attempt never arrived. As late as July 15, 1826, Wright was still trying to obtain 200 additional slaves for the "cheap rate" of $50 each to try the united labor plan (Marie D. Fretageot to William Maclure, August 11, 1826, quoted in Mirabella 405).[30] Yet she herself could afford no more slaves, and it soon became clear that no donations of slaves were forthcoming. Worse, rumors began to swirl, especially among opponents of slavery, that Wright's plan was merely a confidence trick to obtain free labor for her plantation, under the pretense of philanthropic emancipation.[31] Wright, thus, had no constituency for her pilot project. The plan could not succeed.

Yet despite its evident failure as an emancipation scheme, Wright could not simply walk away from Nashoba. She had spent about $10,000—over a quarter of her fortune—on its land and slaves.[32] Moreover, she was publicly and morally committed to both emancipating and colonizing her slaves; thus, she could not simply sell her slaves to recoup her investment, even if she were willing to do so. On top of the potential loss of her slave investments, colonization involved the substantial additional expense of transporting the slaves abroad and equipping them for a lifetime of self-sufficient agriculture. Wright had always insisted Nashoba would pay for itself. She was not prepared to impoverish herself to make good on her much-publicized commitment to the slaves' emancipation and colonization. Above all, emancipating Nashoba's slaves at this juncture would be admitting publicly that there was no way to abolish slavery with no expense to the slaveholders—an admission of failure that she was not yet ready to make.

Instead, she turned on the nation she had misrecognized as a utopia of liberty. Turning bitterly on the white American politicians, leaders, and "citizen philosophers" that she had praised in her book, she now crafted a new oppositional political identity. Race developed a new salience for Wright now, as she began to sneer that despite republican pretensions, the United States of America as a whole was profoundly and indelibly proslavery. Now, for the first time, Wright became an *American* radical, rather than a British one. Jettisoning her utopian idealization of the United States, she remade Nashoba as a utopian community.

Yet even as a utopia, Nashoba was neither egalitarian nor interracial. Rather, it retained the two conditions Wright had stressed in her plan. First, there would be no financial loss to slaveholders (that is, to herself). Second, the new utopia remained committed to colonization.

On December 17, 1826, Wright publicly abandoned both her plan and her now shattered faith in the United States as utopia by signing three deeds that transformed Nashoba from a privately owned model farm into a utopian community and philanthropic trust. The three deeds reorganized Nashoba as a trust, and—adopting some, but not all, of the principles of Robert Owen's failing utopia New Harmony[33]—gave daily governing power to "resident trustees." Now, for the first time, Nashoba became a utopian community of free whites rather than a privately owned model farm. The resident trustees were responsible for making all decisions and administering the property for the "collective benefit of the Negro race" as a whole (Wright, "Frances Wright's Establishment for the Abolition of Slavery" 440).

Nashoba was not, however, an "interracial" utopia: its slaves could never become trustees. They could at best become "coadjutors," residents who could enjoy the community's "benefits" but make no decisions. In fact, the slaves were simply part of Nashoba's movables. According to the trust, slaves must remain enslaved until they had earned their purchase price, when they must be "colonized out of the limits of the United States" and then freed (Wright, "Frances Wright's Establishment for the Abolition of Slavery" 440). Thus, under Nashoba's new guidelines, as under the old, only in Liberia or Haiti could its slaves hope to achieve full social equality.

Moreover, Wright was as unwilling to lose her substantial monetary investment as any other slaveholder. Under the new trust, before the slaves could be freed they were required to purchase themselves, as a group, from the trust for $6,000 plus 6 percent annual interest (Wright, "Frances Wright's Establishment for the Abolition of Slavery" 440). Wright still hoped to prove that slave labor could finance emancipation while providing a good rate of return on slave owners' investments. In short, even in this new "utopian" phase Nashoba was no "egalitarian interracial community."

In establishing this trust, Wright publicly abandoned her grand, failed emancipation scheme. Wright, who always hated admitting mistakes, did not do so now. Instead, she insisted this reorganization simply put Nashoba under the protection of many trustees rather than one individual. Yet despite her brave front, her plan's original rationale—abolishing all American slavery—had disappeared. Only a promise to colonize Nashoba's fifteen slaves and build a temporary school for their children remained.

Yet although Wright refused to admit that she had abandoned her previous utopian goals, she used the occasion of publicizing Nashoba's new structure to attack the nation she had once lauded as utopian. Who should manage Nashoba, she asked? No U.S. governmental body could carry out its mission, she claimed, for under the states' constitutions, political leaders must reflect the "feelings of the majority of the nation" (Wright, "Frances Wright's Establishment for the Abolition of Slavery" 440), and most Americans, she now sneered, were incurably racist. One might imagine Nashoba could be placed under the control of the colonization societies, she continued. Yet these were the creations of wealthy slaveholders, who, Wright now jeered, wanted not to abolish slavery but to remove any inconveniences (presumably troublesome free blacks and slaves) that might force them to abolish slavery.

Wright next turned her sights on religion. Perhaps to insult the slaveholders she had once courted, she conceded that emancipation societies (anathema in the South) were "real friends of the liberty of man" (440). However, the avowed freethinker continued, emancipationists' benevolence was connected with "peculiar tenets of religion" (440). No longer did Wright see the American populace as citizen-philosophers: they were ignorant and prejudiced, hypocritical and self interested, or irritating religious fanatics (440–41).

In short, as Wright set up her own quasi-Owenite utopian community, she publicly repudiated her previous belief in America as utopia. Yet as utopian as her new plan was, it, too, was neither interracial nor egalitarian. Nashoba's continued commitment to colonization and fully compensated emancipation meant that its slaves remained both subordinates and, most fundamentally, property.

Conclusion

Nashoba soon failed as a utopian community. During the summer of 1827, Nashoba's free trustees dragged it through both a public sexual scandal and many private draconian efforts to impose various visionary schemes on the slaves. The most controversial of these schemes were efforts to impose a quasi-Godwinian free love regime upon the colony as a whole—an important aspect of Nashoba's utopian phase which I discuss elsewhere.[34] At the height of this phase, Nashoba was, in fact, interracial although not egalitarian: its trustees included two free mulatto women, who participated fully in these utopian schemes which included forbidding slaves to eat outside the presence of the trustees and removing enslaved children from the authority of their uneducated slave parents.

Wright herself was absent during most of these shenanigans, visiting Europe to regain her health and recruit new trustees. Although absent, she approved the trustees' controversial actions, communicated with them by letter, and enthusiastically defended their unconventional activities to her startled European friends and relations.[35] In December of the same year, in the hold of the ship *Edward* on her way back to the United States, she wrote the famous—in some quarters, infamous—document that gave Nashoba its reputation as an interracial egalitarian community, "Explanatory Notes Respecting the Nature and Objects of the Institution of Nashoba, and of the Principles on which it is Founded. . . ." Written as a public defense of the principles underlying the trustees' scandalous defense of free love, "Explanatory Notes" attacked the institution of marriage as inimical to human happiness and proposed racial amalgamation—miscegenation—as the solution to the United States' race problems. "Explanatory Notes" also, finally, removed Nashoba from the emancipation business, announcing that the community would accept no more donations of slaves unless they were owned by a free trustee who was joining the egalitarian community. At long last, in these "Explanatory Notes," Wright did propose turning Nashoba into an interracial, egalitarian utopia.[36]

Unfortunately, this final, egalitarian, and most famous "Nashoba Plan" was never put into practice. Unbeknownst to Wright, Nashoba had already collapsed and was defunct. Its white trustees had departed. Its long-suffering, hardworking slaves awaited the next futile attempt to render their labor on Wright's "second rate land" profitable to their owner. When Wright arrived home at Nashoba in January 1828, she found her community nearly abandoned. For several months, she remained in Tennessee mourning the utter demise of her plans. By June, she finally concluded that no useful political work could be done in rural Tennessee, delegated the care of Nashoba and its slaves to other hands, and moved on to other types of radical projects.[37]

For the next year or two, Nashoba's slaves remained in bondage, laboring in Tennessee. Then, in January 1830, Wright chartered a ship and—at great personal and financial cost—transported them to Haiti. Once there, she emancipated them. President Jean Pierre Boyer promised her that he would look after them personally (Morris 211–12).[38] No evidence remains to show whether they prospered in their new home, nor whether Wright ever asked any of them whether they desired to emigrate.

What can we learn from this sad story of misrecognition and failed hopes? First, Nashoba makes sense only when situated in the context of British political radicalism. From the moment Wright first glimpsed the United States until her original plan for Nashoba failed, she viewed America as the enlightened opposite of British corruption. She conceived Nashoba to further the cause of the republican utopia she had described in *Views of Manners and Morals*. Because slavery was a relic of British corruption, Wright had faith that Americans would gladly cast it off, if they could afford to do so. Because she saw the United States through the rosy lenses of British radicalism, she truly believed liberty-loving Americans, North and South, would recognize the efficacy of her plan, abolish slavery, and colonize all of the United States' Negroes within eighty-five years, painlessly and with no economic loss to the slaveholders.

Nashoba's collapse in 1826 turned Wright from a British to an American radical. Aware now that the United States was no utopia, she turned on the white Americans whom she had once viewed as allies, condemning them as racist hypocrites. Yet she, too, like any other slaveholder, saw Nashoba's enslaved residents as financial investments. Eventually, and inevitably, Nashoba's second, utopian phase failed, too. Yet even today, we—Wright's liberty-loving descendants—cherish utopian fantasies of Nashoba, at least in our textbooks. Perhaps our desire to see heroism in Nashoba stems from our own civic identification with the United States. Nostalgically, we long to find some project—some insightful radical—that escaped the painful racial realities that have always been interwoven with Americans' republican love of liberty. Such antiracist radicals and histories may well have existed in the 1820s. Unfortunately, such a story cannot be found in the ironic history of Nashoba.

Notes

Gail Bederman, associate professor of history at the University of Notre Dame, is author of *Manliness & Civilization: A Cultural History of Gender and Race in the United States, 1880–1917*. She is writing a prehistory of the American reproductive rights movement, beginning with Mary Wollstonecraft and T. R. Malthus in England, and concluding with Frances Wright, Robert Dale Owen, and Madame Restell (Ann Lohman) in the United States.

Earlier, different versions of this paper were presented at the Women and Enlightenment Conference at York University, the Stanford Humanities Center's Feminist Theory Seminar, Carleton College, the University of Minnesota's Comparative Gender History Seminar, and the University of Notre Dame's Gender/Women's History Group. I thank all the participants and other readers, particularly Jane Rendall, Estelle Freedman, Karen Offen, Joanne Pope Melish, Annette Igra, Anna Clark, Lisa Norling, Elaine Tyler May, Fay Yarbrough, Brandi Brimmer, and Heidi Ardizzone.

1. See also Winthrop D. Jordan and Leon Litwack, *The United States: Conquering a Continent*, vol. 1 (2003), 230. The *Encyclopedia Britannica* entry for "Frances Wright" at http://search.eb.com/eb/article?eu=59241 (accessed March, 7, 2004) likewise inaccurately reports that Wright freed her slaves before she settled them at Nashoba. The three excellent biographies of Wright all provide accurate, detailed narratives of Nashoba's founding, fall, and place in Wright's life: Waterman 92–133; Perkins and Wolfson 123–81; and Morris 87–167. Yet as biographies, all present Nashoba as a story of Wright's personal—rather than *political*—failures. All overstate Robert Owen's influence on Wright's original vision of Nashoba. All ignore or scant Wright's intellectual debts to British philosophic radicalism. Consequently, all three blur the profound political differences between Nashoba's initial stage as a noncommunitarian colonization scheme and its subsequent stage as utopian community. The best short overview of Nashoba is in Nancy Woloch's textbook, *Women and the American Experience* (1999), 159–205, which does an excellent job of tracing Wright's goals, although, understandably, not her political context. Nonbiographical scholarship also tends to depict Nashoba as an Owenite utopia from beginning to end. See, for example, Arthur Bestor, *Backwoods Utopias* (1970), 219–26 and Carol A. Kolmerton, *Women in Utopia* (1998), 111–41. These scholarly tendencies have made it possible for U.S. historians to misrecognize Nashoba as an "interracial anti-slavery utopia." Note that the current essay concentrates on issues of race, slavery, and civic identity, and as such does not consider Nashoba's well-known free love scandal. As I argue elsewhere, Wright's letters began to hint about her new interest in free love in November or December 1826, after it had become clear that her abolition scheme had failed and shortly before she transformed Nashoba into a quasi-Owenite community run by its trustees. See Gail Bederman, *Sex, Politics, and Contraception in England and the United States: A Pre-History of Reproductive Rights, 1793–1831* (forthcoming).
2. See Elie Halévy, *The Growth of Philosophic Radicalism* (1955).
3. See D'Arusmont 9–11; Perkins and Wolfson 8–9, Waterman 16–18, Morris 6–7, 11.
4. See D'Arusmont 11–12; Waterman 26–27; Perkins and Wolfson 8, 12–13; Morris 11.
5. See Waterman 26–28; Perkins and Wolfson 16–18; Morris 12–13.
6. See Rendall, to whom I am indebted for sharing her important articles on women in the Scottish Enlightenment and on Millar and Wright prior to publication.
7. When she wrote these words in her autobiography more than twenty years later, Wright still saw no irony in this question (Waterman 28–29; Morris 23–24).

8. See Waterman 30–55; Perkins and Wolfson 26–33.
9. See Wright's letter on slavery written to the Garnett sisters, probably in October 1820, reprinted in Payne-Gaposchkin 224–25. See also Morris 40.
10. See Perkins and Wolfson 55–56; Morris 42–44; Wright to Julia Garnett, November 22, 1820, in Payne-Gaposchkin 226.
11. Upper and Lower Canada were the only places Wright visited in America where she claimed to find poverty or ignorance.
12. Wright discusses these distinctions most explicitly in her autobiography, written in 1844. From the section explaining Nashoba: "Neither the red savage nor the negro slave can be converted into American citizens, by acts of legislation; and this not because the one is black, nor the other red, but because *the one is a savage, and the other a slave*. . . . In both cases, the circumstances of color and feature increase, though they do not constitute, the difficulty which has until now barred the progress of either race, while placed in juxta-position with one, their superior in knowledge, and therefore necessarily the sovereign disposer of their difficulties. . . . [T]o effect the emancipation of the negro. . . he must be made to go through a real moral, intellectual, and industrial apprenticeship. . . . [F]rom the first generation little comparatively could be expected. . . . The children, brought up distant from their parents in schools of agriculture and industry, might evidently be expected to effect more. . . . In the rising, and, better, in all successive generations, the advancement of the negro race itself in the scale of being might be presented, and its preparation for independence and civilization secured by its acquisition of all the useful arts, and of a familiarity with mechanical power" (D'Arusmont 28–30). The autobiography then immediately turns to explaining Nashoba.
13. See Waterman 62–82; Perkins and Wolfson 60–79; Morris 54–62, 68–77.
14. See also Wright's letter of December 26, 1825, printed in *Le Globe* (Tome IV: N.70) January 23, 1827, 370).
15. See Clare Midgley, *Women against Slavery: The British Campaigns, 1780–1870* (1995), 9–40, on these earliest women antislavery activists, and Bruce Dorsey, "A Gendered History of African Colonization in the Antebellum United States," *Journal of Social History* 23 (2000): 77–103.
16. See also Morris 84–85.
17. Morris 86–94 best describes this journey and its effects on Wright's antislavery plan. Wright herself reports on her thought processes in her letters of January/February 1825, April 12, 1825, and June 8, 1825, reprinted in Payne-Gaposchkin 232–44, and in her autobiography (D'Arusmont, 28).
18. Wright to Garnett, April 12, 1825, quoted in Payne-Gaposchkin 235, describes her "hinting."
19. I am indebted to Joanne Melish, who suggested I consider the Vesey rebellion and whose research pointed me to the undeveloped state of the "slavery as positive good" argument in 1825. See Wright to Garnett, April 12, 1825, quoted in Payne-Gaposchkin 233, 235.
20. For Wright's reports on her conversations with frightened slaveholders about incipient slave rebellions in the Southern United States, see Wright to Garnett, April 12, 1825 and June 8, 1825, quoted in Payne-Gaposchkin 235–36 and 239–40, respectively.
21. An early, more or less complete version of the plan is detailed in Wright to Garnett, June 8, 1825, quoted in Payne-Gaposchkin 240–44.
22. The following discussion is drawn from Wright, "A Plan," October 15, 1825, 58–59. Fay Yarbrough has quite rightly asked how Wright, who recognized the existence of free blacks within the United States, envisioned her plan in relationship to the Unites States' free blacks. The plan was intended to address neither white Americans' color prejudices (which Wright saw as silly) nor the status of free people

of color (who did not concern her very much, either.) Rather, Wright wanted to root out the institution of slavery which she saw as an evil and a corruption of U.S. liberty. As a great admirer of the Haitian revolution, it never occurred to her that racial characteristics would preclude free blacks, if suitably educated and some generations removed from slavery, from behaving as republicans, particularly in Haiti or Liberia. She was, however, willing to be pragmatic about white Americans' ridiculous prejudices about skin color, and, for that reason, willing to accept colonization as a practical necessity in U.S. emancipation. See Wright to Julia and Harriet Garnett, November 12, 1824, Houghton Library, Harvard University, bMSEng1304 (5), also reprinted in Payne-Gaposchkin 230–31. See also Wright to Julia Garnett, June 8, 1825, quoted in Payne-Gaposchkin 240–41.

23. Wright elaborates upon her system and her belief that the superproductivity of "united labor" would soon render traditional slavery completely profitless, in her letter to Julia Garnett, June 8, 1825, quoted in Payne-Gaposchkin 241–42.

24. Lafayette to Wright, August 26, 1825, in Anna B. A. Brown, "A Dream of Emancipation," *New England Magazine* June 30, 1904, 495; Lafayette to Jackson, August 21, 1825, in *Correspondence of Andrew Jackson*, ed. John Spencer Bassett (1928), 290–91.

25. Remaining evidence of Wright's efforts can be found in Wright to Garnett, June 8, 1825, in Payne-Gaposchkin 244–45, in which she describes lobbying New York Governor DeWitt Clinton; see also Jefferson to Wright, August 7, 1825, in *The Writings of Thomas Jefferson*, ed. Andrew A. Lipscomb (1904) 16: 119–21.

26. See Lafayette to Julia Garnett, March 16, 1825, in Garnett Papers, Houghton Library, Harvard University, bMS 1304.1 (23); see also Morris 104.

27. On Wright's work in France as Lafayette's aide, see Waterman 69–78; Perkins and Wolfson 71–84; Morris 70–71. During that time in France, Wright considered herself Lafayette's "adopted daughter"; as a daughter, she could further the political goals of her "father." On female relations' ability to play important political roles, see Catherine Allgor, *Parlor Politics* (2000). Once on her own, however, it was harder for Wright to maneuver in that political world. For the most part, Wright refused to adopt specifically "female" tactics. In this way, she was probably more typical of British bluestocking than American female reform traditions. The literature on women reformers in antebellum United States is voluminous; see, esp. Lori Ginzberg's *Women and the Work of Benevolence* (1990).

28. See John R. Finger, *Tennessee Frontiers: Three Regions in Transition* (2001), 245–49. My thanks to Fay Yarbrough for alerting me to this aspect of Nashoba's history.

29. For the names of Nashoba's enslaved residents, see "Frances Wright's Establishment for the Abolition of Slavery" in *Genius of Universal Emancipation*, February 24, 1827, 440. Wright would eventually purchase Dilly, Willis's wife, and at least one of their children as well.

30. See also Wright to Harriet and Julia Garnett, July 7, 1826, in Payne-Gaposchkin 437, for a similar plan.

31. See, for example, the letter dated "Chester District, S.C. April 6, 1826" in *Genius of Universal Emancipation*, April 29, 1826: 275.

32. See Lafayette to Julia Garnet, June 19, 1826, in Garnett Papers, Houghton Library, Harvard University, bMS 1304.1 (23).

33. Although these documents make it clear that the new Nashoba would be deeply influenced by the utopian ideas of New Harmony, Wright knew from personal experience that New Harmony was on the verge of collapse. On New Harmony's disarray during 1826, see Arthur Bestor, *Backwoods Utopias* (1970), 184–94. Hoping to profit from mistakes made at New Harmony, Wright adopted Owen's ideas

selectively. For example, she made it much harder to become a member through the "trustee" system, and she deeded the property to the trust, rather than retaining private ownership as Owen had. See Wright, "Frances Wright's Establishment for the Abolition of Slavery," 440–41. Soon after Nashoba failed, however, the trustees returned the property (including the slave property) to Wright's private ownership.

34. Waterman 112–20; Perkins and Wolfson 160–72; Morris 139–48. On the Godwinian basis of Nashoba's free love practices, see Gail Bederman, *Sex, Politics, and Contraception in England and the United States: A Pre-History of Reproductive Rights, 1793–1831* (forthcoming).

35. On Wright's support of Nashoba's doctrines, see, for example, James Mylne to Julia Garnett, August 12, 1827, in Garnett Papers, Houghton Library, Harvard University, bMSEng1304.1 (25); Wright to Mesdemoiselles Garnett, August 17, 1827, in Garnett Papers, Houghton Library, Harvard University, bMSEng1304 (22).

36. See Wright, "Nashoba: Explanatory Notes Respecting the Nature and Objects of the Institution of Nashoba. . . ." *Genius of Universal Emancipation*, February 23, 1828: 45–46; March 1, 1828: 52–53; March 8, 1828, 61–62.

37. See Waterman 129–31; Perkins and Wolfson 188–92, 200–07, 270–88; Morris 158–67, 207–13. Wright's post-Nashoba political activities included the editorship of the *New Harmony Gazette*, a series of lectures on infidelity and radical principles, and eventually political activism in New York City. In addition to the biographies, see especially Lori D. Ginzberg, " 'The Hearts of Your Readers Will Shudder': Fanny Wright, Infidelity, and American Freethought" *American Quarterly* 46 (1994): 195–226 and Sean Wilentz, *Chants Democratic* (1984), 176–83, 193–201, 208–16.

38. The personal cost for Wright could not have been greater. As Morris shows, Wright became pregnant on this journey, and this pregnancy stopped her political career.

Works Cited

Clark, Christopher, et al. *Who Built America?* Vol. 1. New York: Worth, 2000.

D'Arusmont, Frances Wright. "Biography and Notes." *Life, Letters, and Lectures 1834–1844*. 1844. New York: Arno, 1972.

Fretageot, Marie Duclos. "To William Maclure." August 11, 1826. *Partnership for Posterity: The Correspondence of William Maclure and Marie Duclos Fretageot, 1820–1833*. Ed. Joseph Mirabella. Indianapolis, IN: Indiana Historical Society, 1994. 405.

Henretta, James A., et al. *America's History*. Vol 1. New York: Worth, 1993.

Madison, James. "To Miss Frances Wright." *Letters and Other Writings of James Madison*. Philadelphia: Lippincott's, 1865. 495–98.

Morris, Celia. *Fanny Wright: Rebel in America*. Urbana, IL: University of Illinois Press, 1984.

Payne-Gaposchkin, Cecilia Helena. "The Nashoba Plan for Removing the Evil of Slavery: Letters of Frances and Camilla Wright, 1820–1829." *Harvard Library Bulletin* 23 (1975): 221–51; 429–61.

Perkins, A. J. G., and Theresa Wolfson. *Frances Wright, Free Enquirer: The Study of a Temperament*. New York: Harper, 1939.

Rendall, Jane. " 'Women that would plague me with rational conversation': Aspiring Women and Scottish Whigs, ca. 1790–1830." *Feminism and the Enlightenment*. Ed. Sarah Knott and Barbara Taylor. NewYork: Palgrave Macmillan, 2005.

———. " 'Enlightened and utopian prospects: The journeys of Robina Millar and Frances Wright 1795–1830." *Enlightenment and Emancipation*. Ed. Peter France and Susan Manning. Lewisburg, PA: Bucknell University Press, forthcoming.

Waterman, William Randall. *Frances Wrightt*. Studies in History, Economics and Public Law 256. New York: Faculty of Columbia University, 1924.

Wright, Frances. "Frances Wright's Establishment for the Abolition of Slavery." *Genius of Universal Emancipation*. February 24, 1827: 440–41.

———. "A Plan." *Genius of Universal Emancipation*. October 15, 1825: 58–59.

———. "From Frances Wright." July 28, 1825. *The Papers of Henry Clay*. Vol. 4. Ed. James F. Hopkins. Lexington: University Press of Kentucky, 1972. 557.

———. "From Frances Wright." September 12–15, 1821. *The Correspondence of Jeremy Bentham*. Vol. 10. Ed. Stephen Conway. Oxford: Clarendon, 1994. 392.

———. *Views of Society and Manners in America*. Ed. Paul R. Baker. Cambridge, MA: Harvard University Press, 1963.

Chapter 5

Outlawing "Coolies": Race, Nation, and Empire in the Age of Emancipation

Moon-Ho Jung

From *American Quarterly*

A vote for Chinese exclusion would mean a vote against slavery, against "cooly importation," a U.S. senator from California warned in 1882. "An adverse vote now is to commission under the broad seal of the United States, all the speculators in human labor, all the importers of human muscle, all the traffickers in human flesh, to ply their infamous trade without impediment under the protection of the American flag, and empty the teeming, seething slave pens of China upon the soil of California!" The other senator from California added that those who had been "so clamorous against what was known as African slavery" had a moral obligation to vote for Chinese exclusion, "when we all know that they are used as slaves by those who bring them to this country, that their labor is for the benefit of those who practically own them." A "coolie," or "cooly," it seemed, was a slave, pure and simple. Representative Horace F. Page (California) elaborated on the same point in the other chamber, branding the "Chinese cooly contract system" and polygamy the "twin relic[s] of the barbarism of slavery." The United States was "the home of the down-trodden and the oppressed," he declared, but "not the home for millions of cooly slaves and serfs who come here under a contract for a term of years to labor, and who neither enjoy nor practice any of our religious characteristics."[1]

Some of their colleagues demanded clarification. If the bill aimed to exclude "coolies," why did it target Chinese laborers wholesale? New England Republicans, in particular, challenged the conflation of "coolies" and "laborers." "All coolies are laborers, but are all Chinese laborers coolies?" inquired a Massachusetts representative. Somewhat flustered, Page claimed that they were synonymous in China and California, where Chinatowns overflowed with "coolies and women of a class that I would not care to mention in this presence." His reply failed to sway the bill's detractors, who assailed its indiscriminate prohibition of Chinese immigration. With the Civil War and Reconstruction fresh in everyone's memory, Senator George F. Hoar of Massachusetts vowed never to "consent to a denial by the United States of the right of every man who desires to improve his condition by honest labor—his labor being no man's property but his own—to go anywhere on the face of the earth that he pleases." There were limits to "honest labor" though. Echoing a sentiment common among the dissenting minority, Hoar called for more exacting words that would strike only at "the evil" associated with "the coming of these people from China, especially the importation of coolies." "It is not importation, but immigration; it is not importation, but the free coming; it is not the slave, or the apprentice, or the prostitute, or the leper, or the thief," he argued, "but the laborer at whom this legislation strikes its blow."[2]

These congressional debates remind us of the extent to which slavery continued to define American culture and politics after emancipation. The language of abolition infused the proceedings on Chinese exclusion, with no legislator challenging the federal government's legal or moral authority to forbid "coolies" from entering the reunited, free nation. Indeed, by the 1880s, alongside the prostitute, there was no more potent symbol of chattel slavery's enduring legacy than the "coolie," a racialized and racializing figure that anti-Chinese (and putatively pro-Chinese) lawmakers condemned.[3] A stand against "coolies" was a stand for America, for freedom. There was no disagreement on that point. The legal exclusion of Chinese laborers in 1882 and the subsequent barrage of anti-Asian laws reflected and exploited this consensus in American culture and politics: "coolies" fell outside the legitimate borders of the United States.

This consensus had taken root in the decades before the Civil War and the abolition of slavery, a result not so much of anti-Chinese rancor in California but of U.S. imperial ambitions in Asia and the Caribbean and broader struggles to demarcate the legal boundary between slavery and freedom. A year before Abraham Lincoln delivered the Emancipation Proclamation on January 1, 1863, he had emblematized this consensus by signing into law a bill designed to divorce "coolies" from America, a little known legislation that reveals the complex origins of U.S. immigration restrictions. While marking the origination of the modern immigration system, Chinese exclusion also signified the culmination of preceding debates over the slave trade and slavery, debates that had turned the attention of proslavery and antislavery Americans not only to Africa and the U.S. South but also to Asia and the Caribbean. There, conspicuously and tenuously at the border between slavery and freedom, they discovered "coolies," upon whom they projected their manifold desires. "Coolies," however, were not a people but a conglomeration of racial imaginings that emerged worldwide in the era of slave emancipation.[4] Ambiguously and then unfailingly linked with slavery and the Caribbean in American culture, "coolies" would eventually make possible the passage of the nation's first restrictions on immigration under the banner of "freedom" and "immigration." The legal and cultural impulse to prohibit "coolies," at home and abroad, also enabled the U.S. nation-state to proclaim itself as "free" and to deepen and defend its imperial presence in Asia and the Americas. Outlawing "coolies," in short, proved pivotal in the reproduction of race, nation, and empire in the age of emancipation.

"Coolies" and Freedom

The word *coolie* was a product of European expansion into Asia and the Americas, embodying the contradictory imperial imperatives of enslavement and emancipation. Of Tamil, Chinese, or other origin, the term was initially popularized in the sixteenth century by Portuguese sailors and merchants across Asia and later was adopted by fellow European traders on the high seas and in port cities. By the eighteenth century, *coolie* had assumed a transcontinental definition of an Indian or Chinese laborer, hired locally or shipped abroad. The word took on a new significance in the nineteenth century, as the beginnings of abolition remade "coolies" into indentured laborers in high demand across the world, particularly in the tropical colonies of the Caribbean. Emerging out of struggles over British emancipation and Cuban slavery in particular, *coolies* and *coolieism*—defined as "the importation of coolies as labourers into foreign countries" by the late nineteenth century—came to denote the systematic shipment and employment of Asian laborers on sugar plantations formerly worked by enslaved Africans.[5] It was during this era of emancipation and Asian migration that the term *cooly* entered the mainstream of American culture, symbolized literally by its relocation from the appendix to the main body of Noah Webster's American dictionary in 1848.[6]

By then, like the word, the idea of importing "coolies" as indentured laborers to combat the uncertainties of emancipation circulated widely around the world. Even before the permanent end to slavery in the British Empire in 1838, sugar planters from the French colony of Bourbon and the British colony of Mauritius, both islands in the Indian Ocean, had begun transporting South Asian workers to their plantations. These initiatives inspired John Gladstone to inquire into the feasibility of procuring a hundred "coolies" for at least five years of labor on his sugar estates in British Guiana. Doubting that black "apprentices"—the status forced upon former slaves for six years in 1834—would work much longer, Gladstone contended that planters had "to endeavor to provide a portion of other labourers whom we might use as a set-off, and when the time for it comes, make us, as far as possible, independent of our negro population." "Coolies" were his solution. A British firm foresaw no difficulty in extending its business from Mauritius to the West Indies, "the natives being perfectly ignorant of the place they go to or the length of voyage they are undertaking." In May 1838, five months before "apprenticeship" came to a premature end, 396 South Asian "coolies" arrived in British Guiana, launching a stream of migrant labor that flowed until World War I.[7]

What happened to the "Gladstone coolies," as they came to be known, exposed a contradiction inherent in coolieism that would bedevil and befuddle planters and government officials in the Americas for decades. Did the recruitment and employment of "coolies" represent a relic of slavery or a harbinger of freedom? Early reports decidedly indicated the former. Upon receiving complaints registered by the British Anti-Slavery Society, British Guiana authorities established a commission to investigate conditions on the six plantations to which the "Gladstone coolies" had been allotted. Witnesses testified that overseers brutally flogged and extorted money from laborers under their supervision. By the end of their contracts in 1843, a quarter of the migrants had died and the vast majority of the survivors elected to return to India. Only sixty remained in British Guiana. Undaunted, the colony's sugar planters proceeded with plans to expand the experiment, but met resistance in India and London. The Indian governor-general prohibited further emigration at the end of 1838, a policy that the secretary for the colonies refused to amend in 1840. "I am not prepared to encounter the responsibility of a measure which may lead to a dreadful loss of life on the one hand," the secretary explained, "or, on the other, to a new system of slavery."[8]

Such inauspicious beginnings failed to derail the mission that Gladstone had inaugurated; West Indian planters soon found a sympathetic hearing in London. They could have their migrant laborers, as long as the state regulated all phases of recruitment, transportation, and employment. Applied to African "immigrants"—those "liberated" from slave smugglers and pressured into indentureship—and then to Asian "coolies" in the 1840s, state intervention was championed in British political circles as the guarantor of freedom. For a time, despite persistent protests and investigations, the employment of "coolies" appeared to signal a departure from the evils of the slave trade, from coercion and servitude, sanctified by voluntary contracts, legal rights, and public subsidies and enforced by the imperial and colonial state apparatus. In practice, however, the system placed a preponderance of power in the hands of planters and their allies, to the detriment of indentured workers who faced criminal prosecution for violating civil contracts. State enforcement on behalf of employers—along with rampant extralegal practices like kidnapping, deception, and corporal punishment—more often than not eclipsed state protection of workers. These contradictions notwithstanding, London and the colonial regimes in India and the West Indies worked together, albeit contentiously at times, to institute the mass migration of laborers bound to five-year indentures as a mainstay of postemancipation life by the 1860s. Coolieism thus became associated with emancipation, but not even the highest aspirations of numerous inquiry commissions and reform measures could erase its roots in slavery and "apprenticeship."[9]

Meanwhile, Cuba, the Caribbean's premier sugar-producing colony in the nineteenth century, magnified the contradictions presented by British West Indian coolieism. Sugar planters there demanded laborers in numbers and conditions that the illicit transatlantic slave trade—prohibited in Anglo-Spanish treaties in 1817 and 1835 and in Spanish law in 1845—could no longer supply by the 1840s, at least not without deep political and economic costs. Following the British example, a Spanish merchant engaged in the slave trade suggested the procurement of Chinese laborers in 1846, four decades before slavery would be abolished in Cuba. Within a year, his firm had made arrangements for two shiploads of "coolies" bound to eight-year contracts with wages fixed at four pesos per month. This experiment initiated and defined a migrant labor system that Cuban planters found indispensable over the next two decades, especially as their recruiting forays in Africa, Mexico, the Canary Islands, and elsewhere failed to yield the results they had hoped for. Ultimately, almost 125,000 Chinese laborers landed in Cuba between 1847 and 1874 to work under conditions approximating slavery, unbeknownst to them and despite legal distinctions and safeguards. Enslaved and indentured labor flourished side by side in Cuba, casting chattel slavery's dark shadow over the "free" aspects of coolieism.[10] British authorities, in response, laid claim to moral superiority through state intervention, in Africa and India as well as in China, whence 17,904 laborers arrived in the British West Indies under conditions similar to the larger system involving close to half a million South Asian migrants.[11]

These developments on the other side of the Gulf of Mexico immediately captured the notice of Americans engaged in their own struggles over slavery. As in British denunciations of the Gladstone experiment, abolitionists wasted no time in vilifying "coolie" labor as a new variant of slavery. New England periodicals related to readers in the 1840s that "coolies" in the British West Indies were "in a state of nudity and hardly any of them decently clothed" and "suffering from severe sickness," with many complaining vociferously and running away. The plight of the early "coolies" was so miserable that "their belief is, that they are slaves" and "the negroes appear sincerely to pity them." Trinidad's officials received and distributed "coolies" like slaves "in pure Baltimore or Cuban style," *Littell's Living Age* reported, while "coolies, half naked, scabby, famishing, helpless from ignorance, and overrun with vermin, infest the highways" of British Guiana. "Coolies" faced a cycle of coercion in that colony, where "the authorities have hounded on them . . . drive[n] them into the lockup house, (surely an illegal act,) and the planters cry out for permission to conclude contracts of indenture, that is, with beguiled strangers, who cannot comprehend the signification thereof." William Lloyd Garrison's *The Liberator* hoped that "the abolitionists of Great Britain will succeed in their efforts to break up entirely a system that produces so much cruelty and misery."[12]

Within a few years though, Caribbean planters' and European officials' propaganda campaigns had their desired effect on American reports, many of which began touting "coolie" labor as a means to expedite and effect emancipation. Chinese emigration heralded a new era across the world, exclaimed an advocate of Chinese labor, that would benefit "both the Chinaman and the Negro, if you can at once relieve the hunger of the former and preserve the freedom of the latter." Four years of Chinese migrants residing in Cuba had proved them to be "laborious, robust—almost as much so as the best Africans—more intelligent, and sufficiently docile, under good management." Similar results prevailed in British Guiana and Hawai'i, but would "prejudice or a mistaken philanthropy" prevent a migration beneficial to all parties? Chinese dispersion across the globe and American expansion across the Pacific and Asia would proceed apace, he concluded. "Instead of the labor-market of the new empires of Oceanica being supplied, like that of Eastern America, by means of violence, and with the captive savages of Negroland, it will be voluntarily occupied by the free and industrious outpourings of China." By 1852, the *New York Times* was imploring U.S. slaveholders to emulate their competitors in the British West Indies, Cuba, and Hawai'i, presenting "coolies" as a conduit toward abolition. "Some happy medium must be struck," an editorial insisted, "and the only medium between forced and voluntary labor, is that offered by the introduction of Orientals."[13] Neither free nor enslaved labor, "coolies" signified an ambiguous contradiction that seemed to hold the potential to advance either.

"Coolies" and Slavery

Humphrey Marshall, the U.S. commissioner to China, likewise felt that "coolies" would spell the end of American slavery. "Should that power [Britain] seriously undertake to populate her West India possessions and her colonies on the coast of South America with Chinese laborers, who have no idea, however, of the right of popular participation in the direction of government," he informed the secretary of state in 1853, "the effect . . . upon the industrial interests of the planting States of the United States, and upon the institutions of the republics of South America, must necessarily be most disastrous to them." Marshall, a Kentucky planter and a future member of the Confederate military and congress, estimated that each Chinese contract laborer cost $80 per year to employ, "far below the cost of slave labor, independent of the risk which the planter runs in his original investment." The Chinese were "patient of labor, tractable, obedient as a slave, and frugal . . . [and] will compel from the earth the maximum production of which it is capable, and, under whatever circumstances, will create a competition against which it must be difficult to struggle." On behalf of American slaveholders, Marshall hoped the president would establish a policy to prevent American ships from advancing the profits of British interests, against whom the United States was competing in the production of tropical goods and Asian commerce. "Coolies," he was convinced, threatened both American imperial ambitions and American slavery.[14]

Marshall articulated a short-lived ideological convergence between U.S. diplomats and slaveholders that would decisively bind "coolies" with slavery in American culture. In the years following his appeal, U.S. officials stationed abroad cast "coolie" labor not only as cheaper than slavery but as a brutal form of slavery that demanded federal intervention. Proslavery ideologues heartily agreed, even as they bristled at the notion of federal meddling in the domestic institution of slavery. The advent of a new system of slavery after emancipation in the Caribbean, they argued, warranted international scorn and laid bare the duplicity of abolition. American slavery, in their view, deserved protection more than ever. On the eve of the Civil War, New England abolitionists and Southern fire-eaters could find common ground in the "coolie" problem, issuing equally strident condemnations that clarified and blurred the limits of slavery and freedom in the process. American calls for the prohibition of "coolie" labor abroad, in turn, also justified and fueled U.S. expansionism in Asia and the Caribbean. Joining the international movement to suppress the "coolie" trade legitimized the U.S. diplomatic mission in China; the abuse of "coolies" in Cuba seemed to affirm the need for American annexation of the Spanish colony, for many, as a slave state. In and through "coolies," American diplomats and slaveholders found ways to promote the U.S. empire, as a beacon of freedom and slavery in the age of emancipation.

Marshall's admonition against the "coolie" trade conveyed America's long-standing commercial aspirations in China, an economic motive that was in full display in response to the tragedy aboard the U.S. ship *Robert Bowne*.[15] In 1852, Captain Lesley Bryson transported a cargo of contract laborers to Hawai'i and then returned to Amoy the following month to carry another 410 "coolies," ostensibly to San Francisco. On the tenth day out at sea, the Chinese passengers rebelled against the officers and crew, killing Bryson and six others and ordering the surviving crew members to guide the ship to Formosa. Instead, the ship ran aground near a small island on the Ryuku archipelago, to which American and British ships were dispatched to round up as many of the "pirates" as possible. Most of the Chinese passengers were never accounted for—only about a hundred were captured—and hundreds probably died from gunshot wounds, suicide, starvation, and disease, in addition to the eight who had been killed during the original insurrection. Peter Parker, the chargé d'affaires of the U.S. delegation in China, conceded that Bryson had administered "injudicious treatment of the coolies"—such as his order to cut off their queues—but insisted that recent mutinies by "this class of Chinese" aboard French and English ships indicated that the uprising might have been "premeditated before the vessel left port."[16]

The mounting evidence against the American captain and the "coolie" trade in general had no effect on Parker's blind defense of his deceased compatriot and U.S. national honor. Bryson's ship was involved in an intensifying trade in Chinese workers around Amoy operated by European and American shippers and their local suppliers, Chinese brokers (or "crimps").

The insatiable global demand for "coolies" manifested locally in an upsurge of kidnappings and fraudulent schemes in the early 1850s, coercive tactics that drove Chinese residents to equate the trade with "pig-dealing."[17] The growing infamy of the "coolie" trade in Amoy could not deter Parker's quest for justice on Bryson's behalf. Although he claimed U.S. jurisdiction over the entire affair, Parker agreed to hand over seventeen individuals, those deemed the "principal actors" by a court of inquiry aboard a U.S. frigate, to Chinese authorities for a speedy trial and punishment. A month later, however, Parker regretted the "most flagrant breach of good faith" committed by the Chinese commissioners who, from the testimony of the accused, had censured Bryson for engaging in "the style of thing called *buying pigs*" and treating his passengers in a "tyrannical" manner. Only one man was found guilty. The U.S. official angrily defended Bryson as "a kind and humane man" and dismissed the suggestion that the passengers had been coerced into signing contracts. "Hereafter the United States will execute their own laws in cases of piracy occurring upon the high seas," Parker declared.[18]

But the violence aboard *Robert Bowne* turned out to be no exception. U.S. officials in Asia dispatched frightening accounts of the trade that Americans back home read about, including the infamous case of the Boston-based *Waverly*. In September 1855, the *Waverly* left Amoy with 353 "coolies" and added 97 others in Swatow before embarking on its chartered voyage to Peru. Within a short span, four passengers had "sprung overboard" and drowned, while a "good many" fell ill, among them the captain, who died soon afterward. Under the circumstances, the first mate, now the acting captain, decided to switch course to the Philippines. Two more "coolies" died before the ship reached Manila, where Spanish authorities placed it under quarantine. Difficult to control from the outset, the new captain wrote in his log, "all of the coolies came aft, with the intention to kill" him two days later. The crew killed "about four or five" in the ensuing struggle and "drove them all down below, between decks"; the captain later killed another "very impudent" passenger. When the other "coolies" attempted to break through the forward hatch, the crew "shoved them down again and shut the hatches on again." When the captain finally decided to allow the passengers on deck eight hours later, he discovered a grisly scene below. Only 150 "coolies" remained alive. The captain's account of "coolies" attacking him and then killing one another, however, could not be corroborated by witnesses, who testified that he had killed and injured the passengers without provocation. The U.S. consul in Manila reported that "the unfortunate beings had perished by suffocation."[19]

Amid such calamities, U.S. officials moved to prevent American citizens from transporting "coolies," a trade that appeared to threaten America's commercial access to China and its international standing. Four years after his defense of the *Robert Bowne*, Peter Parker heard about the *Waverly* disaster en route to take up his appointment as the new U.S. commissioner to China. Armed with verbal instructions from the secretary of state to "discountenance" the "coolie" trade, he wasted no time in issuing a strong "public notification" in January 1856. Parker denounced the trade as "replete with illegalities, immoralities, and revolting and inhuman atrocities, strongly resembling those of the African slave trade in former years, some of them exceeding the horrors of the 'middle passage,' . . . and the foreign name has been rendered odious by this traffic, hundreds and thousands of lives having been inhumanly sacrificed." Parker instructed U.S. citizens "to desist from this irregular and immoral traffic" that imperiled "amicable relations" and "honorable and lawful commerce" between the United States and China, whose government prohibited it. Parker's proclamation generated immediate public outcries back home that further coupled "coolies" with the banned African slave trade. The abolitionist *Liberator* featured articles on the "new slave trade" and chastised Northerners engaged in it as "doughfaces." And departing from its earlier depiction of "coolies" as a vehicle to free labor, the *New York Times* now hoped the federal government would sustain Parker's declaration "with corresponding vigor" and suppress "this abominable trade."[20]

William B. Reed would reinforce Parker's views shortly after being appointed the new U.S. minister to China in 1857. Reed, too, found that shippers blatantly disregarded his public intimidations and general allusions to Chinese and U.S. laws and treaty obligations. In January 1858, he decided to fortify his warnings with a federal statute already on the books, an 1818 law that prohibited U.S. citizens and residents from transporting from Africa or anywhere else "any negro, mulatto, or person of colour, not being an inhabitant, nor held to service by the laws of either of the states or territories of the United States, in any ship, vessel, boat, or other water craft, for the purpose of holding, selling, or otherwise disposing of, such person as a slave, or to be held to service or labour, or be aiding or abetting therein." Despite "some uncertainty" of its applicability and its original intent for "a different evil," Reed argued for the law's relevance. A "Chinese cooly," he rationalized, was surely "a man of color, to be disposed of to be held to service in Cuba."[21]

In contrast to Parker, who had distinguished between the illegality of the "coolie trade" and the legality of "voluntary emigration of Chinese adventurers," Reed felt that "coolies" raised questions far more significant than coercion. It was, to him, a matter of U.S. racial, national, and imperial interests. Beyond "the practical enslavement of a distant and most peculiar race," the prospect of mass migrations of "free" Chinese male laborers also troubled Reed. Such a demographic shift, he believed, would strengthen "the decaying institutions of colonial Spanish America" that ran contrary to U.S. interests. The Chinese would "either amalgamate with the negro race, and thus increase the actual slave population, or maintain a separate existence, their numbers only to be recruited by new arrivals." Reed thought the latter more likely and envisaged a "bloody massacre" borne from the oppression of "a vast aggregation of troublesome populace" in a foreign colony. Driven to prevent such a scenario, he stressed to shippers that "whether the coolies go voluntarily or not to Havana" did not make "the least difference" under the law, if they were transported "under a contract 'to be held to service.' "[22] In his search for a law to suppress the coercive and corrupt trade in "coolies," Reed turned to a slave trade prohibition that, in turn, defined a "coolie." A "coolie," in his mind, was "a man of color" shipped to labor abroad, a gendered, racialized, and classed figure whose migration, voluntary or not, signified the bounds of slavery.

Reed left his post in November 1858, months before federal officials in Washington rescinded his application of the 1818 statute to the "coolie" trade. Secretary of State Lewis Cass, who criticized British and French efforts to obtain "coolie" and African labor for their colonies, had referred Reed's concerns to Attorney General J. S. Black in April 1858. Black finally ruled almost a year later that he considered the "coolie" trade outside the purview of slave trade prohibitions and other "existing laws." "The evil is one which Congress alone can remedy," he concluded. Washington's delayed and deflective reply provided little comfort or direction to the U.S. legation in China that continued to witness the horrors of the trade first-hand. The "cooly trade to the West Indies," Reed had pleaded repeatedly, was "irredeemable slavery under the form of freedom," with results worse than the African slave trade. The "Asiatic" faced a doomed fate in the Caribbean, he prophesied, marked by racial isolation and "a certain and fatal struggle, in which the Asiatic, as the weakest, fails."[23] To U.S. diplomats in China, it was a matter of life and death, a matter of slavery and freedom.

By 1859, the "coolie" trade from China, in which U.S. clippers had become increasingly involved, generated diplomatic crises that both undermined and bolstered Western imperial designs in China. Popular outrage in southern China against kidnapping and deception, sometimes boiling over into mass antiforeigner riots, drove the Chinese imperial court to request assistance from Western diplomats to suppress a trade that flagrantly violated its prohibition against all emigration. The British—motivated by West Indian planters' demand for labor and London's desire to protect its international image—requested a legalized and regulated system of migration instead. The military occupation of Canton (Guangzhou) by British and French troops beginning in 1858 allowed them to exact such a system. Long aware that the imperial decree on emigration carried no weight among Western shippers, Chinese officials in Canton felt empowered and compelled to collaborate with the British to implement a more pragmatic policy. In November 1859, British and local Chinese motives coalesced into a system of voluntary contract migration to the British West Indies from licensed depots in Canton, with regulations intended to avert the violence heretofore employed in the recruitment of "coolies." Lao Ch'ung-kuang, the provincial governor general of Guangdong, then called on other foreign consuls to instruct their citizens to conduct all emigration through Canton under the same guidelines. British and French troops subsequently headed north to Peking (Beijing) and

Figure 5.1 Many U.S. news accounts condemned the inhumanity of the "coolie" trade. From Edgar Holden, "A Chapter on the Coolie Trade," *Harper's New Monthly Magazine* 29 (June 1864): 5.

Source: Courtesy of University of Washington Libraries, Special Collections.

Figure 5.2 They also dehumanized "coolies." From Edgar Holden, "A Chapter on the Coolie Trade," *Harper's New Monthly Magazine* 29 (June 1864): 10.

Source: Courtesy of University of Washington Libraries, Special Collections.

pressured the imperial court to recognize the right of Chinese subjects to emigrate to foreign lands in October 1860.[24]

The regulatory promise of freedom, however, proved illusory, driving U.S. diplomats to lobby more than ever for a new federal law to suppress what they considered a new slave trade. At Lao's insistence, John E. Ward, a Georgia Democrat who replaced Reed, lent his support to inspecting U.S.

vessels docked near but beyond Canton's city limits. The testimony of hundreds of Chinese aboard one particular ship, the secretary of the U.S. legation reported, "exhibited a dismal uniformity of the acts of deception, violence, intimidation, and crafty devices practiced by native crimps, to beguile or force them to go on board boats where they were compelled to assent to the demands of their captors, and go with them on board ship or to the barracoons at Macao." Although these particular passengers won their release, Ward and his consuls could do nothing as the American captain proceeded to Macao, a Portuguese colony, and picked up another shipload of "coolies" for Cuba, a Spanish colony. Ward wished for a law to place such cases under his authority, since neither the Canton system nor consular inspection seemed adequate to the task. "When the consul visits the ships to examine into their condition," he noted, "they are questioned under the painful recollection of what they had already suffered, and what they must still endure if a ready assent to emigrate is not given."[25] The United States had an obligation to outlaw "coolies" on American ships, Ward and his predecessors urged, for the sake of free labor and free trade.

Excepting U.S. diplomats in China, no group of Americans studied and criticized the transport of "coolies" to the Caribbean more assiduously than Southern proslavery ideologues. They, however, drew conclusions that had little to do with ending coercive practices in Asia and the Caribbean; rather, their obsession with the Caribbean and "coolies" developed into a defense of slavery and a rebuttal to abolitionism. The racial and economic failings of emancipation and coolieism, proslavery forces argued, confirmed the natural order of slavery, an order that fanatical abolitionists and politicians had destroyed in the Caribbean. While U.S. officials in China appealed for a federal legislation to suppress the "coolie" trade, slavery's supporters emphasized the futility of state intervention in matters concerning race and labor. American slavery, they asserted, protected the nation from the utter decay experienced in the Caribbean and thereby justified its renewal through new importations from Africa and its expansion southward to Cuba and beyond. Their arguments led to neither but contributed to the emerging consensus in antebellum America that "coolie" labor was an evil to be expunged from America's ships and shores.

Not long after the legal end of slavery in the British Empire, American slavery's defenders charged again and again that abolition heralded a new era of duplicity and hypocrisy, characterized by semantic games rather than genuine humanitarianism. British imperial authorities had imposed the slave trade and slavery upon their colonies in North America, the *United States Magazine* claimed, and now ruled over millions of "absolute slaves" in India and elsewhere. Worse yet, they continued deceptively to sell "negroes" into slavery as "immigrants" and inaugurated "the blackest and worst species of slavery" by transporting "Indian Coolies" to the West Indies. "Humane and pious contrivance!" James Henry Hammond accused the British in his widely circulated letters in defense of slavery. "To alleviate the fancied sufferings of the accursed posterity of Ham, you sacrifice, by a cruel death, two-thirds of the children of the blessed Shem, and demand the applause of Christians, the blessing of Heaven!" Under the ruse of "immigration," Hammond added emphatically, "THE AFRICAN SLAVE TRADE HAS BEEN ACTUALLY REVIVED UNDER THE AUSPICES AND PROTECTION OF THE BRITISH GOVERNMENT." West Indian emancipation was a "magnificent farce" that his "humanity" and American slavery's "full and growing vigor" could not allow on U.S. soil. Reverend Josiah Priest likewise castigated the British for "inveigling . . . a yellow, swarthy race" to labor on the other side of the world, a system at odds with "their seemingly noble generosity in manumitting their slaves" but consistent with their recent indenturing of "the negro"—"ignorant" of legal contracts as a "monkey"—in Africa.[26]

New Orleans-based journalist J. D. B. De Bow was perhaps the most influential figure to incorporate British hypocrisy, conspiracy, and degeneracy into the proslavery argument. Great Britain had been the greatest slave dealer in history, he argued, whose conscience turned to "philanthropy" only out of economic self-interest. His conspiracy theory of emancipation was straightforward: "Liberate your West India slaves; force them [other nations], as you can then, to liberate theirs, and you have the monopoly of the world!" And exposés of the "wide-spread evils" of Caribbean coolieisms became integral to De Bow's derision of British emancipation and defense of American slavery. Emancipation reverted former slaves to "a state of Pagan cannibalism" in the West Indies and drove up the prices of tropical products in Europe, conditions that "made fillibusters [sic] and buccaneers of more than half of christendom." British and Northern abolitionists, De Bow reported, were now shipping "Coolies and Africans" in a "new system" that was "attended with ten times as much of crime and sacrifice of human life" as the slave trade and slavery. Government and newspaper reports on the *Robert Bowne*, *Waverly*, and other disasters, which he quoted extensively, illustrated the "enormities" being committed everyday in Asia and the Caribbean.[27]

To De Bow, the Caribbean demonstrated the moral superiority of the U.S. South and the dire consequences of interfering in the racial order. The "humane conduct" of American slaveholders, he argued, "preserved" human life and the four million American slaves deserved to be spared "the risk of being exposed to evils" characteristic of other plantation societies. After surveying the various migrant contract labor systems of British, French, and Spanish tropical colonies, particularly the "truly frightful" mortality rates on ships and plantations, De Bow asked how they could be accorded "the specious title of *free labor*": "What is the plain English of the whole system? Is it not just this?—that the civilized and powerful races of the earth have discovered that the degraded, barbarous, and weak races, may be induced *voluntarily* to reduce themselves to a slavery more cruel than any that has yet disgraced the earth, and that humanity may compound with its conscience, by pleading that the act is one of *free will*?" Platitudes on "humane principles" and "righteous decrees" might be "all very plausible and very soothing to the conscience" but the truth, he believed, exposed the unconscionable hypocrisy of abolitionism. De Bow demanded that "decisive means" be taken "to arrest this evil in its infancy," lest the entire world be cursed with the "ineradicable evils" of the "coolie" trade, including the specter of race wars between "half savages and half-civilized idolators" in the tropics. Although slavery protected the South for the moment, he concluded, "a successful insurrection of the negroes" incited by abolitionists would prove "an enormous impulse" toward the introduction of "coolies" to the United States.[28]

If freedom could be worse than slavery, as De Bow insisted, other proslavery propagandists such as Daniel Lee wondered how "immigration," as understood and practiced in the Caribbean, might revitalize the institution of slavery in the United States. "Without making the disastrous sacrifice that ruined the planting colonies," Lee proposed, "we may, if it be wise to do so, import Coolies or Africans, under reasonable contracts to serve for a term of years as apprentices, or hirelings, and then be conveyed back to the land of their nativity." The system would not only fill the South's demand for "a muscular force worthy of its destiny," he argued, but also civilize Asia and Africa as these "pupils" returned home, enlightened. His ultimate objective, however, was to reopen the transatlantic slave trade, a movement that witnessed a resurgence in the late 1850s. By 1858, Lee abandoned the idea of recruiting new races of laborers and advocated the sole importation of "African immigrants" under fourteen-year indentures or longer, as Louisiana legislators were then considering. He claimed that the system, once begun, would convert Northerners to the wisdom of Southern ways, allowing the extension of "the term of the African apprenticeship from fourteen years to the duration of his natural life." Lee's reasoning was, in effect, the mirror image of William Reed's attempt to apply the slave trade laws to the "coolie" trade: since the "coolie" trade and African "immigration" to the Caribbean were like the banned African slave trade, the slave trade itself ought to be legalized. Prominent proslavery thinkers such as George Fitzhugh agreed wholeheartedly.[29]

The drive to enslave peoples, at the same time, did not stop proslavery forces from imagining themselves and their nation as liberators—would-be liberators of "coolies" across the oceans as much as U.S. diplomats. U.S. expansionism in the Caribbean, they suggested, would result in the deliverance of slaves and "coolies" from backward despots. Representative Thomas L. Clingman of North Carolina, for example, attempted to shed light on "how this system of transporting and selling into slavery these Coolies is managed by Great Britain and Spain," to drum up congressional support for a more aggressive policy toward "our American Mediterranean" in peril. The mass importation of Chinese "coolies," Mayan Indians, and Africans intermixing with "the present black and mongrel population," he argued, threatened to make Cuba and other islands "desolate," the permanent "abode of savages." Instead, some "*Norman* or *South-man* fillibuster [sic]" ought to go down and force "Cuffee" to produce tropical goods, "which Providence seems to have intended these islands to yield for the benefit of mankind." Senator John Slidell of Louisiana likewise called for the U.S. acquisition of Cuba. In January 1859, he presented a bill to that effect on behalf of the Committee on Foreign Relations, whose accompanying report forecast the humanitarian and financial benefits to come. The United States would put an end to the slave and "coolie" trades—the latter of which resulted in mortality rates and suffering "far worse" than slavery—and thereby improve the value and treatment of Cuban slaves and allow American slaveholders to dominate the world sugar market.[30]

The proslavery argument's critique of Caribbean coolieisms, at the least, frustrated abolitionist attempts to draw sharp contrasts between slavery and freedom and revealed the complex global ties that slavery and coolieism had forged. Developments in Europe, the British West Indies, Cuba, India, China, and Africa produced new anxieties and hopes that informed and challenged universalizing notions. Were the British West Indies really free after emancipation? Weren't Asian and African immigrations merely legalized slave importations? The transport and employment of "coolies" in the Caribbean rendered such questions—whether in diplomatic correspondence from Asia or proslavery pronouncements from the Old South—beyond a black-and-white issue. Initially cast as the "free" advancement from coerced labor, "coolies" came to epitomize slavery in the United States at a time when the national crisis over slavery was about to erupt in open warfare. On the eve of the Civil War, the "coolie" and slave trades had become so intertwined in American culture that an encyclopedic entry for "Slaves and Slave-Trade" devoted a section exclusively to the "Coolie Trade."[31] The project of outlawing "coolies" could not be extricated from the national war over slavery.

Importation and Immigration

The convergent and contrasting denunciations of "coolies" by American diplomats and slaveholders generated simultaneous but distinct initiatives to outlaw "coolies" on U.S. vessels and on U.S. soil. Representative Thomas D. Eliot, a Republican from Massachusetts, led the legislative campaign in the U.S. Congress to ban American participation in the "coolie" trade, beginning with the publication of his report on behalf of the Committee on Commerce in 1860. Encapsulating the frustrations and aspirations of U.S. diplomats in China far more than those of proslavery critics, Eliot and his associates took great pains to distinguish between the status of "coolies" in the British colonies and Cuba. The transport and employment of "East Indian coolies" in British Guiana, Trinidad, and Mauritius, the report argued, were characterized by voluntary contracts and government supervision that obviated outside interference. Chinese migration to California was also "voluntary and profitable mutually to the contracting parties" and, in any case, already subject to federal statutes on passenger ships. The "Chinese coolie trade" to Cuba, on the other hand, was categorically unique and warranted immediate congressional action. That particular trade was "unchristian and inhuman, disgraceful to the merchant and the master, oppressive to the ignorant and betrayed laborers, a reproach upon our national honor, and a crime before God as deeply dyed as that piracy which forfeits life when the coasts of Africa supply its victims." Though targeting "American shipmasters and northern owners" engaged in a trade "as barbarous as the African slave trade"—not Southern slaveholders—the timing and language of the report obviously underscored Eliot's broader antislavery message. [32]

Consistent with a longstanding American rebuke of Cuba as morally backward, the report's geopolitical boundaries also reflected the Republican Party's growing faith in nation-state authority and enduring hope for a peaceful end to slavery. The British Empire stood for state protection, progress, and freedom; the Spanish Empire exemplified state failure, stagnation, and slavery. Antislavery forces therefore vigorously contrasted what the *New York Times* called the "Chinese Coolie-trade" to Cuba and Peru and the "Hindoo Coolie trade" to the British West Indies, which was "not the ally, but the enemy of Slavery." The "East-India Coolies, taken to the British Islands," John S. C. Abbott wrote in his antislavery tract, seemed to "have their rights carefully protected by the British government," whereas "in Cuba the Coolie trade is merely a Chinese slave-trade under the most fraudulent and cruel circumstances." Juxtaposing the "human misery" in Cuba against the "joy and gratitude" in postemancipation British West Indies, Abbott prayed that "the execrable institution" of slavery would "speedily go down" in the United States, "but not in a sea of flame and blood." [33] State regulation and supervision, it seemed, would guarantee and, in essence, define freedom for all.

Slavery's defenders had no patience to draw distinctions among Caribbean coolieisms and demanded the exclusion of "coolies" from America's shores so as to preserve domestic slavery. Between Lincoln's election and inauguration—and during the secession of one state after another—proslavery unionists desperately turned to the Caribbean and "coolies" to sustain their lost cause, with President James Buchanan going so far as to propose the acquisition of Cuba. At a convention called to draft a constitutional amendment to avert a war in February 1861, a delegate from New York recommended the preservation of slavery as a state institution and ridiculed its abolition in England and France. "True, they have abolished slavery by name," he argued, "but they have imported apprentices from Africa, and Coolies from Asia, and have placed them under the worst form of slavery ever known." In considering a provision to prohibit the importation of slaves from abroad, the convention added the phrase "or coolies, or persons held to service or labor" upon the suggestion of a Kentucky delegate, who contended that "the importation of coolies and other persons from China and the East" was "the slave-trade in one of its worst forms." [34]

In a fracturing nation, those who were fighting hardest to uphold slavery attempted to criminalize "coolie" importations first. In March 1861, congressional leaders of the compromise movement proposed multiple drafts of a constitutional amendment that included the retention of slavery below the 36°30' parallel line and the prohibition of the "foreign slave trade" involving "the importation of slaves, coolies, or persons held to service or labor, into the United States and the Territories from places beyond the limits thereof." At the same moment in Mobile, Alabama, the constitutional convention of the Confederate States of America considered an identical clause against "the importation of slaves, coolies, or persons held to service or labor into the Confederate States and their Territories, from any places beyond the limits thereof." Politicians on opposing sides of the secession crisis figured that the preemptive exclusion of "coolies" would shore up slavery in the South.[35]

Antislavery Republicans also moved to put a stop to "coolie" importations during the first year of the Civil War. After settling for congressional resolutions requesting more documents from Buchanan and then Lincoln, Eliot and his allies renewed their attempt to disengage Americans from the "coolie" trade in the now Republican-dominated Congress. Upon the receipt of the Lincoln administration's report on the "Asiatic coolie trade" in December 1861, which attested to the violence of the trade and the failure of government inspection, Eliot proposed an amended bill (H.R. 109) for the House's consideration and pleaded for its passage. Aside from procedural objections to his earlier bill, Eliot argued, he had heard only "a solitary objection" to it from his colleagues. "I refer to Mr. [Henry C.] Burnett [of Kentucky], who is now doing what he can to pull down the Government which he was then under oath to sustain and support," he explained, "and that objection, as I recollect it, was based simply upon the assertion that . . . it might by possibility affect some of his constituents who, as he declared, had some cooly laborers upon their plantations." The House passed the bill.[36]

The Senate then made a significant modification to Eliot's bill. Senator John C. Ten Eyck of New Jersey recommended on behalf of his chamber's Committee on Commerce that the phrase "against their will and without their consent" be struck from H.R. 109. "The committee are of opinion that the cooly trade should be prohibited altogether," Ten Eyck argued. "They are of opinion that persons of this description should not be transported from their homes and sold, under any circumstances; being, as is well known, an inferior race, the committee are of the opinion that these words will afford very little protection to this unfortunate class of people." His racial and moral argument carried the day. The Senate passed the bill with Ten Eyck's amendment; the House concurred two weeks later. And in the throes of military and political battles over slavery, Lincoln signed "An Act to Prohibit the 'Coolie Trade' by American Citizens in American Vessels" in February 1862.[37]

The final version of the bill reproduced the racial logic of the age of emancipation that made the practical enforcement of prohibiting the "coolie" trade a confusing and impossible endeavor. What exactly constituted a "coolie"? And could one ever be emancipated from the status of a "coolie"? The new law answered neither question. Its first section prohibited U.S. citizens and residents from acting as

> master, factor, owner, or otherwise, [to] build, equip, load, or otherwise prepare, any ship or vessel . . . for the purpose of procuring from China . . . or from any other port or place the inhabitants or subjects of China, known as "coolies," to be transported to any foreign country, port, or place whatever, to be disposed of, or sold, or transferred, for any term of years or for any time whatever, as servants or apprentices, or to be held to service or labor.

It was from this section that Ten Eyck removed the words "against their will and without their consent," a clause that might have classified "coolies" more conclusively. Instead, the legislation simply outlawed any shipment of Chinese subjects "known as 'coolies' " abroad "to be held to service or labor." Virtually all Chinese subjects leaving China were known as "coolies." But another section of the law left the door open to Chinese migrations, proclaiming that "any free and voluntary emigration of any Chinese subject" should proceed unabated so long as a U.S. consul attested to the voluntary status of the migrant through a written certificate.[38] The two sections presumably went hand in hand. The United States deplored the importation of human beings; it embraced immigration.

Anti-"Coolie" Legacies

Reflective of the 1862 anti-"coolie" law's origins in wider debates over slavery, postbellum legal battles over its application took place in the U.S. South and its leading antebellum slave market and port city, New Orleans. With the abolition of slavery and the prospect of black enfranchisement, former slaveholders and their allies now looked to the Caribbean and "coolies" for political and economic salvation. A refrain uttered across the region after the war, a journalist reported, was: "We can drive the niggers out and import coolies that will work better, at less expense, and relieve us from this cursed nigger impudence." Alarmed by such brash talk, federal officials responded without delay when the U.S. consulate in Havana reported in 1867 that "certain parties in the State of Louisiana . . . [were] engaged in the business of importing into that state from this Island Chinese or coolies under contracts to serve on stipulated wages for a specified time." The U.S. attorney in New Orleans was dispatched immediately to intercept an American brig en route that was reportedly carrying passengers "purchased" from their Cuban "masters" and signed to contracts establishing "the relation of slavery or servitude." Although the vessel was unquestionably transporting twenty-three Chinese subjects "known as 'coolies' . . . to be held to service or labor" in Louisiana, the U.S. attorney eventually decided to dismiss the case. The failure to obtain consular certificates notwithstanding, he decided, the brig's captain had believed the "coolies" to be "free agents."[39]

The law's creators never contemplated a conflict between the two provisions on "coolies" and "immigrants," rendering its legal enforcement ineffective but its cultural effects enduring. When a labor recruiter from the South requested consular certificates to ship nearly two hundred Chinese workers from Hong Kong to New Orleans in 1869, the local U.S. consul was baffled. "What constitutes a free and voluntary emigrant?" he asked the secretary of state. "What is a 'Coolie' as here defined, and what is a free emigrant?" Discovering that his superiors knew no better and that the passengers appeared to be voluntary, he issued the certificates.[40] If the law did little to stem Chinese migrations to the United States, including to a region vocally demanding "coolies," the racial and cultural logic behind it—that "coolies," in contrast to "immigrants," embodied slavery after emancipation—suffused almost every political debate on Chinese migration. When Senator Charles Sumner tried to remove the word *white* from U.S. naturalization laws in 1870, for instance, his opponents dwelled on the racial image of "coolies" overwhelming the United States back to slavery. "These people are brought here under these infamous coolie contracts," a Nevada Republican exclaimed, "the same contracts that have disgraced humanity in the taking of these poor people to the West India islands and various portions of South America as slaves." As Sumner's resolution went down in defeat, unanimous condemnations of "coolies" echoed universal applause for "immigrants," defined explicitly and implicitly as hailing solely from Europe. The act of outlawing "coolies" racialized "immigrants" as decidedly white and European in American culture, negating the legal space afforded to "free and voluntary" Chinese migrants.[41]

For decades preceding and following the passage of the 1862 law, "coolies" occupied the legal and cultural borderland between slavery and freedom, signifying and enabling critical transitions in U.S. history. The 1862 law, unambiguously framed as an antislavery measure by Eliot and others, established a precedent that few politicians would or could resist. What was, in effect, the last slave trade law would lead to a litany of immigration laws, including the Page Law of 1875 and the Chinese Exclusion Act of 1882, ostensibly targeting "coolies" (and prostitutes) in the name of "immigrants" and freedom. And the perceived existence of coolieism and other forms of bondage—and the moral imperative to prohibit slavery—infected and rationalized U.S. expansionism abroad, from China and Cuba in the 1850s to the Philippines in the 1890s.[42] Locating, defining, and outlawing "coolies" ultimately evolved into an endless and indispensable exercise that facilitated and justified a series of historical transitions—from slave trade laws to racially coded immigration laws, from a slaveholding nation to a "nation of immigrants," and from a continental empire of "manifest destiny" to a liberating empire across the seas. The violent and mythical legacies of those transitions would go a long way toward defining race, nation, and empire in the twentieth century and beyond.

Notes

Moon-Ho Jung is an associate professor of history at the University of Washington, Seattle, and the author of *Coolies and Cane: Race, Labor, and Sugar in the Age of Emancipation* (2006). He is currently working on a book on antiradicalism, anti-Asian racism, and Asian American political struggles from the 1890s to the 1930s. He wishes to thank Tefi Lamson, Moon-Kie Jung, Lisa Lowe, Jodi Melamed, Chandan Reddy, Leti Volpp, Alys Weinbaum, and fellows at the Simpson Center for the Humanities for reading and commenting on earlier drafts.

1. *Congressional Record*, 47th Congress, 1st session, 1482, 1581, 1932, 1936.
2. Ibid., 1934, 1517.
3. On the figure of the prostitute, see Amy Dru Stanley, *From Bondage to Contract: Wage Labor, Marriage, and the Market in the Age of Slave Emancipation* (Cambridge: Cambridge University Press, 1998), esp. 218–63.
4. Scholars of Asian American history all too often stress that Asians in the United States were "immigrants" and not "coolies," presumed to be those coerced to move to the Caribbean (see, for example, Ronald Takaki, *Strangers from a Different Shore: A History of Asian Americans* [Boston, MA: Little, Brown and Company, 1989], 35–36). The habitual assertion of this false binary—"coolies" versus "immigrants"—not only reifies "coolies" and American exceptionalism, but also ironically reproduces the logic and rhetoric of nineteenth-century debates on whether or not Asians in the United States were, in fact, "coolies." No one, in the United States or the Caribbean, was really a "coolie."
5. *The Oxford English Dictionary*, 2nd ed. (Oxford: Clarendon Press, 1989), 891–92; Hugh Tinker, *A New System of Slavery: The Export of Indian Labour Overseas, 1830–1920* (London: Oxford University Press, 1974), 41–43; Robert L. Irick, *Ch'ing Policy toward the Coolie Trade, 1847–1878* (Taipei: Chinese Materials Center, 1982), 2–6; Vijay Prashad, *Everybody Was Kung Fu Fighting: Afro-Asian Connections and the Myth of Cultural Purity* (Boston, MA: Beacon Press, 2001), 71–72.
6. The term *cooly*, defined as an "East Indian porter or carrier," had first appeared in 1842. Noah Webster, *An American Dictionary of the English Language* (New York: White and Sheffield, 1842), 953; Noah Webster and Chauncey A. Goodrich, *An American Dictionary of the English Language* (Springfield: George and Charles Merriam, 1848), 264.
7. Alan H. Adamson, *Sugar without Slaves: The Political Economy of British Guiana, 1838–1904* (New Haven, CT: Yale University Press, 1972), 41–42 (Gladstone quoted on 41); Tinker, *A New System*, 61–63 (quote on 63).
8. Tinker, *A New System* (quote v), 69–70; Adamson, *Sugar without Slaves*, 42–43; Walton Look Lai, *Indentured Labor, Caribbean Sugar: Chinese and Indian Migrants to the British West Indies, 1838–1918* (Baltimore, MD: Johns Hopkins University Press, 1993), 109, 156–57; Dwarka Nath, *A History of Indians in British Guiana* (London: Thomas Nelson and Sons, 1950), 8–21.
9. See, for example: Adamson, *Sugar without Slaves*, 44–56, 104–53; Look Lai, *Indentured Labor, Caribbean Sugar*, 16, 50–86, 107–35; Tinker, *A New System*, 61–287; Walter Rodney, *A History of the Guyanese Working People, 1881–1905* (Baltimore, MD: Johns Hopkins University Press, 1981), 33–42.
10. See, for example: Denise Helly, "Introduction," *The Cuba Commission Report: A Hidden History of the Chinese in Cuba: The Original English-Language Text of 1876* (Baltimore, MD: Johns Hopkins University Press, 1993), 5–27; Evelyn Hu-DeHart, "Chinese Coolie Labour in Cuba in the Nineteenth Century: Free Labour or Neo-slavery?" *Slavery and Abolition* 14.1 (April 1993): 67–83; Rebecca J. Scott,

Slave Emancipation in Cuba: The Transition to Free Labor, 1860–1899 (Princeton, NJ: Princeton University Press, 1985), 29–35, 89–110.

11. Look Lai, *Indentured Labor, Caribbean Sugar*, 19, 37–49, 58–61, 70–75, 87–106; Wally Look Lai, "Chinese Indentured Labor: Migrations to the British West Indies in the Nineteenth Century," *Amerasia Journal* 15.2 (1989): 117–35.

12. "Slavery in Jamaica, W.I.," *Littell's Living Age*, May 30, 1846, 429; "Miscellany: West-India Immigration," Ibid., September 19, 1846, 582; *The Liberator*, April 23, 1847.

13. "The Celestials at Home and Abroad," *Littell's Living Age*, August 14, 1852, 289–91, 297–98; *New York Times*, April 15, May 3, 15, June 14, December 10, 1852.

14. Jules Davids, ed., *American Diplomatic and Public Papers: The United States and China*, ser. 1, vol. 17, *The Treaty System and the Taiping Rebellion, 1842–1860: The Coolie Trade and Chinese Emigration* (Wilmington, DE: Scholarly Resources, 1973), B13–B15; M. Foster Farley, "The Chinese Coolie Trade, 1845–1875," *Journal of Asian and African Studies* 3.3–4 (July and October 1968): 262; Humphrey Marshall to Secretary of State, March 8, 1853, 33rd Congress, 1st session, House Executive Document (HED) 123, 78–82.

15. John Kuo Wei Tchen, *New York before Chinatown: Orientalism and the Shaping of American Culture, 1776–1882* (Baltimore, MD: Johns Hopkins University Press, 1999), 3–59.

16. Robert J. Schwendinger, *Ocean of Bitter Dreams: Maritime Relations between China and the United States, 1850–1915* (Tucson, AZ: Westernlore Press, 1988), 30–37; Irick, *Ch'ing Policy*, 32–34; Peter Parker to Secretary of State Daniel Webster, May 21, June 19, 1852, 34th Congress, 1st session, HED 105, 94–96, 108–10.

17. Schwendinger, *Ocean of Bitter Dreams*, 29–30; Ching-Hwang Yen, *Coolies and Mandarins: China's Protection of Overseas Chinese during the Late Ch'ing Period (1851–1911)* (Singapore: Singapore University Press, 1985), 41–52.

18. Peter Parker to Commodore [J. H.] Aulick, June 5, 1852; J. H. Aulick to [Peter] Parker, June 19, 1852; Peter Parker to Chinese Commissioners, June 22, 1852; Peter Parker to [Secretary of State Daniel] Webster, July 20, 1852; [Chinese Commissioners' Reports], July 9, August 1, 1852; Peter Parker to Seu and Pih, Commissioners, &c., July 12, August 10, 1852; 34th Congress, 1st session, HED 105, 121–22, 127–28, 130–36, 144, 148–49.

19. T. Hart Hyatt to William L. Marcy, June 1, 1856 (including log excerpts), in Davids, *American Diplomatic and Public Papers*, ser. 1, vol. 17, 356–60; H. N. Palmer to Thomas R. Rootes, February 15, 1856 (including log excerpts), 34th Congress, 1st session, Senate Executive Document (SED) 99, 8–10; H. N. Palmer to Secretary of State W. L. Marcy, November 9, December 6, 1855, 34th Congress, 1st session, HED 105, 71–73.

20. Peter Parker to Messrs. Sampson & Tappan, September 8, 1856; Public Notification, January 10, 1856; 35th Congress, 2nd session, SED 22, 1129–30, 625–26; Irick, *Ch'ing Policy*, 53; *The Liberator*, April 18, 25, May 9, 16, 1856; *New York Times*, April 21, 1856.

21. William B. Reed to Secretary of State Lewis Cass, January 13, 1858, 36th Congress, 1st session, SED 30, 59–65. The 1818 law is quoted in Lucy M. Cohen, *Chinese in the Post–Civil War South: A People without a History* (Baton Rouge, LA: Louisiana State University Press, 1984), 37–38.

22. Public Notification, January 10, 1856, 35th Congress, 2nd session, SED 22, 625–26; William B. Reed to Secretary of State Lewis Cass, January 13, 1858; William B. Reed to E. Doty, February 15, 1858; 36th Congress, 1st session, SED 30, 59–65, 203–4.

23. *Harper's Weekly*, April 24, 1858; Lewis Cass to J. S. Black, April 28, 1858; Domestic Letters of the Department of State (National Archives Microfilm M40,

roll 46); J. S. Black to Lewis Cass, March 11, 1859; Miscellaneous Letters of the Department of State (National Archives Microfilm M179, roll 168); General Records of the Department of State, Record Group (RG) 59; National Archives (NA), Washington, DC; William B. Reed to Lewis Cass, September 1, 1858, 36th Congress, 1st session, SED 30, 422–25.

24. Schwendinger, *Ocean of Bitter Dreams*, 47–55, 60–61, 195; Irick, *Ch'ing Policy*, 57–60, 67–104, 148–49; Yen, *Coolies and Mandarins*, 84–100.

25. Governor General Laú to John E. Ward, January 30, February 5, 18, 1860; minutes of an interview between Governor General Laú and U.S. officials, February 1, 1860; John E. Ward to Governor General Laú, February 3, 24, 1860; S. Wells Williams, secretary of the U.S. legation, to John E. Ward, February 7, 20, 1860; John E. Ward to Secretary of State Lewis Cass, February 24, 1860; 36th Congress, 1st session, HED 88, 29–37, 40–46, 48.

26. "Slaves and Slavery," *The United States Magazine and Democratic Review* 19 (October 1846): 243–55; "Gov. Hammond's Letters on Slavery—No. 3," *De Bow's Review* 8 (February 1850): 128–31; Josiah Priest, *Bible Defence of Slavery; and Origin, Fortunes, and History of the Negro Race*, 5th ed. (Glasgow, KY: Rev. W. S. Brown, 1852), 359–60.

27. "The West India Islands," *De Bow's Review* 5 (May and June 1848): 455–500 (quote from 488); "The Coolie Trade," *De Bow's Review* 23 (July 1857): 30–35.

28. "Asiatic Free Colonists in Cuba," *De Bow's Review* 24 (May 1858): 470–71; "The Coolie Trade; or, The Encomienda System of the Nineteenth Century," *De Bow's Review* 27 (September 1859): 296–321.

29. D[aniel] Lee: "Agricultural Apprentices and Laborers," *Southern Cultivator* 12.6 (June 1854): 169–70; "The Future of Cotton Culture in the Southern States, No. II," *Southern Cultivator* 16.3 (March 1858): 90–92; "The Future of Cotton Culture in the Southern States," *Southern Cultivator* 16.5 (May 1858): 137–39; and "Laborers for the South," *Southern Cultivator* 16.8 (August 1858): 233–36; [G.] Fitzhugh, "The Conservative Principle; or, Social Evils and Their Remedies: Part II—Slave Trade," *De Bow's Review* 22 (May 1857): 449–50, 457.

30. Thomas L. Clingman, "Coolies—Cuba and Emancipation," *De Bow's Review* 22 (April 1857): 414–19; "Monthly Record of Current Events," *Harper's New Monthly Magazine* 18 (March 1859): 543–44; "Continental Policy of the United States—The Acquisition of Cuba," *The United States' Democratic Review* 43 (April 1859): 29–30. On the antebellum movement for the annexation of *Cuba*, see Philip S. Foner, *A History of Cuba and Its Relations with the United States*, vol. 2, *1845–1895: From the Era of Annexationism to the Outbreak of the Second War for Independence* (New York: International Publishers, 1963), 9–124.

31. J. Smith Homans and J. Smith Homans Jr., *A Cyclopedia of Commerce and Commercial Navigation*, 2nd ed. (New York: Harper & Brothers, 1859), 1726–29.

32. 36th Congress, 1st session, House Report 443, 1–5, 24.

33. *New York Times*, April 21, 1860; John S. C. Abbott, *South and North, or, Impressions Received during a Trip to Cuba and the South* (1860; New York: Negro Universities Press, 1969), 47–52, 184, 352. A Creole newspaper in British Guiana, on the other hand, described indentured migration as "the enemy, instead of the auxiliary, of freedom" (Look Lai, *Indentured Labor, Caribbean Sugar*, 180).

34. Foner, *A History of Cuba*, vol. 2, 121–22; L. E. Chittenden, *A Report of the Debates and Proceedings in the Secret Sessions of the Conference Convention, for Proposing Amendments to the Constitution of the United States, Held at Washington, DC, in February, AD 1861* (New York: D. Appleton & Company, 1864), 268, 379.

35. 36th Congress, 2nd session, Journal of the Senate, 373–87 (esp. 382, 386); "Monthly Record of Current Events," *Harper's New Monthly Magazine* 22 (April 1861): 689–90; *Journal of the Congress of the Confederate States of America, 1861–1865*, vol. 1 (Washington, DC: Government Printing Office, 1904), 868.

36. 36th Congress, 1st session, HED 88, 1; 37th Congress, 2nd session, HED 16, esp. 1, 3–16, 21–36; *Congressional Globe*, 37th Congress, 2nd session, 350–52. Burnett might have been referring to the Chinese laborers who worked in Kentucky in the 1850s, mostly at iron-refining factories (Cohen, *Chinese in the Post–Civil War South*, 16–19).

37. *Congressional Globe*, 37th Congress, 2nd session, 555–56, 581–82, 593, 838, 849, 855, 911; *Harper's Weekly*, February 15, March 1, 1862.

38. The full text of the 1862 law can be found in Cohen, *Chinese in the Post–Civil War South*, 177–79.

39. Whitelaw Reid, *After the War: A Tour of the Southern States, 1865–1866*, ed. C. Vann Woodward (1866; New York: Harper & Row, 1965), 417; Thos. Savage to William H. Seward, July 12, 1867, Dispatches from U.S. Consuls in Havana, Cuba (NA Microfilm M899, roll 49), RG 59, NA; Cohen, *Chinese in the Post–Civil War South*, 58–61.

40. C. N. Goulding to Hamilton Fish, November 19, 1869, February 9, 1870, Dispatches from U.S. Consuls in Hong Kong (NA Microfilm M108, rolls 6 and 7), RG 59, NA.

41. *Congressional Globe*, 41st Congress, 2nd session, 5121–25, 5148–77 (quote from 5151). These postbellum developments are discussed in greater detail in my *Coolies and Cane: Race, Labor, and Sugar in the Age of Emancipation* (Baltimore, MD: Johns Hopkins University Press, 2006).

42. For the full text and a discussion of the law named after Representative Horace F. Page of California, see George Anthony Peffer, *If They Don't Bring Their Women Here: Chinese Female Immigration before Exclusion* (Urbana, IL: University of Illinois Press, 1999), 32–37, 115–17. On how the antislavery ideology shaped the debates surrounding the U.S. conquest of the Philippines, see Michael Salman, *The Embarrassment of Slavery: Controversies over Bondage and Nationalism in the American Colonial Philippines* (Berkeley, CA: University of California Press, 2001).

Chapter 6

"The Dread Void of Uncertainty": Naming the Dead in the American Civil War

Drew Gilpin Faust

From *Southern Cultures*

We take for granted the obligation of our government to account for the war dead. We expect the military to do everything possible to gather information about our war casualties, to notify their families promptly and respectfully, and to provide the bereaved with the opportunity to reclaim and bury their kin. Eighteen months after the inauguration of combat in Iraq, the Pentagon takes satisfaction that even though more than twelve hundred American soldiers have died, none is missing or unidentified. The contrasting failure to find every American who fought in Vietnam—an estimated 1,950 remain unaccounted for—continues not just as a burden for their grieving families, but as a political force in a POW/MIA movement now more than three decades old.

The United States accepts its persisting obligation to these casualties of war, and the Department of Defense spends more than $100 million a year to identify and recover the approximately eighty-eight thousand soldiers still missing from World War II, Korea, Vietnam, and the Gulf War. Yet the assumption that government bears such a responsibility is in fact quite recent. Only with the Korean War did the United States establish a policy of identifying and bringing home the remains of every dead soldier. Only with World War I did soldiers begin to wear official badges of identity—what came to be known as dog tags. Only with the Civil War did the United States establish a system of national cemeteries and officially acknowledge a responsibility to name and honor the military dead.[1]

There have been many revolutions in warfare in the past two centuries, and the emerging recognition of an obligation to dead and missing soldiers and their families is one of the least visible. Yet changing attitudes and policies concerning the dead and missing may have had a more significant impact than any other transformation, affecting homefront as well as battlefront, civilians as well as soldiers. And it was with the Civil War that this shift in both private and public belief and behavior first became evident, as Americans north and south struggled to find, name, and commemorate every one of the slain. This was a war that fundamentally redefined the relationship of the citizen and the state in its abolition of chattel slavery, but this highly visible affirmation of the individual's right to identity and personhood reflected beliefs about human worth that bore other implications as well. In the face of the Civil War's rising death toll, these assumptions began to yield new attitudes toward the dead and new obligations toward bereaved families (figure 6.1). Bloodier than any other conflict in American history, the Civil War presaged the butchery of World War I's western front and the global carnage of the twentieth century. Approximately 620,000 American soldiers died between 1861 and 1865. A similar rate of death—about 2 percent of the population—would today mean almost 6 million casualties. More Americans died in the Civil War than in all other American wars combined up to Vietnam. Death touched nearly every American, north and south, of the Civil War era, yet the unanticipated scale of the destruction meant that at least half these dead remained unidentified.

The Civil War is often designated the first modern and the last old-fashioned war, and it is perhaps unsurprising to see its treatment of the dead and missing and their families as both alien and familiar. In reporting casualties, notifying kin, and handling corpses, the Civil War yielded policies of inhumane negligence that today seem both appalling and almost unimaginable. Yet at the same time, soldiers and civilians alike often spoke and acted in ways that make the years that separate us from our Civil War predecessors appear not to have altered the fundamental human need for consolation and mourning.

Central to the changes that have occurred since the 1860s is the growing acknowledgment of the importance of information—of knowing whether a soldier is dead or alive, of being able to furnish news or provide the bereaved with the consoling certainty of a loved one's body. Yet at the outset of the Civil War, neither Union nor Confederacy recognized the responsibility to supply such intelligence. There had been no official attention to the Mexican War dead until two years after the conflict ended, when in 1850 the federal government found and reinterred 750 soldiers in an American cemetery in Mexico City. This represented only about 5 percent of those killed in the conflict, and not one body was identified. With the outbreak of the Civil War, both Union and Confederate governments established measures for maintaining records of deceased soldiers, requiring forms to be filled out at army hospitals and to be forwarded in multiple copies to Washington or Richmond. Significantly, however, not one of these copies, or any other sort of official communication, was designated for the family of the slain. And the obstacles even to this plan seemed daunting. Samuel Preston Moore, surgeon general of the Confederate

Figure 6.1   On the battlefield of Antietam. The Civil War left some 620,000 American soldiers dead—more than the total number killed in all other American wars from the Revolution to Vietnam. But whose responsibility would it be to track soldiers' deaths, inform their families, and record their names?

Source: Courtesy of the Collections of the Library of Congress.

army, felt compelled in 1862 to issue a circular deploring the "indifference" of his medical officers to record- keeping, but his exhortations apparently had little effect. A January 1864 article in the *Charleston Mercury* that summarized the preceding year's casualties concluded, "These returns show a great deal of negligence by Captains and Surgeons in reporting the deaths of soldiers."[2]

After more than a year of war, the U.S. government established more elaborate procedures for enumerating the dead, but General Orders #33 was filled with language that acknowledged the obstacles to any real improvement in their identification or treatment. Urging commanders to keep records "when practicable" and "as far as possible," the measure reflected official awareness of the enormous logistical and bureaucratic challenges posed by armies and casualty rates of unprecedented scale. Moreover, the order made no special provision for implementing its goals and designated no special troops for graves registration duties. Instead, burial units would simply be detailed from forces available at the end of any battle. And, like earlier measures, General Orders #33 assumed no responsibility for reporting deaths to those who waited at home.[3]

Journalists at the front struggled to fill the void of official intelligence by gathering information about casualties. In the days after major engagements, Union and Confederate newspapers covered their pages with the eagerly awaited reports. Sarah Palmer of South Carolina reflected the agonies of northerners and southerners alike when she wrote after Second Manassas, "I do feel too anxious to see the papers and get the list of casualties from Co. K and yet I dread to see it." Although civilians crowded news offices and railroad junctions waiting for information, the lists were notoriously inaccurate and incomplete.[4]

The sources of information varied considerably. Sometimes the list of a regiment's dead and wounded was preceded by a statement from a chaplain indicating that he had collected the information; sometimes an officer introduced the list. In some instances, civilians representing charitable organizations assembled the data, recognizing that military officials were too occupied with the concerns of the living to make this a priority. W. P. Price, who represented a South Carolina relief agency, tried to formalize the system, writing from Atlanta in June 1864 that he had made arrangements for colonels of Carolina regiments to furnish him with regular reports, "by which means I hope to be enabled to furnish correct lists." But, he continued, his plan seemed imperiled, "for I regret to state that several important letters sent from the field . . . [with information] have miscarried."[5]

Lists frequently included statements acknowledging the inadequacy of their information. As a Confederate newspaper reported in 1863, "Of Company I, 38 men were lost in action. 31 of these are accounted for as prisoners. The remaining seven must have been killed." Sons or brothers listed as "slightly wounded" often turned out to be dead, and husbands reported as "killed in action" later appeared unharmed. "I have known so many instances where families have been held in agonized suspense for days by the report of relatives being dangerously wounded when they were not," one Confederate wrote from Virginia to an anxious mother in South Carolina. Joseph Willett of New York hastened to write to his sister after the Battle of the Wilderness to explain, "You may have heard before this reaches you that I was killed or wounded but allow me to contradict the Report." Yankee Private Henry Struble was not only listed as a casualty after the Battle of Antietam but assigned a grave after his canteen was found in the hands of a man who died after Struble stopped to aid him. After the war ended Struble sent flowers every Memorial Day to decorate the grave that bore his name and to honor the unknown soldier it sheltered.[6]

More reliable and certainly more consoling were the personal letters custom required that a dead soldier's closest friends and immediate military superiors write to his relatives. These letters emerged as a distinctive genre, predictable in their descriptions of last moments, final words, and, when possible, place and manner of burial. Yet months often passed before soldiers in the field found time, circumstance, or strength to write. And these communications were dependent on the vicissitudes of the postal service that, at least in the Confederacy, grew increasingly unreliable. Southerners complained that by 1864 so many of the postal clerks in Richmond had been conscripted into the army that mail between the Virginia theater and the homefront had entirely broken down.

Voluntary organizations worked to fill the void left by the failure of military or government officials to provide information to families. In the North, both the Christian and Sanitary Commissions, the two most significant Unionwide charitable efforts to grow out of the war, regarded communication with families as a central component of their undertaking. The Christian Commission even proclaimed its commitment in words printed at the top of each page of its stationery: "The U.S. Christian Commission send this sheet as a messenger between the soldier and his home. Let it hasten to those who wait for tidings." Late in 1862, the Sanitary Commission took bolder measures, establishing a "Hospital Directory" in order to centralize information on the name and condition of every soldier admitted to a Union military hospital. On the third floor of the Commission's central office in downtown Washington, DC, three full-time clerks passed their days copying data from the daily reports of dozens of hospitals into large ledgers.[7]

During the directory's first year, some thirteen thousand specific inquiries were submitted and nine thousand answered. By early 1865, more than a million names had been recorded in the office ledgers. Inquiries about soldiers, the Sanitary Commission's Bulletin reported, "were often painful to hear from the harrowing anxiety and persistency with which they are presented." Although the replies were sometimes comforting, they often proved devastating. The superintendent of the Washington office described the daily scene of applicants arriving in person for news: "A mother has not heard anything of her son since the last battle; she hopes he is safe, but would like to be assured—there is no escape—she must be told that he has fallen upon the 'federal altar'; an agony of tears bursts forth which seem as if it would never cease. . . . A father . . . with pale face and tremulous voice, anxious to know, yet dreading to hear, is told that his boy is in the hospital a short distance off; . . . while tears run down his cheeks, and without uttering another word [he] leaves the room."[8]

The Confederacy, lagging behind the North in men and material, also faced greater shortages of information. The South had not experienced the same explosion of voluntary associations that had characterized the North in the prewar years and never developed centralized wartime charitable organizations like the Sanitary or Christian Commissions. But Confederates also sought means to systematize the collection of information about casualties and ways to make that intelligence available to kin. The Louisiana Soldiers Relief Association, for example, promised to provide information to "friends at home" about any Louisiana recruit serving in Virginia, and the Central Association and the South Carolina Relief Depot endeavored to gather information for South Carolinians. Southern religious newspapers often printed "Soldiers' Guides" listing news and location of the killed and wounded.[9]

Less philanthropically inclined individuals also sought to meet the demand for information. In northern cities, entrepreneurs established themselves as agents who would seek missing soldiers for a fee. An enterprise on Bleeker Street in New York City, for example, called itself the "U.S. Army Agency" and advertised in *Harper's Weekly* in 1864 for "Legal heirs seeking information as to whereabouts of Soldiers killed or wounded in battle." In return for their efforts in locating men, they would claim a share of the deceased's back pay or the widow's pension—thus the appeal to "legal heirs."[10]

Even when information was accurate and available, through newspaper casualty lists or the offices of a charitable organization or paid agent, it was often not delivered until long after the fatal event. Weeks or months of waiting were common. In South Carolina, for example, the first casualty lists from the Battle of the Wilderness appeared in newspapers ten days after the engagement they reported. In many cases families wrote desperate letters hoping to discover news of kin from whom they had heard nothing for months or even years. No wonder a Confederate officer took advantage of rank and privilege—and the fortuitous residence of his family near a telegraph line—to send a telegram home after every engagement simply reporting, "I am well."[11]

His decision to take the matter of providing information into his own hands was typical of many Civil War participants, who devised a variety of means to ensure that their fates would be reported to their loved ones. Although no official identification badges were issued by either army, soldiers, aided in some cases by enterprising civilians, devised their own precursors to the dog tag (figure 6.2). A Union burial party, working late on the night of July 4, 1863, to inter the Gettysburg dead, came across the body of a boy of about nineteen. In his pocket they found "a small silver shield with his name, company and regiment upon it." They copied the information on a wooden headboard for his grave and forwarded the shield to his father. Soldiers in the Union army could purchase these badges from sutlers in the field or from a variety of establishments on the homefront that regularly advertised in the press. The badges seem to have been far less readily available in the South, but Confederate soldiers invented their own substitutes. A pocket Bible inscribed with name and address and even instructions about notification of kin served quite effectively.[12]

Figure 6.2   Clara Barton expressed an astute understanding of the new responsibilities of government to dead soldiers and their families, writing to the Secretary of War, "The true patriot willingly loses his life for his country—these poor men have lost not only their lives, but the very record of their death. Common humanity would plead that an effort be made to restore their identity." It was not until World War I did American soldiers wear official dog tags bearing their personal information.

Source: Courtesy of the Collections of the Library of Congress

Stories are legendary of soldiers scribbling their names on bits of paper and pinning them to their uniforms before engagements they expected to be especially bloody—such as Meade's planned attack on Lee's field fortifications at Mine Run in 1863 or Grant's suicidal assault the next year at Cold Harbor. The soldiers' terror that their very identities would be obliterated expressed itself with a grim and almost dispassionate practicality; they confronted the enormity of death with an ingenious attempt to control at least one of its particulars. If a soldier could not save his life, he hoped at least to preserve his name.

Soldiers had many allies among the civilian population in the effort to maintain their identities and to provide for notification of kin. Katherine Wormeley, serving as a nurse in a Union military hospital, used the same method as the fatalistic soldiers. "So many nameless men come down to us, speechless and dying," she reported, "that now we write the names and regiments of the bad cases and fasten them to their clothing, so that if they are speechless when they reach other hands, they may not die like dogs." To die without an identity seemed to Wormeley the equivalent of surrendering one's humanity, of becoming no more than an animal. Nursing pioneer Clara Barton kept a series of small—one imagines pocket—notebooks into which she entered information about the families of dying soldiers so that

Figure 6.3 Clara Barton during the Civil War. Barton recorded details about the families of dying soldiers in her notebooks, so that she would be able to write them when the soldiers died.
Source: Courtesy of the Collections of the Library of Congress.

when time permitted she could write to their survivors (figure 6.3) The diary of T. J. Weatherly, a South Carolina physician who attended Confederate troops in Virginia, served a similar purpose. "Columbus Stephenson, Bethany Church, Iredell County, NoCa," he noted on a torn and undated page, "to be written to about the death &c of Lt. Thomas W. Stephens[on]." It is not hard to envision Dr. Weatherly asking Thomas Stephenson for his father's name and address as he consoled him in his last moments. "AA Hewlett, Summerville Ala for Capt Hewlett; Mrs S Watkins Wadesboro NC for S J Watkins 14th NC," Weatherly's list continued.[13]

Individuals did not just wait for letters or published casualty lists that would provide them with information about the dead and wounded; they also made use of the press to disseminate the knowledge they had been able to acquire. In both the North and South, civilians took out personal ads to announce the condition of prisoners and the fate of the missing. What is most striking about these advertisements is the way they were used to communicate across the divide of the Civil War—to provide southerners with news from the North and vice versa. In 1864, for example, a Richmond paper published a notice placed by Union General Benjamin Butler. Directed to the attention of a Confederate naval surgeon, Butler's advertisement assured his enemy that his son and a friend had been taken prisoner at the end of June: "They are both well and at [the Union prisoner of war camp at] Point Lookout. I have taken leave to write this note to relieve your anxiety." He had spoken to the young prisoner, he explained, in a "personal interview." Butler and the Confederate surgeon had almost certainly been acquainted before the war, and ties of friendship and humanitarianism combined in this instance to yield information about two of the war's unknowns. A personal ad in a Richmond paper announced to "Hon. RWB of South Carolina—your son Nat is a prisoner at Point Lookout, unwounded, and in his usual health, and all his wants shall be supplied." This anonymous northern friend of the family of Robert Barnwell was offering not just the immediate solace of information, but a promise to supplement the meager fare of Union prison camps for the duration of Nat's incarceration.[14]

Families bombarded officers, hospitals, and newspapers with requests for information and traveled by the hundreds to battlefields in search of missing kin. Observers described railroad junctions crowded with frantic civilians in search of news of lost relatives. Oliver Wendell Holmes rushed to Maryland in the aftermath of Antietam to search for his son. When in spite of his worst fears, he found him alive, Holmes described his shifting expectations as in some profound sense a shifting reality: "Our son and brother was dead and is alive again, and was lost and is found." Many of those who sought their loved ones did not share Holmes's happy outcome. Fanny Scott of Virginia began her search for her son Benjamin after several months of silence following the battle of Antietam. She wrote to Robert E. Lee early in 1863. He forwarded her letter across the lines to Union Gen. Joseph Hooker, who promised to have the U.S. Surgeon General survey hospital lists from Maryland (figure 6.4) Lee enclosed Hooker's letter in a reply to Scott and expressed his hopes "that you may hear good news of your son." But two months later Lee forwarded to her a letter sent to him through the lines by a Flag of Truce, which reported, "Diligent and careful inquiry has been made concerning the man referred to in the enclosure and no trace of him can be discovered in any hospital or among the records of the rebel prisoners." Within days, Fanny Scott had submitted a request to Lee for a pass through Union lines to the North to search for her son. Evidently her trip proved fruitless, for at the end of the war she was still seeking information. General E. A. Hitchcock, placed by the Union army in charge of exchange of prisoners, gently responded to Scott's July 15, 1865, request: "From the length of time since the battle of Antietam and you not having heard from your son during all this time, I am very sorry to say that the presumption is

144

Figure 6.4 A mother's quest for knowledge of her son's fate prompted Confederate General Robert E. Lee (left) to correspond with Union General Joseph Hooker (right) in an effort to find out what had happened to the young, Virginia soldier.

Source: Courtesy of the Collections of the Library of Congress.

that he fell a victim to that battle. If he were still living I cannot understand why he should not have found means of making the fact known to you."[15]

The Scott incident illustrates several significant aspects of the problem of the missing in the Civil War. First, it demonstrates the possibility of an individual being entirely lost—a circumstance many civilians found difficult to fathom. The scale of the war presented unprecedented problems of record-keeping; undoubtedly many of those never identified were bodies that could not be connected with names or corpses that were buried too hastily for the names to be procured. But there was another aspect of Civil War death that contributed to the large numbers of unidentified—and would contribute even more dramatically to the nameless ranks of World War I dead. The Civil War obliterated not just names but entire bodies, often leaving nothing left to identify or bury. A Union chaplain described in the aftermath of Gettysburg "little fragments so as hardly to be recognizable as any part of a man." Another soldier wrote in horror of comrades "literally blown to atoms." Many Civil War soldiers actually disappeared, their bodies vaporized by the firepower of this first modern war. This may have been the fate of Benjamin Scott.[16]

Fanny Scott's story demonstrates as well the unifying power of death even amidst the divisive forces of war. General Lee is not above concerning himself with the fall of an individual sparrow—though one assumes that Benjamin Scott was not just an ordinary soldier, but one whose family had some larger claims on Lee's compassion. But the intimacy of this all-American war displays itself strikingly here, as Lee readily corresponds with his Yankee counterpart, who himself acts promptly and decisively to honor his enemy's request. Even as they contemplate the spring campaign that will produce their bloody confrontation at Chancellorsville, Lee and Hooker find themselves on the same side as Fanny Scott in her desperate pursuit of information about her son. Killing enemy soldiers was the goal of each general and of both armies, yet bereavement could unite them in common purpose.

Fanny Scott's 1865 request for information about a son who had by then been gone almost three years suggests the depth and tenacity of the need to secure accurate information about the fate of missing men. General Hitchcock's 1865 letter to Scott seems to reflect a certain incredulity that she had not yet resigned herself to a grim conclusion that he regarded as both undeniable and unavoidable. Yet Fanny Scott's story demonstrates not just the nationally unifying power of death, but also the intensity and the persistence of its hold upon the bereaved. Nine years after the end of the war, Mrs. R. L. Leach was still seeking information about what had happened to her son after he was sent to a hospital ship in Virginia. Unable to admit he must be dead, she explained, "We think some times that he is in Some Insane Hospital." Without further information, she lived in "suspense," even as she acknowledged that "to know he was dead would be better." Jane Mitchell had received a letter after the Battle of Gettysburg from a soldier who described burying a corpse he found rolled in a blanket with her son's name pinned to it, but she never saw the body or found the grave and was never convinced it was really her son. "I would like to find that grave," she wrote. "It was years before I gave up the hope that he would some day appear. I got it into my head that he had been taken prisoner and carried off a long distance but that he would make his way back one day—this I knew was very silly of me but the hope was there nevertheless." The reality of loss was often, as one bereaved South Carolina woman put it, "too hard to realize."[17]

The power and persistence of hope manifested itself dramatically in the responses Union Quartermaster General Montgomery Meigs received when he decided in 1868 to publish in northern magazines a drawing of a soldier who had died unidentified in a Washington military hospital in 1864. This soldier would have been long forgotten if he had not had in his possession the considerable sum of $360. A published announcement seeking his identity also noted that the dead man had left an ambrotype of a child. Letters from women streamed into Meigs's office. While some may indeed have been fortune hunters seeking to claim the money, the great majority display what seems like such poignant desperation that it is difficult to doubt the sincerity of the wrenching tales they tell. Jenny McConkey of Illinois seemed to know she was grasping at straws when she wrote in hopes the unidentified man might be her son, whom she had last heard from in 1862. The photograph of the little boy was hard to explain, for her son was childless, but, she rationalized, he might carry the portrait in any case "as he was very fond of children." A Pennsylvania woman whose husband had last been heard of in the infamous Confederate prison camp at Andersonville described her life as "one constant daze of anxiety" because of her inability to get any information about his fate. Martha Dort wrote explaining that her husband had reportedly been shot while being transferred from one prison to another in 1863, "But that may not be true. Mistakes do often occur." The report of the child's photograph encouraged her to hope, for her husband had carried an ambrotype of their son, aged three or four, wearing plaid pants, with his hands in his pockets. She enclosed fifty cents for a copy of the photograph. Meigs's office returned the money, for the picture did not match her description.[18]

The mysterious soldier was never identified; the child in the ambrotype never provided with the details of his father's death or with his $360 inheritance. But the unknown man had proved the catalyst for an outpouring of despair and hope for women who represented the many thousands of loved ones left not just without husbands, brothers, or sons, but bereft of the kind of information that might enable them truly to mourn. A professor at Gettysburg College who aided many civilians searching for kin after that battle described "aching hearts in which the dread void of uncertainty still remained unsatisfied by positive knowledge." As the war approached its conclusion, the search for "positive knowledge" would intensify in ways that began profoundly to affect both public policy and private behavior.[19]

As early as the summer of 1862, the pressing need for space to bury soldiers dying in hospitals concentrated in and around Washington, DC led Congress to authorize President Lincoln to establish national cemeteries "for the soldiers who shall die in the service of their country." Motivated chiefly by the urgent necessity to dispose of corpses, rather than by any commitment to improvement in identification of deceased soldiers and notification of kin, this measure nevertheless encouraged more accurate record-keeping and marked an acknowledgment by the federal government of responsibility for the war dead. Without any formal policy to implement this Congressional action, the War Department organized cemeteries as emergency circumstances demanded—mainly near concentrations of military hospitals where large numbers of bodies required burial. Under the provisions of this measure, however, five cemeteries of a rather different character were created in the course of the war. These were burial grounds for the dead of a particular battle, usually established when a lull in active operations and the availability of troops for burial duty made such an undertaking possible. In each case, the purpose of the effort extended well beyond simply meeting the need for disposing of the dead. An explicit goal of memorialization lay at the heart of these efforts and made identification of the fallen heroes a central part of the undertaking. Gettysburg represented a particularly important turning point in this transition in official policy toward the war's casualties. The large number of deaths in this bloody battle was obviously an important factor in generating action, but it is not insignificant that this carnage occurred in the North, in a town that had not had the opportunity to grow accustomed to the horrors of constant warfare that had battered Virginia for two long years. Perhaps even more critical was the fact that the North had the resources to respond, resources not available to the hard-pressed Confederacy. Because the attempt to inter the Union dead occurred so soon after that battle, the level of success in identifying the bodies was extremely high; 82 percent were named. Lincoln's presence at the dedication of the cemetery in November 1863, not to mention his delivery of an address that, historian Garry Wills has argued, "remade America," and also signaled the new significance of the dead in public life and ceremony.[20]

Perhaps the very configuration of the cemetery itself can explain the force behind this transformation. The national cemetery at Gettysburg was arranged so that every grave was of equal importance; every dead soldier mattered equally, regardless of rank or station. Changing American attitudes toward the Civil War dead reflected this new conception of citizenship, of the importance of the individual and his place in the American democracy. The citizen had a claim on the state; the state had obligations to the individual. And fundamental to this obligation was the acknowledgment of the citizen as a unique and singular person—a person with a name—in death as in life. It is from this changed understanding of the relationship of the citizen and the state that the government's gradual assumption of responsibility for identifying war dead and notifying kin would emerge in the course of the next century.[21]

The establishment of the National Cemetery system was not the only wartime measure that marked these shifting perceptions. In July 1864, Congress, demonstrating its sense of the inadequacies of military procedures concerning the war dead, passed an act that established a new organizational principle for handling of the war dead, designating a special Graves Registration unit rather than assuming that soldiers could simply be detailed from the line to carry out these duties, as had heretofore been the case. When Confederate General Jubal Early attacked Fort Stevens near Washington, DC, in late 1864, this new unit, under Assistant Quartermaster James Moore, succeeded in identifying every Union body and recording every grave. But during the final operations of the war, men were not spared to serve in registration units, and the principle was abandoned. It represented, nevertheless, a new departure as well as a precursor of organizational methods that would become standard in twentieth-century wars.

The innovations in record-keeping that occurred during the Civil War originated in the North and applied to the treatment of Union dead. This was a result of levels of bureaucratic development and available resources, not of any fundamental difference between northern and southern attitudes about the dead. After Appomattox, these distinctions would become even sharper. Free from the demands of waging war, the North could devote itself more fully to the memorialization of the slain and the needs of the bereaved. The South, however, in losing its nationhood, also lost the official government structures that might have organized efforts to reclaim bodies and notify kin. In addition, the desperate poverty of the defeated South left it with inadequate resources to support many of the living, and thus little to expend upon the dead. Yet white southerners and white southern women in particular endeavored through private and informal means to accomplish many of the same goals pursued by well-funded government efforts in the North. A group of Confederate women in South Carolina, for example, organized to bring their dead home from Antietam; a Memorial Association founded by Richmond ladies in 1866 expended its efforts and all the funds it could raise to identify and bring Confederates back from Gettysburg. And northerners who judged official measures insufficient continued their own private efforts to secure information for the thousands of Americans still searching for news of their kin.

Perhaps the most active of such individuals was Clara Barton, whose wartime endeavors had included forwarding information to the families of the men she treated at the front. Prompted after the end of hostilities by the number of letters she continued to receive from women in search of lost husbands and sons, Barton was determined to develop a more systematic approach to dealing with what she described as the "intense anxiety . . . amounting in many instances almost to insanity" of these petitioners. In the spring of 1865, she founded an organization she named the Office of Correspondence with the Friends of the Missing Men of the United States Army, and she devised a plan to serve as a clearinghouse, publishing the names submitted to her by those in search of kin and requesting information about their fate. "I appeal to you to give such facts relative to the fate of these men as you may recollect or can ascertain," she explained at the top of one published list. "They have been your comrades on march, picket or raid, or in battle, hospital, or prison; and, falling there, the fact and manner of their death may be known *only* to you." Within days of her announcement, Barton had received several hundred letters, and they soon poured in by the thousands. By mid-June 1865, she had published the names of twenty thousand men; by the time she closed the office in 1868 she reported that it had received and answered 63,182 letters and identified twenty-two thousand missing soldiers.[22]

In the summer of 1865, Clara Barton became engaged in another venture, one that would evolve into a major federal commitment to the identification of missing men. Secretary of War Edwin Stanton had learned that a surviving list of soldiers buried at Andersonville corresponded with numbered graves, offering the possibility of identifying and memorializing a great many who had endured the prison camp's extreme suffering and deprivation. Stanton authorized an expedition to be headed by James Moore, the quartermaster who had so successfully employed the new graves registration procedures in 1864 and who was now in charge of battlefield cemeteries. Clara Barton, invited by Stanton almost as an afterthought, joined the endeavor. Though she and Moore grew quickly to resent and even detest one another, their efforts resulted in the identification of 12,912 of the 13,363 recovered bodies. All were reinterred in marked graves, and on August 17 their resting place was dedicated as the Andersonville National Cemetery (figure 6.5).

What Barton had been trying to accomplish through voluntarism and philanthropy, Moore embraced as the responsibility of the state. His duties as quartermaster general in the course of the next five years would be to attempt to identify every slain Union soldier in the eastern theatre and bury them all with the honor they had earned. Across the South, federal agents searched for every Union corpse, buried or unburied. For all the difficulties locating and identifying bodies interred across extended battlefields, the greatest challenge would be finding soldiers scattered all about the countryside—along the line of march, in villages where they had been carried after being wounded, in sites where they had fallen after minor skirmishes too insignificant even to be recorded. Agents reported frequent instances of Union graves desecrated by angry southerners. "This grave," wrote one officer from Georgia "is entirely obliterated as *Mr Brown has plowed and raised corn over it during the last season*. There was a headboard plainly marked which this Brown has knocked down or destroyed." In the aftermath of war, obliterating names and remains could come to seem as important to the defeated as had the killing of enemy soldiers during the war years themselves.

Perhaps the northern agents' most striking observation, however, was their discovery of the role of black southerners in honoring and protecting the Union dead. About two miles from Savannah, one agent reported, lay 77 graves in 4 neat rows, all but 3 identified, all marked with "good painted

GROUNDS AT ANDERSONVILLE, GEORGIA, WHERE ARE BURIED FOURTEEN THOUSAND UNION SOLDIERS WHO DIED IN ANDERSONVILLE PRISON.—SKETCHED BY I. C. SCHOTEL.—[SEE PAGE 624.]

Figure 6.5 On August 17, 1865, Clara Barton raises the National Flag at the dedication of the Andersonville (Georgia) National Cemetery. This sketch, by I. C. Schotel, depicts the dedication of the cemetery grounds where fourteen thousand Union soldiers are interred who died in Andersonville Prison. Known as Camp Sumter, Andersonville was one of the largest of many Confederate military prisons established during the Civil War. It is now the Andersonville National Historic Site, maintained by the National Park Service.

Source: Courtesy of the Collections of the Library of Congress.

headboards and in very good condition." This was the resting place of a unit of U.S. Colored Troops, carefully buried and tended by the freed people of the area. But it was not just black soldiers who received this respectful treatment. Behind an African Colored Church near Bowling Green, Kentucky, for example, 1,134 manicured graves held both black and white Yankee soldiers. One agent noted that in the course of his travels through the South, a black carpenter proved his most useful informant, for he had made coffins and "helped to bury many of the Union dead himself." In the postwar South, the struggle over the war's legacy of freedom included a struggle over the bodies and names of the war's dead.[23]

By 1870, some three hundred thousand men had been reinterred in seventy three national cemeteries, and 58 percent had been identified. This elaborate and costly program undertaken by the federal government in every theater of the war made a forceful statement about the democratization of death and about the significance of the body as the repository of identity and thus of the individual rights for which the nation had fought. But the reinterment program spoke to issues that transcended individualism as well. Gathering the slain into national cemeteries affirmed, to paraphrase Lincoln, that both they and their deaths belonged to the Union, that they had not died in vain, had—in dying that their nation might live—in some sense not died at all. The Civil War transformed death—not just in material ways by preserving bodies and identities in face of war's destructive power—but in ideological ways as well.

The policies toward the dead that evolved in the course of the Civil War represented the assumption of new responsibilities by the federal government— responsibilities to dead soldier citizens, but responsibilities as well to families and to the women so often left alone to head them as the result of war's carnage. Clara Barton may ultimately have lost her personal struggle with James Moore for resources and power, but her understanding of their common goals would not be abandoned—would in fact be embodied in the very program of massive reburial he implemented. After all, she too had worked to compel the government to accept responsibility for the missing and had in 1865 written to the secretary of war to seek federal support for the search for missing men. "The true patriot," she declared,

willingly loses his life for his country—these poor men have lost not only their lives, but the very record of their death. Common humanity would plead that an effort be made to restore their identity. . . . As call after call for "three hundred thousand more" fell upon the stricken homes, the wife released her husband and the mother sent forth her son, and they were nobly given to their country for its necessities: it might take and use them as the bonded officer uses the property given into his hands; it might if needs be use up or lose them, and they would submit without complaint, but never . . . has wife or mother agreed that for the destruction of her treasures no account should be rendered her. I hold these men in the light of Government property unaccounted for.[24]

Barton here explores complex notions of rights, of the mutual obligations that bind state and citizens together. Significantly, at the end of a war about slavery, she situates her discussion in concepts of property in persons. Yet this is not the property of slavery; here the individual freely acts as his own agent, as a true patriot "willingly" ceding control over his life. And here, again in contrast to a system of human bondage that tore families asunder, the wife and mother consent to give up their husband and son "to their country for its necessities."

But this cession of rights, of property in person, remains incomplete. It is, in effect, a contract in which the state must in return accept certain obligations—to provide a record of death, an accounting for the destruction of human treasure. And it is, tellingly, a contract that, in Barton's rendering, is undertaken between women and the state. Women, legally denied the right to make contracts in most of pre–Civil War America, here claim new rights of personhood and citizenship that derive from their wartime sacrifice. In the context of a war of unprecedented mortality, the compelling human-itarian logic that produced emancipation combined with the imperatives of devastating human loss to create a new conception of the relation of the individual and the state. Clara Barton here articulates a notion of citizenship founded in the nation's experience of Civil War and expressed through the powerful shared public need to affirm the individual's right to identity and humanity even in death. Naming the names underscored an emerging awareness of the extent and the perquisites of citizenship as well as of the fundamental obligations of the state; it affirmed the claims of the men who had died as well as those of the wives and mothers left to mourn their loss.[25]

The distinguished European historian Thomas W. Laqueur has written extensively about this issue of naming the dead in the context of twentieth-century wars. He notes a shift in sensibility occurring with World War I. The dead would no longer be "shoveled into the ground and so forgotten," as Tennyson put it, but instead named and memorialized by the hundreds of thousands on monuments and in graveyards across the western front. This new attention to names, Laqueur concludes, represents a significant marker of modernity; it is "the result of the modern notion that everyone has a memorable life to live, or in any case the right to a life story." For the United States, however, this would be a nineteenth rather than a twentieth-century development. The war that freed the slaves established broad claims to rights of citizenship and identity—for blacks as well as whites, for women as well as men, for both the living and the dead.[26]

Notes

Drew Gilpin Faust is Lincoln Professor of History and Dean of the Radcliffe Institute for Advanced Study at Harvard University. She is a past president of the Southern Historical Association and author of five books, including *Mothers of Invention: Women of the Slaveholding South in the American Civil War*, which was a New York Times Notable Book of 1996 and winner of the Francis Parkman Prize.

1. Caroline Alexander, "Letter from Vietnam: Across the River Styx: The Mission to Retrieve the Dead," *The New Yorker*, October 25, 2004, 44–51.

2. Samuel P. Moore, August 14, 1862, in Wayside Hospital, Charleston, Order and Letter Book, South Caroliniana Library, University of South Carolina, Columbia; *Charleston Mercury*, January 27, 1864.

3. Edward Steere, *The Graves Registration Service in World War II*, Quartermaster Historical Studies #21, Historical Section, Office of the Quartermaster (U.S. Government Printing Office, 1951), 4.

4. Sarah J. Palmer to Harriet R. Palmer, September 5, 1862, Palmer Family Papers, South Caroliniana Library.

5. *Daily South Carolinian*, June 16, 1864.

6. *Daily South Carolinian*, July 22, 1863; F. S. Gillespie to Mrs. Carson, July 5, 1864, Carson Family Papers, South Caroliniana Library; Joseph Willett to Dear Sister, June 24, 1864, Elizabeth Cummings Papers, New York Historical Society; Steven R. Stotelmyer, *The Bivouacs of the Dead* (Baltimore, MD: Toomey Press, 1992), 17.

7. *The Sanitary Reporter*, January 15, 1864, 135; J. W. Hoover to Mr. Kuhlman, September 8, 1864, J. W. Hoover Papers, State Historical Society of Wisconsin.

8. "The Hospital Directory," *Sanitary Commission Bulletin* 1(December 15, 1863): 109.

9. *Louisiana Soldiers' Relief Association and Hospital in the City of Richmond, Virginia* (Richmond: Enquirer Book and Job Press, 1862), 30.

10. *Harper's Weekly*, September 13, 1864, 576.

11. *Daily South Carolinian*, May 17,1864; W. D. Rutherford to Mrs. W. D. Rutherford [telegram], July 6, 1862, W. D. Rutherford Papers, South Caroliniana Library.

12. Gregory Coco, *Killed in Action: Eyewitness Accounts of the Last Moments of 100 Union Soldiers Who Died at Gettysburg* (Gettysburg, PA: Thomas Publications, 1992), 76; *Harper's Weekly*, August 1, 1863, September 3, 1864.

13. Katharine Prescott Wormeley, *The Other Side of War: With the Army of the Potomac. Letters from the Headquarters of the United States Sanitary Commission During the Peninsular Campaign in Virginia in 1862* (Boston: Ticknor and Company, 1889), 145; Clara Barton, Journal 1863, Clara Barton Papers, Library of Congress; T. J. Weatherly, Diary, 1864–1865, South Caroliniana Library.

14. *Daily South Carolinian*, July 21, 1864. These were copied by the *Carolinian* "from the Richmond papers."

15. Oliver Wendell Holmes, "My Hunt after 'The Captain,' " *Atlantic* 10 (December 1862): 743; Robert E. Lee to Joseph Hooker, February 14, 1863; Joseph Hooker to Robert E. Lee, February 16, 1863; Robert E. Lee to Fanny Scott, February 18, 1863; Charles S. Venable to Fanny Scott, April 1, 1863; William Alexander Hammond to Robert E. Lee, March 23, 1863; Thomas M. R. Talcott to Fanny Scott, April 18, 1863; E. A. Hitchcock to Fanny Scott, July 25, 1865, all in Scott Family Papers, Virginia Historical Society, Richmond. See Mrs. T. B. Hurlbut to Clara Barton, September 26, 1865, for a description of Confederate general James Longstreet's aid to a northern woman searching for her son. Clara Barton Papers, Library of Congress.

16. Gregory Coco, *A Strange and Blighted Land: Gettysburg, the Aftermath of a Battle* (Thomas Publications, 1995), 48; Robert G. Carter, *Four Brothers in Blue* (Austin, TX: University of Texas Press, 1978), 324–25.

17. Mrs. R. L. Leach to Clara Barton, March 28, 1874, Clara Barton Papers, Library of Congress; Gregory Coco, *Wasted Valor: The Confederate Dead at Gettysburg* (Thomas Publications, 1990), 141; Sarah J. Palmer to Harriet R. Palmer, September 5, 1862. This is the wartime foundation for the postwar reconciliation David Blight describes in *Race and Reunion: The Civil War in American Memory* (Cambridge, MA: Harvard University Press, 2001).

18. Quartermaster General Montgomery C. Meigs to Surgeon General, September 19, 1868, Office of the Quartermaster General: Consolidated Correspondence File, 1794–1915, Portrait of Unknown Soldier, Box 1173, RG 92, National Archives;

Mrs. Jenny McConkey to Meigs, November 4, 1868; Ellen Harback to Meigs, October 26, 1868; Mrs. J. P. Coppersmith to Meigs, November 30, 1868; James M. Truitt to Meigs, November 6, 1868, all in ibid.

19. Coco, *A Strange and Blighted Land*, 306.

20. Garry Wills, *Lincoln at Gettysburg: The Words that Remade America* (New York: Simon and Schuster, 1992).

21. On the revolutionary implications of treating all soldiers equally, see "Our National Cemeteries," *Harper's Monthly Magazine* 33 (August 1866): 311. By contrast, in the American Revolution, "the bodies of the officers and men of the army were interred in ways that emphasized the gap between them," Caroline Cox, *A Proper Sense of Honor: Service and Sacrifice in George Washington's Army* (Chapel Hill, NC: University of North Carolina Press, 2004), 174.

22. Clara Barton to Secretary of War Stanton, draft letter October 1865, final version November 27, 1865, Clara Barton Papers, Library of Congress; "To Returned Soldiers and Others," ibid.

23. Journal of a Trip through Parts of Kentucky, Tennessee, and Georgia for the Purpose of Locating the Scattered Graves of Union Soldiers [1866] RG92 685, National Archives, v. I, 177, 211, 240; v. II, 26. Emphasis in the original.

24. Clara Barton to Edwin Stanton, Secretary of War, October 1865, Clara Barton Papers, Library of Congress.

25. On contract in this period, see Amy Dru Stanley, *From Bondage to Contract: Wage Labor, Marriage and the Market in the Age of Slave Emancipation* (Cambridge University Press, 1998).

26. Thomas W. Laqueur, "Names, Bodies, and the Anxiety of Erasure," *The Social and Political Body*, ed. Theodore R. Schatzki and Wolfgang Natter (New York: Guilford Press, 1996), 123, 135.

Chapter 7

Diplomatic Wives: The Politics of Domesticity and the "Social Game" in the U.S. Foreign Service, 1905–1941

Molly M. Wood

From *The Journal of Women's History*

In the first half of the twentieth century, U.S. Foreign Service officers understood that marriage enhanced their diplomatic careers and generally considered their wives to be partners in the Service. In 1914, U.S. consul Francis Keene wrote to his wife Florence, "You and I, as a team, are, I am confidant, unexcelled in the Service."[1] Career diplomat Earl Packer explained that "the wives carry a terrific burden" in the Foreign Service, while another longtime diplomat, Willard Beaulac, declared, "I know of no field in which a wife can be more helpful."[2] Meanwhile, an outside observer of the U.S. Foreign Service in the 1930s explained that "the wife may serve as a go-between for her husband" by taking part in social interactions with other diplomats and representatives from the host country.[3] At the same time, many American Foreign Service wives also spoke explicitly about their "careers" in the Foreign Service, and the U.S. State Department initiated changes that reflected the Department's dependence on "the tradition of husband and wife teams and of wives' participation in the representational activities of a post."[4] Specifically, the 1924 Rogers Act, which was intended to reform and professionalize the Foreign Service, resulted in administrative changes, such as allowances for rent and entertaining, that directly reflected the growing reliance on the presence of American wives overseas. Furthermore, the new Foreign Service Personnel Board, formed by the Rogers Act to evaluate each Foreign Service officer's eligibility for promotion, explicitly discussed wives' strengths and weaknesses when assessing each officer's merits, noting in particular the success of officers who were "ably seconded" or "ably assisted" by their wives.[5]

At the turn of the twentieth century, many government officials, including President Theodore Roosevelt, concluded that most diplomats were "amateurs" who were more interested in pursuing a "genteel and leisurely life" of "elegance and sophistication" in some foreign capital than in representing growing American interests abroad. In 1905, Roosevelt signed an Executive Order establishing, for the first time, an examination system for lower level prospective diplomatic secretaries, but these reforms were haphazard and only partially successful.[6] Almost twenty years later, State Department officials still lamented, behind closed doors, the poor quality of some of their candidates for overseas posts, including one in 1924 who was "qualified by birth, antecedents and personality" but "greatly hampered by stupidity."[7] Happily, most applicants were more competent, dedicated, and service-oriented than the stereotype suggested, but the fear that inexperienced and incompetent diplomats were jeopardizing efforts to establish American power and influence around the world still worried officials. Calls for reform and modernization finally resulted in the 1924 Rogers Act, which reorganized the Foreign Service and initiated a comprehensive merit promotion system, opening the Service to men of lesser financial means. The reforms initiated by the Rogers Act continued to evolve along the same lines until 1941, when American entry into World War II changed the Foreign Service dramatically in size, purpose, and personnel. The period between 1905 and 1941 therefore provides a finite period of study during which the Foreign Service self-consciously modernized itself in order to better serve the United States's expanding role in the wider world. Through this period, however, the Foreign Service remained relatively small and almost exclusively male. In the wake of the 1920 suffrage victory, less than a dozen women moved into professional positions in the Foreign Service before World War II, yet hundreds of married women accompanied their Foreign Service husbands to diplomatic and consular posts all over the world during the same period.

This article challenges the assumption that because wives held no formal positions in the Foreign Service they played no significant role in the conduct of American diplomacy. In fact, a Foreign Service wife wielded considerable authority and influence as wife, mother, homemaker, hostess, and role model. By operating within conventional gender roles that emphasized domesticity, Foreign Service wives resembled both the wives of British officials in India in the late nineteenth and early twentieth centuries who, as historian Mary Procida has shown, served as "active agents in imperial politics," and the American military wives of the post–World War II era who, as historian Donna Alvah has explained, "actively contribute to [Cold War American] military objectives and American foreign relations."[8] A study of American Foreign Service wives in the first half of the twentieth century suggests ways in which gender helped to create and maintain a positive American presence all over the world, and helped to define the conduct of American diplomacy. An examination of the role of gender in the politics of diplomatic representation will contribute to the growing body of literature on gender and U.S. foreign relations. In the 1980s, a small number of historians, determined to add women to the field of U.S. diplomatic history, produced works on individuals, such as Eleanor Roosevelt and Jeannette Rankin, and groups of women, such as missionaries and peace activists, who clearly influenced U.S. foreign policy.[9] Worried that studies such as these only emphasized the "outsider" status of women in foreign policy, and influenced by groundbreaking theoretical work on gender as an essential category of historical analysis, scholars such as Cynthia Enloe, Emily Rosenberg, Andrew Rotter, and Frank Costigliola, among others, have found gender to be embedded in both the language and conduct of twentieth century U.S. foreign relations.[10] Others, including Margaret Strobel, Ann Stoler, Antoinette Burton, and Laura Wexler, have written convincingly about the ways in which gender has served to legitimize colonial and imperial relationships between nations.[11]

In the Foreign Service, wives managed, without pay, the domestic duties and social obligations that ensured the smooth operation of American missions. They also helped establish a powerful American presence in countries all over the world. Their visibility overseas enhanced American prestige and reflected the very best of the American way of life to other cultures. In order to conduct foreign relations, especially in the pre–World War II years, diplomats spent a great deal of time establishing and maintaining personal relationships with local officials and dignitaries in order to gather information, to report accurately on local conditions, and to represent American positions to their hosts effectively.[12] The political relationships they created were therefore also, by definition, social relationships. As Beaulac has explained, "the social contacts" initiated by diplomats "supplemented our official conversations and helped us to interpret [those conversations]."[13] The Foreign Service establishment understood that formal diplomatic negotiations between officials were complemented by what one observer called the "secret methods of diplomacy" and another Foreign Service officer described as "the process of friendly informed negotiation."[14] Many of these relationships were cultivated outside of the office and at all hours of the day and night, blurring the distinction between private life and public work. Hilary Callen has already described the "diffuseness of the diplomat's role" and noted "the lack of sharp definition of 'public' and 'private' identities" that inevitably "spills over onto his wife."[15] By organizing and managing highly visible social functions, many of which took place in their own homes, Foreign Service wives helped facilitate the exchange of information and messages, official and unofficial, overt and subtle, that defined the conduct of early twentieth-century diplomacy.[16] The success of these social occasions and the efficient conduct of diplomacy therefore depended largely on wives' domestic and social skills, as well as their more intangible function as representatives of the American way of life.

Because the duties and responsibilities of Foreign Service wives reinforced conventional gender roles, scholars are only beginning to recognize the inherently political nature of the work they performed.[17] Maureen

Flanagan has urged scholars to avoid choosing between interpreting "women's activities as socially directed" or as explicitly political, just as Alvah has observed that military wives' "domestic activities and political participation were seen as intertwined." In the context of the early federal period in Washington, D.C., Catherine Allgor has demonstrated that women "appear as political actors in their own right" by "using social events and the 'private sphere' to establish the national capital and build the extraofficial structures so sorely needed in the infant federal republic."[18] American Foreign Service wives used the social arena to create and maintain political relationships, and to send and receive political messages in American missions overseas. More subtly, their domestic presence, in roles as wife, mother, hostess, and homemaker, helped to create an island of American domesticity in a decidedly foreign setting. Diplomatic wives therefore served the same purpose as the wives of colonial administrators in British imperial settings; they were the women who, as Burton has explained, "by virtue of their caretaking functions and their role as transmitters of culture," helped to legitimize the imperial mission as a civilizing mission.[19]

Yet the State Department made little effort to explicitly define and codify the roles they believed wives should play, and indeed made few efforts to define the work of representation in the pre–World War II era beyond the assumption that the American "style of diplomacy must be representative of our way of life," and that American envoys overseas must work at "creating understanding" and "correcting misunderstanding" about the United States. Yet wives recognized their responsibility to "set an example" abroad.[20] One Foreign Service wife in the mid-1930s showed great awareness that she "became a public person or public property" when she married a Foreign Service officer. "Whatever I did," she explained, "was always regarded as not only personal or our own, but as an American also, or wife of a diplomat, also. So how I or the other wives entertained, how we took part in charities, or culture, art, literature, sport [or] fashion, was [all a] part of representation."[21] Wives were also well aware by this time that State Department officials were evaluating them on their ability to create and maintain these kinds of political relationships both within and outside of the embassy. As Lucy Briggs remembered, "In those days, when a man's record was written up, his wife was also commented on. And if she added to his social position in a pleasant way, or if she was helpful in other ways, that was always put down. Or if she was something of a handicap that was put down too."[22] Wives understood that everything they did reflected on their husbands and their country. This work was particularly important as the United States looked to expand its economic and political interests abroad and sought to be perceived widely as a nonimperial power. In the absence of formal colonial or military missions, U.S. Foreign Service wives served as the only significant numbers of American women in quasi-official positions living abroad. The State Department hoped that these wives would serve as exemplars who would, through their domestic presence overseas, introduce the most cultivated Americans to the rest of the world and help project a message of overall goodwill.[23]

Yet Foreign Service wives are still largely ignored as serious subjects of study. Some feminist scholars undoubtedly have been irritated by the way Foreign Service wives universally identified themselves as the "wife of" an American diplomat, or by the apparent concessions these women made to their husbands' careers. Most of the women who became Foreign Service wives between 1905 and 1941 were well educated (many of them college-educated), reflecting the benefits of their class status, but only a few had embarked on careers before marrying, which was not surprising considering the era. Fewer still openly identified themselves as feminists, or had engaged in any kind of traditional political activism. Foreign Service wives in this time period instead appear to have embraced their identity as the "wife of" a diplomat in order to also embrace the opportunities that came with the position. Former Foreign Service wives who were interviewed in the 1980s were therefore perplexed by the desire of a new generation of wives for "careers of their own, outside the Foreign Service." Dorothy Emmerson, who started in the Foreign Service in the 1930s, was frustrated whenever someone asked her if she regretted not pursuing a career, because she assumed that she already did have a career as a Foreign Service wife. Similarly, Naomi Matthews was "a little impatient with women who . . . don't want to be associated with their husbands."[24] Foreign Service wives in the early twentieth century describe themselves not as "helpmates" to their husbands, but as highly visible associates or partners who "joined," rather than "married into," the Foreign Service and who felt a "strong sense of responsibility" and duty to the Foreign Service, just as, for example, the wives of British colonial administrators personally identified themselves with the official British Imperial presence throughout the Empire.[25] American Foreign Service wives recognized that American diplomatic practice depended on them, but they also realized that they benefited in many ways from their status as diplomatic wives.

Before she married Bert Matthews, for instance, Naomi Meffert "loved the thought of life in the Foreign Service" and was "delighted" about Bert's career plans. Reflecting on her life in the Foreign Service many years later, she appreciated the fact that her husband "always said 'we' " when he referred to their life and work in the Foreign Service.[26] Other wives have described their lives in the Foreign Service, and their relationship with their husbands, in very similar ways, reflecting an unconscious illustration of what Hanna Papanek has called the "two person single career." As Eliza Pavalko and Glen Elder explain, some wives are "so highly involved in their husbands' careers" that they believe their work is "a true partnership."[27] This theory, which seems to describe the experiences of many Foreign Service wives, defines the work a wife performs to further her husband's career as something that will also significantly benefit her, both because of the status she gains with her husband's promotions and because of the potential for her own personal fulfillment. Wives in the early twentieth century did not advocate for formal recognition of their roles in the Service, or for freedom from their diplomatic duties in order to pursue other vocations, because they believed they already had important and fulfilling careers in the Service. It was only because a later generation of wives, mostly in the 1960s, advocated for formal changes in the Foreign Service that the State Department issued the 1972 Directive that recognized wives as independent individuals with no formal responsibility to the Foreign Service.

Wives most clearly "assisted" their husbands in the social arena. One wife remembered that her "entire life" in the Foreign Service in the 1930s "was to be devoted to being the best possible hostess."[28] Other wives explained how they "entered into the picture in public relations and making friends," arguing that "one of the best ways to get to know people is to relax over a pleasant meal, and usually a great deal of business was conducted at the same time." Enloe has observed that, given the family backgrounds of most Foreign Service wives, "hostessing was what they had been raised to do."[29] We might misinterpret Enloe's statement as an indictment of Foreign Service wives and their seemingly frivolous lives until reading further about the ways in which, as Enloe explains, "hostessing" should be taken seriously as work, and especially as an integral part of diplomatic activity. As John Foster wrote about the Foreign Service in 1906, "Personal acquaintance with influential people in governmental and political life is often helpful in advancing the business of the legation."[30] It was at the social occasions so crucial to the conduct of diplomacy, where representatives from the host country, the other members of the diplomatic corps, and local dignitaries and visitors mixed and mingled, that these kinds of acquaintances were nurtured. As a gendered responsibility, hostessing reflected common assumptions about women's supposed natural abilities at making people feel comfortable, but the role of "official hostess" was also considered to be a great honor at diplomatic affairs.[31] In order to ensure that the very best women filled this role in the wake of President Roosevelt's 1905 effort to professionalize the service, officials in Washington noted each officer's marital status and assessed whether "the members of his family contribute to his standing and reputation in the community."[32] After the 1924 Rogers Act, the State Department evaluation process became more systematic, as members of the new Foreign Service Personnel Board explicitly discussed the expectations that wives would cultivate a "host of friends" and entertain "with a kindly and likeable disposition."[33]

Yet Foreign Service officers and their wives rarely defined exactly what the wives did, an omission that contributes to the difficulties we face in analyzing their roles and strengthens widespread assumptions about the luxurious nature of Foreign Service life. As one former diplomat's wife explained, "The social aspect of diplomatic life is much maligned," and has generally not been taken seriously outside of the Foreign Service.[34] Therefore, women such as Edith O'Shaughnessy, who organized lavish dinner parties, worried about her clothes, and "cultivated" influential friendships in Vienna in 1910 and 1911, have been dismissed as superficial, when in fact O'Shaughnessy was only doing her job by initiating the social contacts necessary for the conduct of diplomacy (and for her husband's career).[35] Most Foreign Service officers and their wives in the early twentieth century relied on family money to supplement their small Foreign Service salaries and to absorb extra expenses, notably those pertaining to the "social aspects of diplomatic life." They did not receive any allowances for expenses such as rent or entertaining until the 1924 Rogers Act reforms. Generally, therefore, only young men or women of independent means were likely to be successful in the Foreign Service.

Lucy and Ellis Briggs, for instance, were well prepared for this kind of life. Briggs was a Smith College graduate and the daughter of a New York attorney. Her husband was also raised comfortably. He graduated from Dartmouth College and took the new Foreign Service exam several years later in 1925. When the couple married in 1928, Briggs duly observed that "the salaries were extremely small and it was necessary, if you went to any big [important] post, to pay a great deal out of your own pocket."[36] O'Shaughnessy, on the other hand, had no such resources. She hoped marriage would bring social and financial stability, but a series of bad investments left Nelson O'Shaughnessy's father unable to help support the couple. O'Shaugnessy even considered leaving town at the beginning of the social season in Vienna in 1907, because his "humiliating [financial] circumstances" would prevent the couple from participating fully in the important social life of the diplomatic corps. Ultimately, he stayed in town but placed the responsibility on his wife to use her "good sense" to try to find some way to continue their social obligations even in the face of financial distress.[37]

The Foreign Service proved to be a financial disappointment for O'Shaughnessy, but she still relished the excitement of the diplomatic life, as did many other young women. Anna Smith appreciated the chance to pursue an adventure when she married U.S. consul Carl Kemp in 1919. After the untimely death of Kemp's first wife, he proposed to Smith in 1919 and she quickly accepted. Kemp in all likelihood had recognized already the difficulty of carrying on his consular duties without a wife, while the shy and quiet Smith had jumped at the chance to begin a life of travel and adventure.[38] Many Foreign Service wives resembled other groups of women travelers in the way they used their international travel experience as a route to excitement and adventure.[39] Because of their quasi-official status in the Foreign Service, however, wives held unusual positions of responsibility, often acting independently of their husbands. When Foreign Service officers received transfer orders from the State Department, for example, they often moved immediately to the new post and usually lived temporarily in a hotel. They left their wives behind to make all the logistical arrangements for the "arduous" task, in this era of preflight travel, of transporting all the household possessions, the "mounds of luggage," and young children to a new city.[40] Yvonne Jordan recalled the difficulties she encountered when trying to move, with an infant son, from Haiti to Helsinki in 1922. Jordan met and married her husband, Curtis, when he was stationed with the U.S. Army in France after World War I. Jordan took the U.S. Foreign Service exam in Paris in 1919, just before his discharge from the Army. He passed the exam and was posted immediately to Haiti. Less than a year later, he was transferred to Finland, but his wife was so close to delivering their first baby that she had to stay behind, have the baby, and wait seven more weeks before leaving Haiti to catch up to her husband.[41] In addition, she had to arrange and pay for her and the baby's travel out of pocket after being informed by the State Department that "the travel expense fund was exhausted."[42]

As they moved from post to post because of the often haphazard and frustrating nature of overseas assignments, the wife's first responsibility upon arrival at any new post was to find and settle into suitable housing. As Beryl Smedley has stated in her study of the British Foreign Service, "It was a matter of national pride that diplomats should be well-housed." Though the State Department assumed no responsibility for providing its officers with suitable housing, officials still expected that American diplomats and their families should also be "well-housed" in homes that, as the daughter of one former Foreign Service wife explained, "reflected American tastes and customs," in order to most effectively represent the United States overseas.[43] The American home overseas served as an important symbol of American status in the host country. Officials recognized that a wife who finds and "maintains an attractive home" could be "a very real asset to her husband in his task of representing the U.S."[44] Therefore, upon moving to Bucharest in 1919, Kemp was thrilled when she finally found a house with "running water in the dressing room."[45] Such a luxury was important not only for her family's comfort and for the ways in which running water would make it easier to keep an "attractive home," but also because such an amenity was a visible reminder of American prosperity and status. In some remote locations, the homes of American officials might serve as a means of "spreading civilization" or modernization in the same way that Strobel has described the British colonial administrator's home in the "outposts of Empire."[46] Depending on the location, the "American" home was also a key representation of American superiority and sophistication in comparison to the dwellings around it.

Wives quickly learned that their clothing sent similar messages about material prosperity and demonstrated adherence to diplomatic protocol. For instance, Emmerson, who claimed to know "nothing about the Foreign Service" when she married her husband John in 1934, received explicit instructions to "wear a long dress—with train—long sleeves, high neck, hat, gloves, no white, no black" when she was to be presented to the Imperial Family of Japan in 1935. By conforming to these instructions she communicated a message of compliance and goodwill. If she had deviated from protocol in some way, as she once unintentionally did by wearing a dark brown outfit instead of black during mourning for the king of England, she might cause great offense.[47] Wives worried about sending other negative messages with their physical appearance as well, as when O'Shaughnessy worried on the eve of an engagement in Vienna in 1907, "I have of course NOTHING to wear." She meant, of course, that she had nothing *new* to wear to an important social engagement, and she would not want the others in the diplomatic corps to think that the wife of the American Second Secretary did not have enough money to buy new clothes.[48] It was essential that the wife of an American official, in her own representative capacity, maintain her position as a role model. Both feminine clothing and a suitable home served as tangible domestic markers that presented American culture in the most positive manner possible.

Social events held in the home were the primary opportunity to "show off" American culture and prosperity and communicate subtle messages of compliance or disapproval. As Katherine Hughes explained, "Whom a wife invites to the diplomatic residence for tea—or more importantly, whom she does not invite—may or may not reflect her government's policies, but others may perceive that it does."[49] A home that adequately represented the United States also served as an informal but political space for the conduct of diplomacy.[50] As an unofficial space, as Allgor has explained, the home "allows the official players [the diplomats] room to maneuver and negotiate."[51] One observer of the U.S. Foreign Service in 1936 extolled the importance of a "woman's salon" in the home.[52] The more informal nature of the social interactions with wives took some of the pressure off the diplomats and created a more open and friendly environment. A Foreign Service officer relied on his wife to read and interpret both conversations and behavior, and then relay information accurately to him later, since he could not be everywhere at once and because guests would interact differently with his wife than with him. In other words, a Foreign Service wife served in many ways as an extension of her husband. As Briggs explained, "a man who was perhaps not especially gifted was greatly helped by a wife who was friendly and who was interested in what was going on and who was helpful both in personal and professional ways."[53] Cecil Lyon, for instance, relied on his wife, Elsie, to facilitate the exchange of "social and political messages" for him and to "[break] the ice" for him in his new post in Japan, since she had lived there for many years already with her mother and father, and "she had all these Japanese girlfriends" who now "had husbands" with whom Lyon needed to be acquainted in order to do his job as a diplomat.[54]

In their ongoing assessment of Foreign Service officers' social usefulness, specifically their "standing and popularity with the people of the countr[ies] to which [they are] accredited," State Department officials discussed as well their expectations about wives' social activities.[55] They relied on wives to reach out to local women in each host country, and to work with them in local charities and volunteer groups. Because their activities took them into different neighborhoods, wives often knew the local environment, and the locals themselves, better than their husbands who were working all day in the Embassy. As Elizabeth Cabot remembered, when she was in Rio de Janeiro, "I *had* to go to market. I *had* to move around [her emphasis] . . . it made you link up with people."[56] Jordan was commended, in fact, for her particular success in "socializing with the natives."[57] Matthews explained that when she and her husband were in Australia in the 1930s she "was with the Australians much of the time . . . That's what you want to do. That's what you are there for."[58] American Foreign Service wives were therefore seen as role models for the native population, especially the women, with whom they interacted on a regular basis through volunteer work and social calls.

Wives generally divulged few particulars, however, about the volunteer work they performed in the local communities and their other interactions with the locals. Briggs acknowledged that the work was "a very satisfying way to spend your time" but gave few details about the work she performed. Her subsequent comments reveal slightly more about her role. "You're not only helping other people," she stated, "but you're doing the right thing by your husband," and "you're making the Americans welcome."[59] A wife's volunteer activities were more than simple charity. The greater importance was the prestige she brought to her husband and to her position as a role model because her good deeds helped to make Americans "welcome" in the local community. Because there was so much emphasis on creating positive perceptions, however, wives were quite limited in what they could say about a host country or people. As Catherine Cluett remembered, "Regardless of the country, never say you do not like the people."[60] If a wife complained or allowed any classified information to become public, it could be not only embarrassing but potentially dangerous either to American policy or to her husband's career. Another wife remarked, "You have to be very guarded" and "very careful about what you say. You can't give your feelings freely." Sometimes it was easier for wives to pretend they had no interest in or ability to engage in political discourse, as when Emmerson claimed that she "didn't know enough to participate . . . in political discussion." Equally implausibly, she insisted that her husband shared "classified" information with her only once in his entire career, so that she would not have to carry the "burden" of secrecy.[61] The hesitancy to voice political opinions, and the instinct to protect her husband's reputation, remained strong for most wives even many years after retiring from the Service. This reticence limits our understanding of American Foreign Service wives' perceptions of the native populations they encountered, but gives us more insight into the pressure American wives felt as role models.

As a result of this reluctance, very few former Foreign Service wives have written publicly about their lives.[62] The voices of most other former Foreign Service wives have remained largely silent until the Foreign Service Spouse Oral History Program, initiated by the Association of American Foreign Service Women (AAFSW), began in 1986 to interview former Foreign Service spouses.[63] The shared experiences between most interviewers, themselves either current or former Foreign Service wives, and their subjects have given us interview transcripts that are rich in detail, but also reflective of the AAFSW desire to record for the first time the specific kinds of experiences and responsibilities that are absent from the current record. Interviewers therefore steer the conversations to subject home life overseas, travel, the culture and physical landscape of people they encountered overseas, the role of women in different their duties as homemakers, entertaining, volunteer activity, and their children. They seldom ask wives to elaborate on the politics of each post, unless there was a specific crisis—wartime evacuation, revolution, controversial election—and even then, wives focused more on explaining the logistical arrangements that were necessary to weather each storm, only rarely commenting on American policy. While their apparent lack of political engagement in these interviews could be largely attributed to the lingering reticence about discussing politics in public, they also reflected the goals of the AAFSW interviewers, who were interested in showing what wives really did all day long, rather than in rehashing American policy in each post. Wives' opinions about the politics of each situation, or the diplomatic relationship between the United States and each country, are therefore less important than understanding their roles as political players in each specific context. Wives knew their influence did not come through formal discussion of policy. Their political influence, they understood, came much more subtly through their social, domestic, and representational duties and responsibilities.

In each American mission overseas, for instance, wives juggled the personalities and needs unique to each location, playing the diplomatic version of "office politics." Yvonne Jordan arrived in Helsinki in 1922, for example, as the wife of a vice-consul, a very low level position in the Foreign Service hierarchy that should not have required her to play a leading role in the Legation's social life, only to find that she would in fact have to assume a large number of responsibilities since the new American minister in Finland was, as Jordan remembered, "a political appointee from Beloit, Kansas" who had no experience in diplomatic activity and "had never been away" from the United States. "He knew nothing about etiquette, absolutely nothing," Jordan continued, "and he knew nothing about diplomatic life either." His wife came to Helsinki only for a short visit, and then returned to the United States, leaving her husband without a hostess. Since both Jordan and her husband judged the American minister incompetent, her husband took over many of his official duties at the Legation and Jordan "did all his entertaining" and "arrang[ed] all his dinner parties."[64] Everyone, from State Department officials to the American minister to Jordan herself, simply assumed that she would take responsibility for managing the important social aspects of the minister's job and that she would do so with tact and grace, without causing any jealousies or ill will. It was common, in fact, for the wives of other officers at the same post to have to "fill in" as official hostess for bachelor officers.[65] The Jordans reflect here a common complaint among the lower ranking career officers—that the political appointees to high-ranking positions were rarely competent in their conduct of the job, leaving the underpaid and largely unappreciated career men and their wives to pick up the pieces. Naomi Matthews, a young wife in her second post at Sydney, Australia in 1937, found herself in a situation similar to Jordan's when "the wife of the consul was ill and not active much of the time." Matthews was called upon to assume responsibility for many social functions. She concluded that "to be so involved at that age made it very interesting and very exciting," even though she was under the "close scrutiny" of the consul general himself.[66]

Normally, were it not for her illness, it would have been the consul's wife and not the consul himself who would have kept a close eye on Matthews. By custom and practice, since there was no formal protocol training for new Foreign Service wives, the senior-ranking wives trained younger wives in matters of protocol, social etiquette, logistics, and living conditions at different posts.[67] While some wives remembered serving under kind and competent senior wives, it was still widely observed among the junior ranks that there were a rather large number of "some pretty frightful," "difficult," or "unreasonable" women who "tended to terrify the wives of the young officers."[68] Elsie Grew Lyon remembered that there were "always wives who would . . . put you down a few notches" while Matthews acknowledged that such women could "make a young wife miserable," but saw no sense in complaining about it because "it doesn't last forever" and because such mistreatment by these women would hopefully teach younger women "how not to be" when they reached that point in their career. Lucy Briggs said she was "lucky" because she "never had to serve under a very domineering wife."[69]

There was indeed a chasm separating the senior wives from the younger wives that reflected the hierarchical nature of the Foreign Service and created relationships of power and authority between the wives. While senior wives enjoyed status, some security, positions of leadership, and the material benefits of high rank, they also generally carried the most pressing responsibilities. As one longtime Foreign Service wife remembered, "No party is considered a complete success unless the highest ranking officer is at least represented," which meant that "his wife is often called upon to substitute for him."[70] As her husband's prestige grew with increasing rank, the wife was called upon more often to serve as his representative. Some theories about women and work suggest that wives with more duties and responsibilities directly related to their husbands' careers were the most "fulfilled," but many Foreign Service wives looked at the situation more realistically, acknowledging that senior wives had the more difficult and stressful positions (which might account at least partly for their sometimes notoriously bad behavior toward younger wives).[71] Life at the top could be lonely. Many senior wives felt keenly the pressure of the spotlight, which they often referred to as the "goldfish bowl," where "you've got to be so careful" not to offend anyone. Lyon explained, for instance, that "you can't have close ties with people in the Embassy or you're playing favorites."[72] The perception that the American mission treated some members of the diplomatic community better than others could send misleading or even dangerous messages about the relative status of various representatives of different countries.

Foreign Service wives had to avoid not only the jealousies and misunderstandings that could arise between representatives of different countries, but were also responsible for, as one wife described it, "preserving harmony within the official [State Department] family" by keeping a "motherly eye" on the younger wives.[73] Indeed, the role of motherhood and the metaphor of the "official family" were important for defining the wife's roles in the Foreign Service within a nonthreatening discourse of domesticity. Wives regularly, and with enthusiasm, referred to Foreign Service life before World War II as "one big family" where "you sort of knew everybody."[74] Lyon understood better than many the notion of family and duty in the Foreign Service since she and her sisters all grew up in a Foreign Service family headed by Joseph and Alice Grew. It was no coincidence that Lyon and her sisters all married Foreign Service officers, for they all knew exactly what kind of life they wanted. As Lyon's sister Lilla Grew Moffat later remarked, growing up in the service gave them excellent training for "the responsibilities and obligations and duties" of the Foreign Service.[75] As the Grew family understood, childbearing and childrearing were important aspects of the work of representation, for children sent positive and healthy messages out to each host country about American prosperity. Alvah has noted, for instance, that the decision to send military families abroad after World War II reflects "assumptions about women and children as representatives of American understanding and goodwill abroad."[76] In order to complete the job of representation, American diplomats overseas needed to exhibit the ideal American family.

Ironically, because of their many other duties, Foreign Service wives rarely had time to care for their children themselves. As Jordan stated simply, "It was difficult to care for a child" while juggling all her other responsibilities.[77] Many wives exhibited frustrations typical of working mothers, such as the difficulty of finding adequate child care. A nurse or a nanny was necessary so the wife could be free to engage in social activities at all hours of the day and night. One wife was "desperate" to find a nanny two weeks before departing for Buenos Aires "because social life was so intense down there." Another wife in Lima warned Dorothy Emmerson when she arrived, "If you stay in Lima you will not take care of them [her children] because the social life will be extra-ordinarily heavy."[78] The nanny was essential in order to allow wives to perform their social duties, but the nanny was also a matter of American prestige, as was the presence of other domestic servants in the American mission.

The domestic work associated with the conduct of diplomacy could never have happened without the help of native servants. Wives in American missions overseas assumed full responsibility for the hiring, firing, and supervision of servants because they supposedly possessed, as one former Foreign Service wife explained, the "exquisite tact, infinite patience and eternal vigilance" necessary for handling servants most effectively.[79]

(Certainly, these were some of the very same qualities that enabled wives to interact with other diplomats, guests, and officials so effectively at the endless social gatherings.) Many of their supervisory duties, and the difficulties about which they complained, mirrored the experiences of middle-class and upper-class women in the United States, many of whom still lived with domestic servants in their homes in the first few decades of the twentieth century. Women who were running households, whether supervising one or two servants or a whole houseful, invariably complained about the increasing difficulty of finding and retaining competent servants no matter where they lived.[80] Women in the United States specifically complained about the difficulty of finding white, native-born American servants, and were forced to rely either on the labor of black women in the South or immigrant women, most often Irish, in other parts of the United States. Lucy Salmon, who wrote a well-known study of American domestic service at the end of the nineteenth century, noted many of the "difficulties" the "average family" encountered when "assimilating into its domestic life those who are of a different nationality and who consequently hold different industrial, social, religious, and political beliefs."[81] Imagine, then, the difficulties faced by American women who tried to "assimilate" their indigenous servants into an American household in Latin America, India, China, or even Europe.

As Strobel and others have shown, responsibility for servant management in foreign countries could be terribly complex.[82] Yet this responsibility fell directly on the wives, who usually had to "train" their servants to run the house, cook and serve the food, and attend to the family in the proper "American" fashion, thus revealing American domestic superiority. Most servants spoke little English, and few Foreign Service officers (and none of their wives) received any formal language training before taking their new posts, though many wives had studied languages, and others took the initiative to begin to learn new languages when they became engaged to young diplomats. Even if wives were adept at learning new languages, as many of them claimed to be, some had a much easier task than others. Could Kemp really expect to learn "Rumanian" before her arrival in Bucharest? Jordan struggled with Finnish, before giving up and declaring it "a fiendish language."[83] In fact, many wives learned languages more quickly than their husbands, primarily as a result of their intimate daily interaction with their servants. Briggs did not speak any Spanish before going to Peru, but quickly learned to say in Spanish "you must" in order to run the new household and establish her authority with the servants.[84] But the language barrier was not the worst of the cultural problems. Jordan managed eleven household servants in India in the late 1930s, an especially difficult task due to the complicated caste system that strictly dictated the tasks each servant could perform. "Everything was regulated," Jordan recalled, and she had to master the rules in order to "give out the orders" every morning.[85] Another longtime Foreign Service wife noted that supervising the servants was often "in itself a full time job."[86]

Many young Foreign Service wives complained about their servants in an effort to cover up their insecurities, admitting only later that they had initially been very uncomfortable supervising servants. As the daughter of a prominent lawyer in New Rochelle, New York, Briggs had "grown up with servants," but she had "never handled servants [her]self."[87] Many young Foreign Service wives in the 1920s and 1930s, including Briggs, relied on childhood observations of their mothers, their intuition, and perhaps a popular guidebook or ladies' magazine article to help them negotiate the highly personal servant-mistress relationship when they set up their own households.[88] Some young wives also turned to their more senior colleagues, who generally taught them an aspect of diplomatic protocol that Arlie Hochschild has referred to as a "technical message system" or "subterranean communication." This kind of communication with servants through prearranged hand signals or eye contact with trusted servants would enable wives to orchestrate the kinds of large dinner parties expected of important American officials.[89] No wonder Emmerson claimed that supervising servants was, for her, "the most difficult part of the Foreign Service."[90] Servants were, after all, a very visible part of any American home at which diplomatic functions were hosted. The maintenance of the home, and of American prestige and status, depended in part on the visibility and efficiency of those servants working under the supervision of American wives.

Whether these wives working overseas found "trusted" servants or struggled mightily to find good help, they universally reflected the cultural, class, and racial stereotypes evident in an anonymous tongue-in-cheek 1923 article in the *American Consular Bulletin* entitled "A Consul's Wife: An Efficiency Report by One Who Knows." In this brief essay, a new young diplomat's wife "went halfway round the world to take charge of an oriental household of fourteen turbaned and mostly bearded servants."[91] In their unavoidable interactions with servants, wives were thrust into formal positions of authority that added to the burden of perceived racial and class superiority in most parts of the world, while living in a foreign culture about which they understood little. They had always to maintain a distance from the servants. They often covered their fear of the unknown and anxiety about their abilities with predictable stereotypes about domestic servants who were either earnest but inept, or totally incompetent. Matthews, for instance, complimented her servants because they "liked activity" even though they "needed attention, lots of attention," while Kemp remembered in Budapest that "my new cook and maid come tonight and Sunday I hope to have eight for dinner. I trust this maid can serve without dropping everything she touches."[92] Similar complaints were common in the United States, of course, but the stakes were perhaps not quite so high as in the foreign environments where wives' success at "handling" their servants reflected directly on their abilities as models of American domesticity and as unofficial representatives of the U.S. government.

Most of the former Foreign Service wives described in this study went on to long and successful careers in the Foreign Service, followed by active and generally happy retirements. Matthews, Lyon, and Briggs eventually became "ambassadresses," an invented term that nonetheless conveyed an important professional status on the wife of an ambassador. Emmerson became the wife of a minister, Kemp became the wife of a consul general, and the Jordans had a long and successful career in a variety of consular and diplomatic posts. Only O'Shaugnessy left the Foreign Service after an abbreviated tenure when her husband retired from the Service in 1916. While her husband used his training in the law to move into another career, O'Shaugnessy used her experiences as a diplomat's wife to write her well-received book about Mexico in 1916. The book briefly transformed O'Shaugnessy into an authority on Mexico. In the 1916 presidential campaign, she used this political expertise to campaign against President Woodrow Wilson, whose Mexican policies she criticized vehemently.[93] This brief period of political activism was followed by a career of some minor success as an author of fiction in the 1920s.

All of the wives surveyed here, even O'Shaughnessy, saw their quasi-official positions in the Foreign Service as positions of considerable importance and authority. Their work for the Foreign Service gave them status and visibility because a wife's actions, including her choice of wardrobe, her seating of guests at dinner parties, and her "manner toward them," served as a conduit for political messages between diplomats that fell under the radar of official government communication but conveyed, nevertheless, important information.[94] Between 1905 and 1941, many American Foreign Service wives spoke explicitly about their "careers" in the Foreign Service. A scholarly study of the U.S. Foreign Service in 1936 also recognized that wives played important roles in diplomatic posts, indicating that officials in Washington and abroad expected wives would not only oversee the "domestic affairs" of officers, but would also "contribute to the intellectual and social brilliance of the [American] Embassy by attracting people of distinction through her personality and charm."[95] A wife's smooth management of her traditional domestic and social responsibilities—home, family, and entertaining—was therefore crucial for establishing and maintaining American representation in diplomatic missions all over the world.

Notes

Molly M. Wood is associate professor of history at Wittenberg University in Springfield, Ohio, where she teaches U.S. history, U.S. foreign relations, and women's history. She is currently working on a manuscript exploring the roles of women and children in the U.S. Foreign Service. She can be contacted at mwood@wittenberg.edu

1. Francis Keene to Florence Keene, May 25, 1914, Box 3, Keene Papers, Manuscripts Division, Library of Congress, Washington DC.
2. Earl Packer, oral history interview, Foreign Service Oral History Project, Special Collections, Launiger Library, Georgetown University, transcript, p. 23, hereafter FSHOP; and Willard Beaulac, *Career Ambassador* (New York: The Macmillan Company, 1951), 181.

3. Graham Stuart, *American Diplomatic and Consular Practice* (New York: D. Appleton-Century, 1936), 275.

4. See the 1972 Directive reproduced in Homer Calkin, *Women in the Department of State: Their Role in Foreign Affairs* (Washington, DC: Department of State, 1977), Appendix 1.

5. See, for example, Personnel Evaluations, Records of the Foreign Service Personnel Board, 1924–1934, Report of the Board of Review, 1925–1926, Diplomatic Branch, General Records of the U.S. Department of State, RG 59, Stack 250, National Archives, College Park, MD, hereafter GR.

6. Ten years earlier, in 1895, President Grover Cleveland instituted exams for low-level consular officials, but until 1924 the consular and diplomatic services within the Foreign Service remained separate, so Cleveland's Executive Order did not apply to those in the diplomatic service. For more background see Lawrence Gelfand, "Towards a Merit System for the American Diplomatic Service, 1900–1930," *Irish Studies in International Affairs* 2, no. 4 (1988): 49–63; Martin Weil, *A Pretty Good Club* (New York: W. W. Norton, 1978), 21; Rachel West, *The Department of State on the Eve of the First World War* (Athens, GA: University of Georgia Press, 1978); Henry Mattox, *The Twilight of Amateur Diplomacy* (Kent, OH: Kent State University Press, 1989).

7. Minutes of June 24, 1924 meeting, Records of the Foreign Service Personnel Board, 1924, Diplomatic Branch, GR.

8. Mary Procida, *Married to the Empire: Gender, Politics and Imperialism, 1883–1947* (New York: Manchester University Press, 2002), 5. See also Margaret Strobel, *European Women and the Second British Empire* (Bloomington, IN: University of Indiana Press, 1991). On military women see Donna Alvah, " 'Unofficial Ambassadors': American Military Families Overseas and Cold War Foreign Relations, 1945–1965" (PhD diss., University of California at Davis, 2000), 1.

9. See, for example, Edward Crapol, ed., *Women and American Foreign Policy*, 2d ed. (Wilmington, DE: Scholarly Resources, 1992); Jane Hunter, *The Gospel of Gentility* (New Haven, CT: Yale University Press, 1984); and Harriet Alonso, *Peace as a Woman's Issue* (Syracuse, NY: Syracuse University Press, 1993).

10. See Joan Scott, *Gender and the Politics of History* (New York: Columbia University Press, 1988). On gender and U.S. foreign relations, see Cynthia Enloe, *Bananas, Beaches and Bases: Making Feminist Sense of International Politics* (Berkeley, CA: University of California Press, 1990), and *Maneuvers: The International Politics of Militarizing Women's Lives* (Berkeley, CA: University of California Press, 2000). See also Emily Rosenberg, "Gender," *Journal of American History* 77 (June 1990): 116–24; Andrew Rotter, "Gender Relations, Foreign Relations: The United States and South Asia, 1947–1964," *Journal of American History* 81, no. 2 (1994): 518–42; Emily Rosenberg, "Consuming Women: Images of Americanization in the 'American Century,'" *Diplomatic History* 23, no. 3 (1999): 479–97; and Frank Costigliola, "The Nuclear Family: Tropes of Gender and Pathology in the Western Alliance," *Diplomatic History* 21, no. 2 (1997): 163–83.

11. See Strobel, *European Women and the Second British Empire*; Procida, *Married to the Empire*; Ann Stoler, "Rethinking Colonial Categories: European Communities and the Boundaries of Rule," *Comparative Studies in Society and History* 31, no. 1 (1989): 134–61, and "Making Empire Respectable: The Politics of Race and Sexual Morality in 20th Century Colonial Cultures," *American Ethnologist* 16, no. 4 (1989): 634–60; Antoinette Burton, *Burdens of History: British Feminists, Indian Women and Imperial Culture, 1865–1915* (Chapel Hill, NC: University of North Carolina Press, 1994); and Laura Wexler, *Tender Violence: Domestic Visions in an Age of U.S. Imperialism* (Chapel Hill, NC: University of North Carolina Press, 2000).

12. See, for example, Richard Hume Werking, *The Master Architects* (Lexington, KY: University of Kentucky Press, 1977).
13. Beaulac, *Career Ambassador*, 134.
14. John Foster, *The Practice of Diplomacy* (Boston: Houghton Mifflin, 1906), 6; and Beaulac, *Career Ambassador*, 20.
15. Hilary Callen, "The Premise of Dedication: Notes towards an Ethnography of Diplomat's Wives," in *Perceiving Women*, ed. Shirley Ardener (New York: John Wiley and Sons, 1975), 89.
16. Arlie Hochschild, "The Role of the Ambassador's Wife: An Exploratory Study," *Journal of Marriage and the Family* 31, no. 1 (1969): 76.
17. The literature on women and politics is voluminous. See, for example, Maureen Flanagan, "Gender and Urban Political Reform," *American Historical Review* 95 (October 1990): 1032–50; Melanie Gustafson, "Partisan Women in the Progressive Era," *Journal of Women's History* 9 (Summer 1997): 8–30; and Louise Tilly and Patricia Gurin, eds., *Women, Politics and Change* (New York: Russell Sage Foundation, 1990).
18. Flanagan, "Gender and Urban Political Reform," 1033n7; Alvah, "Unofficial Ambassadors," 88; and Catherine Allgor, *Parlor Politics* (Charlottesville, VA: University Press of Virginia, 2000), 1. Karen Blair has coined the term "domestic feminism" to refer to the extension of women's domestic traits into the public sphere in *The Clubwoman as Feminist* (New York: Holmes and Meier Publishers, 1980).
19. Burton, *Burdens of History*, 12; and Strobel, *European Women and the Second British Empire*, 17.
20. Mildred Ringwalt, interview transcript, Associates of the American Foreign Service Worldwide, Special Collections, Lauinger Library, Georgetown University, Washington DC, 13, hereafter AAFSW. Beginning in 1986, the Associates of the American Foreign Service Worldwide (AAFSW), a nonprofit organization founded in 1960 to represent Foreign Service spouses, employees, and retirees, conducted hundreds of interviews with Foreign Service spouses, mostly wives. Copies of these interview transcripts are housed in Special Collections at Georgetown University's Lauinger Library (Washington, DC) as part of their Foreign Service Oral History Project. I am grateful to the Special Collections staff at Georgetown for giving me access to these transcripts when they were still uncataloged. I must express my gratitude as well to Jewell Fenzi, author of *Married to the Foreign Service: An Oral History of the American Diplomatic Spouse* (New York: Twayne, 1994) for her generous personal correspondence, and to Margaret Teich for her help at the AAFSW office in Washington DC. The original interview transcripts are now located at the Association for Diplomatic Studies and Training in Arlington, Virginia.
21. Dagmar Kane, AAFSW, 3.
22. Lucy Briggs, AAFSW, 1–2.
23. There is, of course, a valid argument to be made for the existence of an informal American empire during this period, and certainly there were military missions abroad as well. See Wexler, *Tender Violence*, 52 for a discussion of the "salutary nature of American domesticity and the benign influence of the domestic woman."
24. Dorothy Emmerson, AAFSW, 31; and Naomi Matthews, AAFSW, 11.
25. Many wives use similar language to describe their roles. The text quoted here reflects the reading of numerous interview transcripts. On British wives, see Procida, *Married to the Empire*, 1.
26. Matthews, AAFSW, 4, 11, and 13.
27. Hannah Pampanek as quoted in Eliza Pavalko and Glen Elder, "Women behind the Men," *Gender and Society* 7, no. 4 (1993): 548, 557.
28. Ruth Little, AAFSW, 6.

29. Hilda Lewis, AAFSW, 7; and Enloe, *Bananas, Beaches and Bases*, 96.

30. Foster, *The Practice of Diplomacy*, 115.

31. "Diplomats' Wives Win Hostess Disputes as Roosevelt Bans Chiefs Naming Cousins," *New York Times*, January 12, 1936, 1.

32. See 1907 inspection form quoted in Werking, *Master Architects*, 110.

33. See Personnel Evaluations, Records of the Foreign Service Personnel Board, 1924–1934, Report of the Board of Review, 1925–1926, Diplomatic Branch, GR.

34. Beatrice Russell, *Living in State* (New York: D. McKay, 1959), 83–84; and Hochschild, "The Role of the Ambassador's Wife," 85.

35. Molly Wood, "An American Diplomat's Wife in Mexico" (PhD diss., University of South Carolina, 1998). Allgor has used the term "social work" to describe these interactions in her study of Washington women in the late eighteenth and early nineteenth centuries. See Allgor, *Parlor Politics*.

36. Briggs, AAFSW, 5.

37. Wood, "An American Diplomat's Wife in Mexico," 63–64.

38. Anna Kemp, AAFSW, 1–2 and 33–39.

39. See, for example, Eric Leed, *The Mind of the Traveler* (New York: Basic Books, 1991) for a discussion of the status and expertise conferred upon travelers. The comparison between Foreign Service wives and other women travelers, such as missionaries, is useful for understanding the ways in which American women lived and worked in foreign environments. Because of their semiofficial status, however, and their primary identity as "wives," a more compelling parallel can be drawn with military wives. I am grateful to Donna Alvah for discussions on this topic.

40. Jewell Fenzi, quoted in Elsie Lyon, AAFSW, 10; and Matthews, AAFSW, 8.

41. Yvonne Jordan, AAFSW, 1–2.

42. Ibid., 5. Legislation allowing for travel expenses for families had been passed in 1919, but this money was not yet readily available to most Foreign Service families.

43. Kemp, AAFSW, 52.

44. Beryl Smedley, *Partners in Diplomacy* (London: The Harley Press, 1991), 90; and William Barnes and John Heath Morgan, *The Foreign Service of the U.S.: Origins, Development and Functions* (Washington, DC: Department of State, Historical Office, Bureau of Public Affairs, 1961), 326.

45. Kemp, AAFSW, 40–41.

46. Strobel, *European Women and the Second British Empire*, 17.

47. Emmerson, AAFSW, 1a. Emmerson claimed she did not own a black dress and that the senior wife told her to "go home and stay there until I got a black dress."

48. Wood, "An American Diplomat's Wife in Mexico," 62.

49. Hughes, *Accidental Diplomat*, 16–17.

50. See Fenzi, *Married to the Foreign Service*, 131. See also Strobel's description of women's household responsibilities in the context of the British Empire. Unlike military wives who were housed on military bases, diplomats were responsible for obtaining their own housing.

51. Allgor, *Parlor Politics*, 88–89. See also Enloe, *Bananas, Beaches and Bases*, 97.

52. Stuart, *American Diplomatic and Consular Practice*, 275.

53. Briggs, AAFSW, 1.

54. Ambassador Cecil B. Lyon, oral history interview, October 26 and 27, 1988, FSOHP.

55. Copy of circular no. 14336, June 19, 1908, Department of State, Box 1, O'Shaughnessy Family Papers, New York Public Library, New York.

56. Elizabeth Cabot, AAFSW, 8–9.

57. Jordan, AAFSW, 21.

58. Matthews, AAFSW, 8.

59. Briggs, AAFSW, 16.
60. Cluett, AAFSW, 2.
61. Briggs, AAFSW, 3; Jean Vance, AAFSW, 34; and Emmerson, AAFSW, 28.
62. O'Shaughnessy, who in 1916 published *A Diplomat's Wife in Mexico*, is one exception.
63. Fenzi, *Married to the Foreign Service*, xviii.
64. Jordan, AAFSW, 4 and 17.
65. Very occasionally, a bachelor Foreign Service officer might have another female relative—a sister or mother—serve as his official hostess. The small number of female Foreign Service Officers who served in the 1920s and 1930s were required to be unmarried and clearly posed a dilemma for the State Department officials.
66. Matthews, AAFSW, 6.
67. As Jewell Fenzi has noted, the first official handbook for social matters, "Social Usage in the Foreign Service," was not printed by the Department of State until 1957. *Married in the Foreign Service*, 18.
68. See, for instance, Matthews, AAFSW, 19.
69. Matthews, AAFSW, 19; and Briggs, AAFSW, 30.
70. Russell, *Living in State*, 84.
71. Pavalko and Elder, "Women Behind the Men," 548.
72. Elsie Lyon, AAFSW, 24.
73. Russell, *Living in State*, 84.
74. Matthews, AAFSW, 5.
75. Lilla Grew Moffat, AAFSW, 40.
76. Alvah, "Unofficial Ambassadors," 99.
77. Jordan, AAFSW, 8.
78. Cabot, AAFSW, 11; and Emmerson, AAFSW, 19.
79. Russell, *Living in State*, 48.
80. Katzman, *Seven Days a Week* (New York: Oxford University Press, 1978), 223–24. The numbers of domestic servants in the United States were beginning to fall by the 1920s and 1930s.
81. Lucy Salmon, *Domestic Service* (New York: Arno Press, 1972).
82. Strobel, *European Women and the Second British Empire*, 22.
83. Jordan, AAFSW, 8; and Kemp, AAFSW, 42.
84. Briggs, AAFSW, 17.
85. Jordan, AAFSW, 31–32.
86. Fenzi quoted in Jordan, AAFSW, 31.
87. Emmerson, AAFSW, 22; and Briggs, AAFSW, 86.
88. Katzman, *Seven Days a Week*, 153.
89. Hochschild, "The Role of the Ambassador's Wife," 74n5, 86.
90. Emmerson, AAFSW, 22.
91. *American Consular Bulletin* 5, no. 1 (1923): 8.
92. Kemp, AAFSW, 61; and Matthews, AAFSW, 21.
93. For a full account see Wood, "An American Diplomat's Wife in Mexico," chap. 5.
94. Hochschild, "The Role of the Ambassador's Wife," 79.
95. Stuart, *American Diplomatic and Consular Practice*, 274–75.

Chapter 8

The Flying Machine in the Garden: Parks and Airports, 1918–1938

Janet R. Daly Bednarek

From *Technology and Culture*

Late in the evening of the last day of March 2003, Mayor Richard Daley ordered bulldozers onto the runways at Meigs Field, Chicago's lakefront general aviation airport. By early morning the heavy equipment had carved large X's into the runways, dramatically marking them as closed to air traffic. Though Daley may have hoped this would be the last act in a long conflict with airport supporters, in a last-ditch effort to save the field, a group called Friends of Meigs hastily developed a plan for the dual use of the site as an airport and park. In their proposed scenario, Mayor Daley could have his long-sought lakefront park, and pilots could continue to use the airport, conveniently located near Chicago's downtown. But the Park District of Chicago rejected the proposal in July 2003, seemingly sealing the fate of Meigs Field.

If the effort to promote the dual use of that stretch of Chicago's lakefront as an airport-park seemed perhaps an act of desperation, it nonetheless had historical precedent. In the 1920s, as cities across the country first began to build airports, park officials often took the lead. In some cases they did so in the absence of enabling legislation. In others, states passed laws that formalized initial municipal efforts to respond to aviation developments. The use of parkland for airports and of parks departments or commissions to manage airports sparked a lively debate among park executives, recreation supporters, city planners, and aviation experts between 1928 and 1930. That debate involved long-standing tensions over definitions of the term "park" and was complicated by uncertainty about the future of aviation.

The story of the connection between airports and parks during the 1920s and 1930s weaves together a number of threads in the history of land use and the history of technology. Arguments for dual-use airport-parks highlight a point articulated by Leo Marx in his classic work *The Machine in the Garden*: though some saw conflict in the introduction of technology into natural or naturalistic settings, many Americans welcomed the machine into the garden.[1] Second, as several scholars have pointed out, certain technologies have inspired both utilitarian and nonutilitarian uses. Thus, for example, Cyril Stanley Smith argues that some technologies served artistic purposes before being adopted for more practical applications.[2] And Susan Douglas has noted that the U.S. Navy's early twentieth century efforts to exploit radio technology for military communications were paralleled by a popular movement to adapt the wireless to personal use.[3] The social construction of a technology often involves dialogue between alternate visions, and though one vision may become dominant, the others need not disappear. As Douglas pointed out, radio certainly is most identified with its more practical military and commercial applications, but ham radio operators continue to thrive.

Almost from the beginning, those involved in aviation foresaw practical military uses for the airplane. But on the civilian side competing visions emerged. From the earliest exhibition flyers through the barnstormers and Hollywood scriptwriters, aviation was presented to the public as a form of entertainment. Beginning in the 1920s, however, other aviation boosters, including industry figures and government officials, began working to change its image from one that emphasized thrills and daring to one focused on safety and efficiency that could support commercial applications. By the late 1930s, and certainly by World War II, this second, more utilitarian vision had risen to dominance.[4]

The debate over the nature of the airplane influenced thinking about airports. The vision of the airplane as an entertainment or recreational technology made the use of parkland for airports seem reasonable. When commercial air travel was in its infancy, a significant majority of the American public experienced aviation as a special event—the arrival in town of a famed aviator, an air show or an air race, or other forms of exhibition flying. Additionally, cities wishing to establish airports found it expedient to use their existing power to acquire land for parks. Only as it became more apparent that airplanes would become a form of regular transportation did the plausibility of the airport-park connection diminish. By that time, the late 1930s and early 1940s, the ownership and management of airports was shifting to other organizations, such as airport authorities. The early connection between airports and parks, however, provides an insight into the period when aviation was young and its future still unfolding.

This article will explore the relationship between parks and airports in the 1920s and 1930s. It begins by examining the transformation of the definition of a park from an idealized rural landscape to a location for multiple forms of recreation, both active and passive. Next, it explores the debate over whether airports fit within that new definition. It then outlines the legal framework in which local aviation boosters could employ a city's power to acquire parkland for an airport. The focus then shifts to two case studies: Omaha, Nebraska, and Minneapolis, Minnesota. During the 1920s and 1930s local factors played perhaps the most important role in determining the pattern of airport development. While wider influences—such as the passage of the Air Commerce Act, Charles Lindbergh's celebrated flight, and the work of the Bureau of Air Commerce—certainly set important parameters, local political, economic, and legal conditions shaped decisions. Omaha and Minneapolis represent opposite extremes on a continuum of action during this time period. In Omaha, the link between parks and the airport was important but short-lived, as park officials proved unable to rapidly develop the airport. In Minneapolis it remained in place until 1944, as the park board proved highly capable of managing the facility. In both cases, however, local officials clearly accepted a recreational function for their airports.

The Meaning of Parks

From the time U.S. cities established the first great urban parks in the 1850s until the present, people have argued over what constituted a proper park purpose.[5] Frederick Law Olmsted and Calvert Vaux, designers of New York City's Central Park, envisioned their creation as the antithesis of the city, a completely naturalistic landscape that brought the benefits of a healthful, rural environment to urban dwellers. Exposure to this type of environment, they believed, would provide needed rest to the urban elite and social and moral uplift to the lower classes. Monumental buildings and imposing statuary had no place in this idealized rural landscape. Even as construction of the park began, however, other voices emerged to argue that inspiring parks needed exactly the types of monumental structures the Olmsted-Vaux design banned. Parks, they argued, should have grand ceremonial entrances and house museums and other educational institutions. By the end of the nineteenth century, still others argued that while the passive forms of recreation offered in the Olmsted-Vaux vision had value, city dwellers, especially those of the working class, needed more vigorous recreation. Baseball and other types of organized sports would not only promote health and fitness, but also teach important values, such as fair play and teamwork.[6]

The transformative results of these debates can be seen in the history of Central Park. When the park first opened, both its design and its location on the edge of the city dictated that it would be used primarily by the city's elites. Though, as noted, certain individuals pushed for inclusion of monumental structures and other elements not in keeping with the Olmsted-Vaux vision, for the most part, the park initially reflected the original naturalistic design. Over time, however, the park became more accessible to a greater cross section of the city's population, and later generations of patrons pushed for new facilities. Gradually the park came to include such amenities as baseball diamonds, restaurants, museums, and a zoo. It also changed to accommodate the automobile.[7]

Active recreation represented perhaps the most significant point in the ongoing debate over parks in the first third of the twentieth century. In 1928 the Playground and Recreation Association of America and the American Institute of Park Executives published the results of a major survey of urban parks. Directed by L. H. Weir, a leader in the urban recreation movement, the study began with a survey of park history, which asserted that the rise of the recreation movement had produced a new definition of the urban park. Weir noted that in the 1850s leaders of the park movement, especially Olmsted, had defined parks as places designed to evoke a rural landscape in which city dwellers could enjoy the quiet contemplation of nature—passive recreation. Beginning in the late nineteenth century and progressing during the first quarter of the twentieth, however, many different types of urban open spaces came to be called parks. These included "plazas, squares, ovals, triangles, places, monument sites, promenades, and public gardens" as well as areas dedicated to active recreation, such as golf courses and baseball diamonds. Many parks originally designed according to the Olmsted-Vaux model gradually came to incorporate athletic fields, stadiums, playgrounds, and swimming pools. Weir noted that controversy had often accompanied these changes, but, while acknowledging the value of the ideas of the original park planners, he argued that "the life needs of people which can be expressed in their leisure are far wider than those comprehended in the early conception, and a wide range of active forms of recreation have come to be included." As a result, he concluded, by the late 1920s the term "park" had "come to mean any area of land or water set aside for outdoor recreational purposes, whether it be recreation of a passive or active nature or any of the degrees between those two extremes."[8] It was in the context of this broadened definition that early aviation enthusiasts argued for a connection between airports and parks. Like automobiles, airplanes should also be welcomed into the garden.

Aviation's Early Decades

Early airports were very simple affairs, consisting primarily of large, open, flat, grassy areas. Some had a hangar built along one edge of the field. There were no runways per se, as most fields allowed for all-direction landing. Some did have landing strips, areas where the turf was marked for takeoff and landing, but prepared or paved runways did not appear until the late 1920s. Some airfields had radios and/or telephone service, and those used by the post office gradually acquired lighting. Still, the untrained eye might have had difficulty spotting an airport from the air in the 1920s.

Through most of that decade, aviation remained in many ways a recreational activity. Before the passage of the Air Mail Act of 1925 and the Air Commerce Act of 1926 (the former handing over delivery of airmail to private carriers and the latter establishing regulations for the safe operation of airlines), commercial airlines were not firmly established in the United States.[9] Most people encountered aviation through barnstormers, air racers, or airmail pilots. Military flying also existed, but its public impact was limited and military pilots attracted most attention when participating in air races or various types of long-distance demonstration flights. Barnstormers, on the other hand, traveled the nation thrilling crowds with stunt flying and carrying the adventuresome aloft. Especially in the early 1920s and then again in the 1930s, air races drew huge crowds. The early airmail pilots, pioneering the transcontinental airmail route, emerged as popular heroes. Aviation at this time was largely spectacle, and airport crowds resembled those at the football games and boxing matches so popular in the 1920s.[10]

A 1930 Harvard University study indicated how many people visited airports "on an ordinary day in summer" and "on a week-end in summer." The figures were impressive. A number of cities, including Dallas, Indianapolis, Louisville, Milwaukee, and Minneapolis, reported that ten thousand or more people visited their airports on summer weekends. Dallas's Love Field hosted fifteen to twenty-five thousand on weekends and as many as two thousand "on an ordinary summer day." Yet Dallas reported only six airline arrivals and six departures daily on an average. Obviously, the vast majority of the people visiting the airport were not there as commercial airline passengers. They came because airports and airplanes entertained them (figure 8.1).[11]

Figure 8.1   Charles A. Lindbergh adjusting parachute before testing an experimental airplane, Lambert-St. Louis field, 1925.

Source: Courtesy of the Collections of the Library of Congress.

The park-airport connection also appeared in contemporary city planning documents. The 1929 regional plan for New York City and environs, for example, called for the acquisition of six primary airport sites identified by the Hoover Commission and supported the acquisition of ten additional sites.[12] These recommendations appeared in the part of the plan dedicated to development of open spaces, including country clubs, military reservations, water supply reservations, and public parks as well as airports. The New York planners suggested that parts of the sites acquired for airports could, perhaps, also be used as recreational areas. Further, they noted that sites purchased for airports could be used as parks unless and until they were needed. The planners thus saw airports and parks—or at least recreational open space—as complementary and, to an extent, even interchangeable, though they did recognize the difficulties posed by such dual use.[13]

Further complicating the picture was the fact that airports began to turn to other sorts of recreation—swimming pools, picnic areas, even amusement rides—to generate income. Although managers often looked askance at these uses of the property, airports had trouble operating on a paying basis and needed other sources of income.[14]

Figure 8.2   Washinton-Hoover Airport, looking northeast to the 14th Street Bridge, July 1932. After merging with the nearby Hoover Field in 1930, Washington-Hoover Airport was the first major terminal to be developed in the greater Washington, DC area. The Washington-Hoover Airport site is now part of the property of the Pentagon building.

Source: Historic American Buildings Survey/Historic American Engineering Record, Library of Congress.

The practice of equating airports and parks sparked a sometimes heated debate in the late 1920s and early 1930s. The Harvard University airport study noted that of the forty-seven airports it surveyed, parks departments operated ten, the same number operated by departments of public works. The study's authors tentatively agreed that there were similarities between airport management and park management. Both parks and airports required "a large tract of land [that] must be cleared, graded, drained, surfaced, and landscaped. Structures must be erected and concessions leased or operated, and provisions must be made for the handling of large crowds." Despite the similarities, the report's authors concluded that if airports were to be administered by existing departments of city governments, it was more logical for them to fall under departments of public works, but they qualified their conclusion with the caveat that the decision was "subject of course to special local conditions."[15]

The debate played out more pointedly in the pages of the journal *City Planning*. In January 1930, *City Planning* reprinted a speech by Ulysses S. Grant III, director of public buildings and public parks of the national capital, who argued that parks departments were best qualified to develop and manage airports. Grant's speech drew responses in subsequent issues, some favorable but most opposed to his position. L. H. Weir of the Playground and Recreation Association of America, who in that organization's 1928 study had otherwise supported a broadened definition of parks, was among the critics. Countering the argument that park administrators should respond to the airplane as they had to the automobile, Weir noted that when automobiles were few in number and used largely for purely recreational purposes park administrators had indeed acted to improve existing carriage drives for automobile use. However, once automobiles became a common form of daily transportation, those same administrators began to restrict their use. In the end, while parks departments had provided some early roadways, they had not retained responsibility for the further development of roads and highways. Similarly, although parks had been used as early airfields and some, perhaps, were suitable places for emergency landings, if the airplane was going to become another common form of transportation, it did not make sense for airports to fall under the purview of parks departments.[16]

Gilmore D. Clarke, a landscape architect, and John Nolen, a leading city planner, also wrote to reject the notion that airports should be managed by parks departments, arguing that airports were transportation facilities, not recreational facilities. The editorial board of *City Planning* dismissed the idea as well, also on the grounds that airports were transportation facilities and individuals with expertise in aviation and transportation should manage them. Basically, Clarke, Nolen, and *City Planning* all concluded that parks and airports were not compatible land uses.[17]

In September 1930, Clarence M. Young, the assistant secretary of commerce for aeronautics, weighed in on the issue with an article in *American City*. While noting that both parks and airports were "civic assets" and "essential to a city's present or future well-being—regardless of immediate tangible returns," Young argued that "airports are by no means in the same category as municipal parks." He defined the latter as "mere pleasure centers" while airports were "the very 'highway' terminals through which air travel can flow."[18] Though others arguing against an airport-park connection might have balked at Young's depiction of parks, they surely would have agreed with his definition of airports. And while the future of aviation as a technology was not yet certain, all these critics of the airport-park connection clearly sided with those who anticipated the growth of commercial air transportation.

The Wichita Case

Despite such critics, state legislatures enacted laws that in various ways equated parks with airports. California passed legislation enabling cities and counties to acquire and operate airports in 1927. Not only did the law allow local governments to acquire land for airports, it also permitted them to use previously acquired parkland for airports and explicitly defined an airport as a legitimate park purpose.[19] In the same year, the Illinois legislature permitted local public park commissioners either to use land they already had or to acquire additional land in order to establish simple landing fields—that is, sites where airplanes could take off and land but where they could not be stored, repaired, or fueled. In 1929, the state passed additional legislation allowing parks departments in counties with populations below five hundred thousand to acquire land for the purpose of maintaining and operating airports. The Kentucky legislature in 1928 empowered urban park commissions to use or acquire parkland for airports. In addition, the Kentucky statute specified that the park commission was to set the rules and regulations for any airport it established. And Wisconsin lawmakers in 1927 authorized county park commissions to use or acquire land for airports.[20]

In terms of influence and precedent, the most important developments occurred in Kansas. As early as 1921, that state passed legislation allowing local governments to "acquire by purchase or lease and maintain a municipal field for aviation purposes, and pay the expense of such purchase, lease or maintenance out of the general funds of the city."[21] A problem arose when local aviation boosters in Wichita identified land outside the city limits as the most likely site for a municipal airport. While the city had the power to acquire land for an airport, it could not do so outside the city limits. In 1927, the state legislature passed a law allowing local boards of park commissioners to purchase land beyond city limits for use as parks. The head of the Wichita parks board, L. W. Clapp, apparently an aviation booster himself, declared that an airport could be part of the city's park system. He and the board prepared to move forward on the purchase. The city government, however, opposed the move, and filed a suit against Clapp in a case eventually decided by the Kansas Supreme Court.[22]

In 1928, the court, in an opinion widely reported at the time and frequently cited afterward, not only upheld the legality of the proposed actions of the Wichita Board of Park Commissioners, but also strongly defended the idea that airports constituted a "proper and legitimate" use of parkland. The court determined that "park purposes" had been broadly defined as "race track, bridle trails, boating, waiting room for street cars, baseball diamond, restaurants, museums, conservatories and many other recreational and educational facilities." It declared that while an airport had a commercial aspect, it also had "an important value as a recreation facility similar to city parks, golf courses, equestrian trails, bathing beaches, etc., and it should be a municipal enterprise."[23] The following year, the Kansas state legislature effectively endorsed the court's decision and gave jurisdiction over airports to boards of park commissioners.[24]

In short, by the late 1920s and early 1930s, aviation boosters had plenty of support in law for turning to local parks authorities to establish a municipal airport, though critics of that approach did exist.

Omaha: Finding a Plausible Expedient

Omaha is a case in which aviation boosters exploited the city's authority to purchase parkland to expedite the creation of a municipal airport, something they were able to do because it was seen as plausible by both city government and local courts. Coming in May 1925, Omaha's action followed congressional passage of the Air Mail Act (known also as the Kelly Act) that transferred airmail service from the post office to private companies, but came before any new airmail contracts had been awarded. It also predated by two years the aviation mania that Charles Lindbergh's flight across the Atlantic inspired. And it came well before government policies and technological advances had made commercial passenger aviation much more than the pioneering venture of a few enthusiasts. By convincing the city to purchase parkland without putting the question to a popular vote, civic leaders assured an immediate result despite uncertainty about the extent of public support for aviation in general and a municipal airport in particular. Omaha aviation boosters found city commissioners receptive to the idea that aviation was recreation. And while they hoped to attract one of the new airmail contractors expected to spring up in the wake of the Kelly Act, their first concern was to build an airport for aviation events. Within a short time, again for the sake of expediency, the city shifted responsibility for developing the airfield from the parks department to the street cleaning and maintenance department. Nonetheless, Omaha's municipal airport began as parkland dedicated to aviation.

Like Wichita, Omaha could have acquired land for an airfield under existing law. In 1921 the Nebraska state legislature passed legislation allowing cities of the first or second class (meaning Omaha and Lincoln, the state capital) to acquire land for airports and funding necessary improvements to any such site. The law further authorized the sale of bonds to finance these projects.[25] Despite that legislative authorization and funding, Omaha's first airport came about due to private sector action. Members of the city's Chamber of Commerce established the first public access airport on land owned by another local civic organization. The privately financed AK-SAR-BEN (Nebraska spelled backward) field, west of the city, provided a landing area for the first post office airmail planes. By 1924, however, post office officials had grown dissatisfied with the somewhat remote site. They moved Omaha's airmail service to a military installation, Fort Crook, south of the city in adjacent Sarpy County. Omaha's business leaders reacted negatively to an action that effectively closed the original airport and shifted the city's airmail service to a location not only outside the city, but also outside the county. The following year a committee of local businessmen investigated a number of potential new airport sites within the city limits. They settled on a piece of land north of downtown, near Carter Lake Park. The next step involved financing the purchase and improvement of the land.[26]

The idea of purchasing an airport site using the city's power to acquire parkland first arose at a meeting of the Aerial Transportation Committee of the Omaha Chamber of Commerce.[27] Spearheading the airport drive, this group wanted to avoid a public election over issuing bonds to fund the project. Whether the committee's primary concern was the delay such an election would impose, as suggested in the minutes to the meeting, or a lack of public support (which the razor-thin margin of victory in the eventual vote would confirm) is unclear.[28] It is clear, however, that by the time the Carter Lake site had been selected the group had determined to move forward with convincing the city to purchase the tract as parkland.[29] Though two city commissioners, including the park commissioner, Joseph Hummel, present at a meeting in February 1925, questioned whether the city could legally acquire land for an airport as part of the park system, by March 1925, a majority of the city commission, convinced of the legality of the action, had passed the necessary ordinance. In a message to the commission shortly before the vote, the members of the Aerial Transportation Committee urged immediate action. Their message reflected their own uncertainty over the future of aviation; it noted that even if the Carter Lake site should eventually prove unsuitable for aviation, the land could still be used as a park and would thus prove a good investment.[30]

The city finalized the purchase of the airport site in August 1925. Although some "friendly suits" by landowners remained pending, both the city government and the Chamber of Commerce anticipated that the parks department would soon begin the needed improvements.[31] Hummel, defending the idea that the parks department would take responsibility for the new field, told a local reporter, " 'Aviation is an activity, as golf, tennis, baseball, horseshoes.' "[32]

He was not the only one to assert a link between aviation and recreation. While those who pushed for the establishment of the airport anticipated its use by the airmail service, they also envisioned it as a place to conduct grand public events that would not only inspire a greater "airmindedness" among Omahans, but also promote the city as a center of aviation activity. Over the next two years, however, the link between airports and parks would collapse locally, as Omaha's parks department failed to complete the airfield.

Work began in early 1926 and proceeded slowly throughout that first year. Before the work was completed, members of the Chamber of Commerce made plans to host an event to promote the new airport. In May 1926, Commander Richard Byrd announced that he had circled the North Pole in a Fokker Trimotor piloted by Floyd Bennett. Following his return to the United States, the Guggenheim Fund for the Promotion of Aeronautics sponsored a national tour by Byrd and his plane, the *Josephine Ford,* that arrived at Omaha's still-unfinished airport in October 1926.[33]

But even as the tour landed in Omaha, the Chamber of Commerce was coming to the conclusion that progress in developing the new airport was unsatisfactory. Despite Hummel's support, the parks department proved incapable of bringing about the necessary improvements to the airfield quickly enough to satisfy aviation boosters. In October 1926, Chamber representatives persuaded the city council to allow the street cleaning and maintenance department under Dean Noyes to complete much of the work—mainly grading, providing drainage, and removing tree stumps.[34] Although the airport would remain under parks department jurisdiction for another two years, Noyes and his department carried out the remaining improvements to the grounds during that time.

The relationship between the airport and the parks department further broke down over the issue of building a municipal hangar. In August 1926, Hummel asked the city council for permission to hire an architect to draw up plans for a municipally owned hangar. A certain note of urgency accompanied his request, as the post office planned to award the contract for airmail service on a route through Omaha within the following six months. Chamber of Commerce officials wanted the new airfield to be ready to become the city's airmail airport.[35] When the council approved hiring of an architect to design the hangar, Hummel believed that he could build the structure using parks department funds. In early February 1927, however, the city attorney informed him that existing law did not permit the use of park bond funds for that purpose. The Aerial Transportation Committee then decided to seek an individual or organization to build a hangar using private funds.[36] Though Hummel remained of the opinion that the city ought to build the hangar and make it available to aviators in the same way that the parks department's tourist camps were available to the public, later that year members of the Omaha chapter of the American Legion came forward and agreed to raise the money for the project.[37]

While efforts to bring airmail to Omaha continued during 1927, airport supporters concentrated primarily on planning aviation events. Though the airport still lacked a large municipal hangar, airport boosters decided to dedicate the facility on Sunday, July 10, 1927, during a visit of the Ford Reliability Tour, a contest supported by the Ford Motor Company to promote the development of safer aircraft. Twenty-five thousand people flocked to the airport to see the airplanes and witness the dedication ceremony.[38] The following month, Charles Lindbergh and the Iowa-born aviator Clarence Chamberlin (who had flown with a passenger from New York to Germany shortly after Lindbergh's epic flight to Paris) visited Omaha amid great fanfare. Chamberlin arrived first, lending his support to the American Legion's efforts to raise money for an airport hangar. Plans for Lindbergh's visit two weeks later called for a parade, a public speech, and a banquet. The Chamber hoped that both men would help inspire public enthusiasm for the city's airport. And indeed, the American Legion's fund drive, which had been foundering, concluded successfully in September 1927. The long-awaited hangar was completed in April 1928.[39]

By early 1928, after the parks department's difficulties in improving the field and building a hangar, the Chamber and the city council were ready to turn responsibility for the airport over to the streets department. Even though a local court had settled a suit challenging the city's use of parkland for the airport in the city's favor, on March 13, 1928, the council formally transferred responsibility for the airfield.[40]

Airmail service returned to the city of Omaha proper in November 1930, when Boeing Air Transport moved its operations from the field at Fort Crook to its new hangar at the municipal airport.[41] By then travel by air was growing, despite the onset of the Great Depression, and a future in which airline service would be important began to seem probable. When the city turned responsibility for the airport over to the streets department, it also created an airport commission to oversee aviation activities.[42] Severing the link in Omaha between the parks department and the airport was primarily a response to specific local conditions, particularly the failure of the parks department to expeditiously develop the airport, and not a rejection of aviation as a recreational activity. Local aviation boosters continued to promote popular aviation events, such as the National Air Races held in May 1931 at the municipal airport.

Minneapolis: A Parks Commission Success Story

Minneapolis was another case in which using the parks commission to develop and manage an airfield was an expedient strategy, but there it proved not only plausible but also workable, and the parks commission operated the Minneapolis municipal airport from June 1928 until August 1944. Though use of the airport by commercial airlines grew during the 1930s, recreational or leisure uses remained prominent through the mid-1930s. By late in the decade, however, the complexity and expense of airport management and development had pushed the Board of Park Commissioners in the direction of turning the facility over to an airport commission.

The acreage that would form the heart of Minneapolis's municipal airport first came to the attention of many in the area as the Twin City Motor Speedway, established in 1915 by a number of prominent citizens from

Minneapolis and St. Paul on land adjacent to Fort Snelling. Seeking to dupli-
cate the success of the racetrack at Indianapolis, the speedway hosted its
first 500-mile race on September 4, 1915. Additional races were held in July
1916 and 1917. But the track never became a financial success, and the corporation organized to manage it soon went bankrupt. After World War I,
the head of the Minnesota National Guard approached the state government about establishing an air squadron. In the course of those discussions,
the Aero Club of Minneapolis suggested the site of the old speedway as a
possible location for an airfield. At the time, the land belonged to the
Snelling Field Corporation.[43]

The following year, a number of Minneapolis and St. Paul businessmen,
many of whom were also members of the Aero Club, formed the Twin City
Aero Corporation to lease the land from the Snelling Field Corporation and
prepare the area as a landing field. In May 1920, the post office announced
that it would inaugurate airmail service to the Twin Cities in July "if the landing
field and hangar were ready." Local businessmen soon raised the necessary
funds and the hangar was in place when the first airmail plane arrived on
August 20, 1920. While the arrival of the airmail certainly was a highlight,
the day also included a flying circus and "a double parachute jump by
Charles (Speed) Holman."[44]

The post office suspended airmail service at the end of June 1921, and
military and more event-oriented aviation activities would dominate airfield
use until service resumed in July 1926.[45] In July 1921 the state appropriated
forty-five thousand dollars to build a hangar for the 109th Observation
Squadron, part of the 34th Division Aviation of the state militia. Perhaps
reflecting the predominance of military uses, in 1923 the field was renamed
Wold-Chamberlain Field—Twin City Air Port, in honor of two local military aviators, Ernest G. Wold and Cyrus Foss Chamberlain, who had died
during World War I.[46] In terms of the airport's recreational value, it "was
much like many other flying fields that sprang into use throughout the countryside during that period," where "[o]ccasionally noted fliers from various
parts of the country would drop in."[47]

Until 1926, the airport had been a joint venture, involving business leaders from both Minneapolis and St. Paul. In that year, however, the St. Paul
interests sought to establish an airport nearer by, and by November 1926
the city had opened a new airfield in West St. Paul, across the Mississippi
River. Business and civic leaders in Minneapolis now began to explore how
they might make the existing field Minneapolis's municipal airport. In June
1926 two city aldermen approached the Board of Park Commissioners and
asked if it would be interested in purchasing and operating the airport. The
parks commission was the only municipal agency with the power to purchase land outside the corporate limits of Minneapolis. The Twin City Aero
Corporation offered to sell the field for $126,000, and at the end of
November 1926 the Board of Park Commissioners asked the city's Board of
Estimate and Taxation to authorize the issuance of $150,000 in bonds to
support the purchase.[48]

In early 1927, the State of Minnesota passed legislation permitting city councils or boards of park commissioners in cities of the first class (Minneapolis and St. Paul) to acquire property for and to equip airports. The law limited the amount of bonds that could be issued for such a purpose to $150,000.[49] The connection between the actions taken by the Minneapolis Board of Park Commissioners in late 1926 and the actions of the state legislature in early 1927 is unclear. Though it seemed to endorse the board's action, in fact the new legislation had raised a question: would the city council or the board purchase and build the airport? In April the board notified the city council that it still planned to purchase the airport site, but noted that if the council planned to act under the new legislation the situation would change. The board received the go-ahead for its plans the following month when the council passed a resolution to leave the matter of the airport entirely in the hands of the park commissioners.[50]

The council resolution came shortly after Lindbergh's flight, an event that stirred great interest in aviation locally. In its wake, the Civic and Commerce Association joined with a newly formed Minneapolis chapter of the National Aeronautical Association to promote parks commission action on the airport. By August 1, 1927, the private company that had been leasing the airport from the Snelling Field Corporation was in default, and its lease was cancelled. Two days later, the Board of Park Commissioners voted to acquire the site. Its plans undoubtedly received a boost when, on August 23, 1927, Lindbergh landed there as part of his nationwide tour. It was months, however, before the board and the Snelling Field Corporation came to terms on a price and payment schedule to fit within the $150,000 bond limit and finally completed the sale in August 1928.[51]

Even before the parks commission took possession, military activity at the field increased. In February 1927, Ninth Naval Air District officials announced plans to establish an aviation squadron. A group of local businessmen calling themselves the Minneapolis Committee of One Hundred built a hangar for the new squadron, but gave title to the Board of Park Commissioners. The commissioners in turn agreed to lease the new hangar to the navy for one dollar per year. Thus, when the parks commission took over the field, it had the airmail service hangar built by the Twin City Aero Corporation, a small hangar leased by a local aircraft company, three additional hangars, and a building used by the National Guard's aviation unit. By the end of the first year of operation, two more leased hangars had been built, in addition to the naval reserve hangar. The remains of the old speedway still encircled the field, effectively marking the boundaries of useable land.[52]

Though military activities figured prominently at the field, so did more recreational uses. Sightseeing flights and airplane-watching became popular activities and remained so through the early 1930s. In their operations report for 1929–1930, parks commissioners provided figures illustrating the types of aviation activities at the field. The report noted 2,402 arriving and 2,757 departing passengers on scheduled flights in 1929. For 1930, the numbers rose to 2,810 arriving and 3,148 departing. But they paled in comparison to the number of people who came to the airport to take an aerial tour of the city—14,890 in 1929. Although the number of sightseers declined by half the following year to 7,042, those coming to the airport for recreational flights still outnumbered airline passengers. Only in 1931 did arriving and departing passengers (8,397 and 8,315, respectively) together outnumber sightseers (11,752).[53]

The *Airport News*, founded to publicize activities at the airport, reported that sightseeing, particularly at night, remained popular into the 1930s. In May and June 1933, the paper noted, 1,146 people boarded aircraft for nighttime tours of the city. Through the first six months of 1933, the total stood at 8,227 for all sightseers, day and night. This was at a time when depression conditions had worked to lower the number of scheduled airline passengers to 5,773 for the first half of the year.[54] As late as 1936, when the scheduled airlines enplaned 10,538 passengers, sightseeing operations carried 38,964 people aloft.[55]

People went out to the airport to see the city from the air, and they also went just to see the airplanes. In May 1934, the *Airport News* noted that the monthly operations reports submitted by the airport manager to the park board indicated that 33,200 people had visited the airport in April 1934. While some of these came to the field for flights of some kind, the vast majority simply came to gaze at the airplanes. The September figures were even more impressive, with 111,800 visitors reported.[56] The 1936 report indicated that slightly over one million people had visited the airport during that year.[57] Clearly, during the 1930s the airport provided not only transportation, but also certain types of leisure or recreational opportunities for the people of the Twin Cities.

The Board of Park Commissioners was aware of the debate swirling around the use of parkland for airport purposes. Perhaps not surprisingly, it came down solidly on the side of those who supported the connection between parks and airports. Superintendent of Parks Theodore Wirth, addressing a meeting of the American Institute of Park Executives in 1928, outlined the reasons why, he felt, parks commissions or departments should take responsibility for local airports. First, he cited the recent court decision in favor of the Wichita parks department, agreeing with the court that "airports serve recreational as well as commercial purposes, and the management of such ports is therefore a proper function of park administration." Second, he noted that parks departments either had land suitable for airport use or could purchase such land. Whether he meant that parks departments could purchase such land with or without specific legislative authorization is unclear, but he certainly held that either existing or newly purchased parkland could be used for an airport. He then noted that municipal airports needed to be attractive, well-landscaped areas. This idea was current in the contemporary literature on airports, and Wirth held that parks departments were best qualified to make airport sites "attractive, sanitary, and serviceable to a high degree, just as with any other part of the park system." Finally, Wirth argued, an airport must serve the needs of the public. He noted that parks departments were already organized to serve the public and thus could add airports to their list of facilities operated in the public interest.[58]

The board's annual report for 1929, covering the first year of airport operations under its control, reflected Wirth's confidence in its ability to operate the airport. In addition, it acknowledged both the recreational role of the facility and its more utilitarian purpose as a transportation facility. The board noted two competing ideas about the operation of an airport: that an airport was a municipally owned or operated public utility and as such should be operated at a profit "from the very beginning or within a short period"; and that an airport was infrastructure provided to aid commerce and industry and as such should be paid for out of general taxation. The board argued that the first view would lead to "excessive charges" that would "retard, if not entirely prevent progress and operation of the port." The second would lead to "absurdly low leaseholds" to corporations and other tenants who "could well afford to pay a reasonable rent." Instead of adopting either, the board took a middle path, declaring that cities had an obligation to provide airports and that tenants should "pay a ground rental at all times sufficient to meet the cost of operation, maintenance, and administration." The board saw an airport as "self-sustaining."[59]

In fact, during its first year of operation the airport was self-sustaining, taking in $15,468.94 while expending $14,134.30. But that would be the only time under parks department management that the airport showed a profit. The 1930 report took note of the changed fiscal reality and also reflected a change in the philosophy of the board. No longer did it expect the airport to be self-sustaining. Instead, the board came to the conclusion "that the municipal airport should be subsidized in such a manner as to allow charging what the traffic will bear, yet helping the proponents of this newest method of transportation, air travel, to establish themselves." The report reminded readers "that water and rail transportation was at first subsidized directly by state and governmental aid" and that bus transportation was presently being subsidized indirectly "by both state and federal aid in the building of good roads."[60]

Despite the reversal of fortune, the Board of Park Commissioners continued to operate the airport throughout the 1930s, sponsoring and managing a number of improvements funded by the Work Projects Administration.[61] As long as the two visions—recreational and utilitarian—remained compatible and in rough balance, the park board saw no issues with its continued management of the airport. By the late 1930s, however, the expense and complexity of airport operations had grown, and the board began to look for additional sources of funding and, eventually, an alternative management structure.

In 1938, Congress passed the Civil Aeronautics Act that, among its many provisions, called for a survey of airports with an eye to the development of a federal plan for their improvement. In the wake of this legislation, the United States Conference of Mayors sent a questionnaire to cities across the country as part of an effort to lobby for a permanent program of federal aid for airports. The Minneapolis park board responded with a lengthy argument in favor of federal aid that clearly indicated just how expensive and difficult it had become to own and operate an airport.

While acknowledging that localities did gain from the presence of an airport, the board endorsed the call "for a program of Federal aid to municipal airports for the construction, improvement, development and expansion of needed facilities." It went even further, arguing for funding for "the operation and maintenance of certain municipal airports." The board asserted that the number of improvements required to keep an airport up-to-date were simply too great to be supported by purely local resources. Although it had carried out a number of "extensive improvements," the board still found itself facing "a rather formidable list of desirable and even necessary improvements," including an expanded administration building and more concrete runways, taxiways, and aprons. Further, "the rules and regulations promulgated by the Department of Commerce, which in themselves are entirely justified for the safety and convenience of airplane operation, not infrequently cause the municipality to go to considerable expense to comply with such rules and regulations." The board also mentioned—as war loomed—the amount of military activity at the airport. Military and other federal government operations at the airport (weather bureau, Department of Commerce, communication service) did not pay rents that matched expenses, and that circumstance also served as "a strong argument for additional government subsidies."[62]

The argument for federal subsidies was not in itself an argument for the board to give up management of the airport. However, by the late 1930s the combination of acknowledged need for federal aid, increased use of the airport for transportation purposes, and a desire to make the Minneapolis airport "the major airport in the Northwest" did indeed point to a change in ownership and operation.[63] An airport was no longer just a "suitable tract of land, properly graded and equipped with ground, administration, and safe operating facilities" as the 1929 report of the Board of Park Commissioners described it. Instead, by 1940 the airport required the addition of 435 acres (more than doubling its size), the extension of runways to 5,000 feet, and "the construction of the necessary taxiways, drainage, lighting, fencing, etc." The board's 1940 report indicated that the needed improvements involved moving over two million yards of earth and laying down "approximately 200,000 square yards of concrete."[64] The airport was no longer simply another property belonging to the board, but its major focus. As its 1940 report concluded, "In all likelihood the development of the Minneapolis Municipal Airport during 1941 will constitute the major improvement work of this Board."[65]

The changing view of the airport was undoubtedly reinforced by a study headed by the board for the purpose of planning Minneapolis's postwar aviation future. Published in 1943, this study focused entirely on what would be required to position the city and its airport as an important part of the national air transportation system. It looked at what would be needed

in terms of improvements to the existing airport and assessed sites for a possible second major airport in the area. The study clearly defined the airport
as a transportation facility. No mention was made of any recreational use or
purpose.[66]

In light of these circumstances, the Board of Park Commissioners
endorsed passage of a state bill in 1943 that created the Minneapolis–St. Paul
Metropolitan Airports Commission. The new commission took over
management of the Minneapolis airport in August 1944. Former park
superintendent Theodore Wirth believed that this marked "the beginning of
a new era of aviation development for the metropolitan district." In this
new era, the transportation purpose of the airport would be central; Wirth
predicted that the Twin Cities would develop into "one of the great air
terminals of the United States." This was the same Theodore Wirth who in
1929 had emphasized the recreational nature of airports. By 1944 transportation needs overwhelmingly predominated over the recreational, and
management of the airport needed to reflect that new reality.

Welcoming the Machine

Today commercial aviation is a mass experience, as millions of Americans
travel by air every year. In the 1920s and 1930s, aviation was a mass
phenomenon of a different sort, a recreational activity. Most people experienced flying as spectators, not participants. As people debated the proper
use of the airplane during these decades, they also debated the definition of
an airport. Numerous actors, including parks advocates, local civic leaders,
and aviation professionals contributed to that conversation. As a result of
this and other debates, the definition of a park expanded to embrace a
number of new uses, including aviation. But the definition of an airport nar-
rowed to reflect primarily its transportation function. In consequence,
though airports continued to serve as venues for air shows and visits by
celebrity pilots, and as places to watch a fascinating example of modern
technology, by the 1940s their transportation functions overshadowed their
recreational uses. Both definitions, however, remained elastic enough for
airports to retain certain recreational functions and for parks and airports
to coexist at certain times and under certain circumstances.

While few today would think of an airport as a site for recreation, echoes
of this earlier period remain. Many airports still offer observation decks or
other areas where people can sit and watch so-called airside operations.
Both Ronald Reagan Washington National Airport and Baltimore/
Washington International Airport have adjacent park areas where people
can walk, picnic, and watch airplanes. The International Council of Air
Shows estimates that between fifteen and eighteen million people attend air
shows annually in North America. While military bases hosted a sizable percentage of the more than 260 air shows in 2004, the rest happened at the
nation's municipal airports.[67] And although the number of licensed pilots in
the United States has fallen by approximately two hundred thousand in the

last quarter-century, among the more than six hundred thousand who remain are pilots who annually trek to the convention and air show at Oshkosh, Wisconsin, home of the Experimental Aircraft Association, one of the best attended aviation events in the nation, with a paid attendance, over several days, of approximately seven hundred and fifty thousand.[68]

And in at least one case, in marked contrast to Chicago, a new link between parks and airports has been forged. County commissioners recently purchased Van Sant Airport in Bucks County, Pennsylvania. With commissioners noting that it already contained "many different kinds of parks," the nearly 200-acre facility with its grass runway is the newest addition to the Bucks County park system. While the commissioners carefully asserted the environmental value of preserving this "open space," local users focused on the fact that it offered them an opportunity to have a picnic and watch the vintage airplanes and gliders using the field.[69] Much as their predecessors had in the 1920s and 1930s, the Bucks County commissioners have welcomed the flying machine into one of their gardens.

Notes

Dr. Bednarek is a professor of history at the University of Dayton in Dayton, Ohio. She wishes to acknowledge the feedback and support provided by commentators, particularly Mark Rose, when early versions of this article were presented at conferences organized by the North Carolina First Flight Centennial Commission and the Society for American City and Regional Planning History in 2001. The Office of the Dean, College of Arts and Sciences, University of Dayton provided support for a second research trip to the state archives in St. Paul, Minnesota. The comments of the *Technology and Culture* referees were particularly helpful in identifying additional research sources and clarifying the overall thesis.

1. See Leo Marx, *The Machine in the Garden: Technology and the Pastoral Ideal in America* (Oxford, 1964). On the influence of this work, see Jeffrey L. Meikle, "Leo Marx's *The Machine in the Garden*," *Technology and Culture* 44 (2003): 147–59.
2. Cyril Stanley Smith, "Art, Technology, and Science: Notes on Their Historical Interaction," *Technology and Culture* 11 (1970): 493–549.
3. Susan Douglas, *Inventing American Broadcasting, 1899–1922* (Baltimore, 1987).
4. Dominick A. Pisano, "The Greatest Show Not on Earth: The Confrontation between Utility and Entertainment in Aviation," in *The Airplane in American Culture* (Ann Arbor, MI, 2003), 39–74.
5. In the early 1980s, Galen Cranz published a study of park design in which she suggested that the history of parks in the United States could be divided into four eras: 1850 to 1900; 1900 to 1930; 1930 to 1965; and post–1965. In each, she argued, a certain design ideal emerged to shape park planning. While calling her typology "venturesome and pioneering," Jon Peterson nonetheless offered a number of critiques, among them that parks or open spaces in the United States predated 1850, that Cranz's time periods were too rigid, and that she did not take sufficient account of variations in park design during each period. Taken together, Cranz's work and Peterson's critique strongly suggest that the uses and functions of parks have long been subject to debate. See Galen Cranz, *The Politics of Park Design: A History of Urban Parks in America* (Cambridge, MA, 1982), and Jon Peterson, "The Evolution of Public Open Space in American Cities," *Journal of Urban History* 12 (1985): 75–88.

6. For a discussion of the changing perceptions of the meaning of parkland, see David Schuyler, *The New Urban Landscape: The Redefinition of City Form in Nineteenth-Century America* (Baltimore, MD, 1986), 59–146.

7. See Roy Rosenzweig and Elizabeth Blackmar, *The Park and the People: A History of Central Park* (New York, 1994), 1–11.

8. L. H. Weir, ed., *Parks: A Manual of Municipal and County Parks*, vol. 1 (New York, 1928), xix–xxi.

9. For a sense of early airline history in the United States, the small-scale and often temporary nature of the earliest airlines, and the importance of the Air Mail Act of 1925 in establishing the foundation of U.S. commercial aviation, see R. E. G. Davies, *Airlines of the United States since 1914* (Washington, DC, 1972), 1–15, 31–55.

10. On barnstormers, air racers, and the early airmail pilots, see Roger E. Bilstein, *Flight in America: From the Wrights to the Astronauts*, 3rd ed. (Baltimore, 2001), 60–62; Terry Gwynn-Jones, *Farther and Faster: Aviation's Adventuring Years, 1909–1939* (Washington, DC, 1991), 103–276; William M. Leary, *Aerial Pioneers: The U.S. Air Mail Service, 1918–1927* (Washington, DC, 1985).

11. Henry V. Hubbard et al., *Airports: Their Location, Administration and Legal Basis* (Cambridge, MA, 1930), 146–48.

12. For a discussion of the Hoover Commission's role in identifying possible airport sites in the New York metropolitan area, see David A. Johnson, *Planning the Great Metropolis: The 1929 Regional Plan of New York and Its Environs* (London, 1996), 166.

13. Committee on the Regional Plan of New York and Its Environs, *The Graphic Regional Plan: Atlas and Description, Regional Plan*, vol. 1 (New York, 1929), 336–75.

14. For examples of discussions concerning recreational/amusement activities at airports, see Stratton Coyner, "The Job of the Airport Manager," *American City* 42 (March 1930): 126–28; Major C. C. Mosely, "Hitch Your Airport to the Stars," *Aviation* 34 (November 1935): 16–18; William D. Strohmeier, "More Fun at the Airport," *Aviation* 39 (November 1940): 38–39.

15. Hubbard et al., *Airports*, 57–58, 169. The study also listed airports "built on park lands." In addition to those in the ten cities with airports controlled by parks departments, seven other cities had airports built on parkland. Hubbard, 166.

16. Lieutenant Colonel U.S. Grant III, "Airports and Public Parks," *City Planning* 6 (January 1930): 33–34; L. H. Weir, "The Airport as Transportation Terminal," *City Planning* 6 (April 1930): 119–20.

17. Gilmore D. Clarke, "The Airport Is Specialized Commercial Space," *City Planning* 6 (April 1930): 123–24; John Nolen, "Under What Jurisdiction Public Airports Should Be Placed?" *City Planning* 6 (April 1930): 125–27; "Editorial: Airports," *City Planning* 6 (January 1930): 28–29.

18. Clarence M. Young, "Aeronautics and the Municipality," *American City* 43 (September 1930): 119.

19. Arnold Knauth et al., *1928 United States Aviation Reports* (Baltimore, 1928), 450–51. Published yearly beginning in 1928, the volumes in this series contain reprints of court decisions, state laws, and federal laws and regulations concerning aviation.

20. Ibid., 483, 502–3, 577–78; Ibid., *1929 United States Aviation Reports* (Baltimore, MD, 1929), 524–25.

21. Knauth et al., *1928 United States Aviation Reports*, 495.

22. J. E. Cravey, "Wichita Comes Through," *Airports* 6 (October 1928): 27–28.

23. Knauth et al., *1928 United States Aviation Reports*, 8–16.

24. Ibid., *1929 United States Aviation Reports*, 565–66.

25. Ibid., *1928 United States Aviation Reports* (n. 19 above), 545.

26. Leslie R. Valentine, "The Development of the Omaha Municipal Airfield, 1924–1930" (Master's thesis, University of Nebraska, Omaha, 1980), 18–21.

27. Minutes of the Meeting of the Aerial Transportation Committee, Omaha Chamber of Commerce, July 28, 1924, Special Collections, University Library, University of Nebraska, Omaha (hereafter UNO Special Collections), 27.

28. The city finally held a special airport bond election in October 1928. An analysis of the extremely close vote indicated that voters in working-class wards in the northern and southern sections of the city voted against the measure, while voters in the more affluent western wards voted in favor of the measure. The measure actually failed to pass on election day, but once the absentee ballots were counted it had a margin of 155 votes, 37, 314 to 37,159. Valentine, 48–61.

29. Minutes of the Meeting of the Aerial Transportation Committee, Omaha Chamber of Commerce, January 15, 1925, UNO Special Collections, 54.

30. Minutes of the Aerial Transportation Committee, Omaha Chamber of Commerce, March 23, 1925, UNO Special Collections, 58–59.

31. "Omaha Muny Air Field is Assured," *Omaha Chamber of Commerce Journal* 14, no. 8 (August 15, 1925): 5.

32. Quoted in "Muny Air Field for Omaha Is Approved by Council; Friendly Suits Planned," *Omaha Morning Bee*, August 6, 1925.

33. "Working for Omaha's Interests in Aviation," *Omaha Chamber of Commerce Journal* 15, no. 13 (October 23, 1926): 1.

34. Valentine, "The Development," 34–35.

35. Minutes of the Meeting of the Aerial Transportation Committee, Omaha Chamber of Commerce, September 30, 1926, UNO Special Collections, 55.

36. Minutes of the Meeting of the Aerial Transportation Committee, Omaha Chamber of Commerce, February 4, 1927, UNO Special Collections, 20.

37. Minutes of the Meeting of the Aerial Transportation Committee, Omaha Chamber of Commerce, February 11, 1927, UNO Special Collections, 22; "Legion Works for Air Field Hangar," *Omaha Chamber of Commerce Journal* 16, no. 7 (July 30, 1927): 5.

38. " 'Aviation Day' to Be Gala Event," *Omaha Chamber of Commerce Journal* 16, no. 5 (July 2, 1927): 4; "Omaha Dedicates New Municipal Air Field," *Omaha Chamber of Commerce Journal* 16, no. 6 (July 16, 1927): 1.

39. "Aviation of Prime Interest Now in Omaha," *Omaha Chamber of Commerce Journal* 16, no. 9 (August 27, 1927): 1; "Airport Corporation Organizes," *Omaha Chamber of Commerce Journal* 16, no. 11 (September 24, 1927): 10; "Aviation Needs in Omaha," *Omaha Chamber of Commerce Journal* 16, no. 24 (March 1928): 4.

40. Minutes of the Meeting of the Aerial Transportation Committee, Omaha Chamber of Commerce, January 6, 1928, UNO Special Collections, 9; Valentine (n. 26 above), 69.

41. Valentine, "The Development," 158–59.

42. City of Omaha, Ordinance 13508, June 19, 1928, copy in City of Omaha Recorder's Office, City-County Building, Omaha. That ordinance was soon replaced by a more detailed one; see City of Omaha, Ordinance No. 13581, December 26, 1928, City of Omaha Recorder's Office, City-County Building, Omaha.

43. Theodore Wirth, "Retrospective Glimpses into the History of the Board of Park Commissioners of Minneapolis, Minnesota and the City's Park, Parkway and Playground System," paper presented at the annual meeting of the Board of Park Commissioners, July 16, 1945, 383, 386–87, typescript, Sidney Stolte Collection, Minnesota Work Projects Administration Materials, 1935–1942, P2555, box 1, Minnesota Historical Society, St. Paul (hereafter MHS).

44. Ibid., 387–89.

45. The airmail service came under fire for its high costs following the 1920 elections, and the post office decided to focus primarily on the transcontinental airmail route. It had experimented with feeder routes, such as the one to Minneapolis, but when these failed to garner enough business to justify their existence the service was withdrawn. See Leary (n. 10 above), 145–54.

46. "Short History of the Minneapolis Municipal Airport (Wold-Chamberlain Field) and Memorandum of the Principal Official Transactions from Its Inception up to the Present Time," January 25, 1930, 1, typescript, Manuscript Notebook, Minneapolis (MN) Board of Park Commissioners, P1189–19, MHS.

47. Ibid., 389.

48. Wirth, "Retrospective Glimpses," 389–90.

49. H. F. No. 1387, "A Bill for an act relating to public airports, providing for the organization and administration of public corporations for acquiring, establishing, developing, maintaining, controlling, and operating such airports, and for financing the operations of such corporations, and those of other municipalities owning and operating airports, and appropriating moneys therefore," chap. 500, approved April 19, 1943; copy of text of bill in MHS.

50. Wirth, "Retrospective Glimpses," 389–90.

51. Ibid., 390–91.

52. Ibid., 392–94; "Short History of the Minneapolis Municipal Airport," 3–4.

53. Minneapolis Board of Park Commissioners, *Forty-Eighth Annual Report of the Minneapolis Board of Park Commissioners* (Minneapolis, 1930), chart between 76 and 77, and Minneapolis Board of Park Commissioners, *Forty-Ninth Annual Report of the Minneapolis Board of Park Commissioners* (Minneapolis, MN, 1931), 60, Minneapolis (MN) Board of Park Commissioners Collection, MHS.

54. "Night Sightseeing Flights Popular," *Airport News*, August 12, 1933, 1, 4.

55. Board of Park Commissioners, "Annual Operations Report, 1936," manuscript notebook, P1189–19, MHS.

56. "Thousands of Visitors at Minneapolis Airport during Month of April," *Airport News*, May 15, 1934, 3; "900 Air Passengers Arrive at Minneapolis in Month," *Airport News*, October 26, 1934, 1.

57. Board of Park Commissioners, "Annual Operations Report, 1936."

58. Wirth, "Retrospective Glimpses," 396; "Who Shall Own and Operate the Airports?" *American City* 39 (December 1928): 110. For examples of calls to landscape and beautify airport property, see George B. Ford, "Location, Size, and Layout of Airports," *American City* 37 (September 1927): 301–3; O. J. Swander, "Exceptional Site, Landscaping, Lighting, and Buildings Characterize Wichita Airport," *American City* 44 (April 1931): 109–10.

59. Board of Park Commissioners, *Forty-Seventh Annual Report of the Minneapolis Board of Park Commissioners* (Minneapolis, MN, 1929), 62, Minneapolis (MA) Board of Park Commissioners Collection, MHS.

60. Board of Park Commissioners, *Forty-Eighth Annual Report of the Minneapolis Board of Park Commissioners* (Minneapolis, MN, 1930), 70, Minneapolis (MN) Board of Park Commissioners Collection, MHS.

61. For a sense of the public works projects completed at Wold-Chamberlain Field, see Board of Park Commissioners, "The Story of W. P. A. in the Minneapolis Parks, Parkways and Playgrounds for 1941," 10–27, typescript, Sidney Stolte Collection, Minnesota Work Projects Administration Materials, 1935–1942, P2555, box 1, MHS.

62. Wirth, "Retrospective Glimpses ," 407–9.

63. Board of Park Commissioners, *Fifty-Eighth Annual Report of the Board of Park Commissioners, Minneapolis, Minnesota* (Minneapolis, 1940), 64, Minneapolis (MN) Board of Park Commissioners Collection, MHS.

64. Ibid., 64–66.

65. Ibid., 66.

66. See Board of Park Commissioners, "A Study of Air Terminal Facilities of Minneapolis (March 17, 1943)," MHS.

67. For general information on air shows in North America and precise figures on military bases and municipal airports hosting air shows in 2004, see the website of the International Council of Air shows, http://www.airshows.org, accessed June 16, 2004.

68. For a discussion of the decline in the number of active pilots in the United States and of efforts to reverse that trend, see Janet R. Daly Bednarek and Michael H. Bednarek, *Dreams of Flight: General Aviation in the United States* (College Station, TX, 2003), 124–26. For a history of the Experimental Aircraft Association's annual convention, including attendance figures, see http:// www.airventure.org/ 2004/ about/ history.html, accessed June 16, 2004.

69. Brian Callaway, "It's Just a Flight in the Park," Intelligencer, September 8, 2003; http://www.avweb.com/eletter/archives/avflash/126-full.html# 185665, accessed September 11, 2003.

Chapter 9

Miscegenation and Competing Definitions of Race in Twentieth-Century Louisiana

Michelle Brattain

From *The Journal of Southern History*

Marcus Bruce Christian, an author and professor at Dillard University, observed in the mid-nineteen-fifties that while New Orleans might be known for "gumbo, jambalaya, lagniappe, poor boy sandwiches, pralines, Mardi Gras and Creoles," it also has "another claim to distinction which has not been bruited about very loudly." New Orleans is a place, he wrote, where family lines "waver back and forth across color-lines like wet wash in a high March wind." The city has given to America "more *'passer pour blanches'* [people who pass for white] than any other city in our country." A poet and scholar of black history, Christian anticipated much of the current academic interest in race as a social construction.[1] His meticulous histories of eighteenth- and nineteenth-century families recreated an era when racial lines were more fluid and southern society accepted—or at least expected— interracial sex. In the latter half of Christian's career, as a civil rights struggle charged with anxieties about interracial contact swirled around him, his interests broadened to include the progeny of those early families. Among thousands of newspaper clippings that Christian saved over his lifetime— documenting New Orleans history from the protracted fight over school desegregation to the debate over stereotypical and degrading representations of Africans in Mardi Gras—one finds dozens of society photographs, wedding announcements, and obituaries that he compiled, seemingly in an attempt to discover a similar secret interracial history of the twentieth century. In the margins, he sometimes annotated genealogies, alternate spellings, or anecdotes about similar names encountered on the other side of the color line. In 1959, for example, he noted, and documented, the strange coincidence of a death notice for a man he thought was a "Negro," who had died at an *"all white"* hospital, and speculated on the dead man's familial relationship to a realtor listing a "colored" apartment a couple of weeks later. Of the family name in question, he later wrote to himself, "*Joubert?* What about the white family that says it spells its name *'Jau'* and not *'Jou'*[?]" Christian often wrote simply, as he did on a 1960 photograph of a couple cutting their fiftieth-anniversary cake, the word *miscegenation*.[2] The basis for such judgments was rarely explained. Perhaps it was a distant memory, a rumor, or merely Christian asserting his ability as a black man to spot *passer pour blanches*. Unfortunately he never published his side of these stories.

For the historian who seeks to discover the secret history of the race line in the twentieth century, the record is both as suggestive *and* as cryptic as Marcus Christian's handwritten notes. Though interracial marriage had been illegal in Louisiana since the eighteenth century, it was common knowledge that few families could claim "pure" lineage from any group.[3] Louisianans had a saying in Christian's day that "You can take a bowl of rice and feed all the people of pure-white blood in the city." Local lore also celebrated, from the safe distance of the twentieth century, an exotic past of interracial romance symbolized by the legendary antebellum "quadroon balls." Though white Louisiana revered its cosmopolitan and interracial roots in Spanish, French, Caribbean, and African cultures, it had long ago confined such reverence to memory, adopting a more rigid, binary notion of black and white and the corresponding practices of American segregation. In the twentieth century, the law and racial etiquette absolutely prohibited amorous relationships across the color line. Yet scattered evidence, from anecdotes about "passing" to occasional newspaper reports of arrests on miscegenation charges, lends credence to Christian's hunches about the persistence of interracial relationships. Moreover, whites' concern about "race mixing," the purity of one's lineage, and the maintenance of segregation—in other words, too many whites protesting a little too much—provides grounds for suspecting the existence of significant cracks in racial solidarity. The leaders of Louisiana's White Citizens' Council, for example, frequently proclaimed that miscegenation was the secret, invidious, un-American goal of both the integrationists and the communists.[4] The state's laws formulated increasingly strict definitions of miscegenation and imposed ever-harsher penalties over the course of the first half of the twentieth century. By the 1950s the maximum punishment for a criminal conviction for interracial sex was five years in prison with or without hard labor.[5] The intensity of white anxiety in the twentieth century makes surviving traces of interracial contact more remarkable and compelling.

The realm of law was one of the few venues in which such private relationships became public. Miscegenation law and jurisprudence offer a unique, if somewhat problematic, view of a whole constellation of ideas that twentieth-century Louisianans associated with race. Although court cases permit only a limited view of actors in an artificially controlled context, recent scholarship has demonstrated the rich possibility that legal history affords for providing insight into the construction of race in the United States. An autonomous discourse in its own right, as Eva Saks has argued, miscegenation law consisted of an evolving, self-referential body of ideas and actions that acquired a power of its own, enabling it to create and sustain ideas such as the notion that race is, and resides in, "blood."[6] These statutes and cases also played a paramount role in shaping the legal status of race and racial identity, contributing to a deeply racialized but ostensibly "color blind" jurisprudence based on what Peggy Pascoe has described as a "new modernist racial ideology."[7] Moreover, the law is a matchless arena for witnessing the absurdities of racial belief and the "logic" of racial practice laid out plainly and unapologetically for the historical record.

This essay will focus on racial laws and four major case studies (only one of which is a criminal prosecution) from twentieth-century Louisiana in order to probe the meaning of race and miscegenation for one segregated but irrefutably interracial society in the Jim Crow South.[8] The analysis is based primarily on court records, including testimony, briefs, and exhibits, as well as the judicial decisions and reasoning behind the resolution of each case. In spite of their limitations, these records represent a site where private relations were momentarily exposed and the indeterminate nature of race was often candidly admitted.[9] The courts themselves created a space where people expressed their unofficial "working" definitions of race, providing a fascinating insight into the adaptations of people who lived with the indeterminacy of race yet continued to believe in some essential meaning of the concept. Legal records also permit an examination of the construction of race at the legislative and judicial levels, the use of gender and sexuality in attempts to police the race lines, and, more generally, the evolution of ideas about what race meant in the mid-twentieth-century South.

Two striking conclusions emerge from an analysis of these records. First, Louisianans held much more complicated and historically contingent views of race than the statutes and court decisions alone would suggest. The legal adjudication of race in the twentieth century, as Pascoe has argued, historically had a complex, interdependent relationship with popular and scientific beliefs about race. This essay examines one aspect of that tension. By necessity, politics and the courts represented abstract law that could recognize only black and white, but the people who entered the courts worked with a more practical understanding that was also born of necessity. Most noteworthy about the testimony of people brought into Louisiana courts by miscegenation law is the fluidity and contextual nuance with which many people viewed race. In spite of the mid-twentieth century's increasingly rigid lines of demarcation with regard to race, many ordinary Louisiana citizens instinctively understood and accepted the essentially social nature of racial definitions, and they worked with these definitions in the most private areas of their lives.

Second, though miscegenation law frequently failed to prevent sex across the race line, it served another equally significant function in the twentieth century: a tool to monitor racial boundaries. Louisiana state law had often been able to tame and contain the contradictions of black and white, but by the mid-twentieth century, the demands of massive resistance increasingly brought about more ideological and less practical applications of jurisprudence. Official public records associated with essentially private and gendered actions such as birth and marriage became a gatekeeping mechanism for maintaining segregation in Louisiana schools, sports, and public conveyances. Government-employed bureaucrats carried out increasingly stringent investigations of once-routine applications for marriage licenses, death certificates, and birth certificates in order to police the boundaries of race and expose those who in the past might have "passed" as white or married across race lines. These private points of individual connection with the state, therefore, took on a substantial burden in the maintenance of racial boundaries, the punishment of miscegenation, and the defense of whiteness. The objective of antimiscegenation law was ostensibly to discourage and punish sex across the race line, but it also permitted the state to use gender and private life to control the same boundary. In doing so, it made significant contributions to the redefinition of miscegenation and race itself.

Incidents of "race mixture" and white attempts to control such encounters have a long and infamous history in the South. Although prohibition of interracial sex was typically legislators' stated objective, recent scholarship also underscores the deeply contextual nature of the statutes' various incarnations. In colonial Virginia, where the earliest legislation on interracial liaisons appeared in 1662, the law reflected first the English conception of broadly defined racial hierarchy and later the social and economic dominance of explicitly racial slavery. At all times, colonial law addressed the reality of ongoing racial mixing, even as it represented what A. Leon Higginbotham Jr. and Barbara K. Kopytoff have aptly described as "attempts to patch holes in the fabric of the system."[10]

The solution, as Peter W. Bardaglio puts it, was a legal attempt "not so much to eliminate interracial sexual contacts as to channel them" in directions that bolstered the slave system and existing racial and gender hierarchies.[11] While the specific definitions of the crime and punishment varied, as Charles Robinson notes, "In each colony a violation of the law required some party, man, woman, and/or child, to make restitution by sacrificing freedom." Doubling the fine for interracial fornication, Virginia's assembly, for example, declared in 1662 that an interracial child's status would follow that of the mother. This ruling insured that the most common transgression of the color line—between black women and white men—would not undermine a social system increasingly based on a dichotomy between black slaves and free white persons. Maryland's 1664 antimiscegenation law did not proscribe marriage, but it declared that a white woman who married a slave would serve that slave's master for the remainder of the husband's life and that any offspring would be required to labor for the parish for thirty-one years. After 1692 in Maryland and 1725 in Pennsylvania, free black men who married white women were sentenced to a lifetime of slavery. In the first half of the eighteenth century, Massachusetts, North Carolina, South Carolina, Delaware, and Georgia enacted provisions similar to those of Virginia, Maryland, and Pennsylvania.[12] Colonial officials also singled out white women who had sex with black men for special punishment, a double standard that reflected, among other concerns, a perceived need both to control white female sexuality and to eliminate the threat that interracial offspring posed to the institution of slavery.[13]

Because statutes were created and enforced on a state-by-state basis, it is difficult to generalize about American antimiscegenation law prior to *Loving v. Virginia*, the 1967 U.S. Supreme Court decision that outlawed marriage regulations based on race. By the mid-nineteenth century, though, twenty-one of thirty-four states had passed legislation to proscribe or limit interracial sex. Most banned interracial marriage, but as Charles Robinson and Peter Wallenstein demonstrate in their histories of antimiscegenation law, the level of enforcement and specific penalties varied considerably, even within the South. South Carolina, for example, forbade white women to have children with nonwhite men, but it did not outlaw marriage between them. Alabama and Mississippi, on the other hand, outlawed marriage, but those states did not have an antebellum law prohibiting interracial sex. Only Georgia and Florida explicitly banned interracial cohabitation. However, a lack of specific antimiscegenation laws did not necessarily indicate state lenience, as Robinson shows, for other states occasionally punished interracial sex under adultery or fornication laws, particularly if the case involved a public relationship between a white woman and a black man.[14] Collectively, because many state laws shared a concern with defining races, the whole body of antimiscegenation law made important contributions to the construction of race by establishing local, legal definitions of whiteness and affirming the conception of blackness as an algebraic function of one's "blood."[15] A number of state legislatures decreed how much—one-fourth or one-eighth—black ancestry or "blood" made a person legally black.[16]

Louisiana varied somewhat from the American and southern norms because of its background as a French and Spanish colony. Louisianans historically tolerated interracial unions and grudgingly acknowledged their existence, but most of the state's residents did not condone such relationships. French law, for example, did not initially prevent European settlers in Louisiana from intermarrying or cohabiting with Indians, though French authorities, fearing the material, social, and religious implications of race-mixing (or *métissage*), attempted to stop the practice by promoting the immigration of French women to be wives.[17] The French did introduce an antimiscegenation law in 1724 with severe penalties for interracial sex, but colonial authorities seldom enforced it. Spanish colonial officials, who took control of the territory in 1769, found it equally difficult to prevent interracial sex, even though prohibitions on marriage and on public sexual affairs outside of marriage—known legally as "concubinage"—remained in place. Indeed interracial unions occurred often enough that the French and the Spanish legal systems recognized three distinct populations: Europeans, free people of color, and slaves. When Louisiana became part of the United States, some elements of this system persisted, as Louisiana outlawed marriages between people from three, rather than two, groups: free people of color, black slaves, and whites. However, American laws did not attempt to prohibit or punish concubinage, instead enacting measures to maintain the racial caste system and white supremacy.[18] White society also provided a ritualized outlet for such extramarital unions in quadroon balls, events organized by white entrepreneurs where wealthy white men courted quadroon women. This courting led not to marriage but to a similarly legal and contractual relationship known locally as *plaçage*, whereby a white gentleman supported a young quadroon woman and her mother, provided them with a home, and gave his name to any offspring. But as Monique Guillory has argued, the quadroon balls did not represent a thoroughgoing acceptance of interracial sex, for the whole ritual was carefully contained, institutionalized, and legally limited in contract.[19]

In the early nineteenth century, as moral reformers encouraged the spread of antimiscegenation laws throughout the United States, Louisiana law continued to reflect a greater preoccupation with racial hierarchy and property than with sex.[20] In 1825, for example, the legislature revised the civil code to outlaw the legitimization of biracial children by white fathers, to prohibit children of color from claiming paternity from white fathers, and to make it more difficult for biracial children to receive an inheritance by disallowing all but formal legal acknowledgment as a basis for establishing paternity. Through such measures Louisianans eliminated the old French laws governing support of children born within *plaçage* and protected the interests of white heirs from siblings of color. Interracial marriage remained illegal in the sense that it was legally invalid, but the law did not prescribe punishment for violators.[21]

The Civil War and Reconstruction temporarily undermined but ultimately strengthened most southern antimiscegenation laws. The end of slavery intensified white southern fears of interracial sex, and emancipation was frequently touted as the first step to total social equality and unrestricted sex across the race line (figure 9.1).[22] Indeed, the term *miscegenation* was coined in 1863 in a pamphlet, falsely attributed to the Republican Party, that espoused interracial sex.[23] In their brief return to southern statehouses during the first phase of Reconstruction, former Confederates accordingly attempted to reiterate and strengthen antebellum antimiscegenation laws in black codes and revised state constitutions. When congressional radicals took control of Reconstruction, however, the resulting empowerment of black Republicans throughout the South meant that a number of states effectively eliminated restrictions on interracial relationships, in many cases by simply failing to enforce existing laws. Across the South, in Robinson's words, Reconstruction "blurred the social lines just enough to encourage some blacks and whites to form conspicuous interracial relationships." In 1868, Louisiana became the only southern state to repeal its antimiscegenation laws as a result of black Republican leadership in the legislature. The restoration of white Democratic control in the 1870s, however, resulted in renewed restrictions on formal interracial relationships, if not interracial sex, in every state but Louisiana.[24] Louisiana, for a short while, also remained unique in not adopting antimiscegenation laws during Redemption.

In the 1890s, however, as white southern legislatures codified segregation, many state officials cracked down on interracial relationships with renewed legal vigor. Louisiana's legislature followed suit in 1894 and

Figure 9.1   Isaac and Rosa, emancipated slave children from the Free Schools of Louisiana, ca. 1863.

Source: Courtesy of the Collections of the Library of Congress.

became the last southern state to reintroduce prohibitions on interracial marriage. Fear of interracial promiscuity likewise served as a compelling argument for segregation. Urbanization and industrialization at the turn of the century exacerbated the fears of white southerners because both black and white women moved freely in workplaces, on city streets, on streetcars and trains, and as patrons of commercial amusements—all sites outside the scope of traditional patriarchal and racial authorities. Many whites, in

Edward Ayers's words, found "[t]he sexual charge that might be created among strangers temporarily placed in intimate surroundings" intolerable, even if it did not result in direct physical contact. In 1890, an editorial in a New Orleans newspaper argued in favor of segregated railcars, by stating that any person "who believe[d] that the white race should be kept pure from African taint" opposed the "commingling of the races inevitable in a 'mixed car.' " Articulating what the New Orleans editorial left to the imagination, a Tennessee newspaper recounted one unfortunate white man's horror upon discovering that the young object of an extended flirtation on an unsegregated train was not, in fact, white.[25]

Late nineteenth-century courts also increasingly cited "racial integrity" as the goal of antimiscegenation laws, claiming that interracial unions were biologically unsound and therefore subject to the state's intervention. As the courts repeatedly confronted the failure of such statutes and a growing population of mixed-race persons, proponents of banning interracial sex defended and refined their arguments, which reflected a mixture of scientific racism, eugenics, "reform" impulses, and the desirability of maintaining racial "purity." Significantly, in the late nineteenth and early twentieth centuries, the shift from a law based on slavery to one based on the state's interest in racial integrity and public welfare also created a legislative opening to extend bans beyond black-white liaisons to whites' interactions with other nonwhite groups. Virginia's 1924 racial integrity law, for example, declared that it would be "unlawful for any white person in this State to marry any save a white person, or a person with no other admixture of blood than white and American Indian." The exception granted to American Indians— the so-called Pocahontas clause—also neatly demonstrated the susceptibility of law to current political and social concerns. Whiteness included Indianness as a concession to members of the Virginia elite who otherwise would have no longer been white.[26]

In twentieth-century Louisiana, antimiscegenation jurisprudence continued to reflect concerns with property and, particularly, racial boundaries.[27] As Virginia Dominguez argues, laws banning interracial marriage and cohabitation, as well as statutes that denied nonwhite children the right to inherit or to receive legal acknowledgment of white paternity, "all amount[ed] to legal efforts historically to ensure that relationship by 'blood' did not entail equality of status or through equality of status equal access to property." Moreover, the position of antimiscegenation law in the Louisiana state code suggests the strength of state prohibitions. The code paired prohibition of miscegenation with prohibition of incest of the first order between consanguineous relatives, rather than with other articles that dealt with adultery and second-order incest. In Dominguez's words, the pairing "seems awkward but is telling": white lawmakers equated miscegenation with the most socially abhorrent sexual deviance defined by the law.[28]

If one looks back over Louisiana court records prior to *Loving* v. *Virginia's* invalidation of antimiscegenation laws in 1967 and Louisiana's repeal of its own law in 1972, however, one finds a curious discrepancy between the large amount of white political rhetoric devoted to miscegenation and the small number of cases about sex across the race line. While state laws defining miscegenation and race itself ostensibly sought to insure that interracial sex could not go undiscovered or unpunished, the state's legal record of prosecutions and administrations of related issues in marriage, divorce, and inheritance proceedings is surprisingly sparse. The Louisiana Supreme Court (figure 9.2) reviewed more civil cases related to miscegenation than the highest court of any other southern state, a reflection, perhaps, of its unique cultural heritage, but this represented a total of only nineteen cases between 1868 and 1967.[29]

If one were to take the appellate court's record as the measure of the incidence of interracial sex, it would seem as though such unions almost never happened and, from the white state's point of view, that segregation was working.[30] As Robinson has noted, Louisiana was "a southern state that legally both condemned and tolerated interracial sexual violators." In this respect it resembled other states in the region, as strict antimiscegenation laws did not necessarily result in their strict execution. Rather, they seem to have functioned primarily as a social tool to discourage the public, domestic interracial relationships that were more easily monitored by the law.[31] Between 1894, when Louisiana passed its antimiscegenation statute, and

Figure 9.2   Portrait of Governor Luther Egbert Hall (center) and judges of the Supreme Court of Louisiana, ca. 1913.

Source: Courtesy of the Collections of the Library of Congress.

1967, when antimiscegenation laws were invalidated by the U.S. Supreme Court ruling in *Loving v. Virginia*, only five criminal cases appear in the state case law.[32] Only two criminal cases heard at the appellate level, *State v. Daniel* (1910) and *State v. Harris* (1922), resulted in conviction. Perhaps most surprising is *State of Louisiana v. Brown and Aymond* (1959)—a case prosecuted in the heat of conflict over integration and in which both of the accused confessed—was dismissed by the Louisiana Supreme Court. Yet such cases, even in their rarity, provide a provocative view of wider beliefs and practices.

The *Brown and Aymond* case, for example, not only reveals much about the complex of ideas and white anxieties surrounding miscegenation but also provides many clues to why prosecutions of miscegenation were so rare. The case concerned James Brown, Negro, and Lucille Aymond, white, co-workers at a dry cleaner's shop in the rural, central Louisiana parish of Avoyelles. Local police arrested them after their boss, David Blalock, described their "suspicious" behavior to the sheriff. Blalock had become concerned that Brown and Aymond were too friendly. He said as much to Lucille Aymond and warned her to stay away from Brown. The deputy sheriff arrested Brown and then Aymond. After three hours of questioning, Brown confessed that he and Aymond had had intercourse in the bathroom of the shop one day when Blalock was out. After two hours of questioning, Aymond also confessed to the incident. Their confessions, which were riddled with leading questions, were read into the civil district court record. Both were indicted by the grand jury, tried, and convicted together in the Avoyelles district court, and sentenced to a year of hard labor in the state penitentiary in Angola.[33]

Although Blalock had never seen physical contact between the two, their initial transgression had been a friendship that defied customary racial etiquette. "I told her there was too much familiarity between the two of them," he testified, and "that I'd like for her to stay on her side of the shop and do her work and stay away from his side where his work was." Indeed, Blalock confessed to the court that he had misgivings about hiring a black man to work with Aymond in the first place. "I asked Mrs. Aymond if it was agreeable and all right to have a colored man working along with her and if she could stay in her place and keep him in his place," he explained, "because I don't like to mix the two sexes and two races together." According to Blalock, Aymond had replied that "she had worked with [Brown] before and liked him and thought he was a nice fellow."[34]

When Blalock was pressed to define the "familiarity" he found so objectionable, he replied, "Well, [Aymond] waiting on him, serving him coffee, making him his coffee and bringing it to him, drinking coffee with him. She with her cup and he with his standing together drinking coffee."[35] Of course, drinking coffee together is not ordinarily indicative of sexual intimacy. But by defying the usual lines of servility and putting Aymond in the role of a white female employee serving a black man, their coffee breaks did breach the customs of Jim Crow. Racial etiquette strictly constrained the range of acceptable interactions between black men and white women. For the judge and jury, Aymond and Brown's breaks may have evoked other exchanges with sexual overtones—for example, the image of a secretary serving a boss, also an ostensibly professional relationship but one that labor historians have long understood to be emotionally charged.[36] Blalock made a point of noting that they drank coffee at the "back of the shop" rather than in areas where they would be subject to the scrutiny of customers. Simply putting themselves in such a position, he implied, merited suspicion. He also reported that neighbors were talking about the two and that Aymond and her husband socialized with Brown outside of work, attending boxing matches and traveling together to New Orleans.[37]

The Brown-Aymond affair thus dovetailed with many of the myths perpetuated by overwrought whites in the age of integration—namely, that integrated workplaces, lapses in etiquette, and social mixing were dangerous because they all led to one thing: interracial sex. Prompted by leading questions, Brown and Aymond each portrayed the other in ways that were consistent with clichés about interracial sex. In their confessions, neither admitted to a romantic or consensual affair. According to Brown, Aymond was, in his 1950s parlance, no "lady." She talked "about men and women all the time," Brown charged, "so finally one day she told me if I didn't lay her I would be sorry." In contrast, Aymond portrayed Brown as the aggressor and herself as a penitent victim, who had been inexplicably overwhelmed by Brown's advances: "I don't know what made me do it. It just seemed that when he asked me, I just had to give it to him. I don't know why, I don't know what came over me."[38]

Although Brown and Aymond's defense attorney argued, among other points, that the statute against miscegenation was unconstitutional, the Louisiana Supreme Court took the opportunity to reassert the state's right to regulate sex. Citing two United States Supreme Court rulings, the justices noted that *Pace v. State of Alabama* (1883) held that antimiscegenation laws did not violate the equal protection clause of the Constitution because equal penalties were imposed on each race. Indeed the district attorney noted in his brief that "we most likely could have made a deal with one of the parties, say Mrs. Aymond, to turn State's evidence, but we felt that certainly both were *equally guilty* and that to do so would have been discriminatory." As to the constitutionality of antimiscegenation law, the Louisiana Supreme Court asserted that the law fell "squarely within the police power of the state, which has an interest in maintaining the purity of the races and in preventing the propagation of half-breed children." Then, in an odd twist, the court reworked the arguments put forth in *Brown v. Board of Education* as justification for its own ruling in *State v. Brown and Aymond*. "Half-breed" children found it difficult to be accepted, the Louisiana court declared, and quoting the *Brown* decision, it observed that there is "no doubt that children in such a situation are burdened 'with a feeling of inferiority as to their status in the community that may affect their hearts and minds in a way unlikely ever to be undone.' "[39]

Despite the court's ardent defense of the antimiscegenation laws, details of the case reveal a lack of urgency on the matter at the local level. Blalock did not rush out to report the incident to the police. Nor were Brown and Aymond particularly secretive about their friendship. In fact, Brown had initially been arrested because Blalock charged that Brown had embezzled money from him. Only then had Blalock mentioned his other suspicions to Leon Franklin, a deputy sheriff who decided to conduct his own investigation of possible miscegenation. If the two had not confessed, it is easy to imagine that the charges might have been a subterfuge for Franklin to hassle Brown at the behest of Blalock, who was angry about something else. The questions posed to Brown suggested that Blalock had been suspicious for some time. He even claimed to have caught them in the act. According to a transcript of the interrogation, Franklin asked Brown, "James when Mr. David came to the laundry, one day, he said Miss Lucille come out of the rest room and he didn't see you . . . when he got to the shop no one was in the front part, he called and no one answered, after a few minutes Lucille came out of the rest room straightening her clothes. A little later Mr. David said you came in the front door. He said he then suspicioned something was wrong, and he went into the back and the back door was opened which he said he always kept closed. Was that one of the days you had a sexual intercourse with Lucille?" Brown denied it, but he did so within the rules of Jim Crow, addressing the deputy as "Mr. Leon." Only much later did he admit an affair with Aymond, and then he conceded, "[Y]es, sir, I know it was wrong."[40]

The other important factor with bearing on how to read the historical record was the difficulty of *proving* miscegenation in court. Article 79 of the Louisiana Criminal Code defined it as "the marriage or habitual cohabitation of with knowledge of their difference in race, between a person of the Caucasian or white race and a person of the colored or Negro race."[41] While the court read "cohabit" as including more generally "sexual relations or acts of sexual intercourse," the crime itself was difficult to prove. Sharing a home was "strong, if not convincing, evidence of habitual intercourse," according to the court. Interracial marriages were proof of a violation, but such cases were rarely before the judges. Had Aymond produced some of the "half-breed" children that so concerned the court, they might have served as proof. But in this particular case, the only evidence that illegal sex had taken place was Blalock's suspicion and the confessions. On the witness stand, Blalock admitted that he had not seen Brown and Aymond have any physical contact. The state had, in the court's words, "no other evidence, 'literally none at all.' "Nor would the confessions suffice. A basic rule of criminal law holds that conviction requires a *corpus delicti*, or proof that a crime has been committed. Confessions could not be admitted into the record until the commission of a crime had been established. Thus, the Louisiana Supreme Court ruled that the confessions did not constitute grounds to convict and reversed the lower court's verdict.[42]

The difficulty of proving interracial sex outside of marriage, as demonstrated by *State v. Brown and Aymond*, may explain the sparse court record on the issue at the appellate level. Though many whites told themselves that informed, consensual sex between races was unimaginable, interracial sex did occur; when it occurred secretly, outside of marriage or a home, that circumstance could circumvent the state's usual legal gatekeeping mechanisms.[43] Appellate cases, in spite of their accessibility to historians, might not be the level where most convictions or accusations can be found. Brown and Aymond were atypical in choosing to appeal. Their attorney, armed with the decision in *Perez v. Sharp*, a 1948 California case that overruled the state's antimiscegenation law, may have believed the time was right to challenge the constitutionality of Louisiana's law.[44] The Louisiana Supreme Court, in turn, may have granted a rehearing because the justices wanted to reassert the constitutionality of their state law. Criminal prosecutions probably occurred more often, and perhaps proceeded more successfully, at the local level. The *Times-Picayune*, for example, reported a handful of prosecutions in New Orleans and its vicinity in the postwar years. Marcus Christian kept records on official accusations as well as documents supporting his own suspicions.[45] Furthermore, not all cases went to court. A highly publicized racial identity case involving Ralph Dupas, a professional boxer who sued to obtain a "white" birth certificate necessary to compete in segregated bouts, was preceded by a 1956 miscegenation charge leveled against his brother Peter. That charge was dropped, and at least two couples charged with illegal marriages by the same grand jury resided in states that refused to extradite them.[46]

State v. Brown and Aymond also underlines the persistence of extralegal means to prevent sex across the race line. Communities deployed ostracism and gossip, and because white southern culture would not recognize the willing consent of white women, white anxiety and anger were also channeled into demonizing black men as rapists and using threats of lynching to punish alleged transgressions.[47] Blalock, for example, had first confronted Aymond directly, and his testimony suggested that talking may have also been intended to shame the couple into more discretion, if not an end to their affair.

Miscegenation does appear, however, with some regularity elsewhere in the state's legal record, and these cases suggest ways that couples may have hidden sexual relationships under the cover of more traditional black-white relationships. A large body of civil case law concerning inheritance, succession, and concubinage includes numerous cases of interracial relationships brought to the court's attention throughout the first half of the twentieth century. The significance of this category of law is suggested by the statutory record in Louisiana, which until 1942 addressed miscegenation primarily under laws about concubinage, rather than marriage. As the Louisiana Supreme Court acknowledged in *Succession of Lannes* (1936), "Various kinds of disguises have been utilized by parties to conceal the relation of concubinage—housekeeper, storekeeper, cook, maid, nurse, niece, sister-in-law, etc."[48] The first five categories were particularly meaningful for black women and white men, as black women more often held such jobs in white households. Christian's unpublished manuscript also contains similar anecdotes.[49] Historians have likewise recognized the intimacy inherent in such relationships as well as the sexual vulnerability that employment in white households imposed on black women. In at least a few cases, the record suggests that jobs otherwise conforming to expectations of white-black relationships may have provided cover for illicit relationships.[50]

The relationship between J. W. Jones, white, and his "cook" Amanda Kyle, Negro, seems to have been such a case. Kyle lived in Jones's house from 1904 until 1907 or 1908 and, after that, in a house he built for her on his property. Kyle cooked and kept house for Jones and waited on customers at his store. They did not have children, but, according to the neighbors, "general talk" was that Jones was "keeping" Kyle. One acquaintance even claimed to have found them in bed together. Apparently no one ever reported their activity as criminal. The relationship might have never appeared in the record had Jones not left all of his considerable estate, worth approximately $40,000 in 1926, to Kyle, provoking a challenge from Jones's nieces and nephews.

In court, the nieces and nephews attacked the relationship and charged that Kyle and Jones had lived together in a state of illegal "open concubinage." As defined by Louisiana law, "open concubinage" was more morally repugnant and damaging to community morals than secret concubinage and was therefore punished by limiting the surviving partner's right to inherit from the other's estate.[51] Kyle denied that she was any more to Jones than his cook, and at least a dozen witnesses so testified on her behalf. Interestingly the legal issue was not the relationship per se, but whether it was open or secret, which had a direct bearing on her right to inherit. The court concluded that Kyle and Jones had been a couple, citing among other evidence her access to Jones's cash drawer and their living together, but the court disagreed with Jones's nieces and nephews, concluding that the relationship was secret. Jones hid his relationship while keeping "her in his employ ostensibly as cook and housekeeper and assistant in his store" In fact, by folding the document so that only the signature lines were exposed, he had even kept the contents of his will a secret from the witnesses who signed it. Therefore Kyle was allowed to inherit Jones's estate.[52]

It would of course be a mistake to draw too broad a conclusion from this case, as the employer-employee relationship can be entirely professional, entirely antagonistic, or simply abusive. In many situations, household service subjected women to sexual harassment and made them vulnerable to assault. The white mythology of black hypersexuality historically subjected black women to much abuse that white men described as consensual. But the existence of Amanda Kyle and those involved in a handful of similar cases in the twentieth century does suggest a significant loophole in Jim Crow laws where interracial relationships could escape attention.[53] As many labor historians note, the private and intimate nature of household service historically posed a latent ideological challenge to segregation, even if white society's commitment to having inexpensive and readily available black help always trumped such ideological inconsistencies. Indeed, some historians argue that the figure of an asexual, apolitical, maternal black household worker serving the white home was central to whites' self-image and exercise of power at the turn of the century.[54] It is thus deeply ironic that given white preoccupation with preventing interracial sex as the key to maintaining whiteness, the service of black workers provided a site where interracial intimacy could be hidden or denied. The employer-servant relationship was one that most whites accepted as natural, appropriate, and even benign. Significantly, in the case of J. W. Jones and Amanda Kyle, the neighbors talked, but no one challenged the appropriateness of a white man having a live-in black female housekeeper.

By far the most visible arena of state activism against miscegenation, however, was directed toward *preventing* it, not punishing it. In Louisiana, state definitions of who was white and who was black did not always correspond to social definitions, so antimiscegenation law often required steps to prevent an inadvertent marriage of people across the race line. One of Marcus Christian's strategies in looking for clues to miscegenation, for example, was to scour the *Times-Picayune* white society pages for photographs of racially ambiguous "whites."[55] Interestingly, state officials often worked with some of the same "folk" indicators of race that Christian employed, and they sometimes delayed or denied marriage licenses on the basis of any number of factors: a suspicious surname, an applicant having been born in a locale known to have a large mixed-race population, and simply the officials' own doubts. Local registrars acted on their authority as long-term residents, who "knew" which families were black and which were white. The state bureau of vital statistics and its counterpart in New Orleans (the two offices under the state board of health charged with maintaining records) also used access to vital statistics to verify and maintain the integrity of racial statistics.[56] The requirement that race appear on marriage licenses probably prevented an untold number of persons from unknowingly marrying across the legal line separating black from white. Members of "white" families, when informed that the family had a "touch of the tar brush," might complain, write letters to their state representative, appeal to the directors of the board of health, or even bring a lineup of blue-eyed, blond relatives to the registrar's office, but, according to bureau employees, the angered family often avoided court because of the potential for public exposure.[57]

Licensing of marriage thus provided the state its main legal avenue to intervene against interracial relationships and, in turn, played a singular role in shaping the law of racial identity in Louisiana. Twentieth-century racial identity trials, including those in Louisiana, have received considerable attention from scholars, and the trials in the following case studies generally conform to the dynamics identified in those studies. The legal system in Louisiana, as elsewhere in the United States, defined whiteness in terms of exclusion. It said not what made a person white, but what put a person outside the favored class. As legal scholars and historians have shown, this standard has variously served to defend white supremacy, limit access to citizenship, deprive nonwhite groups of property and civil rights, and maintain "racial integrity."[58] Antimiscegenation law has also played a primary role in defining whiteness and in shaping the legal discourse of race.[59]

In the first half of the twentieth century, Louisiana's legislature and supreme court attempted to eliminate any remaining loopholes allowing marriage between whites and mixed-race persons. In doing so the legislature and court imposed both the notorious "one-drop" rule and the extraordinary legal standard of "no room for doubt" for those who might challenge their legal racial designation. *State v. Treadaway et al.* (1910), for example, considered the legality of a relationship between Octave Treadaway, white, and his companion, Josephine Lightell, an octoroon (commonly understood in Louisiana to be someone "one-eighth Negro"). The law subject to debate in this case was a 1908 statute making interracial concubinage between whites and persons "of the [N]egro or black race" a felony. Given the historic use of the terms *Negro* and *black* in Louisiana, the state supreme court was forced to determine that an "octoroon" was perhaps "colored," but not a "Negro," and therefore not covered by the 1908 law.[60] However, the decision prompted the next session of the state legislature to make a hasty revision of the law to include any "person of the colored or black race. . . . "[61] "Colored," the Louisiana supreme court had decided, was a category broader than "Negro" and included a person of "mixed blood." As Dominguez argues, this case was an important turning point in Louisiana history away from the old tripartite system (black, white, and colored) toward a binary understanding of race (black/white) and reflected a changing ideological climate.[62] In 1938 another intermarriage case, *Sunseri v. Cassagne*, firmly established the "one-drop" rule in Louisiana jurisprudence, as the court decided that any trace of African ancestry required a person to be designated "colored."[63] The case did not involve criminal miscegenation, but the race of a wife and thus the legality of a marriage were at issue.

Sunseri, like all the cases considered in this essay, indicated the important and recurring role that knowledge of race—and particularly the state's control of that knowledge—played in cases involving miscegenation. In Brown and Aymond's case, one argument made by their defense had been that the state had not proven the race of the defendants or their knowledge of each other's race. The statute describing criminal miscegenation specifically noted that violation of the law required knowledge of race by the accused parties. Although the district attorney argued that "the jurors certainly had an opportunity to view the defendants and observe their color," observation often proved less important than knowledge of official records in establishing legal racial identity.[64] Inclusion of that phrase in the law itself gestured toward an important area in Louisiana jurisprudence, as the race of one party was often the issue under litigation.

While *Sunseri* is frequently cited as the preeminent example of white Louisiana's dogmatic inflexibility on matters of black and white, a closer examination of the full case record—a level of documentation often overlooked in legal studies—provides insight into the popular understandings of race that often governed relationships and ultimately decisions about marriage. In 1936, Cyril P. Sunseri, a New Orleans resident facing prosecution for nonpayment of alimony, filed for an annulment of his marriage on the grounds that his wife, Verna Cassagne, was "a person of color." The state supreme court eventually determined that Cassagne was a descendant of Fanny Ducre, a former slave, with traceable African ancestry and therefore annulled the marriage; however, the testimony collected in the civil district court provides a unique and revealing insight into the collective popular perceptions of race in mid-twentieth-century Louisiana. It poignantly speaks to the legal conundrum in distinguishing between representation and essence, as Eva Saks has so ably described. But the record also reveals the essentially epistemological, or socially learned, nature of race in everyday life. The court made a simple black-white decision, but repeatedly witnesses proved reluctant, if not unable, to do the same.[65]

Cyril Sunseri and Verna Cassagne met while she was attending a white high school. In 1935, when she was seventeen, they eloped and then moved in with her mother, Stella Cusachs Cassagne. They lived together for several months, until, according to Verna and Stella Cassagne and several friends of the family, Cyril Sunseri became abusive and Stella Cassagne evicted him from the house. Sunseri claimed that he left on his own accord "when he found out what kind of tramp she was." Because Verna Cassagne was a minor, the case fell under the jurisdiction of the juvenile court, which ordered Sunseri to pay support. Although his reference to Cassagne as a "tramp" deployed a common racial stereotype, he claimed that race was not the issue when they first separated. According to Sunseri, "It must have been three weeks or so after I had left her when someone told me they heard she had colored blood and I started investigating."[66] He contacted a lawyer and his senator and filed for annulment. His case rested on the status of Verna Cassagne's great-great-grandmother Fanny, a slave emancipated in 1837 by Leander Ducre, her white owner who later became her husband. Fanny Ducre was identified on subsequent documents, notarial acts under which she acquired slaves, as "F.W.C.," or "Free woman of color," and "F.C.L.," or *Femme de Couleur Libre*, ambiguous terms that applied in the antebellum period to anyone not recognized as purely "white," but these labels did not necessarily mean someone of African descent or someone who had been a slave. The term *Colored* became synonymous with *Negro* only after the Civil War.[67] Cassagne's lawyers appealed to Louisiana's equivalent of the Virginia Pocahontas clause and argued that Fanny Ducre was an Indian, not a Negro.[68]

The court considered documentary evidence such as certificates of birth, marriage, and death; obituaries; and voter registration records, as well as witness testimony on how the Cassagnes conducted themselves as white people. Verna Cassagne had been born in a white maternity ward, had received her first communion in a white church, had attended white public schools, and had graduated from a white girls' school. Her mother was vice president of the New Orleans Linen Supply Company, a "white organization," according to the court; was a registered white Democratic voter; and had participated in several primary elections—without challenge, the court emphasized. Both women had occupied white seats on buses, streetcars, and trains, and they attended theaters, patronized hotels, and ate at restaurants for whites. Stella Cassagne's explanation for the most damning evidence, Verna's birth certificate identifying her as "colored," was that when a representative of the board of health had come to her home after the birth, she was ill, an aunt, now deceased, had filled out the card, and the board had made a mistake. The original card, according to the chief clerk, had been lost.[69]

Over a dozen witnesses who had known Fanny Ducre and her descendants were called to the stand, and much of the testimony concerned the appearances, both physical and social, of the family members in question. Witnesses disagreed on how to identify a white, a Negro, and an Indian, and they provided wildly contradictory descriptions. Various witnesses described Fanny Ducre as "a nigger woman, plain straight"; "dark skinned"; "black"; "of a copper color" with "long straight black hair"; "someone who always did go for white"; as having "tolerable fair hair, what we call Madagascar hair"; "just like an Indian and nice hair hanging straight back, just as straight as you want"; and always "taken for white people."[70] The distinction between "Indian" and "Negro" proved particularly difficult to pin down in court. Questioning a woman who identified herself as "colored," the district attorney asked, "Aunt Fanny was about your color, wasn't she?" He received the answer, "No, just like I tell you, just like an Indian." When he replied, "Don't tell us that. Tell us what an Indian looks like," she could only add, "Just like an Indian." The court then pressed for elaboration: "What do you mean by an Indian? How did she look?" "Well," the witness replied, "an Indian look a nice color. I can't say, me. You don't see Indian?"[71] The attorneys occasionally tried to pin down descriptions by asking witnesses to compare Fanny to themselves: "Your color is considered brown or yellow, isn't it?" and "Was your hair straight before it went gray?"[72] A woman identified as Fanny's daughter-in-law told the court, "She was black, she was about my color. She couldn't be white, you know I can't be white, can I? She was about my color, no difference in her and me." Even with such direct comparisons, the results were absurd, as the court recognized the subjectivity of descriptions and then entered its own opinion as fact. Of the daughter-in-law, the court "admitted that this witness is a very dark negress, the usual color of a person of Negro race, a full-blooded Negro." The record was peppered with such observations: "It is admitted the witness's hair is kinky."[73]

Though many witnesses entered physical descriptions with some certainty, few made confident pronouncements about the race of a subject in question. Most of the testimony merely underlined the uncertainty of whether Fanny and her descendants were white or black. Some suggested that Fanny and her children had "passed" as white, although the court in this case focused exclusively on the issue of the marriage rather than the question of deliberate deception. Many accounts made it clear that racial definitions were contextual and contingent. When the deputy recorder of births, deaths, and marriages in New Orleans was questioned about the death certificate of one of Fanny Ducre's sons, Drauzin Ducre, he said that he knew the deceased man but was uncertain about Ducre's race, "Well," he told the court, "I wasn't a native over there, but he was always considered colored, but of course I never looked in—had no occasion to look up whether he was or not."[74] Another witness who knew Drauzin Ducre said that "he might be a white man, he never told me, but he always used go with the white people, never come amongst us [colored] at all."[75] Another witness testified that Fanny's other son, Toussaint Ducre, was a "Negro" but looked like a white man. "He could pass anywhere for a white man," she told the court, "and I can prove it because he worked for a white man and went to the St. Charles [Hotel] with him."[76] When the registrar of Lacombe answered questions about Verna Cassagne's mother, Stella Cusachs, she said, "The hearsay was always they [the Cusachs] were colored and that I couldn't prove." When asked whether this was majority opinion in Lacombe, she could say only that "amongst the white people they were always considered colored."[77]

That the testimony about relatives several generations back should be contradictory is perhaps not surprising, but more striking were the conditional terms with which witnesses deployed racial categories with respect to themselves or the defendants. When a resident of Lacombe, who testified as an acquaintance of Fanny Ducre, was asked whether she herself was "colored," she replied, "Well, I will tell you the truth, I can't tell you I am colored and I can't tell you I am white, because I may be Italian, my mother and father, and I can't say if they were white or colored, you understand, a person should come with the truth." The court declared her "light tan or light brown" but did not admit whether she was "colored" or "white." Interestingly, this witness was nevertheless certain about what race Fanny Ducre's daughter should be: "She always did go for white, but she wasn't. She was colored."[78] A friend of the Cassagnes, Pauline Roubion, who lived with Stella Cassagne when the newly wed Sunseris moved in, described herself as being of "Italian descent"—ordinarily a marker for whiteness—but was surprisingly noncommittal when asked about her "race." Asked whether she was white, she replied: "I think I am. . . . Well, maybe, some might think I am colored because I am supposed to be staying with colored people or I stayed with colored people [the Cassagnes]." However, she had never heard anyone say that the Cassagnes were "colored." Verna Cassagne's attorney declared that Roubion was white; Cyril Sunseri's attorney admitted only that "she has the appearance of a white person."[79] Even Sunseri, when asked about his friends, who were not subjects of the proceedings at hand, answered vaguely and said only "I knew them as being white."[80] Neighbors, according to an acquaintance of the Cassagnes, had called them "Negroes," and though the Cassagnes allegedly threatened to file charges, they never did.[81] Verna Cassagne said she had "been taught" that she was of French, Spanish, and English descent. Sunseri's attorneys claimed that the Cassagnes had become known as white only when they moved to New Orleans.[82]

The manner in which witnesses described race was striking—resembling the observations of historians more than the answers one might expect from people living under segregation. However, mid-twentieth-century Louisianans did not believe that race was simply a social construction; most of the people in court, whether they identified themselves as "white" or "colored"—and certainly the ones who ventured speculation about people passing as white—probably did believe that there were genuine categories of "colored" and "white." Their testimony also indicated that they believed that there was a right answer about who belonged in which one. But they also believed that they could be wrong and seem to have intuitively understood the fluidity of one measure and the rigidity of the other.

The operative phrase for many was "to know someone as." Many of the witnesses implicitly recognized the distance between an epistemological understanding of race as something "known" and a kind of absolute, hidden essence of race that supposedly lay behind the legally valid, official designation. Yet they still seemed committed to the metaphysical view that there really was a racial fact of the matter. In other words they admitted that they could not read race on a body or know race with certainty when they encountered a person in day-to-day life. Until a person landed in court or official records were checked, social knowledge was the information that mattered. Even the Louisiana Supreme Court that had granted Verna Cassagne a second opportunity to gather evidence to prove her whiteness, acknowledged the significance of such social validation. In the first trial, the court concluded, "the evidence, while persuasive, is not conclusive and does not warrant us in holding that defendant is a member of the colored race, particularly in view of the overwhelming testimony that she and her immediate associates have always been regarded as members of the white race and have associated with persons of that race," Both the court and the witnesses thus implicitly recognized two sorts of identity, neither of which could be absolutely determined by physical descriptions or, in this case, by documentary records. Unfortunately for Verna Cassagne, on a second hearing the court determined that birth and marriage certificates identifying her mother, her aunts, and herself as colored were more persuasive than testimony from friends and neighbors. Those documents left the court "no alternative" but to conclude that she had "a traceable amount of [N]egro blood" and to annul the marriage.[83]

Such logical conundrums had roots in Louisiana's unique history, a past with which many witnesses in this and other twentieth-century cases had direct experience. The enduring controversy over the racial meaning of *Creole*, for example, illustrated both the ambiguity of racial categories in Louisiana and the long history of white Louisianans' discomfort with that uncertainty. A term adopted in the early nineteenth century to describe Louisiana residents of European descent and to distinguish them from new American settlers, *Creole* was not originally a racial or racially exclusive category. Although, much to the consternation of white Creoles, outsiders occasionally assumed that *Creole* implied mixed blood, locals did not initially insist that the term apply to whites only. Rather, as historian Joseph G. Tregle Jr. notes, white New Orleanians constructed an elaborate myth about Creoles in contrast to Americans, as an exclusive local aristocracy descended from French and Spanish nobility, "renowned for . . . cultural refinement and worldly sophistication. . . . " In doing so, they felt no need to limit their use of *Creole* to whites, as they "perceived no danger from common acceptance of blacks and whites under the Creole rubric, [and] no risk that such definitional partnership might diminish the social status or prerogative of the dominant class."[84]

After the Civil War, however, white Creoles no longer "feigned unconcerned amusement" when outsiders mistakenly assumed that *Creole* meant something other than *white*. In the late nineteenth century, the post-Reconstruction surge of white supremacy, the imposition of segregation, and the fame of George Washington Cable's writings on Louisiana Creoles as racially mixed unleashed an obsessive fixation on race among white New Orleans Creoles.[85] A number of Creole social organizations and scholars claimed the title *Creole* and began defining it as exclusively white. Interestingly, in his research and public addresses, Marcus Christian begged to differ, claiming *Creole* as a category specifically defined as mixed-race descent. Virginia Dominguez's fascinating study of the manipulations and contradictions that shaped self-conceptions of identity in Louisiana in the late twentieth century reveals the long-term significance of such anxieties over whiteness. Many of the self-identified white Creole informants whom she interviewed in the 1970s and 1980s made a point of explaining to her that they were not colored. But the continuing disputes about the racial status of Creoles also implicitly recognized that individual Louisianans could not completely control their own racial identity. "Suspicion" was "part of everyday life," Dominguez concludes, and "[w]hites often grow up afraid to know their own genealogies." Many families, Dominguez found, simply left Louisiana after "rumors spread about their questionable ancestry."[86]

Marriage law took on a substantial part of the burden in drawing and policing the line between black and white. It was one of the few places where the state could bridge the gap between epistemological and metaphysical understandings of race and impose the final authority of its own definition. In Cassagne's case, regulation of marriage had become the tool to prevent any further descendants of the Cassagne family from passing as white in Louisiana. Moreover, it established the standard of proof to be met by any other plaintiff accused of passing or claiming to be legally white. In *Sunseri v. Cassagne*, the court determined that claims against the accuracy of state documents must produce sufficient evidence such that there could be "no room for doubt" that the original classification was wrong. This was an exceptionally stringent burden of proof, as legal scholars have noted, even "more difficult to carry than the criminal 'beyond a reasonable doubt' standard," but the ruling determined judgments in later cases.[87]

The final case considered here, *Villa v. Lacoste*, an annulment case heard before the Louisiana Supreme Court in 1948, revealed ongoing tensions within Louisianans' concepts of racial identity, as witnesses repeatedly demonstrated their adherence to more complex and contingent appraisals of race than the law would allow. This case also underlined the significance of socially understood racial identity, since the evidence suggests that if the couple had not separated, Josephine Lacoste's status as white would have never been questioned. As in the *Sunseri* case, the "discovery" of race happened long after the fact. In order to avoid paying alimony to support his wife, Josephine Lacoste, and their six-year-old son, Charles Stephen Villa sued for an annulment and a disclaimer of paternity, claiming that his wife was Negro, on the basis of a birth certificate identifying her as "colored." The issue for the court was Josephine Lacoste's maternal line. Her father was French and therefore white, but her mother, Catherine Lacoste, was the child of a white woman and an immigrant from the Philippines.[88] How to classify Filipinos in the racial system of New Orleans had been a "bone of contention" among the staff of the board of health for some time.[89] Other persons of Asian descent, including Chinese and Japanese immigrants, were registered by nationality, but Filipino immigrants, who were uncommon outside the western United States and, in the context of Louisiana, certainly exotic, were a gray area for the board of health.[90] Catherine Lacoste had the misfortune of having the birth of her daughter Josephine registered by a deputy recorder who recognized only two categories, white and colored, and considered Asians to be the latter. Although the elder Lacoste, who had registered her grandson's birth on behalf of her daughter, worked in a white job in a white department store, was registered to vote in white Democratic primaries, and was registered as white on her marriage certificate, she obeyed when the recorder said that she could not register the birth of her daughter or grandson as white. "When the man told me to put colored," she explained to the court, "I put colored."[91] She could just as easily have been told to register the child as white because the deputy recorder's successor regarded Filipinos as white.[92]

Although nine states had laws prohibiting marriages between Filipinos and whites, Filipinos were not directly addressed in Louisiana's antimiscegenation statute, which, as written and litigated, reflected its ties to segregation and had applied only to persons of African descent.[93] Rather than arguing in favor of a more abstract "racial integrity" in order to annul the marriage, Villa's attorneys revealed their own commitment to the black-white binary by arguing that Filipinos were actually "Negroes." Citing *Webster's Dictionary*, the *Encyclopaedia Britannica*, and anthropological texts on the Philippines, Villa's lawyers attempted to prove "the existence of Negroes or blacks or Negroid or negritoes in the Philippine Islands, since 'negritoes' was 'Spanish' for 'little Negroes.'" Lacoste's witnesses included an eighty-six-year old friend of her grandfather, who had emigrated with him, and the elderly man made a point of emphasizing that Lacoste's grandfather was a "Blanco Filipino," or white Filipino. Indulging in a little scientific racism of their own, Lacoste's attorneys argued that "in no event can plaintiffs counsel locate an acceptable authority that a 'Filipino Blanco' can be a Negrito. The dwarfish, backward, wholly uncivilized Negritos have virtually no commerce or contact with other inhabitants of the Philippine Islands, and if a single one has come to the United States, it was doubtless as a chained or caged captive."[94] Undaunted, Villa's attorneys still pressed the Negro line, asking her grandfather's Filipino friend whether there were "any colored people at all on the Philippine Islands?" and whether he had ever "seen a Negro in the Philippine Islands?" [95]

Evidence accepted in district court concerning this case, like that considered in *Sunseri*, consisted of both documentary and social evidence of race, and the social evidence took up much of the proceedings. Charles Villa and Josephine Lacoste had known each other since they were teenagers, having met in a hosiery factory where both had worked in "white" jobs. Lacoste had attended white schools; her baby had been delivered in a white maternity ward. She always kept to the white side of the segregation line in public conveyances. When the court asked her if she sat in the white section of the theater, she answered, "Why not? I always placed myself as white." Furthermore, no one "had ever questioned her color."[96] Villa himself said he "never had any suspicion about her color." "It all come up," he told the court, when "a cousin of mine and a relation of hers that ran away and they got married, and a remark was passed [that] they were colored." His mother, who had heard rumors about the color of the Lacostes, "went up there [to the board of health] to satisfy herself, to find out whether it was true or not as far as my wife was concerned."[97] There, she discovered the "colored" birth certificates.

Interestingly, Villa's attorneys did not try to prove that Filipinos generally, rather than "negritoes" specifically, were "colored" or even that they were "Malay," which would have made the marriage illegal in several other states.[98] Neither side referred to resolutions of the issue in states other than Louisiana. For all the witnesses, as well as the lower and higher courts, the important issues were whiteness and blackness. Villa's attorneys tried to link Lacoste to "colored" people in New Orleans, where the family lived. Villa claimed that his wife and mother-in-law visited with a "colored family that lived on the corner. . . . They allow my baby to go in and out the house, like it is one of the family." Visiting might not be proof of sharing the same racial identity, so Villa's attorney's asked him: "They sit down and eat at the same table?" Villa admitted that he had never seen them eating together. Catherine Lacoste, falling back on another Louisiana standby for describing racial ambiguity, said the family on the corner was "Spanish," which in this context also meant white. Another witness for Villa, however, gestured toward another social indicator of race commonly recognized in court, claiming that he knew the neighbors in question were colored because the wife had worked for his mother as household help. Lacoste's counsel brought their white friends forward to attest to the Lacoste family's whiteness. One family friend, asked if she was white, said, "I hope I am."

She reported that she had visited the Lacoste home "quite often" and had "never seen any niggers there."[99]

Charles Villa, who had sought the annulment, apparently also had more flexible views of race than his suit allowed. Two weeks after filing for an annulment, he went to visit Josephine Lacoste, she said, and suggested "we go away, leave town, pack up and leave town." Apparently he believed the rumors about her "colored" blood but nevertheless wanted to reconcile and live somewhere the marriage would be legal. His wife told him "it was no use, that it would still be hanging over my head." She had always been accepted and had access to all the benefits of being white in New Orleans, but she felt it necessary to prove that she was not "colored."[100]

The state supreme court obliged and ruled that the Filipino Lacoste family was mistakenly registered as "colored."[101] In Louisiana, if a person was "not Negro," that was all that mattered for the sake of marriage to a white person. But the court's willingness to override the documentary evidence in this case did not in any way indicate a slackening of the justices' racial views. If anything, it confirmed the significance of the black-white line and the real intent of antimiscegenation statutes, which was to prevent one kind of interracial marriage. As it happened, the rigidity of Louisiana justice on the black/white line served Josephine Lacoste well.

In the late 1950s, the state turned the accoutrements of antimiscegenation law—its records and licensing functions—even more directly to the defense of segregation. Ironically, it was the impending collapse of segregation in other parts of society that led Louisiana state authorities to adopt more stringent procedures to strengthen antimiscegenation law. The shoring up of broad segregation laws and their concurrent discouragement of miscegenation may have contributed to the slim numbers of miscegenation cases in state courts. In the 1950s and early 1960s, in the interest of "racial integrity" and in defiance of school desegregation, Louisiana's legislature passed 131 additional segregation statutes, far more than any other southern state. New laws segregated "all public parks, recreation centers, playgrounds, community centers and other such facilities" and prohibited racial interactions in situations ranging from interracial sporting competition, to shared eating utensils, to the mixture of "black" and "white" blood plasma in hospitals.[102] The newly fortified segregation laws strengthened antimiscegenation efforts by prohibiting the sort of casual contact that many believed led to relationships like that between Lucille Aymond and James Brown and by introducing new measures to prevent accidental unions similar to the one between "white" Cyril Sunseri and "Negro" Verna Cassagne. Significantly, many of the new statutes, including the law determining eligibility for a marriage certificate, placed a much heavier emphasis on the legal designation of race, requiring an official state birth certificate, with seal, designating the applicant's race. In 1955, the state legislature made official documentation of race a requirement for public school registration. In 1958, it became mandatory for marriage license applications. Stoked by massive resistance, the state's attention to the law of racial identity intensified in the decade prior to *Loving v. Virginia*.[103]

In keeping with Louisiana's new segregation laws, in 1957 the New Orleans Board of Health introduced a working "race list" of surnames known to the board as historically "Negro," against which all requests for marriage licenses and other documents were to be double-checked for racial accuracy.[104] This policy aimed to prevent intentional miscegenation and also provided the state a new method to prevent inadvertent interracial marriage and to expose those who, like the members of the Lacoste family, had been "passing" as white. Although it is impossible to know how many marriage licenses were denied as a result, the staff of the board of health were notoriously thorough, conducting extensive genealogical research, even in records out of the state. Between 1957 and 1965, Louisiana court records indicate that a minimum of 4,720 applications for certified copies of birth certificates, undoubtedly many from engaged couples seeking a marriage license, were "flagged" for further inquiry and held back by the board because of questions about race. On a peak day, the board of health office in New Orleans would process as many as seven hundred requests for documents.[105] If a question about race arose, the deputy registrar and office staff simply refused to issue a marriage license. By interposing themselves between men and women who, until the 1950s, would have identified each other as members of the same race and might have been able to marry, the administrators of the law actually introduced a much stricter application of the antimiscegenation laws. In doing so, the board began to compensate for many of the law's weaknesses and, it could be argued, actually contributed to a substantial redefinition of what comprised miscegenation in marriage.

The new segregation laws also represented a historic turning point in the construction of race, by enhancing the state's ability to control the terms of definition in Louisiana. In public schools, for example, where "social evidence" had once prevailed and Cyril Sunseri first met Verna Cassagne, the state now enacted a screening process for all pupils and required for entry an official birth certificate designating race.[106] Therefore, such records permitted state officials not only to enforce customary segregation but also to enforce segregation laws according to a strict *legal* definition of black and white. Rigorous bureaucratic procedures also allowed the state to make such determinations of race *first* and thus circumvent the usual social process of racial definition by imposing stricter separation between those people it chose to define as white or black. In the 1960s, the board's defenders argued that race was not "an accidental quality which can be acquired by association with other races . . . through fraud, misrepresentation and deceit." It was "substance of the being, an inherited trait, acquired from ancestry genetically."[107]

As this examination of miscegenation case law has demonstrated, however, such definitions had not always prevailed in Louisiana. For the first half of the twentieth century, race was, in spite of the one-drop designation, "known" as it was brokered, negotiated, tested, and asserted in day-to-day life between individuals. The state held that there was a meaningful difference between being "known as" one race and "legally" belonging to a racial category, but case studies of miscegenation prior to the 1960s reveal the inability, and perhaps unwillingness in some cases, of ordinary folks to make such distinctions when they courted, became engaged, or simply had sex. In the guise of other relationships, some Louisiana couples like J. W. Jones and Amanda Kyle and James Brown and Lucille Aymond circumvented the law's intent. But even when it came to conventional and legally sanctioned relationships like marriage, the successful separation of races depended upon the "proper" outcome of countless situations and personal exchanges in school admissions, housing rentals, hotel registrations, voter registrations, the streets, workplaces, bars, dance halls, and all other public spaces.

The small numbers of miscegenation prosecutions in the twentieth century may indicate that Louisianans accepted prohibitions on sexual relationships with people socially defined as racially different, but there are also suggestions that Marcus Christian's hunches were probably right. Antimiscegenation law repeatedly failed. As Eva Saks has argued, antimiscegenation law has historically been "committed to the separation of *looked like* (possession of whiteness without legal title to it) from *was* (good title to whiteness)."[108] The many witnesses called on behalf of miscegenation proceedings—and undoubtedly an even greater number of betrothed who never appeared in court—repeatedly demonstrated the failure of the people to uphold or respect that commitment. In doing so, ordinary Louisianans not only crafted and enforced their own definition of acceptable marriages, but also became the primary, if only temporary, architects of the construction of race at mid-century.

Notes

Ms. Brattain is an associate professor of history at Georgia State University.

1. "Sheep Goats and Passer Pour Blanches," unpublished manuscript by Marcus Christian, Folder "Ebony Magazine research re passe pour blanc," Box 12, Series XIII.l: Historical Manuscripts, Marcus Bruce Christian Papers (Special Collections, Earl K. Long Library, University of New Orleans; hereinafter cited as Christian Papers). On Christian, see Marilyn S. Hessler, "Marcus Christian: The Man and His Collection," *Louisiana history* 28 (Winter 1987–1988): 37–55; and Jerah Johnson, "Marcus B. Christian and the WPA History of Black People in Louisiana," *Louisiana history* 20 (Winter 1979–1980): 113–15. I would like to thank Jennifer Gonzalez for her research assistance and Andrew Milne, Krystyn Moon, and the anonymous readers for the *Journal of Southern history* for their criticisms and suggestions.

2. Christian saved the clipping of an August 22, 1959, death notice for a man named Ernest Joubert and wrote to himself "Mercy Hospital is white *all white. Check*"; on a clipping of the obituaries dated August 23, 1959, he editorialized: "Those who notice a Negro 'passing' remember him best who know him longer. No Ernest Joubert listed here??? Bakay-Baham??? Private burial? No Joubert listed in next day's death in Picayune, also"; on a clipping dated September 8, 1959, Christian circled the name "Joubert" in an ad for a "colored" apartment and wrote to himself: "The man who died, Sr.?" See Christian's clippings from the New Orleans *Times-Picayune*, dated (handwritten on each clipping) August 22, August 23, and September 8, 1859, in Folder "January-July 1960," Box 16, all in Series VI: Clippings, Christian Papers; emphasis

appears in originals (as underlining). For the 1960 photograph of the fiftieth-anniversary celebration, see a clipping dated January 28, 1960, in the same folder.

3. Interracial marriage was prohibited by both French and Spanish colonial authorities in Louisiana. American lawmakers maintained that prohibition, outlawing interracial marriage in 1808. More detail on the legal history of interracial sex follows below. For a discussion of the myths of racial purity in Louisiana, see Virginia R. Dominguez, *White by Definition: Social Classification in Creole Louisiana* (New Brunswick, NJ, 1986), 185–204.

4. See, for example, the Citizens' Council's pamphlet "What is the Citizens' Council? Defender of Racial Integrity, States Rights, and the Constitution," in Folder "Citizen's Council of Greater New Orleans," Series 1963, Box S63–65, in Mayor Victor H, Schiro Records (Louisiana Division, City Archives and Special Collections, New Orleans Public Library; hereinafter cited as New Orleans Public Library); "Citizen Council Canvass Slated," New Orleans *Times-Picayune*, January 27, 1956, p, 13, col, 1; and Glen Jeansonne, *Leander Perez: Boss of the Delta* (Baton Rouge, LA, 1977), 222–25.

5. The statute under which Brown and Aymond were charged was La, R, S, 14:79 (Article 79 of Louisiana's revised statutes, criminal code). The code and the legal punishment are cited in *State of Louisiana v. James Brown and Lucille Aymond*, 236 La, 562, 108 So, 2d 233 (1959), The full text of the statute appears in the published *Louisiana Revised Civil Code*, 1128–1130 (1949), Older copies of published Louisiana statutes (which are no longer valid) are available for research at the Louisiana State Supreme Court Library in New Orleans.

6. As numerous scholars have argued, miscegenation law is not a mere by-product of racial ideas; it contributes to the construction and reconstruction of those ideas. See, for example, Eva Saks, "Representing Miscegenation Law," *Raritan* 8 (Fall 1988): 39–69; Peggy Pascoe, "Miscegenation Law, Court Cases, and Ideologies of 'Race' in Twentieth-Century America," *Journal of American History* 83 (June 1996): 44–69; Peter W, Bardaglio, " 'Shamefull Matches': The Regulation of Interracial Sex and Marriage in the South before 1900," in Martha Hodes, ed., *Sex, Love, Race: Crossing Boundaries in North American History* (New York, 1999), 112–38; and Barbara J. Fields, "Ideology and Race in American History," in J, Morgan Kousser and James M, McPherson, eds,. *Region, Race, and Reconstruction: Essays in Honor of C. Vann Woodward* (New York, 1982), 143–77.

7. Pascoe, "Miscegenation Law," 7.

8. A note on the language of race in this essay: Though I regard race as nothing more than a social construction, as a historian I also recognize the significance, power, and reality of a racial label or designation in its historical context. Accordingly, I use the words of contemporaries since that is the meaning or designation that matters historically. If they describe someone as "Negro," or "colored," so do I. Although some may find this antiquated racial language of the courts problematic, I think that recognizing race as a social construction requires a scholar to treat the idea as historically bounded and thus refuse to translate their words/ideas into seemingly equivalent twenty-first-century terms. The only change that I have made as a concession to style is to regularize the capitalization of *Negro*. My approach to the cases concerning racial identity is similar. I do not make any claims as to what might be the "proper" racial designation for a person, since I do not believe that there is one. What mattered historically was the designation that prevailed at the time, either in the court or in a subject's community more generally. Similarly, if a person was regarded as one race by their peers and another by the courts, the person did, in a very real sense, possess two racial identities. Self-identity, social identity, and legal identity were separate entities, and each possessed very real historical implications that demand that scholars recognize the validity of each.

9. For a discussion of the limitations of legal records, see note 30 and text below.

10. A. Leon Higginbotham Jr. and Barbara K. Kopytoff, "Racial Purity and Interracial Sex in the Law of Colonial and Antebellum Virginia," in Werner Sollors, ed., *Interracialism: Black-White Intermarriage in American History. Literature, and Law* (New York, 2000), 81–139 (quotation on p. 84).

11. Bardaglio, ' "Shamefull Matches,' " 112–38 (quotation on p. 113); Peter Wallenstein, *Tell the Court I Love My Wife: Race, Marriage and the Law—An American History* (New York, 2002), 13–38. On the South specifically, see Charles F. Robinson, *Dangerous Liaisons: Sex and Love in the Segregated South* (Fayetteville, Ark., 2003), 1–21. On the legal treatment of miscegenation in the colonial period, see also Kathleen M. Brown, *Good Wives, Nasty Wenches, and Anxious Patriarchs: Gender, Race, and Power in Colonial Virginia* (Chapel Hill, NC, 1996), chap. 6; Martha Hodes, *White Women, Black Men: Illicit Sex in the Nineteenth-Century South* (New Haven, CT, 1997), chap. 2; Joshua D. Rothman, *Notorious in the Neighborhood: Sex and Families Across the Color Line in Virginia, 1787–1861* (Chapel Hill, NC, 2003); Paul Finkelman, "Crimes of Love, Misdemeanors of Passion: The Regulation of Race and Sex in the Colonial South," in Catherine Clinton and Michele Gillespie, eds. *The Devil's Lane: Sex and Race in the Early South* (New York, 1997), 124–35; Karen A. Getman, "Sexual Control in the Slaveholding South; The Implementation and Maintenance of a Racial Caste System," *Harvard Women's Law Journal* (1984): 121–34; Joel Williamson, *New People: Miscegenation and Mulattoes in the United States* (New York, 1980), chap. 1; A. Leon Higginbotham Jr., *In the Matter of Color: Race and the American Legal Process*, vol. I; *The Colonial Period* (New York, 1978), 44–47, 108, 139, 231, 269, 286, 309; and Higginbotham and Kopytoff, "Racial Purity and Interracial Sex."

12. Robinson, *Dangerous Liaisons*, 2–4 (quotation on p. 4).

13. Getman, "Sexual Control," 126; Anne Firor Scott, *The Southern Lady: From Pedestal to Politics, 1830–1930* (Chicago, 1970), chap. 1; Cathetine Clinton, *The Plantation Mistress: Woman's World in the Old South* (New York, 1982), 87–94; Brown, *Good Wives, Nasty Wenches, and Anxious Patriarchs*, 187–211; Hodes, *White Women, Black Men*, 4–5.

14. Robinson provides an instructive overview that reveals the great diversity of state statutes and enforcement practices. In general, states seem to have acted to preserve white male authority, as laws were enforced and penalties assigned at white lawmakers' discretion. In practice this meant that most cases punished public relationships between white women and black men. See Robinson, *Dangerous Liaisons*, 8–20; and Wallenstein, *Tell the Court I Love My Wife*, 51–123.

15. Louisiana and South Carolina were exceptions to the law of racial definition, as South Carolina did not introduce a strict legal definition of blackness and whiteness and Louisiana still recognized more than two racial categories. F. James Davis, *Who Is Black? One Nation's Definition* (University Park, PA, 2001), 34–38. On Louisiana, see below and Dominguez, *White by Definition*. On South Carolina, see Michael P. Johnson and James L. Roark, *Black Masters: A Free Family of Color in the Old South* (New York, 1984). For a twentieth-century example of the relationship between miscegenation law and the law of racial identity, see Victoria E. Bynum, " 'White Negroes' in Segregated Mississippi; Miscegenation, Racial Identity, and the Law," *Journal of Southern History* 64 (May 1998): 247–76.

16. For a comparative and synthetic account of such legal conceptions of race and blood, see Davis, *Who Is Black?* 1–16, 61–80. For a discussion of the relationship between "blood" and miscegenation, see Saks, "Representing Miscegenation Law"; and Davis, *Who Is Black?* 17–30. On Louisiana, see Dominguez, *White by Definition*, chap. 3; and Anthony G. Barthelemy, "Light, Bright, Damn *Near* White; Race, the

Politics of Genealogy, and the Strange Case of Susie Guillory," in Sybil Kein, ed., *Creole: The History and Legacy of Louisiana's Free People of Color* (Baton Rouge, LA, 2000), 252–75.

17. According to Jennifer M. Spear, French authorities' preference for intraracial relationships was motivated by a number of concerns, but primary among them was the belief that Indian women's sexuality and their willingness to abandon unhappy conjugal unions made them ill-suited to the establishment of family and farm, two projects essential to imperial success in the Louisiana/French system of racial classification. Spear, " 'They Need Wives'; Metissage and the Regulation of Sexuality in French Louisiana, 1699–1730," in Hodes, ed., *Sex, Love, Race*, 35–59.

18. On the history and development of antimiscegenation law in Louisiana under French, Spanish, and American authorities, see Charles F. Robinson II, "The Antimiscegenation Conversation: Love's Legislated Limits (1868–1967)" (PhD diss., University of Houston, TX, 1998), 112–15; and Gwendolyn Midlo Hall, *Africans in Colonial Louisiana: The Development of Afro-Creole Culture in the Eighteenth Century* (Baton Rouge, LA, 1992).

19. Monique Guillory, "Some Enchanted Evening on the Auction Block: The Cultural Legacy of the New Orleans Quadroon Balls" (PhD diss., New York University, 1999). On quadroon balls, see also Joan M. Martin, "*Plaçage* and the Louisiana *Gens de Couleur Libre:* How Race and Sex Defined the Lifestyles of Free Women of Color," in Keen, ed., *Creole*, 57–70; Marcus Christian, "Manuscript 19," Folder "White Men and Negro Women," Box 14, Series XIII.1: Historical Manuscripts, Christian Papers; Domínguez, *White by Definition*, 1311; Davis, *Who is Black?*, 45; and John W. Blassingame, *Black New Orleans: 1860–1880* (Chicago, 1973), 17–19.

20. As Robinson notes, this was the general trend, but again, generalizations are defied by a few exceptional states. Robinson, *Dangerous Liaisons*, 8–9. Massachusetts eliminated antimiscegenation law in 1843, and Iowa eliminated it in 1851. Many state laws continued from the colonial period, as in the case of Virginia and Maryland. Massachusetts reenacted its colonial law in 1786. Maine and Rhode Island enacted laws in 1821 and 1798, respectively. For a discussion of the spread of state laws and specific state statutes in the early national period, see Wallenstein, *Tell the Court I Love My Wife*, chap. 3. On Massachusetts, Maine, Rhode Island, Virginia, and Maryland, see ibid., 40–41.

21. Robinson, "Antimiscegenation Conversation," 114–17; Harriet Spiller Daggett, *Legal Essays on Family Law* (Baton Rouge, LA, 1935), 25–29.

22. On the frequent appearance of the subject of interracial sex in mid-nineteenth-century political discourse, see Wallenstein, *Tell the Court I Love My Wife*, 50–63.

23. On the origin of the term *miscegenation*, see Sidney Kaplan, "The Miscegenation Issue in the Election of 1864," *Journal of Negro History* 34 (July 1949): 274–343; Hodes, *White Women, Black Men*, 144; and Wallenstein, *Tell the Court I Love My Wife*, 51–52.

24. Robinson, *Dangerous Liaisons*, 30 (quotation). Robinson notes that Redemption ushered in many new state antimiscegenation laws, but the impact of these laws was limited and primarily aimed at formal relationships such as marriage. His survey of southern legal cases indicates that enforcement was uneven, as white authorities feared federal intervention and were reluctant to circumscribe interracial sex between white men and black women, ibid., 49–59.

25. Edward L. Ayers, *The Promise of the New South: Life after Reconstruction* (New York, 1992), 140 (first quotation), 139 (other quotations). On anxieties related to women's increased presence in public spheres of work and amusement, see Glenda Gilmore, *Gender and Jim Crow: Women and the Politics of White Supremacy in North Carolina, 1896–1920* (Chapel Hill, NC, 1996), 72–76.

26. Paul A. Lombardo, "Medicine, Eugenics, and the Supreme Court: From Coercive Sterilization to Reproductive Freedom," *Journal of Contemporary Health Law and Policy* 13 (Fall 1996): 21 (quotations); Lisa Lindquist Dorr, "Arm in Arm: Gender, Eugenics and Virginia's Racial Integrity Acts of the *1920s*," *Journal of Women's History* 11 (Spring 1999): 143; Pascoe "Miscegenation Law"; Paul A. Lombardo, "Miscegenation, Eugenics, and Racism: Historical Footnotes to *Loving* v. *Virginia,* " *U.C. Davis Law Review* 21 (Winter 1988–1989): 421–52; Richard B Sherman, " 'The Last Stand': The Fight for Racial Integrity in Virginia in the 1920s," *Journal of Southern History* 54 (February 1988): 69–92.

27. The state's complex and conspiratorial system of policing the practice of self-identification of race is perhaps the most notorious in modern America. The state's practices regarding racial identity have received an extraordinary amount of scholarly and public attention since the early 1980s, when Susan Guillory Phipps, a Louisiana native, unsuccessfully sued the state to have her racial designation changed to white. On Phipps, see Barthelemy, "Light, Bright, Damn *Near* White," 259–66; Calvin Trillin, "American Chronicles: Black or White," *New Yorker*, April, 14 1986, pp. 62–78; and Dominguez, *White by Definition*, 52–53.

28. Dominguez, *White by Definition*, 57–62 (first quotation on p. 57; second quotation on p. 62).

29. Analyzing the evolution of Louisiana's antimiscegenation jurisprudence, Robinson remarks, "It appears that for Louisiana any abhorrence that whites might have felt for interracial sex was balanced by the undeniable fact of its frequent occurrence." "Antimiscegenation Conversation," 128–31 (quotation on p. 128; figures on p. 131). Civil cases involving miscegenation outnumbered criminal cases throughout the United States. Peggy Pascoe has systematically examined all appeals court cases in which miscegenation played a role, and among these cases she found 132 civil and 95 criminal cases. See Pascoe, "Miscegenation Law," 50*n*15.

30. The paucity of cases at this level also points to a number of problems in relying on legal records, and appellate cases in particular. Though appellate cases provide quick access to essential cases that established subsequent case law and, equally important, have the advantage of being published, indexed, complete with full records of testimony, exhibits, and briefs, they are in Pascoe's words, "by definition atypical." Chosen for their legal merits, they are in no way a representative sample. Nor can they be used to gauge the frequency of illegal sex or the number of civil suits and local prosecutions related to miscegenation. Nor, as Randall Kennedy argues, do they reveal much about the influence of miscegenation law on "the way in which people actually lived their lives," since other factors like social disapproval and, for black men, the fear of lynching may have been more significant. For a discussion of appellate cases, see Pascoe, "Miscegenation Laws," 50*n*15; and on the limitations of the law as a source, see Randall Kennedy, "The Enforcement of Anti-Miscegenation Laws," in Sollors, ed., *Interracialism*, 140–62 (quotation on p. 146). However, in the 1930s, at least one scholar argued that antimiscegenation laws, coupled with social sanctions, may have been a deterrent. Daggett, *Legal Essays on Family Law*, especially chap. 1, "The Legal Aspect of Amalgamation in Louisiana."

31. Robinson, "Antimiscegenation Conversation," 128 (quotation); Robinson, *Dangerous Liaisons*, 113.

32. Those cases were *State v. Treadaway et al.*, 126 La. 300, 52 So. 500 (1910); *State v. Daniel*, 141 La. 900, 75 So. 836 (1917); *State v. Harris*, 150 La. 383, 90 So. 686 (1922); *City of New Orleans v. Miller et al.*, 142 La. 163, 76 So. 596 (1917); *State v. Brown*, 236 La. 562, 108 So. 2d. 233 (1959). There are some inherent difficulties in counting cases, however, including how one decides which cases to count. Some cases clearly involve miscegenation, such as the divorce cases cited below in which the race of one party determined the legality of the marriage, but the case itself does not cite miscegenation or miscegenation law explicitly. In other examples, the case may

mention miscegenation and in so doing document an accusation or an occurrence of miscegenation (and therefore the state's knowledge of an accusation of miscegenation), but the case itself involves a different legal matter. A sixth criminal case, *State v. Bertrand et al.*, 123 La. 575, 49 So. 199 (1909), does cite a couple indicted for criminal miscegenation, but the legal matter in this particular appellate case concerns the forfeiture of bail, because the defendant, Eugene Bertrand, failed to appear in court. The case does not mention whether the couple was convicted but does note that the accused, Eugene Bertrand, was in jail at the time. The miscegenation case would have been before the district, rather than the appellate court. Another case appearing indirectly in the appellate records is that of Edward and Ezilda Von Buelow, who were charged with criminal miscegenation, but the case itself concerns an insurance claim. Edward Von Buelow committed suicide before his trial, and his widow sued her life insurance company for his benefits. *Ezilda Von Buelow, Testamentary Executrix v. The Life Insurance Company of Virginia*, 9 Teiss. 143 (1912).

33. Brief on Behalf of the Defendants, in case files of *State of Louisiana v. James Brown and Lucille Aymond*, 236 La. 562, 108 So. 2d 233 (1959), Louisiana Supreme Court Records (Louisiana Supreme Court Clerk's Office, New Orleans).

34. Quotations from transcript of testimony of David Blalock before the civil district court. May 29, 1958, Avoyelles Parish; Brief on Behalf of the State of Louisiana, Plaintiff-Appellee, both in case files of *State of Louisiana v. James Brown and Lucille Aymond*.

35. Quoted in transcript of testimony of David Blalock, ibid.

36. Rosabeth Moss Kanter, for example, notes that the relationship is often highly personalized and compared to that between man and wife. See Kanter, *Men and Women of the Corporation* (New York, 1977), 76, 86–91.

37. Quoted in transcript of testimony of David Blalock before the civil district court. May 29, 1958, Avoyelles Parish; Brief on Behalf of the State of Louisiana, Plaintiff-Appellee, both in case files of *State of Louisiana v. James Brown and Lucille Aymond*.

38. Brown and Aymond confessions, as cited in Brief on Behalf of the Defendants, in case files of *State of Louisiana v. James Brown and Lucille Aymond*.

39. *State of Louisiana v. James Brown and Lucille Aymond*, 236 La. at 567.

40. Brief on Behalf of the Defendants, in case files *State of Louisiana v. James Brown and Lucille Aymond*.

41. La R.S. 14:79 as cited in *State of Louisiana v. James Brown and Lucille Aymond*.

42. *State of Louisiana v. James Brown and Lucille Aymond*, 236 La. at 569 (first and second quotations) and 575 (third quotation).

43. On the creation of the myth of white female purity, see Hodes, *White Women, Black Men*, 5, 160–61, 177, 181, 186, 197–202, 261–25. Hodes links the evolution of white beliefs about interracial sex, white women's purity, and black men's sexual predation to escalating violence against black men. Ibid., 178–208.

44. *Andrea D. Perez et al. v. W. G. Sharp*, 32 Cal. 2d 711, 198 P. 2d 17 (1948) ruled that California's laws prohibiting marriages between whites and members of other racial groups were invalid. In the case, Perez, a "white" woman, and Sylvester Davis, a "Negro" man, were denied license to marry by the Los Angeles clerk of court. However, California did not remove the antimiscegenation law from the California Civil Code until 1959. On *Perez*, see Pascoe "Miscegenation Law," 61–63; and Leti Volpp, "American Mestizo: Filipinos and Antimiscegenation Laws in California," *U.C. Davis Law Review* 33 (Summer 2000): 824.

45. See for example. New Orleans *Times-Picayune*, July 7, 1959; and Christian's clippings from the *Times-Picayune* dated (handwritten on the clippings) October 18, January 28, May 5, and May 26, 1959, in Folder "Jan-June 1959," Box 14; and September 11, 1960, in Folder "July-Dec 1960," Box 16, both boxes in Series VI: Clippings, Christian Papers.

46. On Dupas see Michelle Brattain, "Passing, Racial Boundaries, and the Social Construction of Race in Twentieth Century New Orleans," paper presented at conference entitled "Race, Place, and the American Experience," Tuscaloosa, AL, March 10, 2002; and "Miscegenation Charges Denied," New Orleans *Times-Picayune*, July 12, 1956, p. 5, col. 5.

47. On the demonization of black male sexuality in the twentieth century, see Jacquelyn Dowd Hall, " 'The Mind that Burns in Each Body'; Women, Rape, and Racial Violence," in Ann Snitow, Christine Stansell, and Sharon Thompson, eds., *Powers of Desire: The Politics of Sexuality* (New York, 1983), 328–49; Randall Kennedy, *Interracial Intimacies: Sex, Marriage. Identity, and Adoption* (New York, 2003), 189–200; and James Goodman, *Stories of Scottsboro* (New York, 1994). Bryant Simon notes that rumor played a significant and unique role in the way whites talked about racial issues that they otherwise dared not confront. See Simon's new introduction to Howard W. Odum, *Race and Rumors of Race . . .* (Baltimore, MD, 1997; originally published in 1943), viii–ix.

48. For an extended discussion of the court's treatment of concubinage, see *Succession of Lannes*, 187 La. 17, 40 (quotation), 174 So. 94 (1936).

49. See Christian, unpublished manuscript chapter titled "White men, Negro women," p. 202, in Folder "White men, Negro Women," Box 14, Series XIII: Historical Manuscripts, Christian Papers.

50. Every case that I found concerned a white man and a black woman. Presumably the same sorts of disguises might have hidden relationships between black men and white women, although black female employees more typically held jobs that would have required them to live in a white household. On black women's household employment, see Jacqueline Jones, *Labor of Love, Labor of Sorrow: Black Women, Work, and the Family from Slavery to the Present* (New York, 1985); Elizabeth Clark-Lewis, *Living In, Living Out: African American Domestics in Washington, D.C, 1910–1940* (Washington, DC, 1994); Brenda Clegg Gray, *Black Female Domestics During the Depression in New York City, 1930–1940* (New York, 1993); and Tera W. Hunter, *To 'Joy My Freedom: Southern Black Women's lives and Labors after the Civil War* (Cambridge, MA, 1997).

51. *Jones et al. v. Kyle*, 168 La. 728, 733 (first, second, and third quotations), 735 (other quotations), 123 So. 306 (1929). In determining the "open" or "secret" status of the relationship between Jones and Kyle, the state relied upon the decision in *Succession of Jahraus*, 114 La. 456, 38 So. 417 (1905), which provided an extended discussion of the legal history of this distinction from the original French law to the state of Louisiana's civil code and Louisiana case law up to 1905. As the court explained in *Jahraus*, the framers of the Louisiana Civil Code had two concerns. They wished to discourage "unseemly scandals which resulted from permitting scrutiny into the private lives of people who were dead and no longer able to defend themselves," but they also wished "in the interests of public morals, of making some distinction between people who lived together as man and wife under the solemn sanction of marriage, and those who maintained practically the same status, openly and publicly, without the sanction of marriage." *Succession of Jahraus*, 114 La. at 462. See also *Succession of Lannes*, 187 17, which provides another extended discussion of the history of the law regarding "open concubinage" and its intent to discourage public immorality.

52. *Jones et al. v. Kyle*, 168 La. at 735.

53. See also, for example, the case *of Hodges' Heirs v. Kelt et al.*, 125 La. 87, 51 So. 77 (1910). In *Hodges*, the dispute over the estate of John E. Hodges resulted from the long-term relationship between Hodges, white, and his partner, Eliza Kline, Negro, who lived with him as an employee for nearly thirty years. In his will, Hodges

identified Kline as "my true and faithful servant who has been in my employ for the last 28 years" (p. 94), but he left his entire estate to Kline and their seven children.

54. See Grace Elizabeth Hale, *Making Whiteness: The Culture of Segregation in the South 1890–1940* (New York, 1998), 94–114.

55. See various clippings in Series VI: Clippings from American and English Publications, Christian Papers.

56. Louisiana had two bureaus of vital statistics, one serving New Orleans and the other serving the rest of the state.

57. See, for example, the appeals recorded in Minutes of the Board of Health, bound volume. New Orleans Health Department Records (New Orleans Public Library); *Naomi Drake v. Department of Health*, City of New Orleans Civil Service Commission, Appeal No. 391, in Civil Service Department Minutes, Classified City Employees, 1965, microfilm AI300, roll #66–155 (New Orleans Public Library).

58. On whiteness and law, see Ian Haney López. *White by Law: The Legal Construction of Race* (New York, 1996); Davis, *Who is Black?* Cheryl 1. Harris, "Whiteness as Property," *Harvard Law Review* 106 (June 1993): 1707–91. Kimberly Crenshaw et al., eds., *Critical Race Theory: The Key Writings that Formed the Movement* (New York, 1995); and Richard Delgado, ed., *Critical Race Theory: The Cutting Edge* (Philadelphia, 1995). On New Orleans see Kennedy, *Interracial Intimacies*, 324–25; Dominguez, *White by Definition;* Paul Finkelman, "The Crime of Color," *Tulane Law Review* 67 (June 1993): 2063–112; Raymond T. Diamond and Robert J. Cottrol, "Codifying Caste: Louisiana's Racial Classification Scheme and the Fourteenth Amendment," *Loyola Law Review* 29 (Spring 1983): 255–85; and Robert Westley, "First-Time Encounters: 'Passing' Revisited and Demystification as a Critical Practice," *Yale Law and Policy Review* 18 (2000): 297.

59. Saks, "Representing Miscegenation Law"; Pascoe, "Miscegenation Law."

60. *State v. Treadaway et al.*, 126 La. 300, 301 (second and third quotations), 52 So. 500 (1910). The law cited in *Treadaway* is section 1 of Act No. 87 of 1908. Quotations are taken from the text of the *Treadaway* decision to indicate the court's technical language for racial identities. Octave Treadaway's companion is identified as Josephine Lightell in the case file of *State v. Octave Treadaway et al.*, Louisiana Supreme Court Records, 1813–1920 (Special Collections, Earl K. Long Library, University of New Orleans).

61. Domínguez, *White by Definition*, 31–32 (quotation on p. 32). See also Christian, editorial notes, undated. Folder "Ebony Magazine research re passé pour blanc," Box 12, Series XIII. 1: Historical Manuscripts, Christian Papers.

62. Domínguez, *White by Definition*, 30–38.

63. *Sunseri v. Cassagne*, 191 La. 209, 185 So. 1 (1938). On the legal significance of this standard, see Diamond and Cottrol, "Codifying Caste."

64. Brief on Behalf of the State of Louisiana, Plaintiff-Appellee, in case files of *State of Louisiana v. James Brown and Lucille Aymond.*

65. *Sunseri v. Cassagne*, 191 La. at 211 (quotation); *Sunseri* v. *Cassagne*, 195 La. 19, 196 So. 7 (1940); Saks, "Representing Miscegenation Law."

66. See transcript of testimony of Cyril Cassagne, Case No 219–350, Civil District Court Orleans Parish, 1936, included in case files of *Sunseri v. Cassagne*, 191 La. 209, Louisiana Supreme Court Records (Louisiana Supreme Court Clerk's Office).

67. *Sunseri v. Cassagne*, 191 La. at 214.

68. Brief on behalf of Verna Cassagne, included in case files of *Sunseri v. Cassagne.* The status of Indians as white people or persons of color changed over time. In 1810, the superior court in the territory of Orleans decided in *Adelte v. Beauregard* that Indians were considered persons of color. Marriage between whites and Indians was illegal until Louisiana's antimiscegenation law was repealed in 1870. In 1894, when

antimiscegenation laws were reenacted, Indians were still classified as persons of color and therefore not permitted to marry whites. In 1920, state law declared marriage between Indians and persons "colored and black" miscegenation, and after that Indians were treated as not "colored." Virginia Dominguez points out that in the 1930s the attorney general was "explicitly stating that marriage between white persons and Indians was not prohibited . . . " For a full account, see Dominguez, *White by Definition*, 34. Given that marriage between whites and Indians or whites and persons of color was prohibited in 1837, in theory Fanny Ducre should not have been able to marry Leander Ducre if she was identified as either an Indian or a person of color, but the record does not explain the circumstances of the marriage.

69. Petition and Affidavit from *Cyril P. Sunseri v. Verna Cassagne*, No 219–350, Civil District Court, Parish of Orleans, included in case files of *Sunseri v. Cassagne*. See also the transcript of the testimony of Stella Cassagne before the civil district court, ibid.

70. The nine quotations (in order) are from transcripts of the testimony of Toussaint Ducre; Marie Atlow; Rose Green Ducre; C. Harry Culbertson; Marie Atlow; Marie Atlow; Marie Atlow; Mary Parker; Rene Pierre, all before the civil district court, ibid.

71. Transcript of testimony of Mary Parker before the civil district court, ibid.

72. The court, in transcript of testimony of Mary Parker before the civil district court, ibid.

73. The court (second and third quotations) and Rose Green Ducre (first quotation), in transcript of testimony of Rose Green Ducre before the civil district court, ibid.

74. Transcript of testimony of P. Henry Lanause before the civil district court, ibid.

75. Transcript of testimony of Rene Pierre before the civil district court, ibid.

76. Transcript of testimony of Rose Green Ducre before the civil district court, ibid.

77. Transcript of testimony of Mrs. Emma Villarrubia, registrar of Lacombe, before the civil district court, ibid

78. Transcript of testimony of Marie Atlow before the civil district court,ibid.

79. Transcript of testimony of Pauline Roubion before the civil district court, ibid.

80. Transcript of testimony of Cyril Sunseri before the civil district court, ibid.

81. Transcript of testimony of Mrs. George Obitz before the civil district court, ibid.

82. *Sunseri v. Cassagne*, 195 La. 19 (1938). Quotation from Transcript of testimony of Verna Cassagne before the civil district court, included in case files of *Sunseri v. Cassagne*.

83. *Sunseri* v. *Cassagne*, 191 La. at 222 (first quotation); *Sunseri v. Cassagne*, 195 La. at 21(third quotation), 27 (second quotation).

84. Joseph G. Tregle Jr., "Creoles and Americans," in Arnold R. Hirsch and Joseph Logsdon, eds., *Creole New Orleans: Race and Americanization* (Baton Rouge. 1992), 134–35 (first quotation on p. 135), 139 (second quotation).

85. Tregle, "Creoles and Americans," 139 (quotations), 172–81.

86. On the "Creole controversy," see Domínguez, *White by Definition*, 149–81 (quotations on p. 159).

87. *Sunseri v. Cassagne*, 195 La. at 22 (first quotation); Diamond and Cottrol, "Codifying Caste," 282 (second quotation). Raymond T. Diamond and Robert J. Cottrol have argued that the state's racial classification system served primarily to prevent a person "labeled black because of heredity" from escaping such categorization. See Diamond and Cottrol, "Codifying Caste," 281–85 (quotation on p. 282).

88. *Villa V. Lacoste et at.*, 213 La. 654, 35 So. 2d 419 (1948). When Lacoste sued Villa for support, he answered her suit by attacking the marriage as null and void because she was "colored." The circumstances surrounding the case are explained in the Brief

on behalf of Villa, March 13, 1948, in case files of *Villa v. Lacoste et al.*, 213 La. 654, 35 So. 2d 419 (1948), Louisiana Supreme Court Records (Louisiana Supreme Court Clerk's Office).

89. Quotation is from transcript of testimony of Mr. Prudhomme, deputy recorder, before the civil district court, included in case files of *Villa v. Lacoste et al.* Apparently the issue had also appeared in civil district court on a number of occasions, according to Lacoste's attorney. See brief on behalf of Josephine Lacoste, March 29, 1948, included in case files of *Villa v. Lacoste et al.*

90. Although the United States had a considerable number of Filipino immigrants in 1948, the majority of them resided in the West, with more than three-quarters of them living in California. According to U.S. law, Filipinos were U.S. nationals, free to migrate between the Philippines and the U.S. but ineligible for naturalization. U.S. policy had, since 1790, limited naturalization to "free white persons" with the exception of African Americans and African immigrants, who were naturalized, by the Fourteenth Amendment in 1868 and the Naturalization Act of 1870, respectively. Passage of the Tydings-McDuffie Act of 1934 promised the Philippines independence, immediately restricted Filipino immigration, and ultimately intended to exclude all Filipino immigrants after independence, which was eventually granted in 1946. In 1946, passage of the Luce-Celler Bill provided naturalization rights to Filipinos who had migrated prior to 1934 but placed a quota on future immigration. Megumi Dick Osumi, "Asians and California's Anti-Miscegenation Laws," in Nobuya Tsuchida et al., eds., *Asian and Pacific American Experiences: Women's Perspectives* (Minneapolis, 1982), 1–30; Barbara M. Posadas, *The Filipino Americans* (Westport, 1999), 23–27 (quotation on p. 23), 35–36. On race and naturalization, see also Haney López, *White by Law*.

91. Brief on behalf of Josephine Lacoste, March 29, 1948, included in case files of *Villa v. Lacoste et al.*

92. ibid.

93. Nine states had laws prohibiting marriage between "Malays," the racial group to which Filipinos were traditionally assigned, and "whites." Arizona, California, Maryland, Nevada, South Dakota, Utah, and Wyoming had statutes specifically prohibiting white-Malay marriages. Georgia and Virginia laws on marriage did not specifically prohibit Malay-white marriages, but those states did prohibit marriages between whites and nonwhites and in other laws defined Malays as not white. See "American Mestizo," 800–1; and Rachel F. Moran, *Interracial Intimacy: The Regulation of Race and Romance* (Chicago, 2001), 38–41.

94. Brief on behalf of Josephine Lacoste, March 29, 1948, included in case files of *Villa v. Lacoste et al.*

95. Transcript of testimony of Raymond Cabilash, ibid.

96. Transcript of testimony of Josephine Lacoste, ibid.

97. Transcript of testimony of Charles Villa, ibid.

98. For a more contemporary discussion of the racial status of Filipinos, see Emory S. Bogardus, "What Race Are Filipinos?" *Sociology and Social Research* 16 (January–February 1932): 274–79.

99. Transcript of testimony of Stephen Villa; and transcript of testimony of Mrs. John J. Gilbert, included in case files of *Villa v. Lacoste et al.*

100. Transcript of testimony of Josephine Lacoste, ibid.

101. *Villa v. Lacoste et al.*, 213 La. 654.

102. See Brattain, "Passing, Racial Boundaries, and the Social Construction of Race in Twentieth Century New Orleans"; and Jeansonne, *Leander Perez*, 233–35.

103. On schools, see Marcus Christian's notes on *Bush v. Orleans Parish School Board*, Folder "Bush v. Orleans," Box 5, Series XI, Historical source materials, Christian

Papers; and New Orleans *Times-Picayune*, September 8, 1955, p. 26, col. 3. The new requirements for marriage licenses were implemented by Act 160, House Bill 596, approved July 1, 1958.

104. On the race list, see Domínguez, *White by Definition*, 36–37; Trillin, "American Chronicles," 62–78; and Brattain, "Passing, Racial Boundaries, and the Social Construction of Race in Twentieth Century New Orleans."

105. *Naomi M. Drake v. Dept. of Health* (1965), appeal from the Civil Service Commission of the City of New Orleans, no. 391, transcript of hearings, vol. 1, p. 16, Civil Service Files (New Orleans Public Library).

106. On the requirement of birth certificates for school registration, see New Orleans *Times-Picayune*, September 8, 1955, p. 26, col. 3.

107. Brief on behalf of Drake, in *Naomi M. Drake v. Dept of Health* (1965), transcript of hearings, vol. 3, pp. 722–23, Civil Service Files.

108. Saks, "Representing Miscegenation Law," 58.

Chapter 10

The Long Civil Rights Movement and the Political Uses of the Past

Jacquelyn Dowd Hall

From *The Journal of American History*

The black revolution is much more than a struggle for the rights of Negroes. It is forcing America to face all its interrelated flaws—racism, poverty, militarism, and materialism. It is exposing evils that are rooted deeply in the whole structure of our society . . . and suggests that radical reconstruction of society is the real issue to be faced.

—Martin Luther King Jr.

Stories are wonderful things. And they are dangerous.

—Thomas King

The civil rights movement circulates through American memory in forms and through channels that are at once powerful, dangerous, and hotly contested. Civil rights memorials jostle with the South's ubiquitous monuments to its Confederate past. Exemplary scholarship and documentaries abound, and participants have produced wave after wave of autobiographical accounts, at least two hundred to date. Images of the movement appear and reappear each year on Martin Luther King Jr. Day and during Black History Month. Yet remembrance is always a form of forgetting, and the dominant narrative of the civil rights movement—distilled from history and memory, twisted by ideology and political contestation, and embedded in heritage tours, museums, public rituals, textbooks, and various artifacts of mass culture—distorts and suppresses as much as it reveals.[1]

Centering on what Bayard Rustin in 1965 called the "classical" phase of the struggle, the dominant narrative chronicles a short civil rights movement that begins with the 1954 *Brown v. Board of Education* decision, proceeds through public protests, and culminates with the passage of the Civil Rights Act of 1964 and the Voting Rights Act of 1965.[2] Then comes the decline. After a season of moral clarity, the country is beset by the Vietnam War, urban riots, and reaction against the excesses of the late 1960s and the 1970s, understood variously as student rebellion, black militancy, feminism, busing, affirmative action, or an overweening welfare state. A so-called white backlash sets the stage for the conservative interregnum that, for good or ill, depending on one's ideological persuasion, marks the beginning of another story, the story that surrounds us now.

Martin Luther King Jr. is this narrative's defining figure—frozen in 1963, proclaiming "I have a dream" during the march on the Mall. Endlessly reproduced and selectively quoted, his speeches retain their majesty yet lose their political bite. We hear little of the King who believed that "the racial issue that we confront in America is not a sectional but a national problem" and who attacked segregation in the urban North. Erased altogether is the King who opposed the Vietnam War and linked racism at home to militarism and imperialism abroad. Gone is King the democratic socialist who advocated unionization, planned the Poor People's Campaign, and was assassinated in 1968 while supporting a sanitation workers' strike.[3]

By confining the civil rights struggle to the South, to bowdlerized heroes, to a single halcyon decade, and to limited, noneconomic objectives, the master narrative simultaneously elevates and diminishes the movement. It ensures the status of the classical phase as a triumphal moment in a larger American progress narrative, yet it undermines its *gravitas*. It prevents one of the most remarkable mass movements in American history from speaking effectively to the challenges of our time.

While the narrative I have recounted has multiple sources, this essay emphasizes how the movement's meaning has been distorted and reified by a New Right bent on reversing its gains. I will then trace the contours of what I take to be a more robust, more progressive, and *truer* story—the story of a "long civil rights movement" that took root in the liberal and radical milieu of the late 1930s, was intimately tied to the "rise and fall of the New Deal Order," accelerated during World War II, stretched far beyond the South, was continuously and ferociously contested, and in the 1960s and 1970s inspired a "movement of movements" that "def[ies] any narrative of collapse."[4]

Integral to that more expansive story is the dialectic between the movement and the so-called backlash against it, a wall of resistance that did not appear suddenly in the much-maligned 1970s, but arose in tandem with the civil rights offensive in the aftermath of World War II and culminated under the aegis of the New Right. The economic dimensions of the movement lie at the core of my concerns, and throughout I will draw attention to the interweavings of gender, class, and race. In this essay, however, racial narratives and dilemmas will take center stage, for, as Lani Guinier and Gerald

Torres suggest, "Those who are racially marginalized are like the miner's canary: their distress is the first sign of a danger that threatens us all."[5]

A desire to understand and honor the movement lies at the heart of the rich and evolving literature on the 1950s and early 1960s, and that era's chroniclers have helped endow the struggle with an aura of cultural legitimacy that both reflects and reinforces its profound legal, political, and social effects. By placing the world-shaking events of the classical phase in the context of a longer story, I want to buttress that representational project and reinforce the moral authority of those who fought for change in those years. At the same time, I want to make civil rights harder. Harder to celebrate as a natural progression of American values. Harder to cast as a satisfying morality tale. Most of all, harder to simplify, appropriate, and contain.[6]

The Political Uses of Racial Narratives

The roots of the dominant narrative lie in the dance between the movement's strategists and the media's response. In one dramatic protest after another, civil rights activists couched their demands in the language of democratic rights and Christian universalism; demonstrated their own respectability and courage; and pitted coercive nonviolence against guns, nightsticks, and fists. Played out in the courts, in legislative chambers, in workplaces, and in the streets, those social dramas toppled the South's system of disfranchisement and de jure or legalized segregation by forcing the hand of federal officials and bringing local governments to their knees. The mass media, in turn, made the protests "one of the great news stories of the modern era," but they did so very selectively. Journalists' interest waxed and waned along with activists' ability to generate charismatic personalities (who were usually men) and telegenic confrontations, preferably those in which white villains rained down terror on nonviolent demonstrators dressed in their Sunday best. Brought into American living rooms by the seductive new medium of television and replayed ever since, such scenes seem to come out of nowhere, to have no precedents, no historical roots. To compound that distortion, the national press's overwhelmingly sympathetic, if misleading, coverage changed abruptly in the mid-1960s with the advent of black power and black uprisings in the urban North. Training a hostile eye on those developments, the cameras turned away from the South, ignoring the southern campaign's evolving goals, obscuring interregional connections and similarities, and creating a narrative breach between what people think of as "the movement" and the ongoing popular struggles of the late 1960s and the 1970s.[7]

Early studies of the black freedom movement often hewed closely to the journalistic "rough draft of history," replicating its judgments and trajectory. More recent histories, memoirs, and documentaries have struggled to loosen its hold.[8] Why, then, has the dominant narrative seemed only to consolidate its power? The answer lies, in part, in the rise of other storytellers— the architects of the New Right, an alliance of corporate power brokers, old-style conservative intellectuals, and "neoconservatives" (disillusioned liberals and socialists turned cold war hawks).

The Old Right, North and South, had been on the wrong side of the revolution, opposing the civil rights movement and reviling its leaders in the name of property rights, states' rights, anticommunism, and the God-given, biological inferiority of blacks. Largely moribund by the 1960s, the conservative movement reinvented itself in the 1970s, first by incorporating neoconservatives who eschewed old-fashioned racism and then by embracing an ideal of formal equality, focusing on blacks' ostensible failings, and positioning itself as the true inheritor of the civil rights legacy.[9] Like all bids for discursive and political power, this one required the warrant of the past, and the dominant narrative of the civil rights movement was ready at hand. Reworking that narrative for their own purposes, these new "color-blind conservatives" ignored the complexity and dynamism of the movement, its growing focus on structural inequality, and its "radical reconstruction" goals. Instead, they insisted that color blindness—defined as the elimination of racial classifications and the establishment of formal equality before the law—was the movement's singular objective, the principle for which King and the *Brown* decision, in particular, stood. They admitted that racism, understood as individual bigotry, did exist—"in the distant past" and primarily in the South—a concession that surely would have taken the Old Right by surprise.[10] But after legalized Jim Crow was dismantled, such irrationalities diminished to insignificance. In the absence of overtly discriminatory laws and with the waning of conscious bias, American institutions became basically fair. Free to compete in a market-driven society, African Americans thereafter bore the onus of their own failure or success. If stark group inequalities persisted, black attitudes, behavior, and family structures were to blame. The race-conscious remedies devised in the late 1960s and 1970s to implement the movement's victories, such as majority-minority voting districts, minority business set-asides, affirmative action, and two-way busing, were not the handiwork of the authentic civil rights movement at all. Foisted on an unwitting public by a "liberal elite" made up of judges, intellectuals, and government bureaucrats, those policies not only betrayed the movement's original goals, they also had little effect on the economic progress blacks enjoyed in the late 1960s and 1970s, which was caused not by grassroots activism or governmental intervention but by impersonal market forces. In fact, the remedies themselves became the cause of our problems, creating resentment among whites, subverting self-reliance among blacks, and encouraging "balkanization" when nationalism and assimilation should be our goals.[11] It was up to color-blind conservatives to restore the original purpose of civil rights laws, which was to prevent isolated acts of wrongdoing against individuals, rather than, as many civil rights activists and legal experts claimed, to redress present, institutionalized manifestations of historical injustices against blacks as a group.[12]

Germinated in well-funded right-wing think tanks and broadcast to the general public, this racial narrative had wide appeal, in part because it conformed to white, middle-class interests and flattered national vanities and in part because it resonated with ideals of individual effort and merit that are widely shared. The American creed of free-market individualism, in combination with the ideological victories of the movement (which ensured that white supremacy must "hide its face"), made the rhetoric of color blindness central to the "war of ideas" initiated by the New Right in the 1970s. With Ronald Reagan's presidential victory in 1980, and even more so after the Republican sweep of Congress in 1994, that rhetoric entrenched itself in public policy. Dovetailing with the retreat from race-specific remedies among centrist liberals, it crossed traditional political boundaries, and it now shapes the thinking of "a great many people of good will."[13]

Clearly, the stories we tell about the civil rights movement matter; they shape how we see our own world. "Facts" must be interpreted, and those interpretations—narrated by powerful storytellers, portrayed in public events, acted upon in laws and policies and court decisions, and grounded in institutions—become primary sources of human action. Those who aspire to affect public opinion and policy and thus to participate in "the endless struggle over our collective destiny" must always ask themselves not only "which stories to advance, contest, and accept as 'true,' " but also how to discipline those stories with research and experience and to advance them with power. In the world of symbolic politics, the answers to those questions determine who will prevail.[14]

In that spirit, I will turn now to a story of my own—the story of the long civil rights movement and of the resistance to it. Throughout, I will draw on the work of a wide range of historians, tying together stories usually told separately in order to alter common understandings of the black freedom struggle (and of how we arrived at the dilemmas of the new millennium) in at least six major ways. First, this new, longer and broader narrative undermines the trope of the South as the nation's "opposite other," an image that southernizes racism and shields from scrutiny both the economic dimensions of southern white supremacy and the institutionalized patterns of exploitation, segregation, and discrimination in other regions of the country—patterns that survived the civil rights movement and now define the South's racial landscape as well. Second, this narrative emphasizes the gordian knot that ties race to class and civil rights to workers' rights. Third, it suggests that women's activism and gender dynamics were central both to the freedom movement and to the backlash against it. Fourth, it makes visible modern civil rights struggles in the North, Midwest, and West, which entered a new phase with the turn to black nationalism in the mid-1960s but had begun at least a quarter century before. Fifth, it directs attention to the effort to "make use of the reforms won by the civil rights movement" in the 1970s, after the national movement's alleged demise.[15] And finally, it construes the Reagan-Bush ascendancy not simply as a backlash against the "movement of movements" of the late 1960s and 1970s, but as a development with deep historical roots.

The Long Backlash

Two great internal migrations gave rise both to the long civil rights movement and to the interests and ideologies that would ultimately feed the most telling resistance to it: the exodus of African Americans to the cities of the South, North, and West precipitated by the collapse of the southern sharecropping system and the mass suburbanization of whites. Accelerating during World War II, those vast relocations of people and resources transformed the racial geography of the country. Each responded to and acted on the other. They were fatefully, although often invisibly, entwined.[16]

Gender, class, region, and race—all shaped both migration experiences. Because discrimination in the North shunted black men into the meanest factory jobs, women carried the burden of a double day. Relegated mainly to domestic service, they combined wage earning not only with homemaking but with kin work and social networking, practices that were rooted in the folk and family traditions of the South, bound neighborhoods together, and provided the safety net that discriminatory welfare policies denied. Such networks also helped to blur urban-rural boundaries, ensuring that struggles in the city and the countryside would be mutually reinforcing.[17]

As rural black folk grappled with the planter-dominated policies and practices that exploited their labor and drove them from the land, urban migrants fought to "keep Mississippi out of California" and the "plantation mentality" out of the cities of the South.[18] Indeed, the resonance of the plantation metaphor for blacks throughout the country suggests the depth and durability of rural memories and interregional connections. In one sense, however, the metaphor is misleading. For black migrants who made their way to the "promised land" found themselves confronting not Mississippi in California but indigenous forms of discrimination and de facto segregation— the result not of custom, as "de facto" implies, but of a combination of individual choices and governmental policies (some blatant and some race neutral on their face) that had the effect, and often the intent, of barring African Americans from access to decent jobs, schools, and homes, as well as to the commercialized leisure spaces that increasingly symbolized "making it in America" for white ethnics en route to the middle class.

Ironically, New Deal programs helped to erect those racial barriers. In tandem with the higher wages won by the newly empowered unions of the Congress of Industrial Organizations (CIO), the expansion of the welfare state mitigated the terrible insecurity of working-class life for blacks and whites alike. Yet the "gendered" and "raced" imagination of New Deal reformers also built racial and gender inequality into the very foundation of the modern state.[19] Those inequalities were intensified by the concessions exacted both by conservative Republican congressmen and by southern Democrats, who owed their congressional seniority and thus their domination of key committees to the South's constricted electorate and one-party rule.

One manifestation of systemic inequality was a two-track welfare system rooted in a "family wage" ideal that figured the worker as a full-time breadwinner who supported children and a dependent, non-wage-earning wife at home—an ideal from which most people of color were excluded. When unemployment insurance was enacted in 1935, for example, it did not extend to agricultural and domestic workers, whom reformers did not see as independent, full-time breadwinners, and on whom the South's low-wage economy depended. As a result, 55 percent of all African American workers and 87 percent of all wage-earning African American women were excluded from one of the chief benefits of the New Deal. In lieu of such protections, African Americans were dependent on—and stigmatized by—the stingy, means-tested programs known as "welfare" today.[20]

As metropolitan populations exploded, a mad scramble for housing brought African Americans face to face with another limitation of the New Deal: white men benefited disproportionately from the G.I. Bill of Rights, a mammoth social welfare program for returning veterans passed by Congress at the end of World War II. In combination with an equally ambitious housing program, the G.I. Bill drew aspiring ethnic workers and the white middle class out of the city, away from black neighbors, and into ever-expanding suburban rims. Centuries of racial denigration, compounded by divisions built into the two-track welfare system, predisposed white urbanites to fear black migrants. But what came to be known as "white flight" was caused not just by individual attitudes but also by a panoply of profit- and government-driven policies. Local zoning boards and highway building choices equated "black" with "blight," frightening away white buyers and steering investment away from black urban neighborhoods. Blockbusting real estate agents stampeded whites into selling cheap and blacks into buying dear. Redlining banks denied mortgages to African Americans and to buyers in "mixed" neighborhoods. Most important, the Federal Housing Administration pursued lending policies that not only favored but practically mandated racial homogeneity.[21]

Encouraged by tax incentives, highway building programs, and a desire to outflank the new unions, factories and businesses moved to the suburbs as well, eroding the cities' tax base, damaging infrastructure, and eviscerating municipal services. The growth of segregated suburbs also exacerbated the trend toward almost complete segregation in urban schools. The practice of supporting public education through local taxes and the fiercely guarded divide between urban and suburban school districts, combined with conscious, racially motivated choices regarding the siting of schools and the assignment of pupils, relegated black migrants to schools that were often as separate and as unequal as those they had left behind.[22]

This cascading process of migration, job discrimination, suburbanization, and race-coded New Deal reform had three major effects. First, over the course of the 1940s race became increasingly spatialized, rendering invisible to whites the accumulated race and class privileges that undergirded what suburbanites came to see as the rightful fruits of their own labor. Second, the "suburban frontier" spawned a new homeowners' politics based on low taxes, property rights, neighborhood autonomy, and a shrinking sense of social responsibility, all of which became entangled with racial identity in ways that would prove extremely difficult to undo.[23] Finally, African Americans, already burdened by the social and economic deprivations of slavery and Jim Crow, found themselves disadvantaged by employment practices and state policies that amounted to affirmative action for whites. In a society where a home represented most families' single most important asset, for example, differential access to mortgages and housing markets and the racial valuation of neighborhoods translated into enormous inequalities. Passed on from generation to generation, those inequalities persist to this day. Short-circuiting the generational accumulation of wealth and social capital that propelled other ethnic minorities into the expanding post–World War II middle class, those policies left a legacy of racial inequality that has yet to be seriously addressed.[24]

Southern Strategies

We now have a copious literature on postwar suburbanization and the deepening of segregation in the North and West. But too often, the already segregated, rural, backward South figures in this story only as a footnote or an exception to the rule. In fact, because southern cities grew up in the age of New Deal reform, the automobile, and suburban sprawl, the modern South might better be seen as a paradigm.[25]

Looking back from the perspective of the dominant narrative, it is easy to see a peculiar system of legal segregation as the South's defining feature. But spatial separation was never the white South's major goal. Black and white southerners engaged in constant and nuanced interactions, moderated by personal ties, economic interests, and class and gender dynamics and marked by cultural exchange.[26] Taking place as they did within a context of racial hierarchy, those interactions did not diminish segregation's perniciousness and power. Yet given the ubiquity of black-white contact and the crucial role of blacks as a source of cheap labor, what we think of as the age of segregation might better be called the age of "racial capitalism," for segregation was only one instrument of white supremacy, and white supremacy entailed not only racial domination, but also economic practices. Pursued by an industrial and agricultural oligarchy to aggrandize themselves and forward a particular development strategy for the region, those practices involved low taxes, minimal investment in human capital, the separation and political immobilization of the black and white southern poor, the exploitation of non-unionized, undereducated black and white labor, and the patriarchal control of families and local institutions.[27]

That strategy created a particularly brutal and openly racialized social system, especially in the Deep South. But its basic doctrines—racial and class subordination, limited government regulation, a union-free workplace, and a racially divided working class—dovetailed seamlessly with an ethic of laissez-faire capitalism rooted deeply in American soil.[28] This is not to minimize regional differences. It is, however, to suggest that the further we move away from the campaigns that overturned the South's distinctive system of state-sponsored segregation, the easier it is to see the broader and ultimately more durable patterns of privilege and exploitation that were American, not southern, in their origins and consequences.

Those common patterns meant that the South's postwar prosperity could narrow regional differences without eliminating racial gaps. Change began in earnest in the 1940s and accelerated in the 1950s and 1960s, as southern Democrats, responding selectively to the activist New Deal state (rather than opposing it, as observers often assume), used their congressional seniority to garner a disproportionate share of defense spending while demanding local and state control over federal programs for housing, hospital construction, education, and the like. That strategy helped raise wages and triple regional incomes in the 1940s, but it also blunted federal antidiscrimination efforts.[29] At the same time, southern industrialists, like their counterparts in other regions, reacted to rising wages and to the labor militancy that followed World War II by installing laborsaving machinery and eliminating the jobs held by blacks, while whites monopolized the new skilled and white-collar jobs, which demanded qualifications denied to blacks by both educational inequities and discriminatory practices that barred them from learning on the job. Thus even as the South prospered, racial disparities widened.[30]

Much of the South's new technical and managerial workforce, moreover, was imported from the urban North. Before World War II, the chief goal of most southern politicians was to maintain the South's isolation and the captive labor supply on which the sharecropping system depended. Afterward, boosterism became these leaders' *raison d'être* and "the selling of the South" began. Low corporate taxes, low welfare benefits, and "look-the-other-way environmental policies," coupled with federally financed highway-building campaigns, attracted northern industry and an influx of northern-born, Republican-bred branch managers, supervisors, and technicians.[31] Those newcomers settled with their southern-born counterparts in class- and race-marked enclaves created by the same ostensibly race-neutral public policies that spatialized race in the North. With mushrooming suburbanization came the attitudes and advantages that would undergird the South's version of homeowner politics—the politics of the long backlash everywhere. Richard M. Nixon's "southern strategy" which attacked welfare, busing, and affirmative action in order to bring white southerners into the Republican fold, targeted such voters: middle-class suburbanites, including skilled workers from outside the South and young families who had come of age after the *Brown* decision and were uncomfortable with the openly racist rhetoric of massive resistance. Aimed also at white workers in the urban North, that strategy helped make the South a chief stronghold of the Republican Party as over the next quarter century, the party cast off its moderates and set about dismantling the New Deal order.[32]

The Long Civil Rights Movement

Yet the outcome was not inevitable. It would take many years of astute and aggressive organizing to bring today's conservative regime to power. It took such effort because another force also rose from the caldron of the Great Depression and crested in the 1940s: a powerful social movement sparked by the alchemy of laborites, civil rights activists, progressive New Dealers, and black and white radicals, some of whom were associated with the Communist Party. Robert Korstad calls it "civil rights unionism," Martha Biondi the "Black Popular Front"; both terms signal the movement's commitment to building coalitions, the expansiveness of its social democratic vision, and the importance of its black radical and laborite leadership. A national movement with a vital southern wing, civil rights unionism was not just a precursor of the modern civil rights movement. It was its decisive first phase.[33]

The link between race and class lay at the heart of the movement's political imagination. Historians have depicted the postwar years as the moment when race eclipsed class as the defining issue of American liberalism.[34] But among civil rights unionists, neither class nor race trumped the other, and both were expansively understood. Proceeding from the assumption that, from the founding of the Republic, racism has been bound up with economic exploitation, civil rights unionists sought to combine protection from discrimination with universalistic social welfare policies and individual rights with labor rights. For them, workplace democracy, union wages, and fair and full employment went hand in hand with open, affordable housing, political enfranchisement, educational equity, and an enhanced safety net, including health care for all.[35]

The realization of this vision depended on the answers to two questions. First, could the black-labor-left coalition reform the social policies forged during the Great Depression, extending to blacks the social and economic citizenship the New Deal had provided to an expanding state-subsidized middle class and an upper echelon of male workers? Second, could the coalition take advantage of the New Deal and the surge of progressive thought and politics in the American South to break the grip of the southern oligarchy in the region?[36]

Extending the New Deal and reforming the South were two sides of the same coin because seven out of ten African Americans still lived in the former Confederate states and because conservative southern Democrats possessed such disproportionate power in Congress.[37] To challenge the southern Democrats' congressional stranglehold, the movement had to enfranchise black and white southern workers and bring them into the house of labor, thus creating a constituency on which the region's emerging pro-civil rights, prolabor politicians could rely. If the project failed and the conservative wing of the southern Democratic Party triumphed, the South would become a magnet for runaway industries and a power base for a national conservative movement, undercutting the northern bastions of organized labor and unraveling the New Deal.[38]

During the 1940s half a million unionized black workers, North and South, put themselves in the front ranks of the effort. The "Double V" campaign, for victory over fascism abroad and racism at home; the prolabor policies of the Roosevelt administration; the booming economy which made labor scarce and triggered the biggest jump in black earnings since emancipation; the militancy of the black- and Left-led unions; the return of black veterans—all taken together "generated a rights consciousness that gave working-class black militancy a moral justification in some ways as powerful as that evoked by [Afro-Christianity] a generation later."[39]

International events deepened and broadened that consciousness. African Americans and their allies were among the first to grasp the enormity of the Nazi persecution of the Jews and to drive home the parallels between racism and anti-Semitism. In so doing, they used revulsion against the Holocaust to undermine racism at home and to "turn world opinion against Jim Crow." A "rising wind" of popular anticolonialism, inspired by the national liberation struggles in Africa and Asia that erupted after the war, also legitimized black aspirations and linked the denial of civil rights at home to the exploitation of the colonized peoples around the globe as well as to racially exclusive immigration and naturalization laws.[40]

At the same time, Popular Front culture encouraged labor feminism, a multiclass, union-oriented strand within the women's movement in which black women played a central role. Women joined the labor movement in record numbers in the 1940s, and by the end of the decade they had moved into leadership positions. The labor feminists among them fought for access to jobs, fair treatment, and expanded social supports within their unions and on the shop floor. They aimed to "de-gender" the idea of the family wage by asserting that women too were breadwinners. They also wanted to transform "the masculine pattern" of work, first by eliminating all invidious distinctions between male and female workers and then by demanding innovations, such as federally funded child care, that addressed the burdens of women's double day. Paralleling and reinforcing labor feminism, women in the Communist movement launched a women's liberation campaign. Articulated by Claudia Jones, the leading black woman leader in the Communist Party, and pushed forward by the Congress of American Women, the concept of the triple oppression of black women—by virtue of their race, class, and gender—stood at the center of a tradition of left or progressive feminism that saw women's issues as inseparable from those of race and class.[41]

Spurred by this broad insurgency, as well as by the turn of black leaders from "parallelism" (the creation of black institutions and the demand for separate but equal public services) to a push for full inclusion, black political activism soared and barriers to economic and political democracy tumbled. The Wagner Act and the National War Labor Board helped workers temper the power of corporations and forward the dream of workplace democracy that had animated American reform consciousness since the Progressive Era. In response to pressure from below, led mainly by

A. Philip Randolph and the Brotherhood of Sleeping Car Porters, President Franklin D. Roosevelt established a Fair Employment Practices Committee (FEPC) in 1941, putting racial discrimination on the national agenda for the first time since Reconstruction. In 1944 the Supreme Court brought a half century of acquiescence in political exclusion to an end when it declared the white primary unconstitutional. Rivaling in importance the later and more celebrated *Brown* decision, *Smith v. Allwright* sparked a major, South-wide voter registration drive. Other victories included the desegregation of the military, the outlawing of racial restrictive covenants and segregation in interstate commerce and graduate education, and the equalization of the salaries of black and white teachers in some southern states.[42]

The Chill of the Cold War

Those breakthroughs contributed to the movement's momentum, but they also met fierce resistance, as the long backlash accelerated. In the late 1940s, northern business interests joined conservative southern Democrats in a drive to roll back labor's wartime gains, protect the South's cheap labor supply, and halt the expansion of the New Deal. Their weapon of choice was a mass-based but elite-manipulated anticommunist crusade that would profoundly alter the cultural and political terrain.

The chief target was New Deal labor law. Like antidiscrimination and affirmative action programs in the 1960s and 1970s, the FEPC had enraged the conservative alliance, which defended the employer's right to hire and fire at will and equated fair hiring practices with quotas. After the war, probusiness conservatives quashed the campaign for a permanent FEPC, the chief item on the black-labor-left legislative agenda, in part by framing their opposition in the powerful new language of the cold war. Sen. Strom Thurmond of South Carolina, for instance, painted the FEPC as a violation of the "American" principle of "local self-government" by a "federal police state" reminiscent of the Soviet Union. By demonizing the Communists in the labor movement, conservatives also pushed the Taft-Hartley Act through Congress. Under Taft-Hartley's restrictions, the CIO expelled its left-wing unions, tempered its fight for social welfare programs that would benefit the whole working class, and settled for an increasingly bureaucratized system of collective bargaining that secured higher wages and private welfare protections for its own members, mainly white male workers in heavy industries. Despite this so-called labor-management accord, American corporations remained fundamentally hostile toward both unions and the regulatory state, leaving even the workers who profited from the constricted collective bargaining system vulnerable to a renewed corporate offensive in the 1970s and 1980s, an offensive that, in combination with economic stagnation, deindustrialization, and automation, would cripple the trade-union movement for years to come.[43]

To be sure, even as domestic anticommunism helped drive labor to the right and weaken civil rights unionism's institutional base, it gave civil rights advocates a potent weapon: the argument that the United States' treatment of its black citizens undermined its credibility abroad. At a time when the State Department was laboring to draw a stark contrast between American democracy and Soviet terror, win the allegiance of the newly independent nations of Asia and Africa, and claim leadership of the "free world," competition with the Soviet Union gave government officials a compelling reason to ameliorate black discontent and, above all, to manage the image of American race relations abroad. As a result, civil rights leaders who were willing to mute their criticism of American foreign policy and distance themselves from the Left gained a degree of access to the halls of power they had never had before. On balance, historians have emphasized the effectiveness of this strategy and viewed the movement's successes in the 1950s as "at least in part a product of the Cold War."[44] Seen through the optic of the long civil rights movement, however, civil rights look less like a product of the cold war and more like a casualty.

That is so because antifascism and anticolonialism had *already* internationalized the race issue and, by linking the fate of African Americans to that of oppressed people everywhere, had given their cause a transcendent meaning. Anticommunism, on the other hand, stifled the social democratic impulses that antifascism and anticolonialism encouraged, replacing them with a cold war racial liberalism that, at best, failed to deliver on its promise of reform (with the partial exception of the judiciary, the federal government took no effective action throughout the 1950s) and, at worst, colluded with the right-wing red scare to narrow the ideological ground on which civil rights activists could stand. To take just one example: Both left-wing and centrist black leaders seized the opportunity offered by the 1945 founding of the United Nations (UN) to define the plight of African Americans as a "human rights" issue, a concept that in UN treaties denoted not just freedom from political and legal discrimination but also the right to education, health care, housing, and employment. Although eager to convince emerging African nations of America's racial progress, the State Department blocked that endeavor, insulating the internal affairs of the United States from the oversight of the UN while carefully separating protected civil liberties from economic justice and branding the whole campaign for a robust human rights program a Soviet plot. Thwarted in its efforts, the National Association for the Advancement of Colored People (NAACP) abandoned both economic issues and the battle against segregation in the North and devoted its considerable resources to clear-cut cases of de jure segregation in the South, thus severing its ties to the black Popular Front and increasingly weakening the link between race and class.[45]

The presidential campaign of 1948 marked both the high point and the demise of the postwar black-labor-left coalition. The coalition found a national voice in Henry Wallace, a New Dealer who broke with the Democratic Party and ran for president on a third-party ticket. Courting the black vote with a progressive civil rights platform, Democratic Party candidate Harry S. Truman trounced Wallace but alienated the Dixiecrats, conservative southern congressmen who bolted the Democratic convention and formed their own party—a way station, as it turned out, on a road that would lead many conservative white southerners to support George C. Wallace briefly and then, with the election of Richard M. Nixon in 1972, move in large numbers to the Republican Party.[46]

The Dixiecrats also left another legacy. They perfected a combination of race- and red-baiting that defeated the South's leading New Deal politicians in the critical election of 1950 and, ten years later, allowed segregationists to claim that the civil rights movement was "communist inspired." Red-baiting thus got a second lease on life, spawning a dense network of "little HUACs" and "little FBIs," local imitations of the House Committee on Un-American Activities and the Federal Bureau of Investigation, throughout the South. Led by some of the region's most powerful politicians, notably Mississippi's James Eastland, those agencies hounded "subversives" of every sort, from veterans of the black-labor-left alliance, to local NAACP officials, to gay teachers, to national civil rights leaders, thus extending McCarthyism well into the 1960s, long after it had fallen into disrepute at the national level.[47]

The Classical Phase of the Movement

In the South, perhaps more than anywhere else in the country, the cold war destroyed Popular Front institutions and diverted the civil rights movement into new channels. When the so-called classical phase of the movement erupted in the late 1950s and 1960s, it involved blacks and whites, south-erners and northerners, local people and federal officials, secularists and men and women of faith. It also extended far beyond the South, and throughout the country it drew on multiple, competing ideological strands. But on the ground, in the South, the movement's ability to rally participants, stymie its enemies, and break through the fog of the cold war came largely from the prophetic tradition within the black church. Cold war liberals counseled patience while countering international criticism by suggesting that racism was not woven into American institutions; it was limited to the South, a retrograde region that economic development would eventually bring into line with an otherwise democratic nation. By contrast, southern civil rights activists, mobilizing the latent themes of justice and deliverance in an otherworldly religion, demanded "freedom now," not gradual, top-down amelioration. That prophetic vision gave believers the courage to engage history as an ongoing process of reconstruction to risk everything for ideals they might never see fulfilled.[48]

Those ideals have often been misconstrued, not only by those on the right who reduce them to color blindness but also by those on the left who stress the southern movement's limitations. In their zeal to make up for inatten-tion to the freedom struggle in the North and West, for instance, urban historians sometimes draw a misleading contrast between a northern embrace of economics and black power and a southern commitment to a minimalist program of interracialism and integration. That dichotomy ignores both the long history of nonviolent struggles against segregation in the North and the fact that black southerners were schooled in a quest *both* for access and for self-determination that dated back to emancipation, a quest that called forth strategies ranging from tactical alliances across the color line, to the building of separate institutions, to migration, to economic boycotts and direct action.[49] In both regions, the success of the movement depended not just on idealism and courage, but on a keen understanding and ready use of the fulcrums of power.

There was, moreover, nothing minimalist about dismantling Jim Crow, a system built as much on economic exploitation as on de jure and de facto spatial separation. In the minds of movement activists, integration was never about "racial mingling" or "merely sitting next to whites in school," as it is sometimes caricatured now.[50] Nor did it imply assimilation into static white-defined institutions, however much whites assumed that it did. True integration was and is an expansive and radical goal, not an ending or abolition of something that once was—the legal separation of bodies by race—but a process of transforming institutions and building an equitable, democratic, multiracial, and multiethnic society.[51]

The 1963 March on Washington which came at the height of what figures in the dominant narrative as the good, color-blind movement, is a case in point. Today's conservatives make much of Martin Luther King's dream that "children will one day live in a nation where they will not be judged by the color of their skin but by the content of their character." But virtually nothing in the dominant narrative would lead us to expect an image of the march that showed women carrying signs demanding jobs for all, decent housing, fair pay, and equal rights "*NOW*," thus asserting both their racial solidarity and their identities as activists and workers and thereby the equals of men.[52] Nothing in the dominant story reminds us that this demonstration which mobilized people from all walks of life and from every part of the country was a "march for jobs and freedom"—and that from early on women were in the front ranks, helping to link race, class, and gender and thus foreshadowing both black feminism and the expansive movement of movements the civil rights struggle set in motion (figures 10.1 and 10.2). [53]

In recent years we have learned more and more about the continuities between the 1940s and the 1960s, especially about the civil rights activists who came to political consciousness in the earlier period and then groomed and guided the young men and women who stepped forward in later years. E. D. Nixon, the stalwart NAACP leader who recruited King for the Montgomery bus boycott, was a veteran of the Brotherhood of Sleeping Car Porters, the black-led union that was central to the movement in the 1940s. Ella Baker passed on to the Student Nonviolent Coordinating Committee (SNCC) the radical pedagogy and organizing style she had learned both from her upbringing in the rural South and from the left-wing politics of Harlem in the 1930s and 1940s. Bayard Rustin, one of the movement's most brilliant strategists, had been "an eager young explorer of the American left, broadly defined." Anne Braden, a white southerner who became, as Angela

Figure 10.1 Protesters at the 1963 Civil Rights March on Washington, DC, carry signs for equal rights, integrated schools, decent housing, and an end to bias.

Source: Courtesy of the Collections of the Library of Congress.

Figure 10.2 Photographers, riding on the back of a truck, photograph civil rights leaders, including Martin Luther King, Jr., and the crowd carrying signs, as they take part in the 1963 Civil Rights March on Washington, DC.

Source: Courtesy of the Collections of the Library of Congress.

Y. Davis put it, a "legend" to young radicals, worked for Left-led unions in the late 1940s and continues to carry the banner of antiracism to this day. Frances Pauley got her start working for the New Deal in Georgia, helped mobilize white women on behalf of desegregation, and spent the rest of her life in the fight for civil rights and against poverty.[54]

The differences and discontinuities, however, were critical as well. The activists of the 1960s relied on independent protest organizations; they could not ground their battle in growing, vibrant, social democratic unions. They also suffered from a rupture in the narrative, a void at the center of the story of the modern civil rights struggle that is only now beginning to be filled. Many young activists of the 1960s saw their efforts as a new departure and themselves as a unique generation, not as actors with much to learn from an earlier, labor-infused civil rights tradition. Persecution, censorship, and self-censorship reinforced that generational divide by sidelining independent black radicals, thus whitening the memory and historiography of the Left and leaving later generations with an understanding of black politics that dichotomizes nationalism and integrationism. The civil rights unionism of the 1940s—which combined a principled and tactical belief in interracial organizing with a strong emphasis on black culture and institutions—was lost to memory. As the movement waned and contrary political forces resumed power, that loss left a vacuum for the current dominant narrative to fill.[55]

Beyond Declension

In the dominant narrative, the decline of the movement follows hard on the heels of the Civil Rights and Voting Rights acts, and the popular struggles of the 1970s become nothing more than identity politics, divisive squabbles that promoted tribalism, alienated white workers, and swelled the ranks of the New Right.[56] The view of the 1970s as a tragic denouement belittles second-wave feminism and other movements that emerged from the black freedom struggle and institutionalized themselves even as they served as the New Right's antagonists and foils. It also erases from popular memory the way the victories of the early 1960s coalesced into a lasting social revolution, as thousands of ordinary people pushed through the doors the movement had opened and worked to create new, integrated institutions where none had existed before.[57]

The literature on the post-sixties is still in its infancy, and except in accounts of the women's and gay rights movements, scholars left, right, and center have told stories of declension. A burst of new work on the black power movement, however, has departed from that model, documenting "an African American . . . political renaissance" in the 1970s, in which advocates of black political power put forth a program of urban reform that echoed the demands raised thirty years before.[58] Studies of other aspects of the black freedom movement in the North also offer powerful evidence that the civil rights movement did not die when it "went north" in the late 1960s, in part because it had been north all along. Still needed is more research on all aspects of the movement of movements in the post-sixties that rivals in nuance and complexity what we know about the classical phase.[59]

The studies that we do have reveal overlapping grassroots struggles. One struggle involved the move from token to comprehensive school desegregation in the South, which took place not during the turbulent short civil rights movement, but in the 1970s, after the media spotlight had swung away from the region. Another involved the desegregation of the workplace and the widespread acceptance of fair employment practices as a worthy goal. Like civil rights unionism, both of those advances have been forgotten or distorted. Both deserve to move from the margins to the center of the civil rights saga. Both, moreover, belong not to the past, but to the present, not to a story of rightwing triumph and over-and-done-with declension, but to an ongoing project whose key crises may still lie ahead.

The *Brown* decision and the rock-throwing mobs of Little Rock occupy pride of place in the popular narrative of school desegregation in the South. Barely noted is another critical turning point, a case in which black and white southerners grappled directly with the spatialization of race in the region. In *Swann v. Charlotte-Mecklenburg Board of Education* (1971), a case originating in North Carolina, civil rights lawyers exposed the artificial distinction between de jure and de facto segregation by demonstrating beyond a doubt that governmental policies, not benign-sounding customs, had created an almost totally segregated school system. " 'I lived here for twenty-four years without knowing what was going on,' " commented Judge James McMillan, who handed down a historic decision ordering twoway busing of black children to wealthy white suburbs and suburban children to city schools. A vigorous white homeowners' movement fought the decision tooth and nail, couching its opposition, not in the discredited rhetoric of massive resistance that surrounded the Little Rock debacle, but in a language of color blindness that resonated nationwide.[60]

More surprising, given how busing has come to symbolize all that went wrong with the dream of integration, a coalition of blue-collar activists, women's groups, white liberals, and black parents arose to defeat the homeowners' movement. Moreover, Charlotte took the unusual step of maintaining one of its historically black high schools rather than tearing it down and putting the burden on black students to sink or swim in hostile, whitedominated institutions. That school—West Charlotte High School—launched an experiment in true integration that reverberates to this day. Although many of the city's white students decamped to private schools, as they did throughout the South, Charlotte's success became such a point of civic pride that when the presidential candidate Ronald Reagan announced, during a campaign stop in 1984, that court-ordered busing "takes innocent children out of the neighborhood schools and makes them pawns in a social experiment that nobody wants," his largely Republican audience responded with an "awkward silence" that spoke louder than words.[61] Twenty years later, interviews conducted separately by the Southern Oral History

Program and by researchers at Columbia University's Teachers College suggested that, especially for students at West Charlotte High during the peak
years of integration, confronting racial differences and crossing racial
boundaries was life changing in ways that test scores and statistics cannot
capture. They treasured the experience, felt that it had dissipated "the
hostility and the hate" of early years, and struggled to maintain a degree of
diversity in their later lives.[62]

By the 1980s aggressive court supervision plus ongoing pressure from
black parents and students and their white allies had done what no one could
have predicted: they had endowed the South with the most integrated school
systems in the country, an achievement that has virtually disappeared from
the master narrative and barely registers even in scholarly accounts of the
movement. The era of desegregation was marked by other forms of political
and economic progress as well, most notably the surge in black voter registration and the election of black officials after the Voting Rights Act of 1965
and the desegregation of the workforce, as grassroots activists took advantage
of Title VII of the Civil Rights Act, which barred employment discrimination
by race and sex. Each of those advances reinforced the other. Black voters
acquired a leverage with school boards and access to public employment they
had never enjoyed before. As black students escaped from schools of concentrated poverty and took advantage of preschool and after-school programs,
smaller classes, superior facilities, and other benefits long monopolized by
suburban schools, a growing percentage attended college and entered managerial and professional positions. In a society in which economic status was
increasingly determined by education, the black middle class expanded.[63]
Nothing, perhaps, reflects the success of this push for political representation,
jobs, and education more vividly than the phenomenon of return migration to
the South. In the 1970s African Americans, who for more than half a century
had fled or been pushed from the region, began answering a "call to home."
Drawn by new opportunities, they returned in droves, not just to the cities,
but to the small towns and rural areas of the region.[64]

As blacks sought to reclaim the South and the South rejoined the country, however, the country was moving, seemingly inexorably, toward resegregation. In 1973 and 1974 the Supreme Court made two fateful decisions,
each of which "insulated predominately white suburban school districts
from the constitutional imperatives of *Brown* . . . and offered white parents
in urban districts fearful of school desegregation havens of predominately
white public schools to which they could flee." Ignoring the public policies
that had created the white enclaves in the first place, the Supreme Court in
Milliken v. Bradley (1974) exempted the suburbs around Detroit from
desegregation plans on the grounds that they had not engaged in recent,
intentional acts of discrimination. In *San Antonio Independent School
District v. Rodriguez* (1973), the Court ruled that the states faced no
obligation under the federal Constitution to equalize funding among
school districts. By the early 1990s, the Reagan-Bush courts were lifting the
court-ordered desegregation plans of the 1970s, even in states where dual

school systems had been required by law. After only two decades, the courts effectively abandoned the effort to enforce desegregation. By the late 1990s, judges had gone so far as to prohibit school boards from voluntarily using considerations of race (and thus of history and social reality) to maintain their hard-won progress toward integration.[65]

Throughout the South and the country, except in the Northeast, which never experienced significant desegregation, resegregation is now proceeding apace. Often blamed on the reflexive racism connoted by the all-purpose term "white flight" or, more recently, on black disillusionment with integration, that reversal can be better understood as the outcome, in an atmosphere of judicial hostility, of long-term failures to limit residential segregation, halt the decay of inner cities, prevent urban sprawl, address growing class divisions, and alter school-funding arrangements that favor suburban schools. Under such circumstances, it is no wonder that middle-class parents of both races feel acute pressure to buy homes in neighborhoods with reputable, well-financed schools and that parents in now hypersegregated inner cities sometimes demand the resources they hope will provide their children with a separate but equal education. Those pressures, moreover, have intensified as the No Child Left Behind Act, passed in 2002, has shifted the focus of educational policy away from funding and onto accountability and assessment in ways that often punish resource-poor schools, drive away the best teachers and better-off students, and deepen poverty and segregation. And yet, in spite of everything, large majorities of both whites and blacks maintain a commitment to integration—a commitment that public policy makers and pundits have done nothing to promote and are doing their best to squander.[66]

If the continuing story of school desegregation has been obscured by a narrative of post-1965 declension, the struggle for economic justice has been erased altogether. That struggle took many forms. In Seattle, Washington, the Congress of Racial Equality (CORE) launched its first direct-action campaign against employment discrimination in 1961 and followed up in 1964 with one of the most ambitious campaigns in the nation. In Memphis, Tennessee, black workers persisted in seeing civil rights and workers' rights as two aspects of the same struggle; the 1968 sanitation strike—best known as the context of King's assassination—was part of a decades-long push by black workers to attain better workplace conditions and fair wages. In Oakland, California, and other places, the Black Panthers called for a redistribution of economic and political power in cities devastated by four decades of failed metropolitan policies.[67]

More likely to be included in the prevailing narrative is President Lyndon B. Johnson's War on Poverty, an ambitious effort not only to join the issues of economics and civil rights, but also to expand the New Deal in order to address the economic inequalities embedded in American institutions. Launched in 1965, the program fell far short of its goals, not, as conservatives would have it, because it "threw money" at problems that only private enterprise and individual effort could solve, but because it did not go nearly far enough and because the minimally funded initiatives it did launch focused so heavily on "supply side" solutions such as job training, rather than on full employment, unionization, and the redistribution of economic resources. Nevertheless, the Great Society yielded lasting and important results (Medicaid and Head Start come immediately to mind), and it turned many activists in the direction of structural economic solutions.[68]

By contrast, the grassroots movement set in motion by Title VII of the Civil Rights Act of 1964 has been among the least noted of the movement's economic dimensions. Thousands of men and women, including a persistent and evolving network of labor feminists, pursued their rights under that historic law by signing petitions, filing class-action lawsuits, seeking affirmative action policies that specified hiring goals and timetables, and stepping forward to become courageous pioneers, the first of their race or sex to brave the minefields of long-segregated occupations. Once on the job, black workers became the most avid of new union members, and the understanding of workplace rights they brought with them inspired a surge of organizing in the public sector, which became one of the brightest spots in an otherwise-bleak landscape for organized labor. In combination, government intervention and grassroots action made 1965–1975 the breakthrough period for black economic progress, especially in the South. That victory inspired Latinos and others to make similar demands and adopt similar strategies. As a result, legal protection of individuals from workplace discrimination was extended to a large majority of Americans, including not only people of color and all women, but also the elderly and the disabled.[69]

In the early 1970s, moreover, a remarkable union democracy movement sought to revitalize the labor movement, and a wave of strikes swept the country, suggesting that the white workers now seen as preordained "Reagan Democrats" were by no means united, and that their allegiance was "up for grabs."[70] At the same time, a little-noticed cohort of civil rights veterans threw in their lot with the labor movement and launched labor support campaigns. As rank-and-file workers, rising labor leaders, labor lawyers, and the like, they joined other civil rights activists in an effort to "raise issues of economic equality . . . to the moral high ground earlier occupied by the assault against de jure segregation."[71]

Like the battle to desegregate the public schools, the struggle for economic justice met formidable barriers. Some were deep-seated, such as American individualism, the intensification of capital flight, and the legacy of anticommunism, which, in combination with the New Right's "war of ideas," tainted all attempts at redistribution. Others were produced by the unique economic crisis of the 1970s. Brought on by the simultaneous rise of unemployment and inflation known as "stagflation," the crisis galvanized a corporate offensive against unions and accelerated an ongoing process of economic restructuring that forwarded the emergence of a service economy and destroyed not only the strongholds of organized labor in the rust belt, but the South's traditional industries as well. At the same time, economic change in Latin America and the alteration of immigration restrictions in the 1960s sent millions of Latinos searching for work in northern cities. This wave of Third World immigration created new hybrid identities and spawned new liberation movements. But as the labor supply swelled and the blue-collar jobs opened up by Title VII evaporated, communities of color suffered from shocking rates of unemployment, and inner cities turned into burnt-out wastelands from which few could hope to escape.[72]

As layoffs skyrocketed, moreover, increasing numbers of white male workers, influenced by conservatives' pseudopopulist claims, blamed affirmative action, despite conclusive evidence that employers' efforts to hire and promote blacks and women did not lead to significant "reverse discrimination." As Thomas Sugrue has noted, "Long-term economic restructuring was inscrutable to most white workers. But affirmative action was an easy target"—in part because powerful stories and storytellers made it so.[73] The struggle for the equal rights amendment and abortion rights had a similar impact on some working-class wives. Dependent on men in an atmosphere of deepening economic insecurity and inundated with New Right attacks on the women's movement as an antifamily, elitist plot, they opposed reform in part out of fear that feminism would "free men first," leaving women with no claim to male protection and support.[74]

These developments helped to propel the New Right to power and encouraged the Reagan administration's efforts to gut antidiscrimination enforcement mechanisms. This deregulation of the labor market forwarded a resurgence of antiblack discrimination based on "hidden preferences and stereotypes" that are well documented but almost impossible to prove and thus helped reverse almost two decades of black economic gains.[75] Still, as Nancy MacLean argues, the right wing's triumph was by no means complete, in part because Reagan's efforts aroused a storm of opposition from advocacy groups, and in part because many large corporations, after years of resistance, embraced affirmative action, albeit in the new, watered-down form of "diversity"—a move designed, not to forward redistributive justice, but to help businesses reach new consumers and operate in global markets. The result is a stalemate that underscores both the ground won by advocates of economic access and the need for broader federal action to promote full employment, tame corporate power, and protect unions. On the one hand, government policy, driven by grassroots pressure, succeeded in cracking the edifice of racial discrimination erected over time by both employers and white-dominated unions. On the other, economic restructuring drove home how far beyond the reach of governmental protections against discrimination workers' dilemmas often lay. Without a strong collective voice, workers had no means of defending themselves against unfair labor practices (as opposed to willful bias against individuals) or of countering corporate control of the state. Nor could they build on and expand the legacy of civil rights unionism by transforming the fight for fair employment into an antiracist, antisexist, social democratic project for the twenty-first century.[76]

Conclusion

The challenges faced by the civil rights movement stemmed from what Martin Luther King Jr. called "evils that are rooted deeply in the whole structure of our society," evils that reflected not just the legacy of slavery but also the perpetuation of that legacy during subsequent generations by racialized state policies that wove white privilege into the fabric of American culture and institutions.[77] Despite the movement's undeniable triumphs, those evils persist and in some ways have been compounded. The resegregation of the public schools; the hypersegregation of inner cities; the soaring unemployment rates among black and Latino youths; the erosion of minority voting rights; the weakening of the labor movement; the wealth and income gap that is returning the United States to pre–New Deal conditions; the unraveling of the social safety net; the ever-increasing ability of placeless capital to move at will; the malignant growth of the "prison-industrial complex,"which far outstrips apartheid-era South Africa in incarcerating black men—those historical legacies cannot be waved away by declaring victory, mandating formal, race-neutral public policies, and allowing market forces to rule.[78]

Nor, of course, will understanding how the past weighs on the present in itself resolve current dilemmas. But it can help cut through the miasma of evasion and confusion that cripples our creativity from the start. For many white Americans have moved through what the critical theorist Walter Benjamin termed "this storm . . . we call progress" without coming to terms with the past.[79] That lack of accounting opens the way to a color-blind conservatism that is breathtakingly ahistorical and blind to social facts. It impoverishes public discourse, discourages investment in public institutions, and undermines our will to address the inequalities and injustices that surround us now.

The narratives spun by the new conservatives maintain a strong hold on the public imagination, in part because they have been repeated so often and broadcast so widely, and in part because they avoid uncomfortable questions about the relationship between cumulative white advantage and present social ills. Yet there is reason to hope that countervailing stories could make themselves heard and could even, under the right circumstances, prevail. Opinion poll after poll indicates that white racial attitudes have changed dramatically since World War II, that support for the principles of integration and equal treatment remains high (even as approval of governmental intervention to accomplish those goals has declined), and that most white as well as black Americans continue to favor the keystones of the New Deal order.[80] Those attitudes should not be underestimated. They do not mean that hidden or even overt biases have disappeared or that sedimented, institutional inequalities have been eliminated. But they are the ground in which new understandings of today's problems can take root. Those understandings must grapple both with history, which explodes the notion that racial disparities are caused by black failings, and with the abundant evidence that the distress of people of color today is indeed "the first sign of a danger that threatens us all." That danger—whose signs range from the every-family-for-itself scramble for "good schools" to the high cost of "prisons, police, mopping-up health care services, and other reactive measures"—if amplified by public storytellers, could combine with antiracist principles to create a climate in which fresh solutions to social problems can emerge.[81]

Historians can and must play a central role in a struggle that turns so centrally on understanding the legacy of the past. But how can we make ourselves heard without reducing history to the formulaic mantras on which political narratives usually rely? To tell our stories both truly and effectively, we need modes of writing and speaking that emphasize individual agency, the *sine qua non* of narrative, while also dramatizing the hidden history of policies and institutions—the publicly sanctioned choices that continually shape and reshape the social landscape and yet are often invisible to citizens trained in not seeing and in thinking exclusively in ahistorical, personal terms. We cannot settle for simple dichotomies (especially those that pit race against class, race-targeted against universalistic remedies, and so-called identity politics against economic policy and unionization), no matter how seductive they might be. Finally, we must forego easy closure and satisfying upward or downward arcs.

Only such novel forms of storytelling can convey what it means to have lived through an undefeated but unfinished revolution, a world-defining social movement that has experienced both reversals and victories and whose victories are now, once again, being partially reversed.[82] Both the victories and the reversals call us to action, as citizens and as historians with powerful stories to tell. Both are part of a long and ongoing civil rights movement. Both can help us imagine—for our own times—a new way of life, a continuing revolution.

Notes

Jacquelyn Dowd Hall is Julia Cherry Spruill Professor of History at the University of North Carolina and director of the Southern Oral History Program. This article is a revised version of the presidential address delivered to the convention of the Organization of American Historians in Boston on March 27, 2004.

Writing this essay led me to conversation with a far-flung network of friends and colleagues, and I thank them for their encouragement and generous sharing of ideas. Among them were Jefferson Cowie, Jane Dailey, Matthew Lassiter, Nelson Lichtenstein, Eric Lott, Nancy MacLean, Bryant Simon, and Karen Kruse Thomas. Laura Edwards, Drew Faust, Glenda Gilmore, Jeanne Grimm, Pamela Grundy, Bethany Johnson, Robert Korstad, Joanne Meyerowitz, Timothy McCarthy, Joe Mosnier, Kathryn Nasstrom, Della Pollock, Jennifer Ritterhouse, and Sarah Thuesen also offered astute comments on the manuscript in its various iterations. I benefited especially from Bethany Johnson's research and editorial skills, and Elizabeth More provided additional research assistance. A fellowship at the Radcliffe Institute for Advanced Study provided an ideal community in which to think and write.

1. On civil rights autobiographies and histories, see Kathryn L. Nasstrom, "Between Memory and History: Autobiographies of the Civil Rights Movement and the Writing of a New Civil Rights History," National Endowment for the Humanities Lecture, University of San Francisco, April 29, 2002 (in Jacquelyn Dowd Hall's possession); Steven F. Lawson, "Freedom Then, Freedom Now: The Historiography of the Civil

Rights Movement," *American Historical Review* 96 (April 1991): 456–71; Adam Fairclough, "Historians and the Civil Rights Movement,"*Journal of American Studies* 24 (December 1990): 387–98; Charles M. Payne, *I've Got the Light of Freedom: The Organizing Tradition and the Mississippi Freedom Struggle* (Berkeley, CA, 1995), 413–41; Charles W. Eagles, "Toward New Histories of the Civil Rights Era," *Journal of Southern History* 66 (November 2000): 815–48; and Kevin Gaines, "The Historiography of the Struggle for Black Equality since 1945," in *A Companion to Post–1945 America*, ed. Jean-Christophe Agnew and Roy Rosenzweig (Malden, MA, 2002), 211–34. In contrast to the vast literature on what the movement was and what it did, the scholarship on how it is remembered is scattered and thin. For examples, see David A. Zonderman, review of the Martin Luther King Jr. National Historic Site, Birmingham Civil Rights Institute, and National Civil Rights Museum, *Journal of American History* 91 (June 2004): 174–83; Kathryn L. Nasstrom, "Down to Now: Memory, Narrative, and Women's Leadership in the Civil Rights Movement in Atlanta, Georgia," *Gender and History* 11 (April 1999): 113–44; Terrie L. Epstein, "Tales from Two Textbooks: A Comparison of the Civil Rights Movement in Two Secondary History Textbooks," *Social Studies* 85 (May–June 1994): 121–26; William A. Link, review of the film *The Road to Brown*, by William A. Ellwood, Mykola Kulish, and Gary Weimberg, *History of Education Quarterly* 31 (Winter 1991–1992): 523–26; and an anthology in progress: Leigh Raiford and Renee Romano, eds., " 'Freedom Is a Constant Struggle': The Civil Rights Movement in United States Memory" (in Leigh Raiford and Renee Romano's possession).

2. Bayard Rustin, *Down the Line: The Collected Writings of Bayard Rustin* (Chicago, 1971), 111–22, esp. 111.

3. Martin Luther King Jr., "The Rising Tide of Racial Consciousness (1960)," in *I Have a Dream: Writings and Speeches That Changed the World*, ed. James Melvin Washington (San Francisco, CA, 1992), 67. For early protests against the tendency to idolize King and to ignore his radicalism and that of the grassroots, see "A Round Table: Martin Luther King Jr.," *Journal of American History* 74 (September 1987): 436–81. For a call for attention to the later King years, see Michael Honey, "Labor and Civil Rights Movements at the Cross-Roads: Martin Luther King, Black Workers, and the Memphis Sanitation Strike," paper delivered at the annual meeting of the Organization of American Historians, Memphis, TN, April 2003 (in Hall's possession).

4. Steve Fraser and Gary Gerstle, eds., *The Rise and Fall of the New Deal Order, 1930–1980* (Princeton, NJ, 1989); Van Gosse, "A Movement of Movements: The Definition and Periodization of the New Left," in *Companion to Post–1945 America*, ed. Agnew and Rosenzweig, 277–302, esp. 282.

5. The meaning of race and racism in America has always been inflected by ethnic exclusions and identities, and it has been complicated by the demographic changes in the late twentieth century. In this essay, however, I limit my focus to the black-white divide. Lani Guinier and Gerald Torres, *The Miner's Canary: Enlisting Race, Resisting Power, Transforming Democracy* (Cambridge, MA, 2002), 11.

6. Kevin Mattson, "Civil Rights Made Harder," *Reviews in American History* 30 (December 2002): 663–70.

7. Julian Bond, "The Media and the Movement: Looking Back from the Southern Front," in *Media, Culture, and the Modern African American Freedom Struggle*, ed. Brian Ward (Gainesville, FL, 2001), 16–40, esp. 32. See also Robert J. Norrell, "One Thing We Did Right: Reflections on the Movement," in *New Directions in Civil Rights Studies*, ed. Armstead L. Robinson and Patricia Sullivan (Charlottesville, VA, 1991), 72–73, 77; and Payne, *I've Got the Light of Freedom*, 391–405.

8. Payne, *I've Got the Light of Freedom*, 391. For works that stress the events of the classical phase but also highlight the long trajectory of the movement, see ibid.; Manning

Marable, *Race, Reform, and Rebellion: The Second Reconstruction in Black America, 1945–1990* (Jackson, MS, 1991); Steven F. Lawson, *Running for Freedom: Civil Rights and Black Politics in America since 1941* (New York, 1997); Adam Fairclough, *Race and Democracy: The Civil Rights Struggle in Louisiana, 1915–1972* (Athens, GA, 1995); and Greta De Jong, *A Different Day: African American Struggles for Justice in Rural Louisiana, 1900–1970* (Chapel Hill, 2002). Community studies tend to blur the boundaries of the dominant narrative, and biographies often illuminate North/South linkages and the fluidity and diversity of the movement. See, for example, George Lipsitz, *A Life in the Struggle: Ivory Perry and the Culture of Opposition* (Philadelphia, PA, 1995). For a growing chorus of calls for a broader scholarly focus, see Robert Korstad and Nelson Lichtenstein, "Opportunities Found and Lost: Labor, Radicals, and the Early Civil Rights Movement," *Journal of American History* 75 (December 1988): 786–811; Timothy B. Tyson, "Robert F. Williams, 'Black Power,' and the Roots of the African American Freedom Struggle," ibid., 85 (September 1998), 540–70; Julian Bond, "The Politics of Civil Rights History," in *New Directions in Civil Rights Studies*, ed. Robinson and Sullivan, 8–16; Payne, *I've Got the Light of Freedom*, 3, 391–405, 413–41; Charles Payne, "Debating the Civil Rights Movement: The View from the Trenches," in *Debating the Civil Rights Movement, 1945–1968*, by Steven F. Lawson and Charles Payne (Lanham, MD, 1998), 108–11; Peniel E. Joseph, "Waiting till the Midnight Hour: Reconceptualizing the Heroic Period of the Civil Rights Movement, 1954–1965," *Souls*, 2 (Spring 2000): 6–17; Jacquelyn Dowd Hall, "Mobilizing Memory: Broadening Our View of the Civil Rights Movement," *Chronicle of Higher Education* (July 27, 2001): B7–B11; Nell Irvin Painter, "America Needs to Reexamine Its Civil Rights History," *Journal of Blacks in Higher Education* (August 31, 2001): 132–34; Brian Ward, "Introduction: Forgotten Wails and Master Narratives: Media, Culture, and Memories of the Modern African American Freedom Struggle," in *Media, Culture, and the Modern African American Freedom Struggle*, ed. Ward, 1–15; Robert O. Self, *American Babylon: Race and the Struggle for Postwar Oakland* (Princeton, 2003), 10–11, 330–31; Evelyn Brooks Higginbotham, "Foreword," in *Freedom North: Black Freedom Struggles outside the South, 1940–1980*, ed. Jeanne Theoharis and Komozi Woodard (New York, 2003), viii–xvi; Jeanne Theoharis, "Introduction," ibid., 1–15; Van Gosse, "Postmodern America: A New Democratic Order in the Second Gilded Age," in *The World the Sixties Made: Politics and Culture in Recent America*, ed. Van Gosse and Richard Moser (Philadelphia, PA, 2003), 1–36; Jack Dougherty, *More Than One Struggle: The Evolution of Black School Reform in Milwaukee* (Chapel Hill, NC, 2004), 1–4; and Nikhil Pal Singh, *Black Is a Country: Race and the Unfinished Struggle for Democracy* (Cambridge, MA, 2004), 4–14.

9. For a bracing look at the reinvention of the Right in the 1970s, see Nancy MacLean, *"Freedom Is Not Enough": How the Fight over Jobs and Justice Changed America* (Cambridge, MA, forthcoming), chap. 7. I am indebted to MacLean for sharing her work with me. For the metamorphosis of conservatism in the West and South, see Lisa McGirr, *Suburban Warriors: The Origins of the New American Right* (Princeton, NJ, 2001); Anders Walker, "The Ghost of Jim Crow: Law, Culture, and the Subversion of Civil Rights, 1954–1965" (Ph.D. diss., Yale University, 2003); Anders Walker, "Legislating Virtue: How Segregationists Disguised Racial Discrimination as Moral Reform Following *Brown v. Board of Education*," *Duke Law Journal* 47 (November 1997): 399–424; Matthew D. Lassiter and Andrew B. Lewis, eds., *The Moderates' Dilemma: Massive Resistance to School Desegregation in Virginia* (Charlottesville, 1998); Matthew D. Lassiter, "The Suburban Origins of 'Color-Blind' Conservatism: Middle-Class Consciousness in the Charlotte Busing Crisis," *Journal of Urban History* (May 30, 2004): 549–82; and Richard A. Pride, *The Political Use of Racial Narratives: School Desegregation in Mobile, Alabama, 1954–97* (Urbana, IL, 2002).

10. The quotation is from Ernest Van den Haag, "Reverse Discrimination: A Brief against It," *National Review* (April 29, 1977): 493, cited in MacLean," *Freedom Is Not Enough*," chap. 7.

11. Proponents of this new racial orthodoxy differ in tone and, to a lesser extent, in ideas. I am stressing the interventions of those who present themselves as the voice of the reasoned, informed center or as "racial realists," in Alan Wolfe's phrase. I refer to them as "new conservatives" or "color-blind conservatives." For racial realism, see Alan Wolfe, "Enough Blame to Go Around," *New York Times Book Review*, June 12, 1998, p. 12; Philip Klinkner, "The 'Racial Realism' Hoax," *Nation*, December 14, 1998, pp. 33–38; "Letters," ibid., January, 25, 1999, p. 24; and Michael K. Brown et al., *Whitewashing Race: The Myth of a Color-Blind Society* (Berkeley, CA, 2003), 5–12, 224. For the spectrum and evolution of new conservative writing on race, see Charles A. Murray, *Losing Ground: American Social Policy, 1950–1980* (New York, 1984); Thomas Sowell, *Civil Rights: Rhetoric or Reality?* (New York, 1984); Dinesh D'Souza, *The End of Racism: Principles for a Multiracial Society* (New York, 1995); Stephan Thernstrom and Abigail Thernstrom, *America in Black and White: One Nation, Indivisible* (New York, 1997); Jim Sleeper, *Liberal Racism* (New York, 1997); Tamar Jacoby, *Someone Else's House: America's Unfinished Struggle for Integration* (New York, 1998); Shelby Steele, *A Dream Deferred: The Second Betrayal of Black Freedom in America* (New York, 1998); and Abigail Thernstrom and Stephan Thernstrom, *No Excuses: Closing the Racial Gap in Learning* (New York, 2003). Critiques of color-blind conservatives, which dispute the conservatives's understanding of history, interpretation of civil rights law, and research, include Brown et al., *Whitewashing Race;* J. Morgan Kousser, *Colorblind Injustice: Minority Voting Rights and the Undoing of the Second Reconstruction* (Chapel Hill, NC, 1999); K. Anthony Appiah and Amy Gutmann, *Color Conscious: The Political Morality of Race* (Princeton, NJ, 1996); Stephen Steinberg, *Turning Back: The Retreat from Racial Justice in American Thought and Policy* (Boston, MA, 2001); MacLean, "*Freedom Is Not Enough*"; and Alice O'Connor, "Malign Neglect," *Du Bois Review* 1 (November 2004), forthcoming.

12. This formulation is drawn from Kimberlé Williams Crenshaw, "Race, Reform, and Retrenchment: Transformation and Legitimation in Antidiscrimination Law," in *Critical Race Theory: The Key Writings That Formed the Movement*, ed. Kimberlé Crenshaw et al. (New York, 1995), 105.

13. Gosse, "Postmodern America," 5; Brown et al., *Whitewashing Race*, 224. We have little scholarship on the mushrooming of conservative think tanks and foundations and their role in training and supporting policy intellectuals and marketers and thus in shaping the terms of American political debate. This lack of attention leaves intact the assumption that the current assault on the gains of the civil rights movement results from a more or less spontaneous shift in public opinion that proponents of racial and gender justice often feel helpless to combat. For a start, see Leon Howell, *Funding the War of Ideas: A Report to the United Church Board for Homeland Ministries* (Cleveland, 1995); Jean Stefancic and Richard Delgado, *No Mercy: How Conservative Think Tanks and Foundations Changed America's Social Agenda* (Philadelphia, 1996); David Callahan, *$1 Billion for Ideas: Conservative Think Tanks in the 1990s* (Washington, DC, 1999); Lee Cokorinos, *The Assault on Diversity: An Organized Challenge to Racial and Gender Justice* (Lanham, MD, 2003); and Andrew Rich, *Think Tanks, Public Policy, and the Politics of Expertise* (New York, 2004).

14. Pride, *Political Use of Racial Narratives*, 4–20, 244–72, esp. 9 and 272.

15. Nancy MacLean, "Redesigning Dixie with Affirmative Action: Race, Gender, and the Desegregation of the Southern Textile Mill World," in *Gender and the Southern Body Politic: Essays and Comments*, ed. Nancy Bercaw (Jackson, MS, 2000), 163.

16. On the reshaping of cities by the two internal migrations, see Robert O. Self and Thomas J. Sugrue, "The Power of Place: Race, Political Economy, and Identity in the Postwar Metropolis," in *Companion to Post–1945 America*, ed. Agnew and Rosenzweig, 20–43.

17. Robert O. Self, " 'Negro Leadership and Negro Money': African American Political Organizing in Oakland before the Panthers," in *Freedom North*, ed. Theoharis and Woodard, 99–100. For the long-neglected topic of women and migration, see Darlene Clark Hine, "Black Migration to the Urban Midwest: The Gender Dimension, 1915–1945," in *The Great Migration in Historical Perspective: New Dimensions of Race, Class, and Gender*, ed. Joe William Trotter Jr. (Bloomington, IN, 1991), 127–46; Kimberley L. Phillips, *Alabama North: African-American Migrants, Community, and Working-Class Activism in Cleveland, 1915–1945* (Urbana, IL, 1999); Gretchen Lemke-Santangelo, *Abiding Courage: African American Migrant Women and the East Bay Community* (Chapel Hill, 1996); Megan Taylor Shockley, *"We, Too, Are Americans": African American Women in Detroit and Richmond, 1940–54* (Urbana, 2004); and Laurie Beth Green, "Battling the Plantation Mentality: Consciousness, Culture, and the Politics of Race, Class, and Gender in Memphis, 1940–1968" (Ph.D. diss., University of Chicago, 1999).

18. Self, *American Babylon*, 88; Laurie B. Green, "Race, Gender, and Labor in 1960s Memphis: 'I AM A MAN' and the Meaning of Freedom," *Journal of Urban History* 30 (March 2004): 467.

19. Alice Kessler-Harris, *In Pursuit of Equity: Women, Men, and the Quest for Economic Citizenship in Twentieth-Century America* (New York, 2001).

20. Nelson Lichtenstein, *State of the Union: A Century of American Labor* (Princeton, NJ, 2002), 96. On gender, race, and welfare, see Kessler-Harris, *In Pursuit of Equity*; Linda Gordon, ed., *Women, the State, and Welfare* (Madison, WI, 1990); Linda Gordon, *Pitied but Not Entitled: Single Mothers and the History of Welfare, 1890–1935* (New York, 1994); and Michael K. Brown, *Race, Money, and the American Welfare State* (Ithaca, 1999). For changes in the family-wage system as the key theme of post–World War II women's history, see Nancy MacLean, "Postwar Women's History: The 'Second Wave' or the End of the Family Wage?" in *Companion to Post–1945 America*, ed. Agnew and Rosenzweig, 235–59.

21. My discussion of white ethnic workers, the middle class, and the spatialization of race draws on the work of brilliant urban historians, especially Kenneth T. Jackson, "Race, Ethnicity, and Real Estate Appraisal: The Home Owners Loan Corporation and the Federal Housing Administration," *Journal of Urban History* 6 (August 1980): 419–52; Kenneth T. Jackson, *Crabgrass Frontier: The Suburbanization of the United States* (New York, 1985); Thomas W. Hanchett, *Sorting Out the New South City: Race, Class, and Urban Development in Charlotte, 1875–1975* (Chapel Hill, NC, 1998); Thomas J. Sugrue, "Crabgrass-Roots Politics: Race, Rights, and the Reaction against Liberalism in the Urban North, 1940–1964," *Journal of American History* 82 (September 1995): 551–78; Arnold R. Hirsch, *Making the Second Ghetto: Race and Housing in Chicago, 1940–1960* (New York, 1983); Thomas J. Sugrue, *The Origins of the Urban Crisis: Race and Inequality in Postwar Detroit* (Princeton, 1996); Kevin Fox Gotham, "Urban Space, Restrictive Covenants, and the Origins of Racial Residential Segregation in a U.S. City, 1900–50," *International Journal of Urban and Regional Research* 24 (September 2000): 616–33; Self, *American Babylon*; Martha Biondi, *To Stand and Fight: The Struggle for Civil Rights in Postwar New York City* (Cambridge, MA, 2003), 112–36, 223–49; Lizabeth Cohen, *A Consumer's Republic: The Politics of Mass Consumption in Postwar America* (New York, 2003); Kenneth D. Durr, *Behind the Backlash: White Working-Class Politics in Baltimore, 1940–1980* (Chapel Hill, 2003); and Bryant Simon,

Boardwalk of Dreams: Atlantic City and the Fate of Urban America (New York, 2004). I am also indebted to Douglas S. Massey and Nancy A. Denton, *American Apartheid: Segregation and the Making of the Underclass* (Cambridge, MA, 1993); and Brown, *Race, Money, and the American Welfare State.* On how veterans' benefits disadvantaged blacks, see Brown et al., *Whitewashing Race,* 75–77.

22. Biondi, *To Stand and Fight,* 241–49.

23. Self, *American Babylon,* 333–34.

24. Melvin L. Oliver and Thomas M. Shapiro, *Black Wealth/White Wealth: A New Perspective on Racial Inequality* (New York, 1995).

25. For the argument that the South "traveled almost directly from the countryside to suburbia" and that "the southern city became the quintessential suburban city," see David R. Goldfield, *Promised Land: The South since 1945* (Arlington Heights, IL, 1987), 153, 34.

26. On such black-white interactions, see Diane Miller Sommerville, *Rape and Race in the Nineteenth-Century South* (Chapel Hill, 2004); and Jennifer Lynn Ritterhouse, "Learning Race: Racial Etiquette and the Socialization of Children in the Jim Crow South" (Ph.D. diss., University of North Carolina, Chapel Hill, 1999).

27. For the argument that racialism arose in feudal Europe before Europe's encounter with Africa and that capitalism and racialism evolved together to produce "a modern world system of 'racial capitalism' dependent on slavery, violence, imperialism, and genocide," see Cedric J. Robinson, *Black Marxism: The Making of the Black Radical Tradition* (1983; Chapel Hill, NC, 2000), 2–3; and Robin D. G. Kelley, "Foreword," ibid., esp. xiii. I use "racial capitalism" to emphasize that unfettered capitalism as well as racialism produced the Jim Crow system and to suggest similarities between the North and the South. For such uses of the term by southern historians, see Hall, "Mobilizing Memory," B8; Robert Rodgers Korstad, *Civil Rights Unionism: Tobacco Workers and the Struggle for Democracy in the Mid-Twentieth-Century South* (Chapel Hill, NC, 2003), 55; and Brian Kelly, "Sentinels for New South Industry: Booker T. Washington, Industrial Accommodation, and Black Workers in the Jim Crow South," *Labor History* 44 (August 2003): 339. On the patriarchal political culture of the black belt elite, see Kari A. Frederickson, *The Dixiecrat Revolt and the End of the Solid South, 1932–1968* (Chapel Hill, NC, 2001).

28. Robert Korstad, "Class and Caste: Unraveling the Mysteries of the New South Regime," paper delivered at the W. E. B. Du Bois Institute Colloquium Series, Harvard University, Cambridge, MA, Februry 18, 2004 (in Hall's possession).

29. Bruce J. Schulman, *From Cotton Belt to Sunbelt: Federal Policy, Economic Development, and the Transformation of the South, 1938–1980* (New York, 1991), 112–73; Samuel Lubell, *The Future of American Politics* (New York, 1951), 100, 111–12; Karen Kruse Thomas, "Southern Racial Politics and Federal Health Policy in the Careers of Three Southern Senators: Allen Ellender of Louisiana, Lister Hill of Alabama, and Claude Pepper of Florida," paper delivered at the Organization of American Historians Southern Regional Conference, Atlanta, GA, July 10, 2004 (in Hall's possession).

30. Gavin Wright, "Economic Consequences of the Southern Protest Movement," in *New Directions in Civil Rights Studies,* ed. Robinson and Sullivan, 174–78; Brown et al., *Whitewashing Race,* 72–73. On how mechanization undercut labor and eliminated jobs for blacks, see Korstad, *Civil Rights Unionism,* 277–81.

31. Gavin Wright, "The Civil Rights Revolution as Economic History," *Journal of Economic History* 59 (June 1999): esp. 285. For the argument that much of the South's continuing distinctiveness rests less on its history of racism than on its devotion to the conservative economic tenets of racial capitalism, see ibid.

32. This paragraph draws on James C. Cobb, *The Selling of the South: The Southern Crusade for Industrial Development, 1936–1980* (Baton Rouge, 1982); Schulman, *From Cotton Belt to Sunbelt*; Brown, *Race, Money, and the American Welfare State*; Lubell, *Future of American Politics*, 100, 111–12; Hanchett, *Sorting Out the New South City*, 89–182, 223–56; Bruce J. Schulman, *The Seventies: The Great Shift in American Culture, Society, and Politics* (New York, 2001), 36–37; Dan T. Carter, *The Politics of Rage: George Wallace, the Origins of the New Conservatism, and the Transformation of American Politics* (New York, 1995), 326–27, 399; Lassiter, "Suburban Origins of 'Color-Blind' Conservatism," 549–82; and Jefferson Cowie, "Nixon's Class Struggle: Romancing the New Right Worker, 1969–1973," *Labor History* 43 (August 2002): 257–83. For a more sympathetic treatment of Nixon's southern policies, see Dean J. Kotlowski, *Nixon's Civil Rights: Politics, Principle, and Policy* (Cambridge, MA, 2001), 1–43.

33. Korstad, *Civil Rights Unionism*; Biondi, *To Stand and Fight*, 6. In this essay I use the term "civil rights unionism" to highlight the conjunction of race and class interests in black- and Left-led unions and progressive organizations. On the Popular Front, see Michael Denning, *The Cultural Front: The Laboring of American Culture in the Twentieth Century* (New York, 1996). Important early studies focused on civil rights activism in the late 1930s and the 1940s. See, for example, Richard M. Dalfiume, "The 'Forgotten Years' of the Negro Revolution," *Journal of American History* 55 (June 1968): 90–106; and Harvard Sitkoff, *A New Deal for Blacks: The Emergence of Civil Rights as a National Issue* (New York, 1978). Still, only in the 1990s did civil rights historians begin to see the 1940s as a watershed comparable to the 1870s and the 1960s. See, for example, Michael K. Honey, *Southern Labor and Black Civil Rights: Organizing Memphis Workers* (Urbana, IL, 1993); Patricia Sullivan, *Days of Hope: Race and Democracy in the New Deal Era* (Chapel Hill, NC, 1996); Penny M. Von Eschen, *Race against Empire: Black Americans and Anticolonialism, 1937–1957* (Ithaca, NY, 1997); Barbara Dianne Savage, *Broadcasting Freedom: Radio, War, and the Politics of Race, 1938–1948* (Chapel Hill, 1999); John Egerton, *Speak Now against the Day: The Generation before the Civil Rights Movement in the South* (New York, 1994); Carol Anderson, *Eyes off the Prize: The United Nations and the African American Struggle for Human Rights, 1944–1955* (New York, 2003); Risa Lauren Goluboff, "The Work of Civil Rights in the 1940s: The Department of Justice, the NAACP, and African-American Agricultural Labor" (PhD diss., Princeton University, NJ, 2003); and Glenda Gilmore, "Defying Dixie: African Americans and Their Allies, 1915–1945," book in progress (in Glenda Gilmore's possession). For a contrary view of the 1940s as a decade of quiescence, see Harvard Sitkoff, "African American Militancy in the World War II South: Another Perspective," in *Remaking Dixie: The Impact of World War II on the American South*, ed. Neil R. McMillen (Jackson, MS, 1997), 70–92.

34. On the 1940s as the beginning of an era in which progressives elevated race over class, see Gary Gerstle, "The Protean Character of American Liberalism," *American Historical Review* 99 (October 1994): 1043–73; and Peter J. Kellogg, "Civil Rights Consciousness in the 1940s," *Historian* 42 (no. 1, 1979): 18–41, esp. 22–25. For contrary views of the decade, see Denning, *Cultural Front*, 467; and Goluboff, "Work of Civil Rights."

35. Korstad, *Civil Rights Unionism*, 3; Biondi, *To Stand and Fight*, 16; Self, *American Babylon*, 2–3, 6; Alan Derickson, " 'Take Health from the List of Luxuries': Labor and the Right to Health Care, 1915–1949," *Labor History* 41 (May 2000): 171–87.

36. What Alex Lichtenstein has called the "Southern Front" was signaled by union successes in the region, a spike in National Association for the Advancement of Colored People (NAACP) membership and voter registration among blacks, local

activism by African Americans and white workers, and an influx into Washington of prolabor, antiracist, southern New Dealers. See Alex Lichtenstein, "The Cold War and the 'Negro Question, ' " *Radical History Review* 72 (Fall 1998): 186; Anthony P. Dunbar, *Against the Grain: Southern Radicals and Prophets, 1929–1959* (Charlottesville, VA, 1981); Linda Reed, *Simple Decency and Common Sense: The Southern Conference Movement, 1938–1963* (Bloomington, 1991); Sullivan, *Days of Hope*; Korstad, *Civil Rights Unionism*; and Egerton, *Speak Now against the Day*.

37. According to the U.S. census of 1940, out of 12,672,971 African Americans, 8,873,631 lived in the eleven former Confederate states. University of Virginia Geospatial and Statistical Data Center, *United States Historical Census Data Browser* <http://fisher.lib.virginia.edu/census/> (accessed September 2004).

38. Sullivan, *Days of Hope*; Michael Goldfield, *The Color of Politics: Race and the Mainsprings of American Politics* (New York, 1997), 231–61; Brown, *Race, Money*, 99–134; Ira Katznelson, Kim Geiger, and Daniel Kryder, "Limiting Liberalism: The Southern Veto in Congress, 1933–1950," *Political Science Quarterly* 108 (Summer 1993): 283–306; Korstad and Lichtenstein, "Opportunities Found and Lost," 786–811; Korstad, *Civil Rights Unionism*, 4–5.

39. Dalfiume, " 'Forgotten Years' of the Negro Revolution," 90–106; Biondi, *To Stand and Fight*, 5; Korstad and Lichtenstein, "Opportunities Found and Lost," esp. 787; and Eric Arnesen, *Brotherhoods of Color: Black Railroad Workers and the Struggle for Equality* (Cambridge, MA, 2001).

40. Nikhil Pal Singh, "Culture/Wars: Recoding Empire in an Age of Democracy," *American Quarterly* 50 (September 1998): 474; Norrell, "One Thing We Did Right," 68–69. For the statement on "world opinion," see Gilmore, "Defying Dixie." Brenda Gayle Plummer, *Rising Wind: Black Americans and U.S. Foreign Affairs, 1935–1960* (Chapel Hill, NC, 1996); Von Eschen, *Race against Empire*.

41. This discussion of labor feminism is drawn from Dorothy Sue Cobble, "Lost Visions of Equality: The Labor Movement Origins of the Next Women's Movement," paper delivered at the annual meeting of the Organization of American Historians, Washington, DC, April 13, 2002 (in Hall's possession), esp. 13; and Dorothy Sue Cobble, *The Other Women's Movement: Workplace Justice and Social Rights in Modern America* (Princeton, NJ, 2004), 8–9, 94–144, esp. 8. For an earlier use of the term "labor feminism," see Jacquelyn Dowd Hall, "O. Delight Smith's Progressive Era: Labor, Feminism, and Reform in the Urban South," in *Visible Women: New Essays on American Activism*, ed. Nancy A. Hewitt and Suzanne Lebsock (Urbana, IL, 1993), 166–98. For left feminism more generally, see Kate Weigand, *Red Feminism: American Communism and the Making of Women's Liberation* (Baltimore, MD, 2001); Gerald Horne, *Race Woman: The Lives of Shirley Graham Du Bois* (New York, 2000); Amy Swerdlow, "The Congress of American Women: Left-Feminist Peace Politics in the Cold War," in *U.S. History as Women's History: New Feminist Essays*, ed. Linda K. Kerber, Alice Kessler-Harris, and Kathryn Kish Sklar (Chapel Hill, NC, 1995), 296–312; Daniel Horowitz, *Betty Friedan and the Making of* The Feminine Mystique: *The American Left, the Cold War, and Modern Feminism* (Amherst, MA, 1998), 50–152; and Gerda Lerner, *Fireweed: A Political Autobiography* (Philadelphia, 2002), 256–74.

42. Lichtenstein, *State of the Union*, 4–11; Dalfiume, " 'Forgotten Years' of the Negro Revolution," 90–106; Biondi, *To Stand and Fight*, 4; Darlene Clark Hine, *Black Victory: The Rise and Fall of the White Primary in Texas* (Columbia, MO, 2003); *Smith v. Allwright*, 321 U.S. 649 (1944); Amilcar Shabazz, *Advancing Democracy: African Americans and the Struggle for Access and Equity in Higher Education in Texas* (Chapel Hill, 2004). On "parallelism," see Darlene Clark Hine, "Black

Professionals and Race Consciousness: Origins of the Civil Rights Movement, 1890–1950," *Journal of American History* 89 (March 2003):1280. On salary equalization and the improvement of black schools in the 1940s and early 1950s, see Sonya Ramsey, "More Than the Three R's: The Educational, Economic, and Cultural Experiences of African American Female Public School Teachers in Nashville, Tennessee, 1869–1893" (Ph.D. diss., University of North Carolina, Chapel Hill, 2000); Adam Fairclough, *Teaching Equality: Black Schools in the Age of Jim Crow* (Athens, 2001), 58–60; Sarah Caroline Thuesen, "Classes of Citizenship: The Culture and Politics of Black Public Education in North Carolina, 1919–1960" (Ph.D. diss., University of North Carolina, Chapel Hill, 2003); and James J. Heckman, "The Central Role of the South in Accounting for the Economic Progress of Black Americans," *American Economic Review* 80 (May 1990): 242–46.

43. Frederickson, *Dixiecrat Revolt*, 7; Lichtenstein, *State of the Union*, 114–40; Nelson Lichtenstein, "Union Strategies," *Dissent* 49 (Summer 2002): 75. For the battle over the Fair Employment Practices Committee (FEPC), see also Merl E. Reed, *Seedtime for the Modern Civil Rights Movement: The President's Committee on Fair Employment Practice, 1941–1946* (Baton Rouge, LA, 1991).

44. Mary L. Dudziak, *Cold War Civil Rights: Race and the Image of American Democracy* (Princeton, NJ, 2000), 12.

45. Anderson, *Eyes off the Prize*; Von Eschen, *Race against Empire*; Gerald Horne, *Communist Front? The Civil Rights Congress, 1946–1956* (London, 1988); U.S. Civil Rights Congress, *We Charge Genocide: The Historic Petition to the United Nations for Relief from a Crime of the United States Government against the Negro People*, ed. William L. Patterson (1951; New York, 1970); Mark V. Tushnet, *The NAACP's Legal Strategy against Segregated Education, 1925–1950* (Chapel Hill, NC, 1987); Goluboff, "Work of Civil Rights."

46. Frederickson, *Dixiecrat Revolt*; Carter, *Politics of Rage*.

47. Jeff Woods, *Black Struggle, Red Scare: Segregation and Anti-Communism in the South, 1948–1968* (Baton Rouge, LA, 2004); Catherine Fosl, *Subversive Southerner: Anne Braden and the Struggle for Racial Justice in the Cold War South* (New York, 2002); Chris Myers, "The Senator and the Sharecropper: James O. Eastland, Fannie Lou Hamer, and the Struggle for Freedom at Home and Abroad" (Ph.D. diss., University of North Carolina, Chapel Hill, in progress, in Hall's possession); Stacy Braukman, "Anticommunism and the Politics of Sex and Race in Florida, 1954–1965" (Ph.D. diss., University of North Carolina, Chapel Hill, 1999); Stacy Braukman, " 'Nothing Else Matters but Sex': Cold War Narratives of Deviance and the Search for Lesbian Teachers in Florida, 1959–1963," *Feminist Studies* 27 (Fall 2001): 553–75. For a prescient study of the 1950 election, "the first trial runs of a Republican-Southern political alliance," in which North Carolina's Frank Porter Graham and Florida's Claude Pepper were defeated, see Lubell, *Future of American Politics*, 100–128, esp. 108.

48. David L. Chappell, *A Stone of Hope: Prophetic Religion and the Death of Jim Crow* (Chapel Hill, NC, 2004); Richard Moser, "Was It the End or Just a Beginning? American Storytelling and the History of the Sixties," in *World the Sixties Made*, ed. Gosse and Moser, 37–51. For an emphasis on the relative quiescence of the institutional black church and the strategic brilliance, rather than the idealism, of the movement's grassroots participants, see Payne, *I've Got the Light of Freedom*. See also Aldon D. Morris, *The Origins of the Civil Rights Movement: Black Communities Organizing for Change* (New York, 1984). For conflicting perspectives on the religious basis of segregationist thought, see Chappell, *Stone of Hope*; and Jane Dailey, "Sex, Segregation, and the Sacred after *Brown*," *Journal of American History* 91 (June 2004): 119–44.

49. Steven Hahn, *A Nation under Our Feet: Black Political Struggles in the Rural South, from Slavery to the Great Migration* (Cambridge, MA, 2003).

50. For examples of the caricature, see *Wall Street Journal*, July 21, 1999, p. A22; Tamar Jacoby, "A Surprise, but Not a Success," *Atlantic Monthly* 289 (May 2002): 114; Raymond Wolters, "From *Brown* to *Green* and Back: The Changing Meaning of Desegregation," *Journal of Southern History* 70 (May 2004): 321; and Ann Coulter, "Racial Profiling in University Admissions," *Human Events*, April 9, 2001, p. 7. For a contrary view, see *Los Angeles Sentinel*, March 31, 1994, p. A4.

51. John A. Powell, "A New Theory of Integrated Education: *True Integration*," paper delivered at the conference "The Resegregation of Southern Schools? A Crucial Moment in the History (and the Future) of Public Schooling in America," University of North Carolina Law School, Chapel Hill, NC, August 30, 2002 (in Hall's possession).

52. For an example of the "content of our character" mantra, see *Wall Street Journal*, January 19, 1998, p. 1. For more accurate views of the March on Washington, see Higginbotham, "Foreword," viii–xiv; Theoharis, "Introduction," 1–15; and Juan Williams, "A Great Day in Washington: The March on Washington for Jobs and Freedom Was America at Its Best," *Crisis* 110 (July–August 2003): 24–30.

53. My gloss of this photograph draws on Green, "Race, Gender, and Labor in 1960s Memphis," 465–89; and Nasstrom, "Down to Now." On the recent literature giving attention to women and the cultural work of gender in the movement, see Michele Mitchell, "Silences Broken, Silences Kept: Gender and Sexuality in African-American History," *Gender and History* 11 (November 1999): 433–44; and Steven F. Lawson, "Civil Rights and Black Liberation," in *Companion to American Women's History*, ed. Nancy A. Hewitt (Malden, MA, 2002), 397–413.

54. Payne, *I've Got the Light of Freedom*, 404–17; Barbara Ransby, *Ella Baker and the Black Freedom Movement: A Radical Democratic Vision* (Chapel Hill, 2003); John D'Emilio, *Lost Prophet: The Life and Times of Bayard Rustin* (New York, 2003), 36; Kathryn L. Nasstrom, *Everybody's Grandmother and Nobody's Fool: Frances Freeborn Pauley and the Struggle for Social Justice* (Ithaca, NY, 2000). For Angela Davis's statement, see Fosl, *Subversive Southerner* 10. Other black radicals, sidelined by McCarthyism, took up artistic endeavors that influenced the political and aesthetic imagination of generations to come. See Rebeccah E. Welch, "Black Art and Activism in Postwar New York, 1950–1965" (Ph.D. diss., New York University, 2002).

55. Korstad, *Civil Rights Unionism*, 413–19. For the suggestion that such historical amnesia extended to early voter registration drives, sit-ins, and legal battles, see August Meier, "Epilogue: Toward a Synthesis of Civil Rights History," in *New Directions in Civil Rights Studies*, ed. Robinson and Sullivan, 214–15; and Nasstrom, "Down to Now." For an example of southern movement activists seeking out the radical history they had been denied, see the thematic issue "No More Moanin': Voices of Southern Struggle," *Southern Exposure* 1 (Winter 1974–1975). The black studies and women's history movements were, in part, outcomes of this search for historical roots.

56. For an influential expression of this view, see Todd Gitlin, *The Twilight of Common Dreams: Why America Is Wracked by Culture Wars* (New York, 1995). For a rejoinder, see Gosse and Moser, eds., *World the Sixties Made*; and Gosse, "Movement of Movements," 278.

57. Sara M. Evans, "Beyond Declension: Feminist Radicalism in the 1970s and 1980s," in *World the Sixties Made*, ed. Gosse and Moser, 52–66, esp. 63; MacLean, "*Freedom Is Not Enough*," introduction, chaps. 5, 7, and epilogue.

58. Robert Self, "'To Plan Our Liberation': Black Power and the Politics of Place in Oakland, California, 1965–1977," *Journal of Urban History* 26 (September 2000): 759–92, esp. 787. See Charles E. Jones, ed., *The Black Panther Party (Reconsidered)*

(Baltimore, MD, 1998); Komozi Woodard, *A Nation within a Nation: Amiri Baraka (LeRoi Jones) and Black Power Politics* (Chapel Hill, NC, 1999); Kathleen Cleaver and George Katsiaficas, eds., *Liberation, Imagination, and the Black Panther Party: A New Look at the Panthers and Their Legacy* (New York, 2001); Peniel E. Joseph, "Black Liberation without Apology: Reconceptualizing the Black Power Movement," *Black Scholar* 31 (Fall–Winter 2001–2002): 2–19; and Self, *American Babylon*.

59. Theoharis and Woodard, eds., *Freedom North*; Gosse, "Movement of Movements," 277–302.

60. *Swann v. Charlotte-Mecklenburg Board of Education*, 402 U.S. 1 (1971); Lassiter, "Suburban Origins of 'Color-Blind' Conservatism," 555.

61. Lassiter, "Suburban Origins of 'Color-Blind' Conservatism," 549–82, esp. 576. See also Frye Gaillard, *The Dream Long Deferred* (Chapel Hill, 1988); and Davison M. Douglas, *Reading, Writing, and Race: The Desegregation of the Charlotte Schools* (Chapel Hill, 1995). For the closing of black schools and other results of white control of the process of school desegregation, see David S. Cecelski, *Along Freedom Road: Hyde County, North Carolina, and the Fate of Black Schools in the South* (Chapel Hill, 1994); Barbara Shircliffe, We Got the Best of That World': A Case for the Study of Nostalgia in the Oral History of School Segregation," *Oral History Review* 28 (Summer–Fall 2001): 59–84; and James Leloudis, George Noblit, and Sarah Thuesen, "What Was Lost: African American Accounts of School Desegregation," paper delivered at the annual meeting of the Organization of American Historians, Boston, MA, March 2004 (in Hall's possession).

62. *Charlotte Observer*, October 9, 1999, p. 19A; Pamela Grundy, "A Sense of Pride: Segregation, Desegregation, and Community at West Charlotte High School," paper delivered at the conference "Listening for a Change: Transforming Landscapes and People," Southern Oral History Program/North Carolina Humanities Council Teachers' Institute, June 24–30, 2001, Chapel Hill (in Hall's possession); Pamela Grundy, "Race and Desegregation: "'West Charlotte High School" <http://www. ibiblio.org/sohp/research/lfac/lfac_31b.html> (accessed July 2004); Amy Stuart Wells et al., "How Desegregation Changed Us: The Effects of Racially Mixed Schools on Students and Society: A Study of Desegregated High Schools and Their Class of 1980 Graduates" < http://cms.tc.columbia.edu/ i /a/ 782_ASWells041504.pdf > (accessed November 2004); and Amy Stuart Wells et al., *In Search of Brown* (Cambridge, MA, 2005). For the quotation about West Charlotte High School graduates' experiences, see Arthur Griffin interview by Pamela Grundy, May 5, 1999, "Listening for a Change: West Charlotte High School Project," series K, Southern Oral History Program Collection, Southern Historical Collection (Wilson Library, University of North Carolina, Chapel Hill). A collection finding aid is available at http://www.lib.unc.edu/mss/inv.html (accessed September 2004).

63. For this dynamic in one southern county, see Pride, *Political Use of Racial Narratives*, 244. For the reciprocal relationship between jobs and education, see Wright, "Civil Rights Revolution as Economic History," 280. On black political advances, see Steven F. Lawson, *In Pursuit of Power: Southern Blacks and Electoral Politics, 1965–1982* (New York, 1985).

64. Carol B. Stack, *Call to Home: African Americans Reclaim the Rural South* (New York, 1996); Wright, "Civil Rights Revolution as Economic History," 281.

65. Sheryll Cashin, *The Failures of Integration: How Race and Class Are Undermining the American Dream* (New York, 2004), esp. 212; *Milliken v. Bradley*, 418 U.S. 717 (1974); *San Antonio Independent School District v. Rodriguez*, 411 U.S. 1 (1973); Gary Orfield, Susan E. Eaton, and the Harvard Project on School Desegregation, *Dismantling Desegregation: The Quiet Reversal of* Brown v. Board of Education (New York, 1996); Gary Orfield and the Harvard Civil Rights Project, "Schools

More Separate: Consequences of a Decade of Resegregation," July 2001
<http://www.civilrightsproject.harvard.edu/research/deseg/Schools_More_Separate.
pdf > (accessed July 2004); James T. Patterson, Brown v. Board of Education: *A
Civil Rights Milestone and Its Troubled Legacy* (New York, 2001), 191–205;
Richard Kluger, *Simple Justice: The History of* Brown v. Board of Education *and
Black America's Struggle for Equality* (New York, 2004), 751–89; John Charles
Boger, "Education's 'Perfect Storm'?: Racial Resegregation, High Stakes Testing, and
School Resource Inequities: The Case of North Carolina," *North Carolina Law
Review* 81 (May 2003): 1375–1462, esp. 1379; John Charles Boger, "Willful
Colorblindness: The New Racial Piety and the Resegregation of Public Schools,"
ibid., 78 (September 2000): 1719–96.

66. Cashin, *Failures of Integration*, 232–36, 11–12; Boger, "Education's 'Perfect
Storm'?"

67. Quintard Taylor, "The Civil Rights Movement in the American West: Black Protest
in Seattle, 1960–1970," *Journal of Negro History* 80 (Winter 1995–1996): 4–5;
Green, "Race, Gender, and Labor in 1960s Memphis," 465–89; Honey, "Labor and
Civil Rights Movements at the Cross-Roads"; Honey, *Southern Labor and Black
Civil Rights*; Michael K. Honey, *Black Workers Remember: An Oral History of
Segregation, Unionism, and the Freedom Struggle* (Berkeley, CA, 1999); Steve Estes,
" 'I AM A MAN!': Race, Masculinity, and the 1968 Memphis Sanitation Strike,"
Labor History 41 (May 2000): 153–70; Self, *American Babylon*, 227, 291–327;
Gaines, "Historiography of the Struggle for Black Equality since 1945," 229; Self
and Sugrue, "Power of Place," 30–31.

68. For an astute overview, see William H. Chafe, *The Unfinished Journey: America
since World War II* (New York, 1995), 236–43. For a critique of the Great Society's
limitations, see Ira Katznelson, "Was the Great Society a Lost Opportunity?" in *Rise
and Fall of the New Deal Order*, ed. Gerstle and Fraser, 185–211. See also Jill
Quadagno, *The Color of Welfare: How Racism Undermined the War on Poverty*
(New York, 1994).

69. This discussion of the struggle for economic inclusion is drawn from Nancy
MacLean, "*Freedom Is Not Enough*"; Timothy J. Minchin, *Hiring the Black
Worker: The Racial Integration of the Southern Textile Industry, 1960–1980*
(Chapel Hill, 1999); Timothy J. Minchin, *The Color of Work: The Struggle for Civil
Rights in the Southern Paper Industry, 1945–1980* (Chapel Hill, NC, 2001); Wright,
"Civil Rights Revolution as Economic History"; Heckman, "Central Role of the
South in Accounting for the Economic Progress of Black Americans," 242–46;
Lichtenstein, *State of the Union*, 3; Cobble, *Other Women's Movement*, 180–205;
and Thomas J. Sugrue, "Affirmative Action from Below: Civil Rights, the Building
Trades, and the Politics of Racial Equality in the Urban North, 1945–1969," *Journal
of American History* 91 (June 2004): 145–73.

70. Cowie, "Nixon's Class Struggle," 257–83, esp. 264; Jefferson Cowie, " 'Vigorously
Left, Right, and Center': The Crosscurrents of Working-Class America in the
1970s," in *America in the Seventies*, ed. Beth Bailey and David Farber (Lawrence,
KS, 2004), 75–106; Joshua B. Freeman, "Labor during the American Century:
Work, Workers, and Unions since 1945," in *Companion to Post–1945 America*, ed.
Agnew and Rosenzweig, 202; Richard Moser, "Autoworkers at Lordstown:
Workplace Democracy and American Citizenship," in *World the Sixties Made*, ed.
Gosse and Moser, 289–315. For a remarkable instance of 1970s labor insurgency
(the basis for the Academy Award-winning film *Norma Rae*), see James A. Hodges,
"J. P. Stevens and the Union: Struggle for the South," in *Race, Class, and Community
in Southern Labor History*, ed. Gary M. Fink and Merl E. Reed (Tuscaloosa, AL,
1994), 53–64.

71. Peter B. Levy, *The New Left and Labor in the 1960s* (Urbana, 1994); Keiran Taylor, "A Turn to the Working Class: The New Left, Black Liberation, and the Struggle for Economic Justice, 1968–1979" (Ph.D. diss., University of North Carolina, Chapel Hill, in progress, in Hall's possession); Korstad and Lichtenstein, "Opportunities Found and Lost," esp. 811.

72. See MacLean, "*Freedom Is Not Enough,*" chap. 7; Lichtenstein, *State of the Union,* 195; Jefferson Cowie, *Capital Moves: RCA's Seventy-Year Quest for Cheap Labor* (Ithaca, NY, 1999); Cowie, " 'Vigorously Left, Right, and Center,' " 99–100; Thomas Byrne Edsall, *The New Politics of Inequality* (New York, 1984), 107–40; and Mae M. Ngai, *Impossible Subjects: Illegal Aliens and the Making of Modern America* (Princeton, NJ, 2004), 228–70.

73. Brown et al., *Whitewashing Race,* 164–92; Sugrue, "Affirmative Action from Below," 172.

74. Deirdre English, "The Fear That Feminism Will Free Men First," in *Powers of Desire: The Politics of Sexuality,* ed. Ann Snitow, Christine Stansell, and Sharon Thompson (New York, 1983), 477–83. Studies of women and the New Right include Jane J. Mansbridge, *Why We Lost the ERA* (Chicago, 1986); Donald G. Mathews and Jane Sherron De Hart, *Sex, Gender, and the Politics of ERA: A State and the Nation* (New York, 1990); Susan Faludi, *Backlash: The Undeclared War against American Women* (New York, 1991); Jane Sherron De Hart, "Gender on the Right: Meanings behind the Existential Scream," *Gender and History* 3 (Autumn 1991): 246–67; Kristin Luker, *Abortion and the Politics of Motherhood* (Berkeley, CA, 1984); Rebecca E. Klatch, *Women of the New Right* (Philadelphia, PA, 1987); and Marjorie Julian Spruill, "Countdown to Houston: The 1977 International Women's Year Conferences and the Polarization of American Women," paper delivered at the annual meeting of the Southern Historical Association, Houston, TX, November 8, 2003 (in Hall's possession).

75. Brown et al., *Whitewashing Race,* 80–85, 185–92, esp. 185. See also William A. Darity Jr. and Samuel L. Myers Jr., *Persistent Disparity: Race and Economic Inequality in the United States since 1945* (Northampton, 1998); and William A. Darity Jr. and Patrick L. Mason, "Evidence on Discrimination in Employment: Codes of Color, Codes of Gender," *Journal of Economic Perspectives* 12 (Spring 1998): 63–90. Recent Supreme Court decisions on minority contracting programs have gone a long way toward gutting Title VII. See *Richmond v. J. A. Croson Company,* 488 U.S. 469 (1989); and *Adarand Constructors v. Pena,* 515 U.S. 200 (1995). Cf. Brown et al., *Whitewashing Race,* 187–88.

76. MacLean, "*Freedom Is Not Enough,*" chap. 9; Lichtenstein, *State of the Union,* 178–211. For a critique of the focus of civil rights organizations on enforcement of Title VII that argues that job-training and antidiscrimination programs were poor substitutes for economic planning to preserve well-paying blue-collar jobs, see Judith Stein, *Running Steel, Running America: Race, Economic Policy, and the Decline of Liberalism* (Chapel Hill, NC, 1998). For a black labor leftist's view of the movement's trajectory, 1950–1980, see J. Hunter O'Dell, "Notes on the Movement: Then, Now, and Tomorrow," *Southern Exposure* 9 (Spring 1981): 6–11.

77. Martin Luther King Jr., "A Testament of Hope," in *A Testament of Hope: The Essential Writings of Martin Luther King, Jr.,* ed. James M. Washington (San Francisco, CA, 1986), 315. See also David Halberstam, "The Second Coming of Martin Luther King," *Harper's Magazine* 235 (August 1967): 39–51.

78. Craig Haney and Philip Zimbardo, "The Past and Future of U.S. Prison Policy: Twenty-Five Years after the Stanford Prison Experiment," *American Psychologist* 53 (July 1998): 714; Joy James, ed., *The Angela Y. Davis Reader* (Malden, MA, 1998), 29–110.

79. Walter Benjamin, "Theses on the Philosophy of History," in *Illuminations*, ed. Hannah Arendt (New York, 1969), 258.

80. For white attitudes as revealed in survey data, see Lawrence D. Bobo and Ryan A. Smith, "From Jim Crow Racism to Laissez-Faire Racism: The Transformation of Racial Attitudes," in *Beyond Pluralism: The Conception of Groups and Group Identities in America*, ed. Wendy F. Katkin, Ned Landsman, and Andrea Tyree (Urbana, IL, 1998), 182–220; Brown et al., *Whitewashing Race*, 248–49; Pride, *Political Use of Racial Narratives*, 238; Cokorinos, *Assault on Diversity*, 6. For evidence that the Reagan administration's effort was not driven by, but drove, a change in public opinion, see Thomas Ferguson and Joel Rogers, *Right Turn: The Decline of the Democrats and the Future of American Politics* (New York, 1986), 3–39.

81. Guinier and Torres, *Miner's Canary*, 11; Brown et al., *Whitewashing Race*, 249.

82. Gosse, "Movement of Movements," 277–78.

Other Articles Nominated for the 2007 Competition

Dirlik Arif, "The End of Colonialism?" *Boundary* 2 (Spring 2005): 1–31.

Bruce E. Baker, "Lynch Law Reversed: The Rape of Lula Sherman, the Lynching of Manse Waldrop, and the Debate Over Lynching in the 1880s" *American Nineteenth Century History* 6 (September 2005): 273–29.

Rebecca Bales, "Winema and the Modoc War: One Woman's Struggle for Peace," *Prologue* 37 (Spring 2005): 24–35.

Alan C. Braddock, " 'Jeff College Boys': Thomas Eakins, Dr. Forbes and Anatomical Fraternity in Postbellum Philadelphia," *American Quarterly* 57 (June 2005): 355–83.

Kingsley M. Bray, " 'We Belong to the North': The Flights of the Northern Indians from the White River Agencies," *Montana: The Magazine of Western History* 55 (Summer 2005): 28–47.

Lynn E. Couturier, "The Influence of the Eugenics Movement on Physical Movement Education in the United States" *Sport History Review* 36 (May 2005): 21–42.

Edward E. Curtis IV, "African-American Islamization Reconsidered: Black History Narratives and Muslim Identity," *Journal of the American Academy of Religion* 73 (Sept. 2005): 659–84.

Ruth Feldstein, " 'I Don't Trust You Anymore': Nina Simone, Culture, and Black Activism in the 1960s," *Journal of American History* 91 (March 2005): 1349–79.

Gretchen Heefner, " 'A Symbol of a New Frontier': Hawaiian Statehood, Anti-Colonialism and Winning the Cold War," *Pacific Historical Review* 74 (November 2005): 511–44.

Sean P. Holmes, "All the World's A Stage: The Actors Strike of 1919," *Journal of American History* 91 (March 2005): 1291–1317.

Mark W. Janis, "Dred Scott and International Law," *Columbia Journal of Transnational Law* 43, no. 3 (2005): 763–810.

S. J. Kleinberg, "Children's and Mothers' Wage Labor in Three Eastern U.S. Cities, 1880–1920," *Social Science History* 29 (Spring 2005): 45–76.

Dean Kotlowski, "With All Deliberate Delay: Kennedy, Johnson and School Desegregation" *Journal of Policy History* 17, no. 2 (2005): 155–92.

Drew Lopenzina, " 'Good Indian': Charles Eastman and the Warrior as Civil Servant," *American Indian Quarterly* 27 (Summer-Fall 2003): 727–57.

Christopher Malone, "Race Formation, Voting Rights, and Democratization in the Antebellum North," *New Political Science* 27 (June 2005): 177–98.

William G. Martin, "Global Movements before 'Globalization': Black Movements as World-Historical Movements," *Review: Fernand Braudel Center* 28 no.1(2005): 7–28.

Carolyn M. Moehling, " 'She Has Suddenly Become Powerful': Youth Employment and Household Decision-Making in the Early Twentieth Century," *Journal of Economic History* 65 (June 2005): 414–38.

W. Scott Poole, "Memory and the Abolitionist Heritage: Thomas Wentworth Higginson and the Universal Meaning of the Civil War," *Civil War History* (June 2005): 202–17.

Matthias Reiss, "Bronzed Bodies Behind the Barbed Wire: Masculinity and the Treatment of German Prisoners of War in the United States during World War II," *Journal of Military History* 69 (April 2005): 475–504.

Laurence Shore, "The Enduring Power of Racism: A Reconsideration of Winthrop Jordan's White Over Black," *History and Theory* 44 (May 2005): 195–226.

Josh Sides, "Excavating the Postwar Sex District in San Francisco," *Journal of Urban History* 32 (March 2006): 355–79.

Whitney Walton, "Internationalism and the Junior Year Abroad: American Students in France in the 1920s and 1930s," *Diplomatic History* 29 (April 2005): 255–78.

Reginald Washington, "Sealing the Sacred Bonds of Holy Matrimony: Freedmen's Bureau Marriage Records," *Prologue* 37 (Spring 2005): 58–65.

Joan Waugh, " 'Pageantry of Woe': The Funeral of Ulysses S. Grant," *Civil War History* 51 (June 2005): 151–74.

Gray H. Whaley, "Oregon, Illahee, and the Empire Republic: A Case Study of American Colonialism, 1843–1858," *Western Historical Quarterly* 36 (Summer 2005): 157–78.

Rachel Wheeler, "Hendrick Aupaumut: Christian-Mahican Prophet," *Journal of the Early Republic* 25 (Summer 2005): 187–220.

Charles Vert Willie and Sarah Susannah Willie, "Black, White, and Brown: The Transformation of Public Education in America," *Teachers College Record* 107 (March 2005): 475–95.

Index